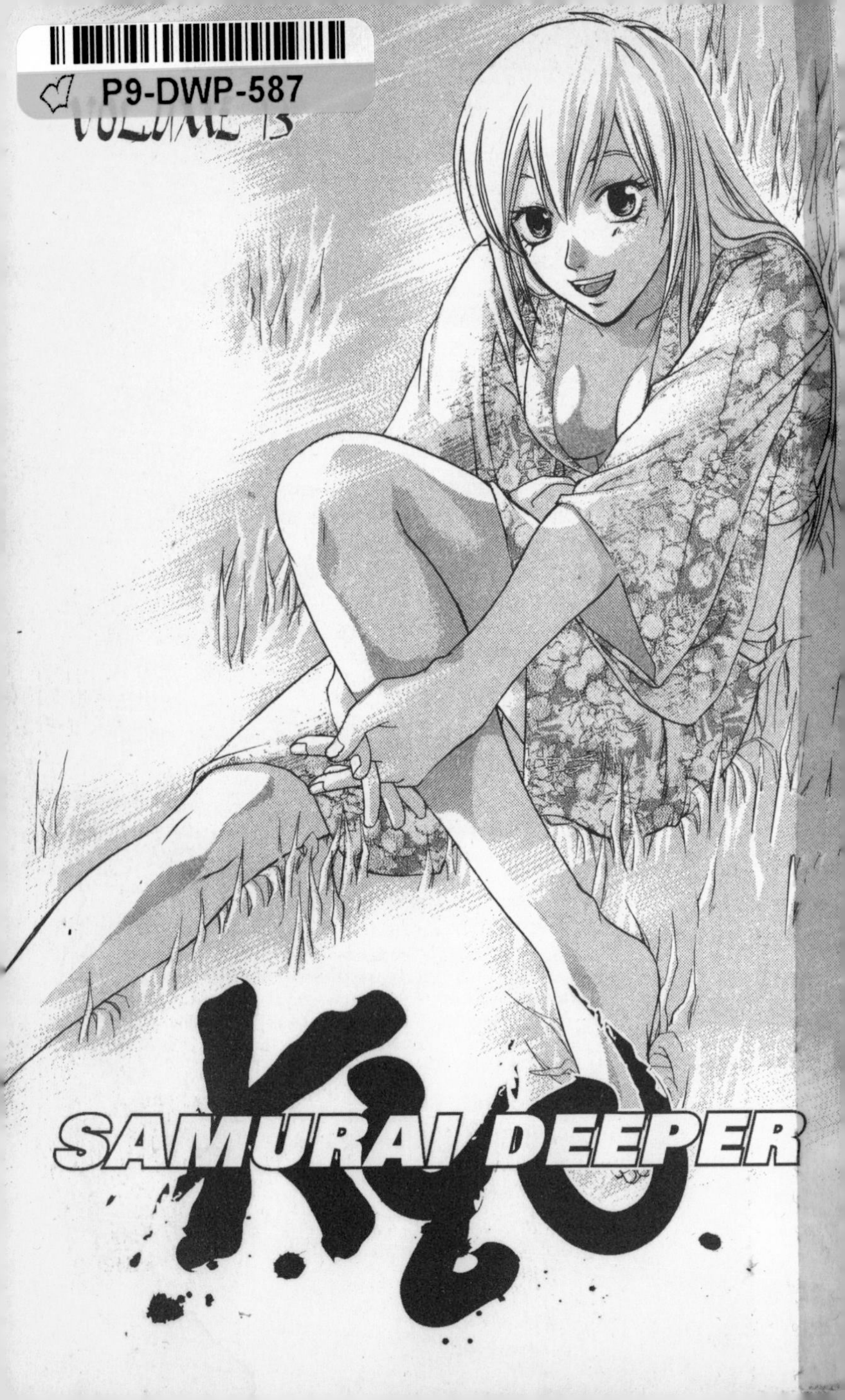
VOLUME 13
SAMURAI DEEPER
KYO

Samurai Deeper Kyo Vol. 13
Created by Akimine Kamijyo

Translation - Alexander O. Smith
Script Editor - Rich Amtower
Copy Editor - Suzanne Waldman
Retouch and Lettering - Patrick Tran
Production Artist - Jason Milligan
Cover Design - Seth Cable

Editor - Aaron Suhr
Digital Imaging Manager - Chris Buford
Pre-Press Manager - Antonio DePietro
Production Managers - Jennifer Miller and Mutsumi Miyazaki
Art Director - Matt Alford
Managing Editor - Jill Freshney
VP of Production - Ron Klamert
Editor-In-Chief - Mike Kiley
President and C.O.O. - John Parker
Publisher and C.E.O. - Stuart Levy

A  TOKYOPOP® Manga

TOKYOPOP Inc.
5900 Wilshire Blvd. Suite 2000
Los Angeles, CA 90036

E-mail: info@TOKYOPOP.com
Come visit us online at www.TOKYOPOP.com

ISBN: 1-59532-453-4

First TOKYOPOP printing: June 2005
10 9 8 7 6 5 4 3 2 1
Printed in the USA

SAMURAI DEEPER Kyo

Vol. 13
by Akimine Kamijyo

HAMBURG // LONDON // LOS ANGELES // TOKYO

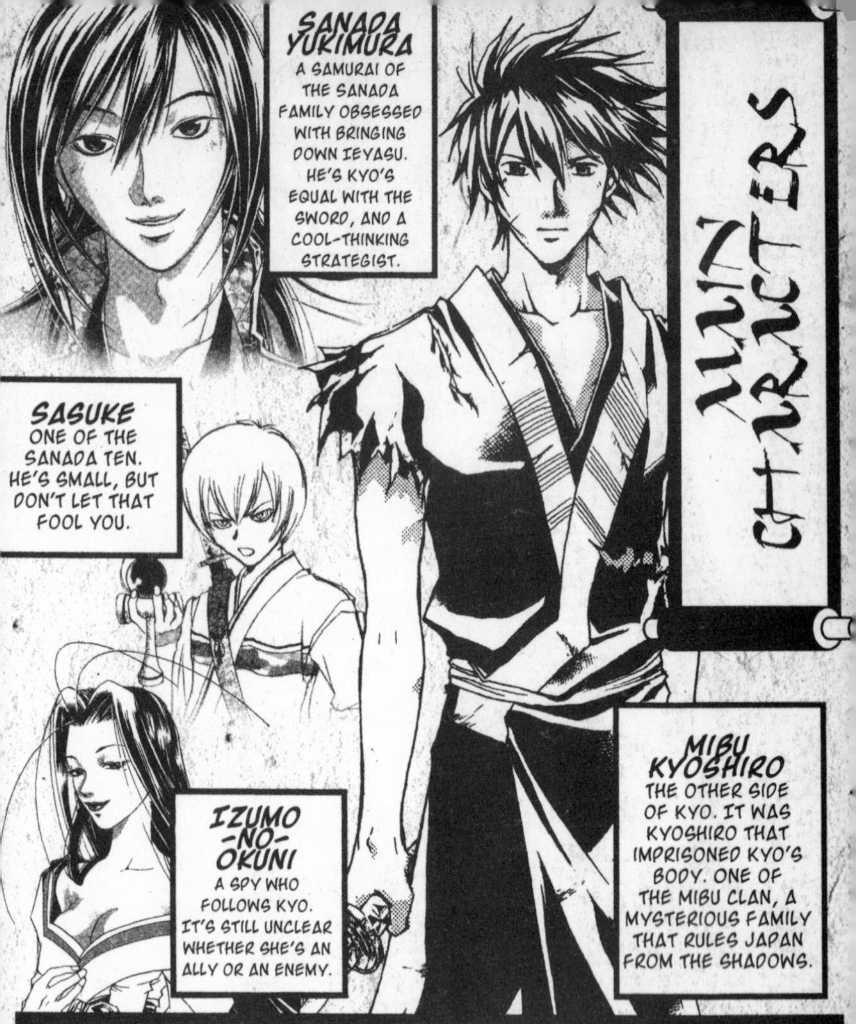
MAIN CHARACTERS
SANADA YUKIMURA
A SAMURAI OF THE SANADA FAMILY OBSESSED WITH BRINGING DOWN IEYASU. HE'S KYO'S EQUAL WITH THE SWORD, AND A COOL-THINKING STRATEGIST.
SASUKE
ONE OF THE SANADA TEN. HE'S SMALL, BUT DON'T LET THAT FOOL YOU.
MIBU KYOSHIRO
THE OTHER SIDE OF KYO. IT WAS KYOSHIRO THAT IMPRISONED KYO'S BODY. ONE OF THE MIBU CLAN, A MYSTERIOUS FAMILY THAT RULES JAPAN FROM THE SHADOWS.
IZUMO-NO-OKUNI
A SPY WHO FOLLOWS KYO. IT'S STILL UNCLEAR WHETHER SHE'S AN ALLY OR AN ENEMY.

THE STORY

FOUR YEARS HAVE PASSED SINCE THE BATTLE OF SEKIGAHARA.
YUYA AND KYOSHIRO MEET AND BEGIN TO TRAVEL TOGETHER, BUT YUYA SOON LEARNS THAT KYOSHIRO HAS ANOTHER SIDE: THE CRUEL AND POWERFUL SAMURAI KYO.
AS THE TWO KYOS FIGHT FOR DOMINANCE, THEY PICK UP TWO MORE TRAVELING COMPANIONS, BENITORA AND YUKIMURA, AND LEAVE EDO, HEADING WEST. THEIR DESTINATION: THE AOKIGAHARA FOREST AT THE BASE OF MT. FUJI, WHERE KYO'S BODY LIES HIDDEN...BUT ON THE WAY, THEY ARE ASSAILED BY THE SIXTH DEMON KING, ODA NOBUNAGA, AND HIS TWELVE GOD SHOGUNS! A BATTLE ENSUES, AND BLOOD IS SPILLED UPON BLOOD. JUST AS KYO SEEMS ABOUT TO RECLAIM HIS BODY, IT IS SNATCHED AWAY BY AN OLD FRIEND--AKIRA.

THE PARTY SETS OUT TOWARD KYOTO, HOT ON AKIRA'S TRAIL WHEN THEY ENCOUNTER BONTENMARU, ANOTHER OF THE FOUR EMPERORS. HE LEADS THEM TO THE HOME OF KYO'S MASTER, MURAMASA. THERE, A DEADLY BATTLE ENSUES BETWEEN KYO AND SHINREI, A MIBU CLAN ASSASSIN, ENDING WITH YUYA HIT BY A SECRET MIBU TECHNIQUE THAT ENSURES HER DEATH IN 60 DAYS!

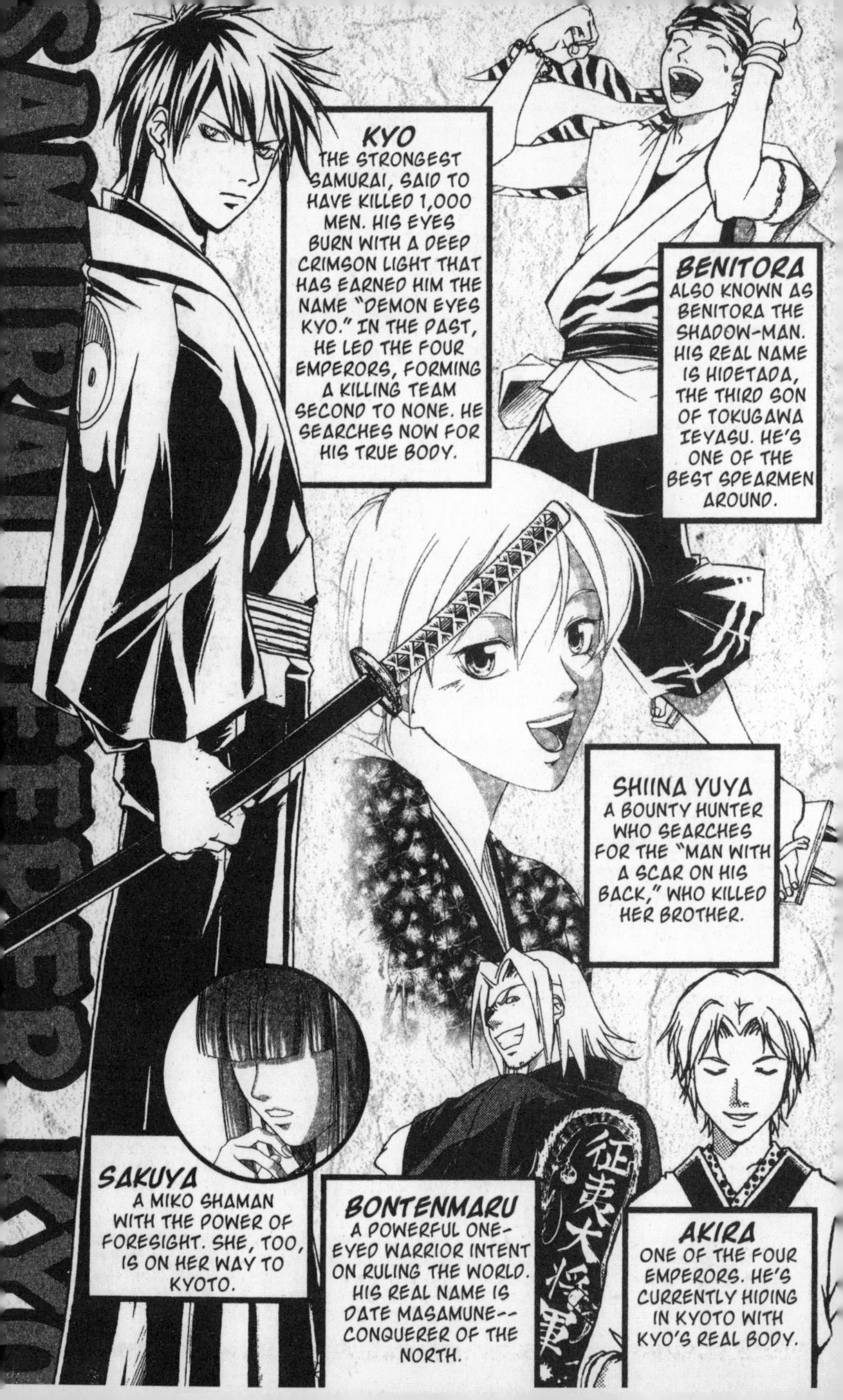
KYO
THE STRONGEST SAMURAI, SAID TO HAVE KILLED 1,000 MEN. HIS EYES BURN WITH A DEEP CRIMSON LIGHT THAT HAS EARNED HIM THE NAME "DEMON EYES KYO." IN THE PAST, HE LED THE FOUR EMPERORS, FORMING A KILLING TEAM SECOND TO NONE. HE SEARCHES NOW FOR HIS TRUE BODY.
BENITORA
ALSO KNOWN AS BENITORA THE SHADOW-MAN. HIS REAL NAME IS HIDETADA, THE THIRD SON OF TOKUGAWA IEYASU. HE'S ONE OF THE BEST SPEARMEN AROUND.
SHIINA YUYA
A BOUNTY HUNTER WHO SEARCHES FOR THE "MAN WITH A SCAR ON HIS BACK," WHO KILLED HER BROTHER.
AKIRA
ONE OF THE FOUR EMPERORS. HE'S CURRENTLY HIDING IN KYOTO WITH KYO'S REAL BODY.
BONTENMARU
A POWERFUL ONE-EYED WARRIOR INTENT ON RULING THE WORLD. HIS REAL NAME IS DATE MASAMUNE--CONQUERER OF THE NORTH.
SAKUYA
A MIKO SHAMAN WITH THE POWER OF FORESIGHT. SHE, TOO, IS ON HER WAY TO KYOTO.

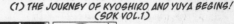

WHERE DID KYO MEET ALL HIS FRIENDS? WHO DID THEY FIGHT? SWIFTER THAN KYO CAN SWING HIS SWORD, HERE'S A RECAP OF ALL THAT'S HAPPENED IN SDK SO FAR!

OF KYO!

一 (1) THE JOURNEY OF KYOSHIRO AND YUYA BEGINS! (SDK VOL.1)

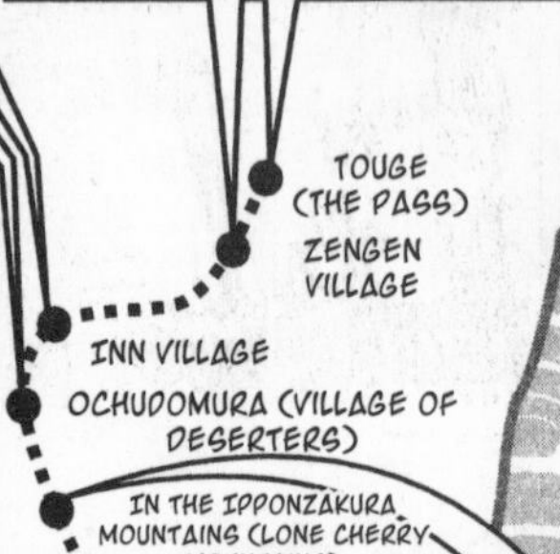

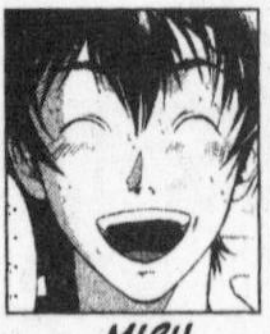

▲ MIBU KYOSHIRO

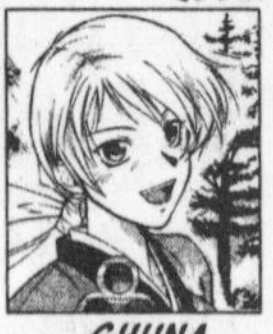

▲ SHIINA YUYA

THE BEAUTIFUL BOUNTY HUNTER YUYA MEETS MIBU KYOSHIRO BY CHANCE (OR WAS IT FATE?!). WHEN THEY FOUGHT THE BANTOUJI BROTHERS, KYOSHIRO'S OTHER SIDE WAS REVEALED: THAT OF DEMON EYES KYO!

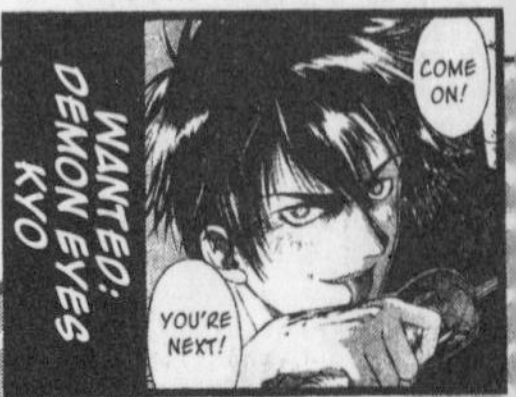

WANTED: DEMON EYES KYO
COME ON!
YOU'RE NEXT!

二 (2) THE WOMAN IZUMO-NO-OKUNI (SDK VOL.1-2)

THEY MEET THE WOMAN IZUMO-NO-OKUNI IN AN INN TOWN--AND SHE SEEMS TO KNOW A LOT ABOUT KYO AND KYOSHIRO'S PAST. THEN, IN THE VILLAGE OF DESERTERS, KYO AWAKENS AND SHOWS HIS FULL STRENGTH!

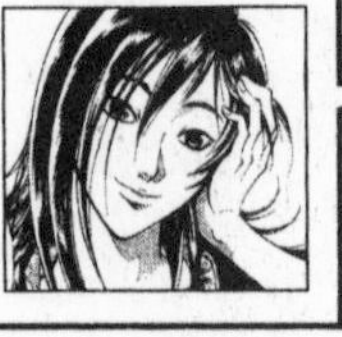

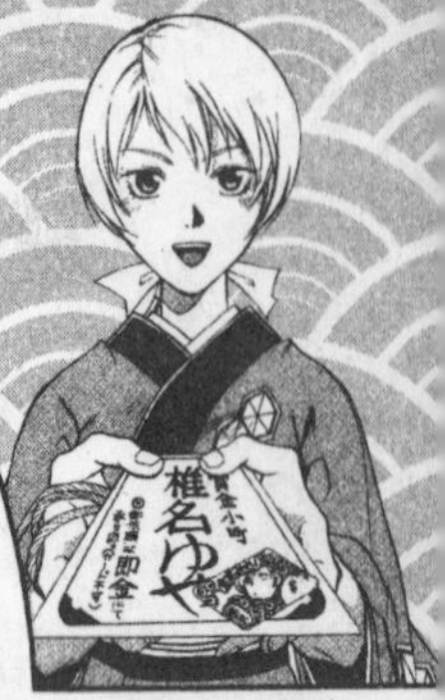

TOUGE (THE PASS)
ZENGEN VILLAGE
INN VILLAGE
OCHUDOMURA (VILLAGE OF DESERTERS)
IN THE IPPONZAKURA MOUNTAINS (LONE CHERRY MOUNTAINS)
TEAHOUSE IN THE PASS
EDO
THE FOREST OF AOKIGAHARA
HAKONE
MT. FUJI

四 KYO AND YUKIMURA MEET! (SDK VOL.3)

A DRUNK CALLS OUT TO THEM AT A TEAHOUSE--AND TURNS OUT TO BE A SWORDSMAN OF SUCH SKILL HE CAN SLIP PAST EVEN KYO'S DEFENSES!

▶ SANADA YUKIMURA

三 BENITORA JOINS THE PARTY! (SDK VOL. 2-3)

THE PARTY GETS INTO A FIGHT WITH A TREASURE-SEEKING GROUP OF ASSASSINS KNOWN AS THE KITOU FAMILY SANSAISHU. ONE OF THEIR NUMBER, BENITORA, ENDS UP JOINING SIDES WITH KYO. KYO FIGHTS THE SHIROKARASU (WHITE CROW) AND FULLY AWAKENS! KYOSHIRO, HOWEVER, IS NOWHERE TO BE SEEN.

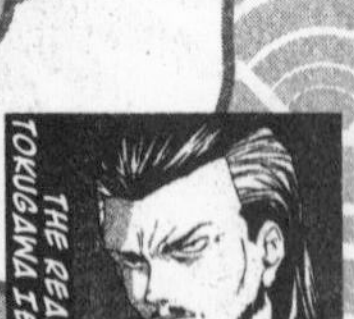

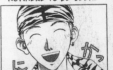

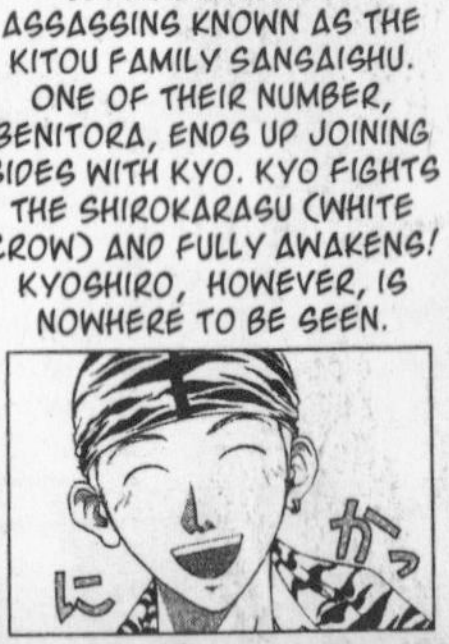

に
かっ

BENITORA ▶

THE REAL TOKUGAWA IEYASU

五 FIGHT BEFORE THE SHOGUN! (SDK VOL.3-5)

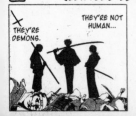

KYO, YUKIMURA, AND BENITORA ENTER A TOURNEY HELD BY THE RULER OF THE LAND, TOKUGAWA IEYASU. BUT THE TOURNEY WAS A TRAP! SET UPON BY TOKUGAWA'S ELITES, THE THREE MANAGE TO DESTROY THEM ALL WITHOUT BREAKING A SWEAT! THEN YUKIMURA TELLS KYO A SECRET: THE LOCATION OF HIS BODY!

THEY'RE NOT HUMAN...
THEY'RE DEMONS.

IN JUST 3 MINUTES!

LEARN THE LEGEND

六 (6) MORTAL COMBAT VERSUS ODA NOBUNAGA AND THE TWELVE GOD SHOGUNS! (SDK VOL. 5-10)

KYO'S BODY LIES HIDDEN IN THE DEEPEST REACHES OF THE AOKIGAHARA FOREST AT THE FOOT OF MT. FUJI. BUT BETWEEN KYO AND HIS BODY STAND THE TWELVE--GUARDIANS OF THE MASTER, ODA NOBUNAGA. AFTER A STRING OF BLOODY BATTLES, KYO'S DEMONBLADE, MURAMASA, RELIEVES NOBUNAGA'S BODY OF ITS HEAD, BUT AKIRA MAKES HIS ESCAPE WITH KYO'S BODY!

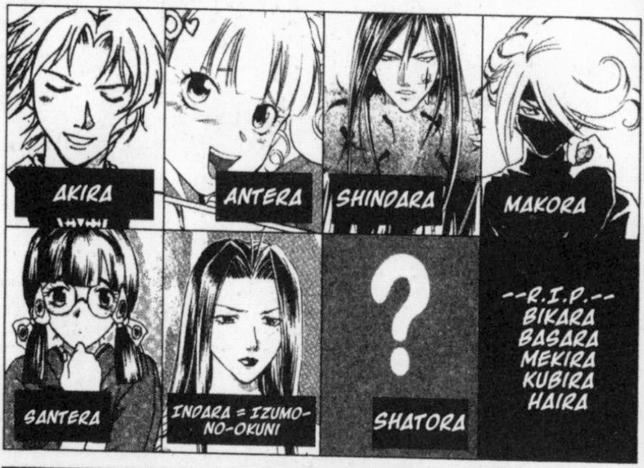
AKIRA
ANTERA
SHINDARA
MAKORA
SANTERA
INDARA = IZUMO-NO-OKUNI
?
SHATORA
--R.I.P.--
BIKARA
BASARA
MEKIRA
KUBIRA
HAIRA

NOBUNAGA AWAITS THE TIME OF HIS RESURRECTION IN THE VILLAGE OF THE MIBU, DEEP WITHIN THE LAND OF THE FIRE LOTUS.

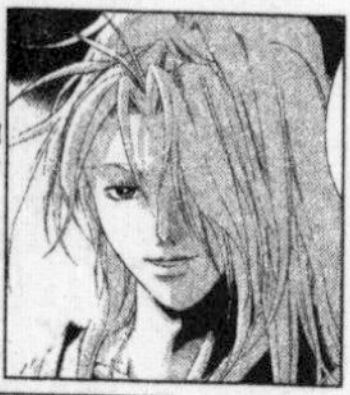

▲ ODA NOBUNAGA

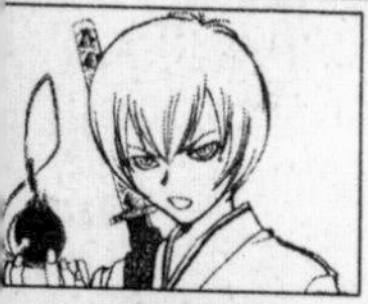

◀ SASUKE

ONE OF THE SANADA TEN. HE RETURNED TO THE FOREST WHERE HE WAS BORN ON YUKIMURA'S ORDERS.

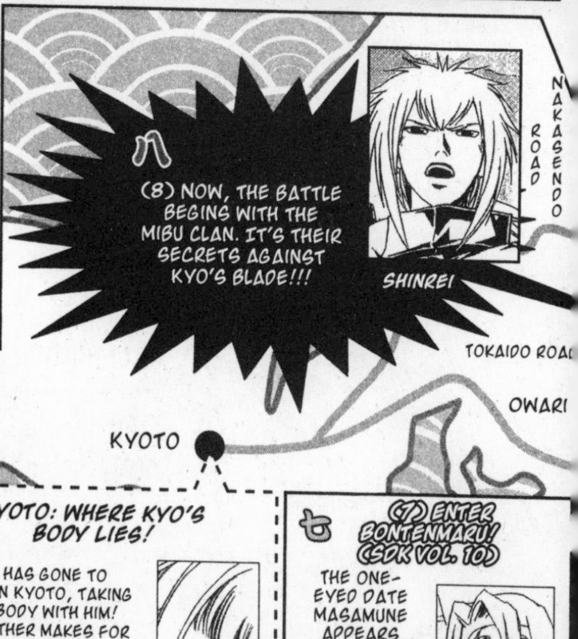
NAKASENDO ROAD
SHINREI
TOKAIDO ROAD
OWARI
KYOTO

八 (8) NOW, THE BATTLE BEGINS WITH THE MIBU CLAN. IT'S THEIR SECRETS AGAINST KYO'S BLADE!!!

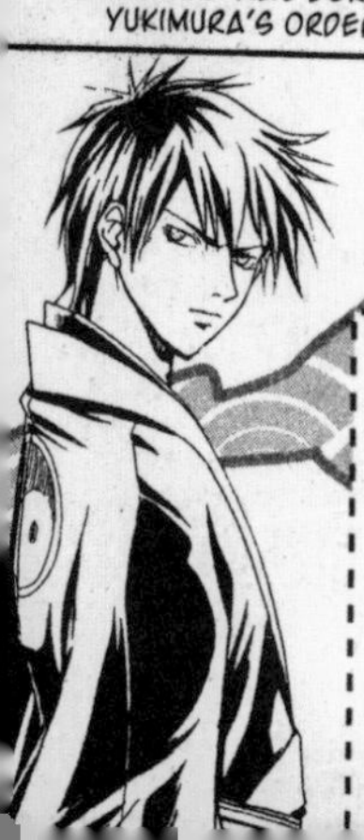

KYOTO: WHERE KYO'S BODY LIES!

AKIRA HAS GONE TO GROUND IN KYOTO, TAKING KYO'S BODY WITH HIM! BUT ANOTHER MAKES FOR KYOTO: KYO'S BELOVED SAKUYA HAS LEFT THE PROTECTION OF THE SANADAS!

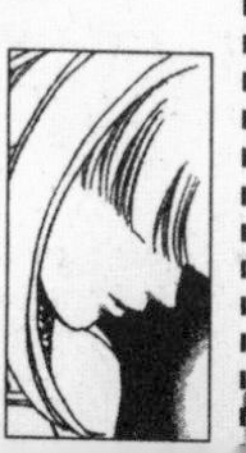

七 (7) ENTER BONTENMARU! (SDK VOL. 10)

THE ONE-EYED DATE MASAMUNE APPEARS BEFORE KYO AND LEADS THE PARTY TO KYO'S MASTER, MURAMASA.

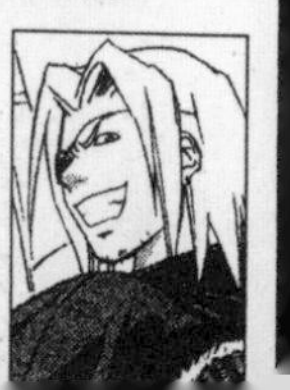

My second idea for a giveaway phone strap. I truly feel this is my masterpiece. An all-around amazing strap!

C'mon, it's cool

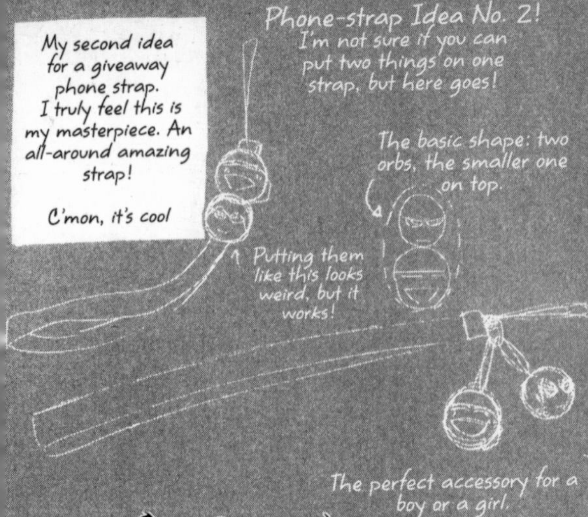
Phone-strap Idea No. 2!
I'm not sure if you can put two things on one strap, but here goes!
The basic shape: two orbs, the smaller one on top.
Putting them like this looks weird, but it works!
The perfect accessory for a boy or a girl.

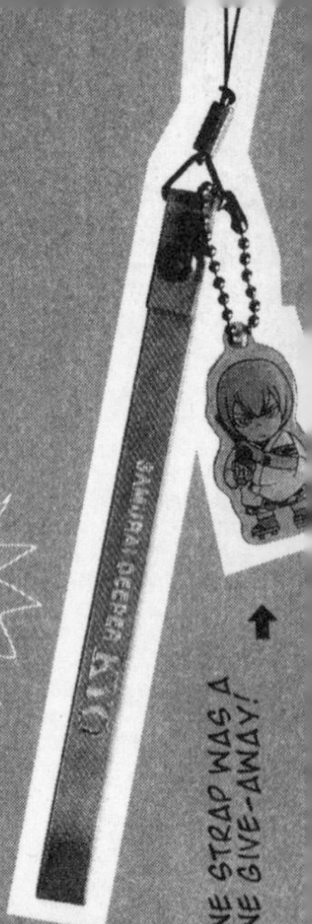
SAMURAI DEEPER KYO

THIS PHONE STRAP WAS A MAGAZINE GIVE-AWAY!

SAMURAI DEEPER KYO

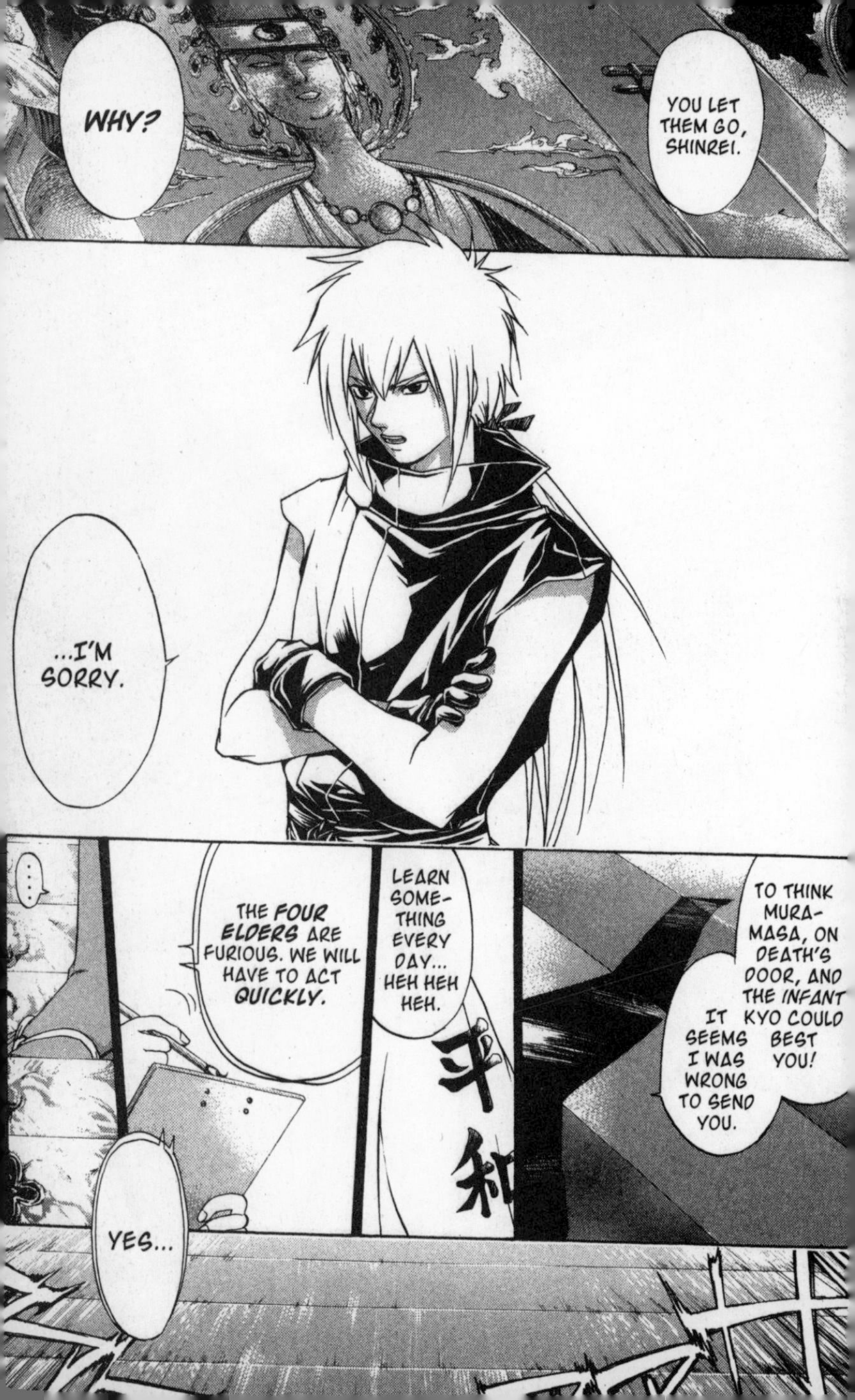

YOU LET THEM GO, SHINREI.
WHY?
...I'M SORRY.
TO THINK MURAMASA, ON DEATH'S DOOR, AND THE *INFANT* KYO COULD BEST YOU!
IT SEEMS I WAS WRONG TO SEND YOU.
LEARN SOMETHING EVERY DAY... HEH HEH HEH.
...
THE *FOUR ELDERS* ARE FURIOUS. WE WILL HAVE TO ACT *QUICKLY*.
YES...

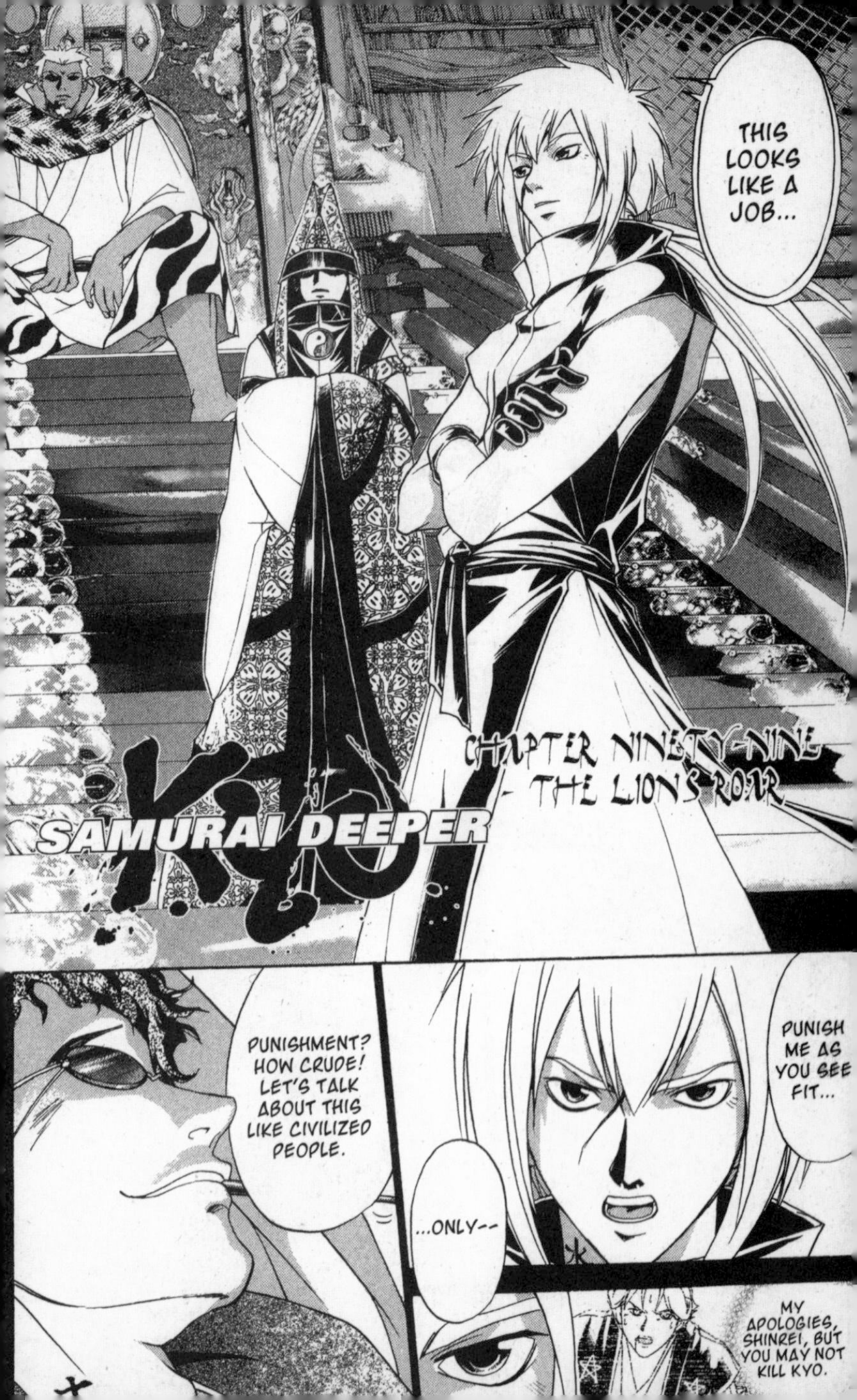
THIS LOOKS LIKE A JOB...
CHAPTER NINETY-NINE - THE LIONS ROAR
SAMURAI DEEPER KYO
PUNISH ME AS YOU SEE FIT...
...ONLY--
MY APOLOGIES, SHINREI, BUT YOU MAY NOT KILL KYO.
PUNISHMENT? HOW CRUDE! LET'S TALK ABOUT THIS LIKE CIVILIZED PEOPLE.

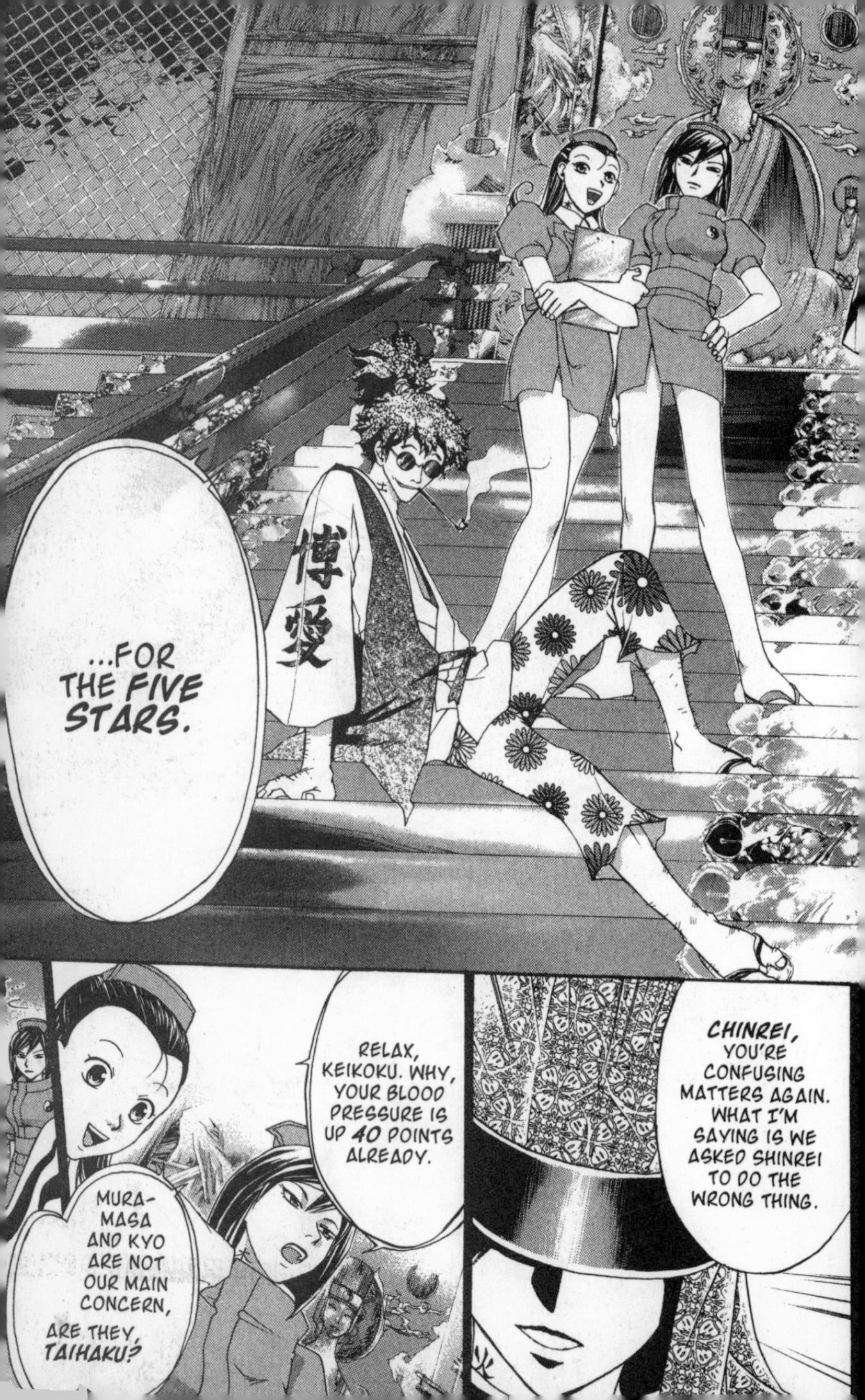
博愛
...FOR THE FIVE STARS.
CHINREI, YOU'RE CONFUSING MATTERS AGAIN. WHAT I'M SAYING IS WE ASKED SHINREI TO DO THE WRONG THING.
RELAX, KEIKOKU. WHY, YOUR BLOOD PRESSURE IS UP 40 POINTS ALREADY.
MURA-MASA AND KYO ARE NOT OUR MAIN CONCERN, ARE THEY, TAIHAKU?

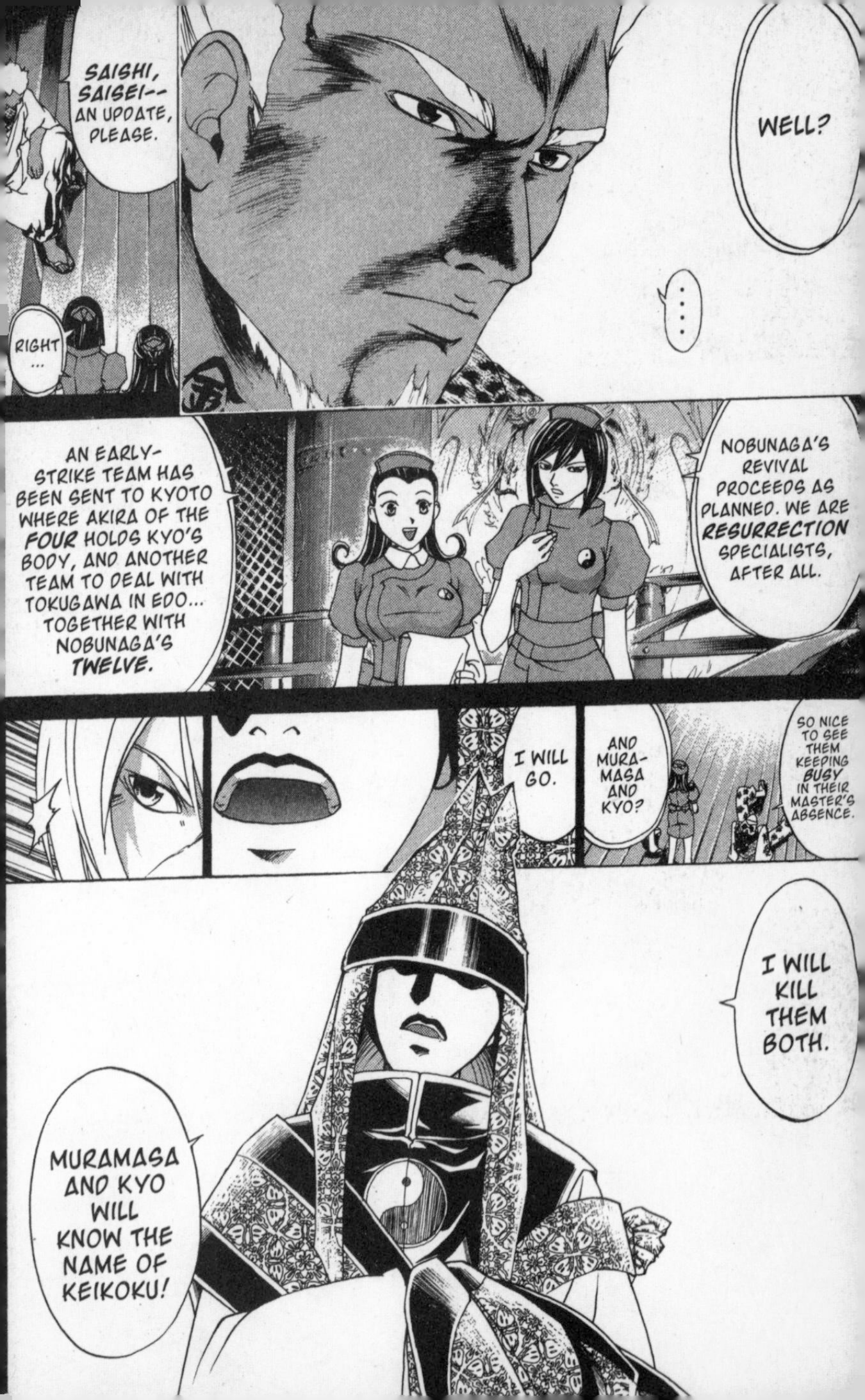
WELL?
...
SAISHI, SAISEI-- AN UPDATE, PLEASE.
RIGHT...
NOBUNAGA'S REVIVAL PROCEEDS AS PLANNED. WE ARE RESURRECTION SPECIALISTS, AFTER ALL.
AN EARLY-STRIKE TEAM HAS BEEN SENT TO KYOTO WHERE AKIRA OF THE FOUR HOLDS KYO'S BODY, AND ANOTHER TEAM TO DEAL WITH TOKUGAWA IN EDO... TOGETHER WITH NOBUNAGA'S TWELVE.
SO NICE TO SEE THEM KEEPING BUSY IN THEIR MASTER'S ABSENCE.
AND MURAMASA AND KYO?
I WILL GO.
I WILL KILL THEM BOTH.
MURAMASA AND KYO WILL KNOW THE NAME OF KEIKOKU!

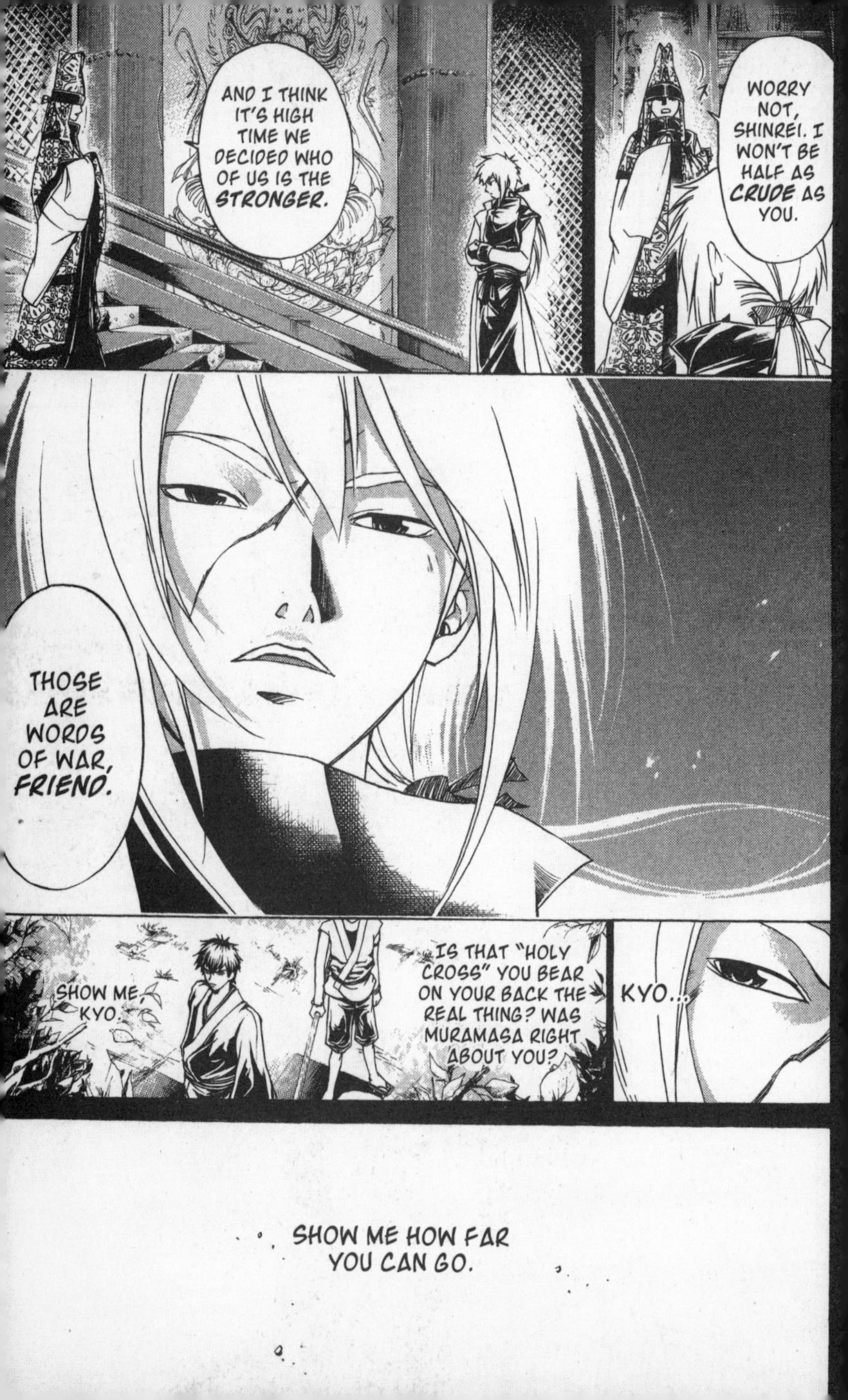
WORRY NOT, SHINREI. I WON'T BE HALF AS *CRUDE* AS YOU.
AND I THINK IT'S HIGH TIME WE DECIDED WHO OF US IS THE *STRONGER*.
THOSE ARE WORDS OF WAR, *FRIEND*.
KYO...
IS THAT "HOLY CROSS" YOU BEAR ON YOUR BACK THE REAL THING? WAS MURAMASA RIGHT ABOUT YOU?
SHOW ME, KYO.
SHOW ME HOW FAR YOU CAN GO.

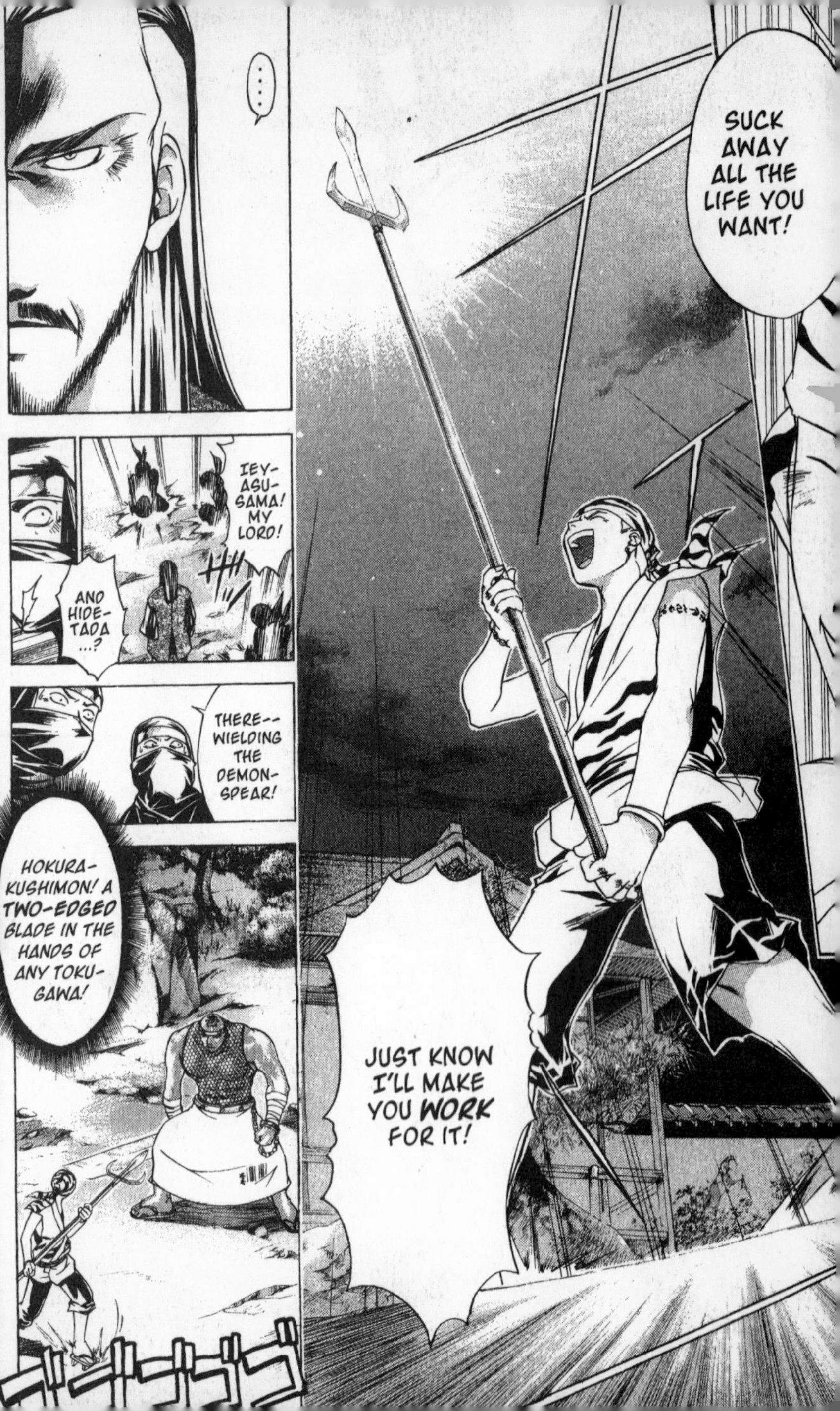
SUCK AWAY ALL THE LIFE YOU WANT!
JUST KNOW I'LL MAKE YOU **WORK** FOR IT!
....
IEY-ASU-SAMA! MY LORD!
AND HIDE-TADA...?
THERE--WIELDING THE DEMON-SPEAR!
HOKURA-KUSHIMON! A **TWO-EDGED** BLADE IN THE HANDS OF ANY TOKU-GAWA!

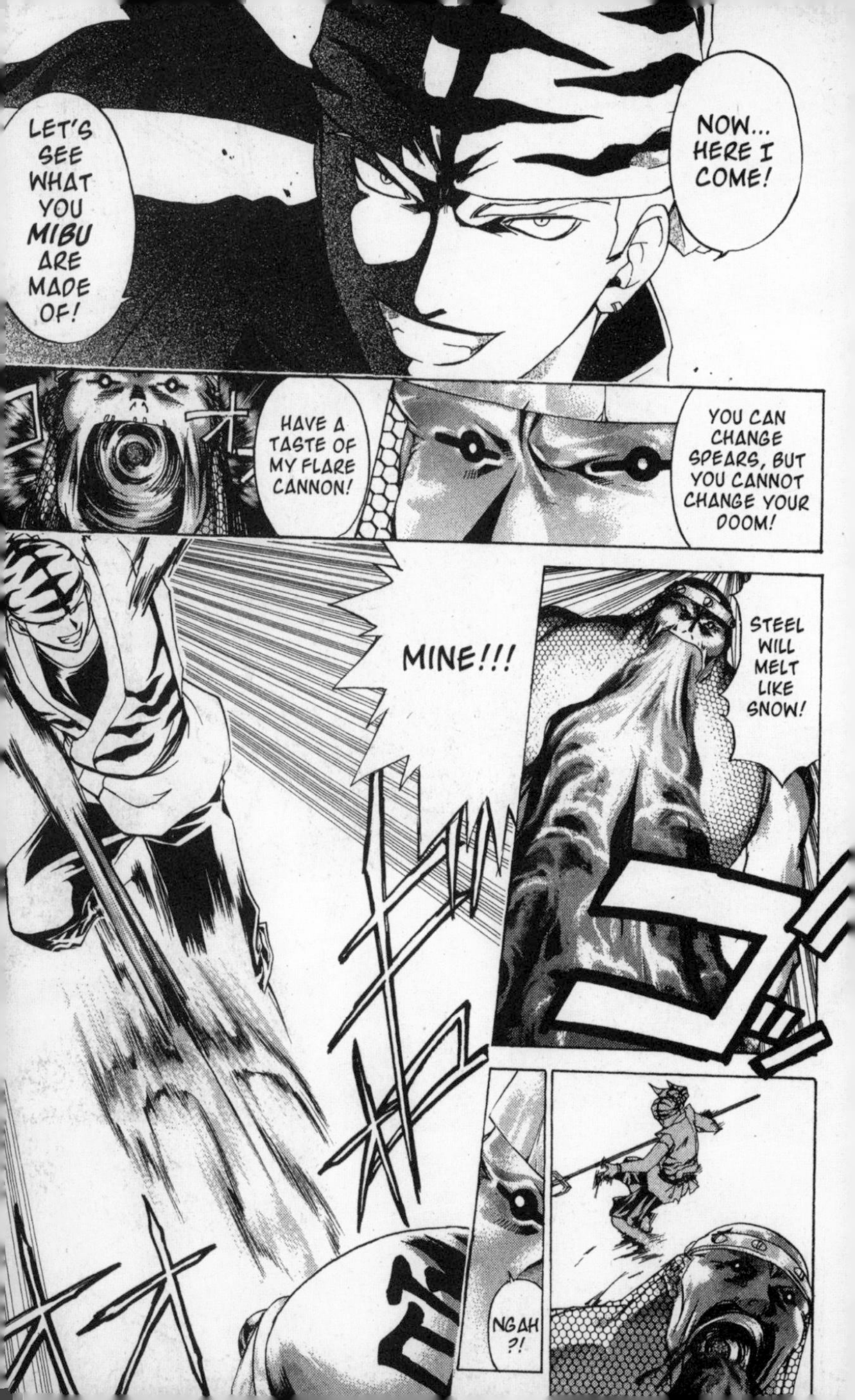
NOW... HERE I COME!
LET'S SEE WHAT YOU MIBU ARE MADE OF!
YOU CAN CHANGE SPEARS, BUT YOU CANNOT CHANGE YOUR DOOM!
HAVE A TASTE OF MY FLARE CANNON!
STEEL WILL MELT LIKE SNOW!
MINE!!!
NGAH ?!

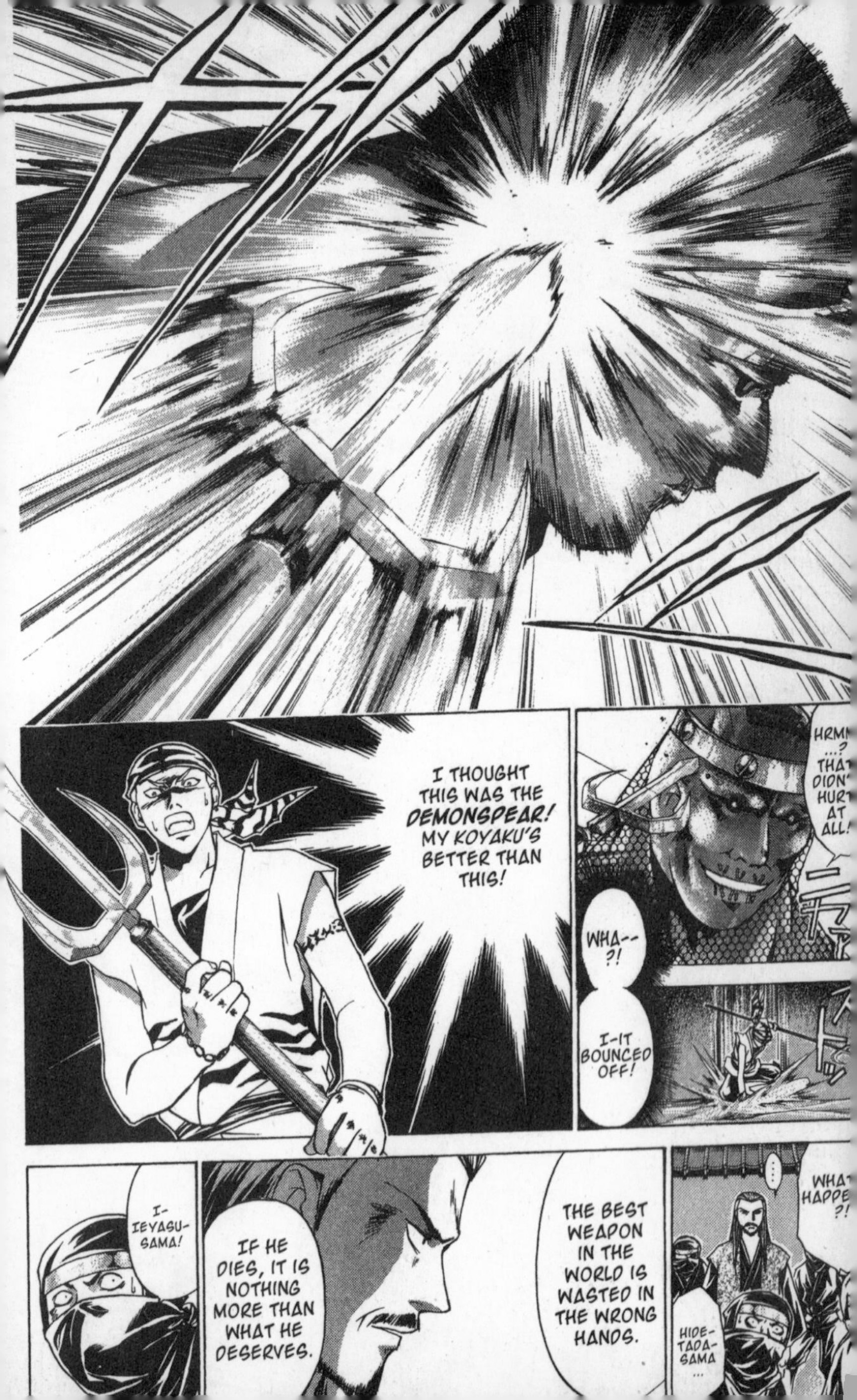
HRMM ...? THAT DIDN' HURT AT ALL!
WHA--?!
I-IT BOUNCED OFF!
I THOUGHT THIS WAS THE *DEMONSPEAR!* MY KOYAKU'S BETTER THAN THIS!
WHAT HAPPE ?!
...
HIDE-TADA-SAMA ...
THE BEST WEAPON IN THE WORLD IS WASTED IN THE WRONG HANDS.
IF HE DIES, IT IS NOTHING MORE THAN WHAT HE DESERVES.
I-IEYASU-SAMA!

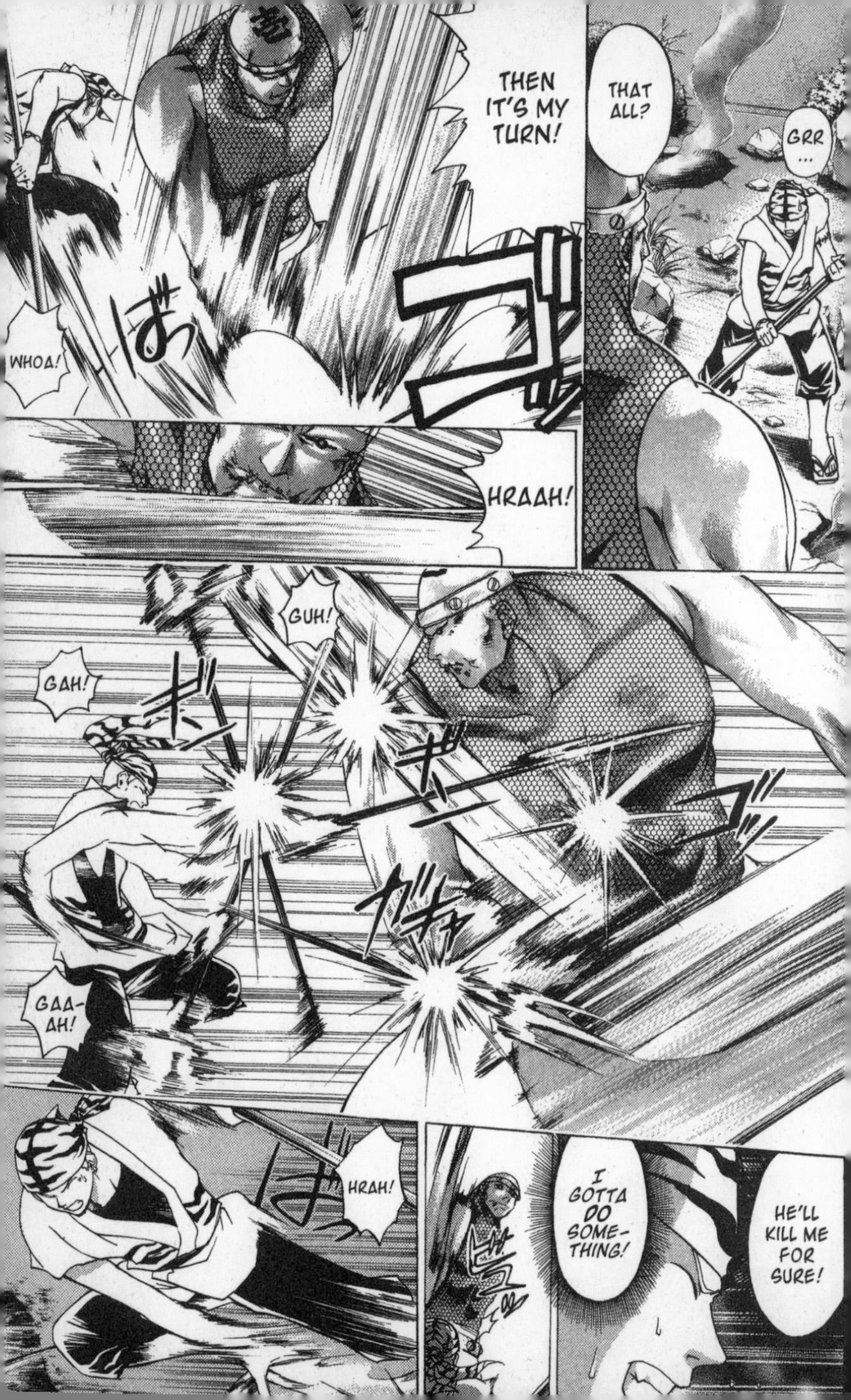
GRR ...
THAT ALL?
THEN IT'S MY TURN!
ゴッ
ばっ
WHOA!
HRAAH!
GUH!
GAH!
GAA-AH!
HE'LL KILL ME FOR SURE!
I GOTTA DO SOME-THING!
HRAH!

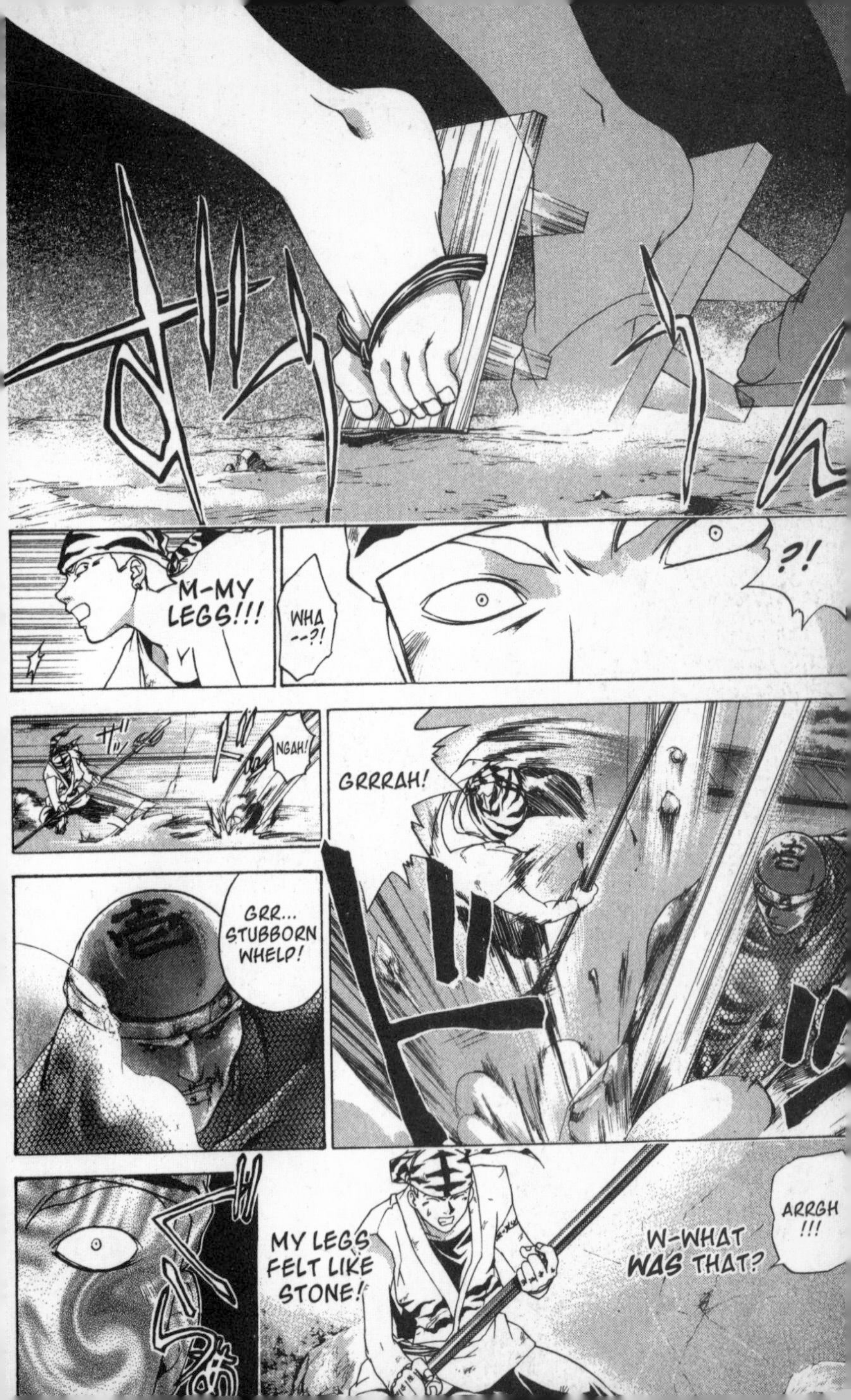
?!
WHA --?!
M-MY LEGS!!!
GRRRAH!
NGAH!
GRR... STUBBORN WHELP!
ARRGH!!!
W-WHAT WAS THAT?
MY LEGS FELT LIKE STONE!

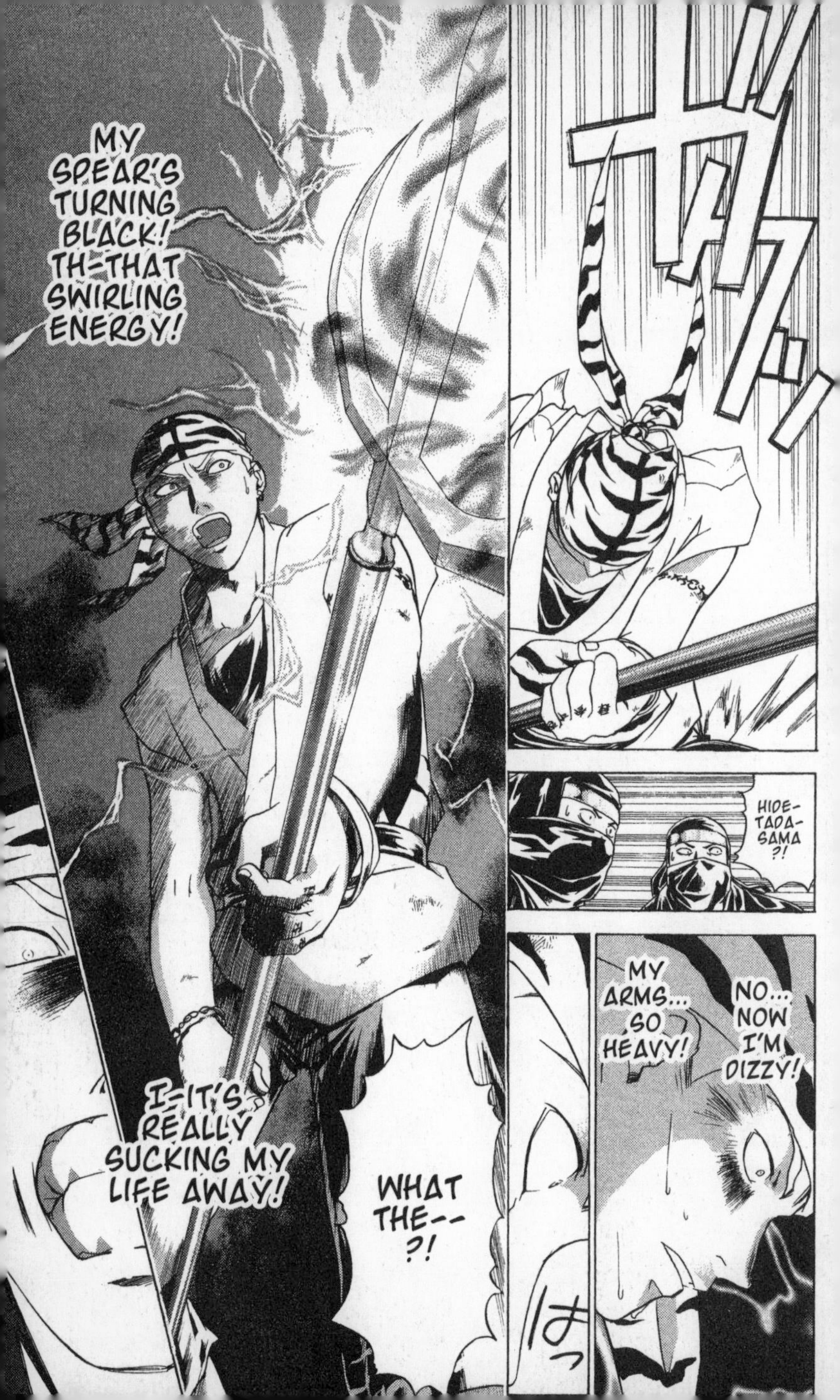
HIDE-TADA-SAMA?!
NO... NOW I'M DIZZY!
MY ARMS... SO HEAVY!
はっ
MY SPEAR'S TURNING BLACK! TH-THAT SWIRLING ENERGY!
I-IT'S REALLY SUCKING MY LIFE AWAY!
WHAT THE--?!

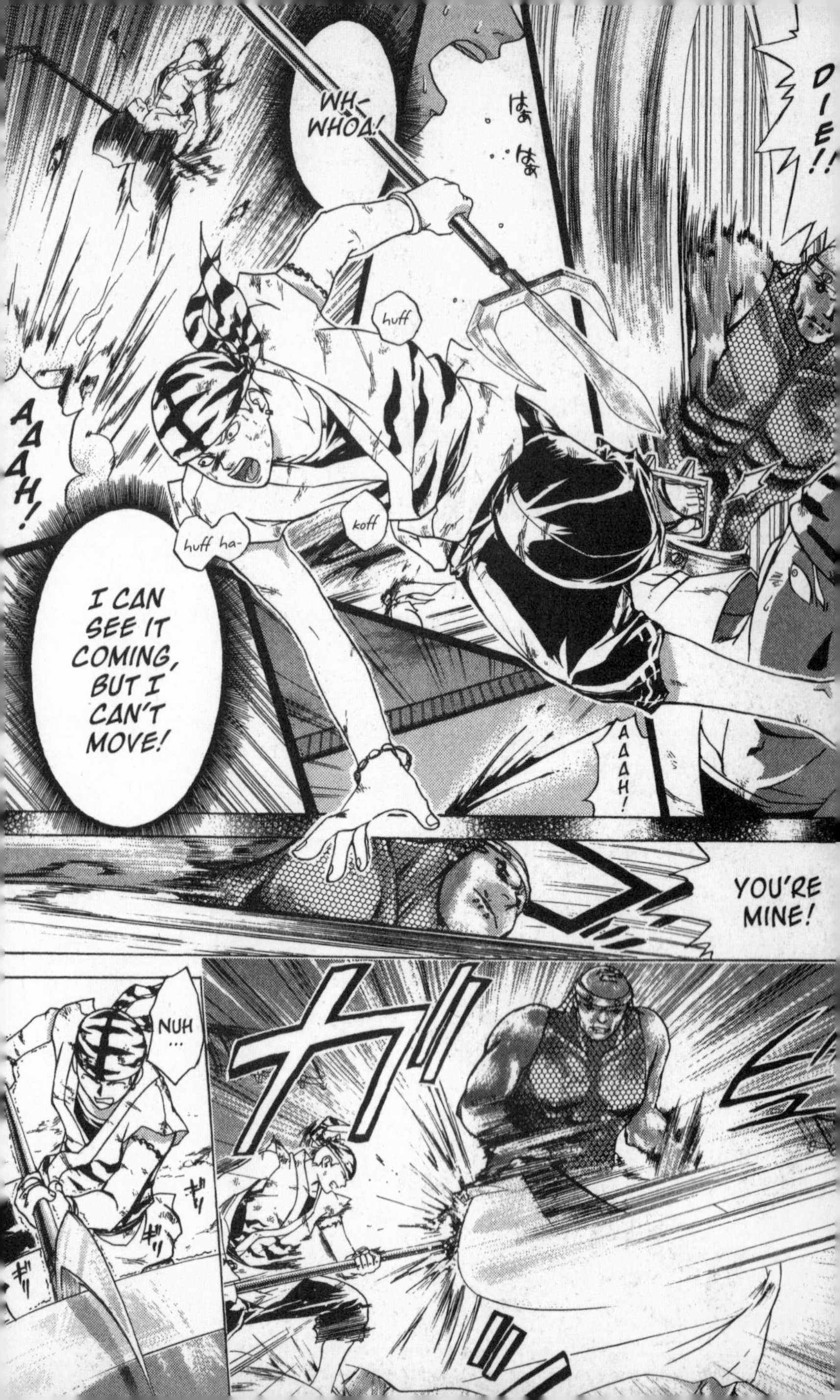
DIE!!
はぁ はぁ
WH-WHOA!
huff
koff
huff ha-
AAAH!
AAAH!
I CAN SEE IT COMING, BUT I CAN'T MOVE!
YOU'RE MINE!
NUH ...
ギリ
ギリ
ギリ

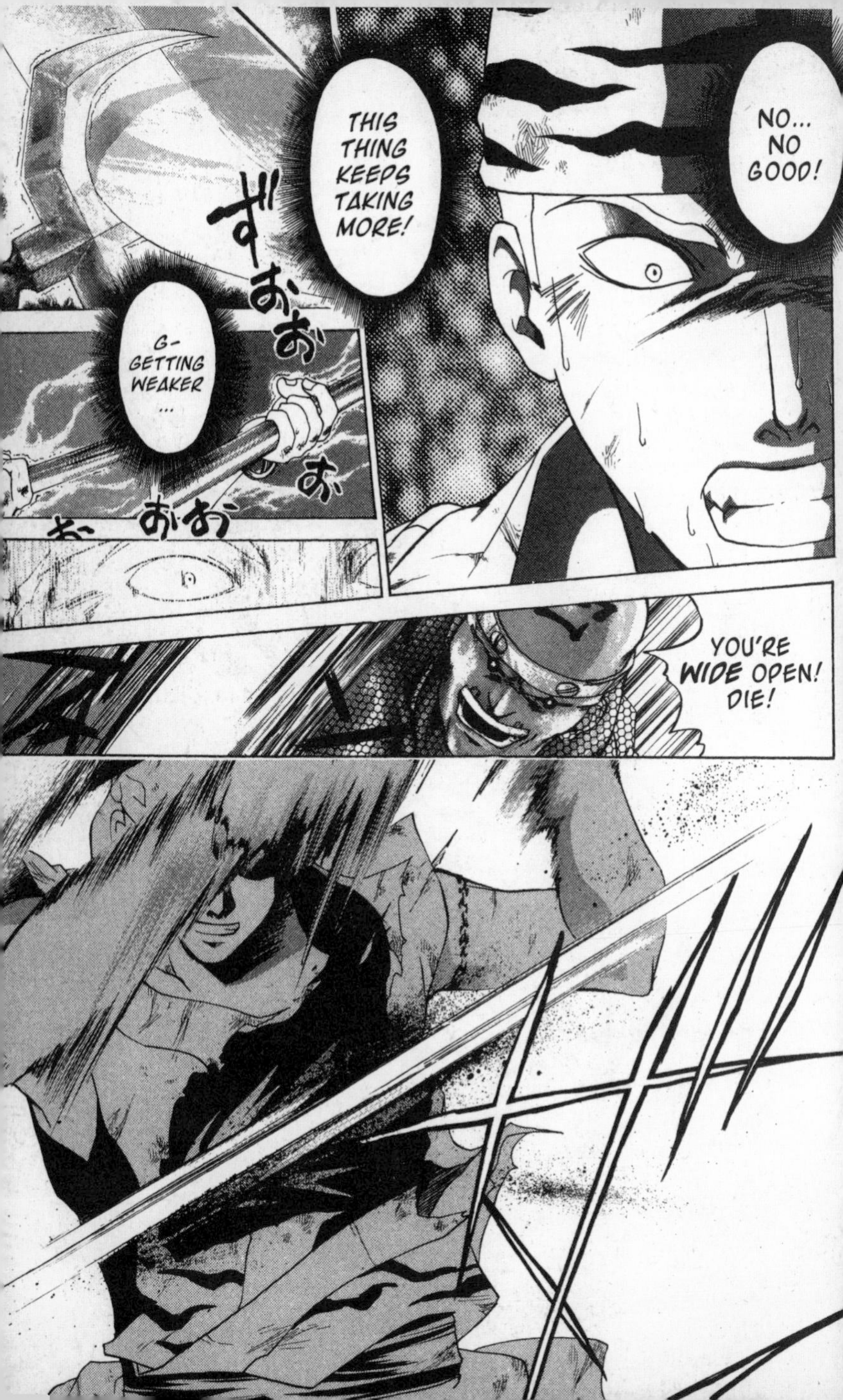

NO... NO GOOD!
THIS THING KEEPS TAKING MORE!
ずおおおおおお
G-GETTING WEAKER...
YOU'RE **WIDE** OPEN! DIE!

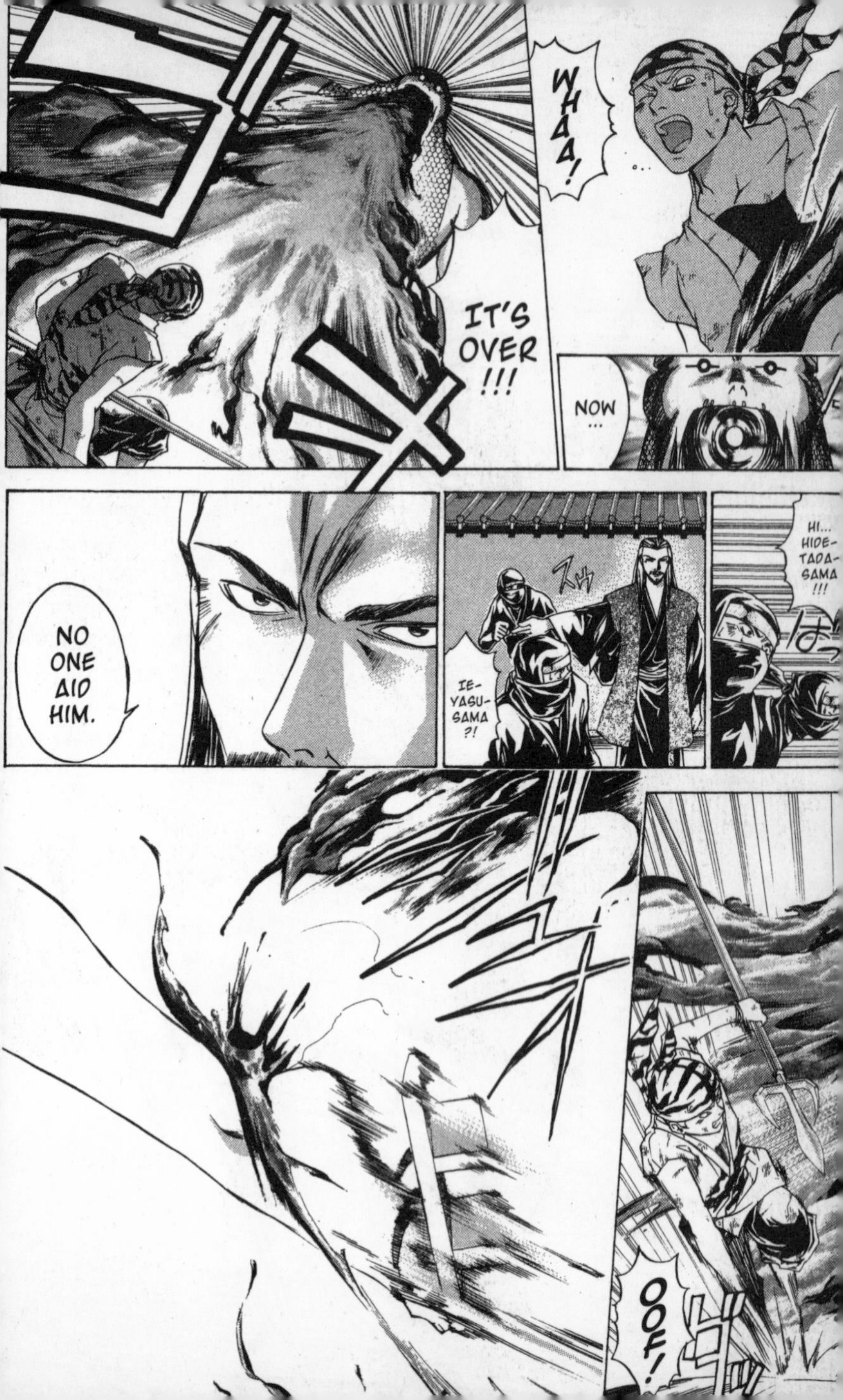
WHAAA!
NOW...
IT'S OVER!!!
HI... HIDETADA-SAMA!!!
IE-YASU-SAMA?!
NO ONE AID HIM.
OOF!

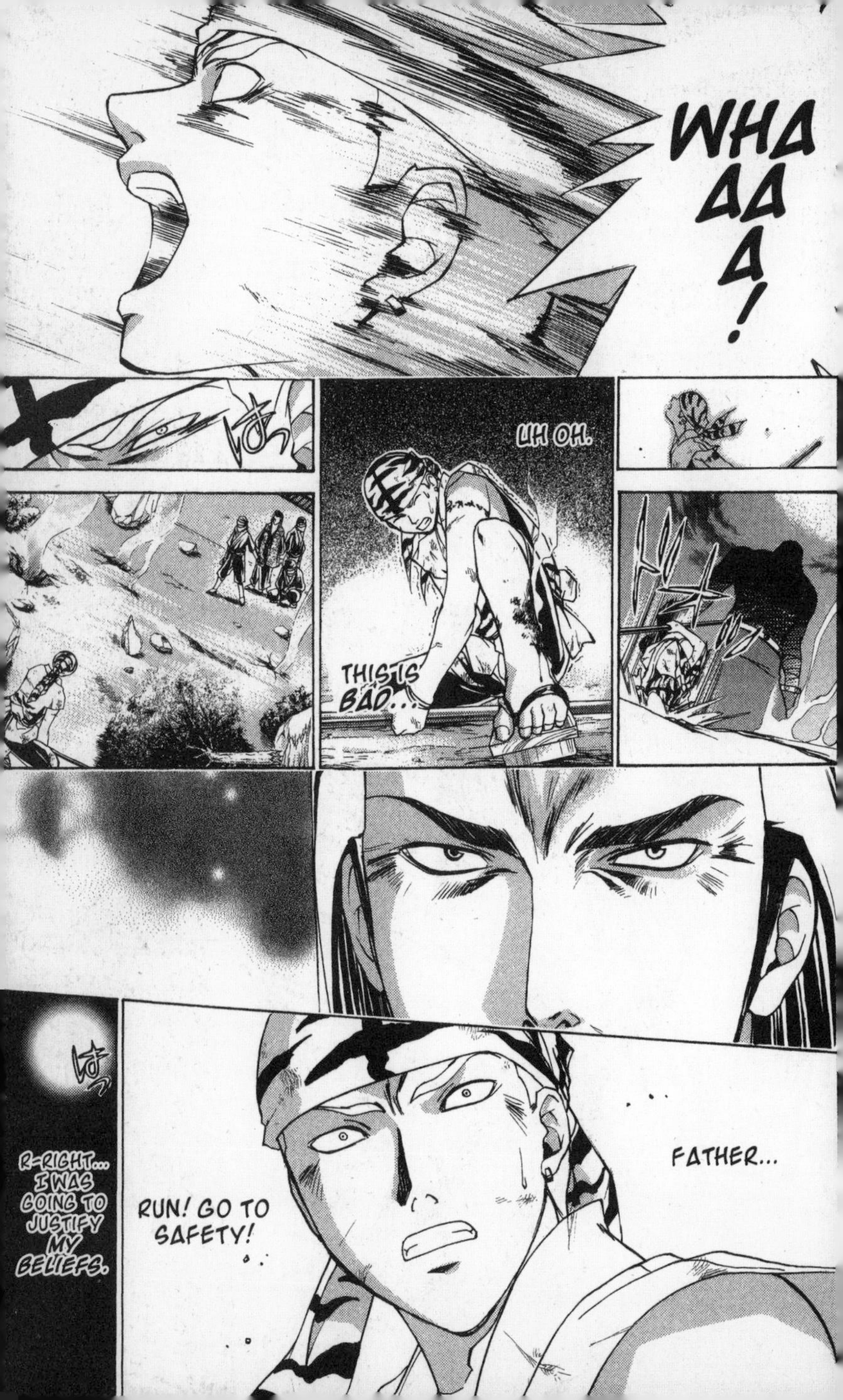
WHAAAA!
UH OH.
THIS IS BAD...
FATHER...
RUN! GO TO SAFETY!
R-RIGHT... I WAS GOING TO JUSTIFY MY BELIEFS.

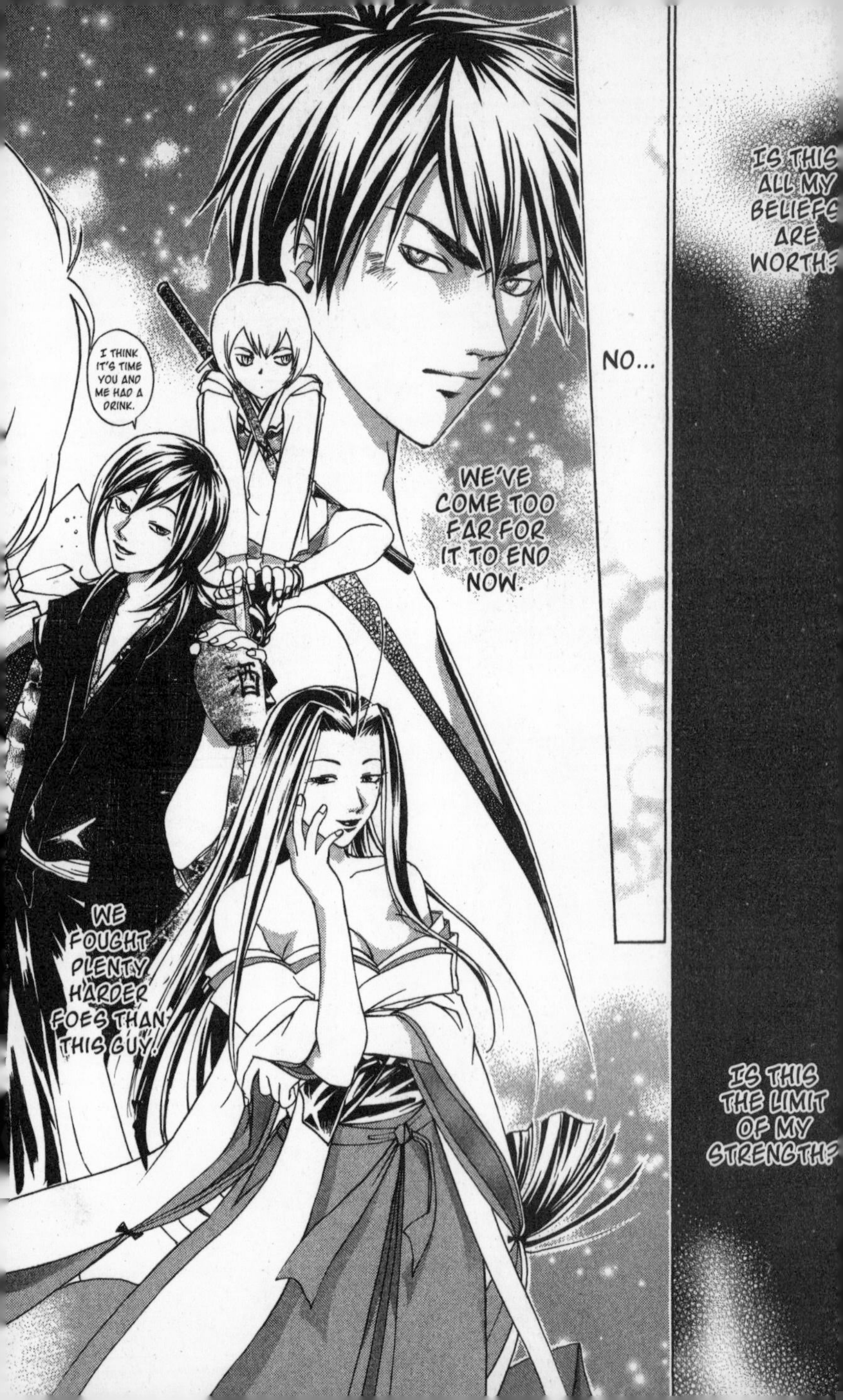
IS THIS ALL MY BELIEFS ARE WORTH?
IS THIS THE LIMIT OF MY STRENGTH?
NO...
WE'VE COME TOO FAR FOR IT TO END NOW.
I THINK IT'S TIME YOU AND ME HAD A DRINK.
WE FOUGHT PLENTY HARDER FOES THAN THIS GUY!

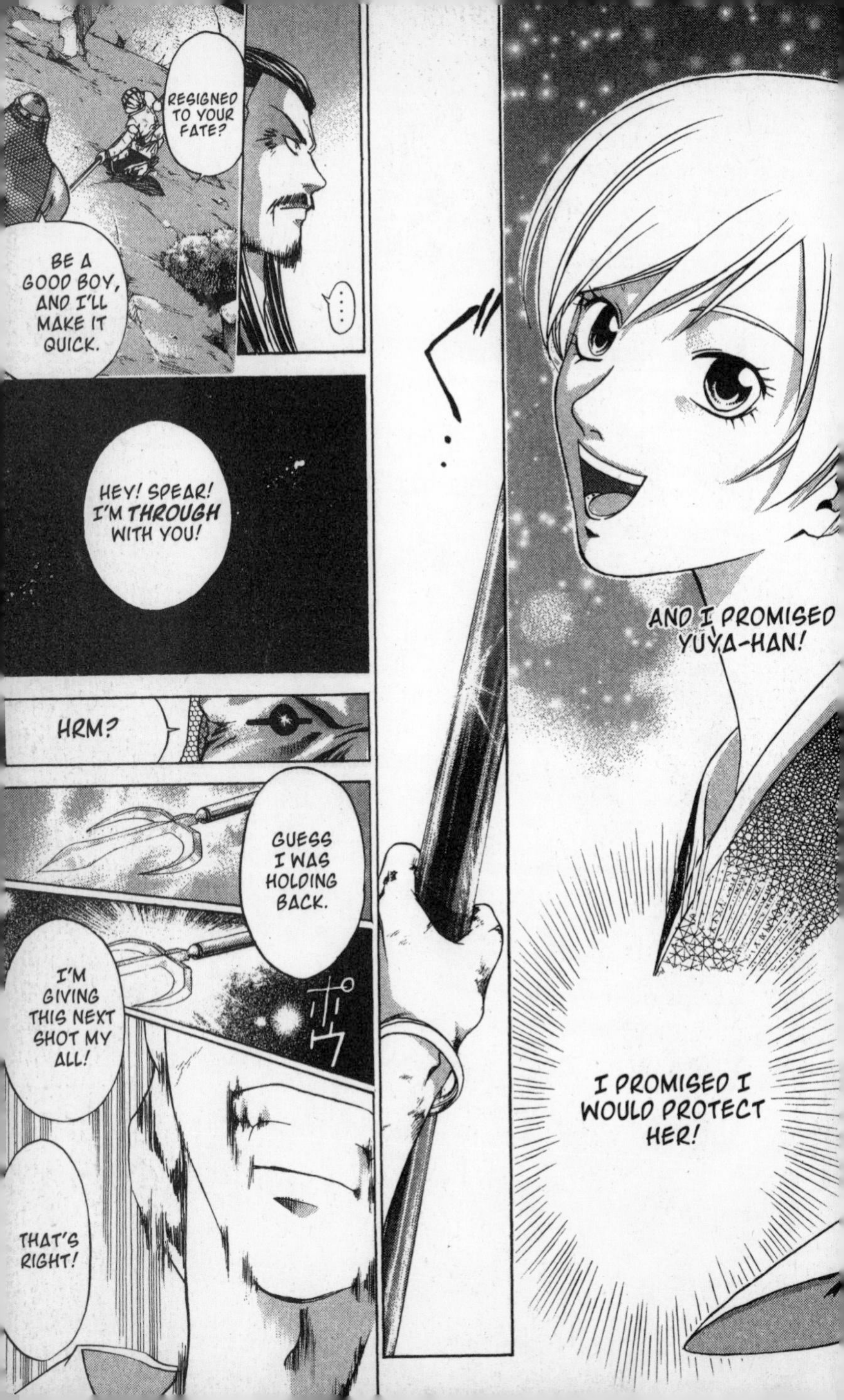
RESIGNED TO YOUR FATE?
BE A GOOD BOY, AND I'LL MAKE IT QUICK.
...
HEY! SPEAR! I'M THROUGH WITH YOU!
HRM?
GUESS I WAS HOLDING BACK.
I'M GIVING THIS NEXT SHOT MY ALL!
THAT'S RIGHT!
AND I PROMISED YUYA-HAN!
I PROMISED I WOULD PROTECT HER!

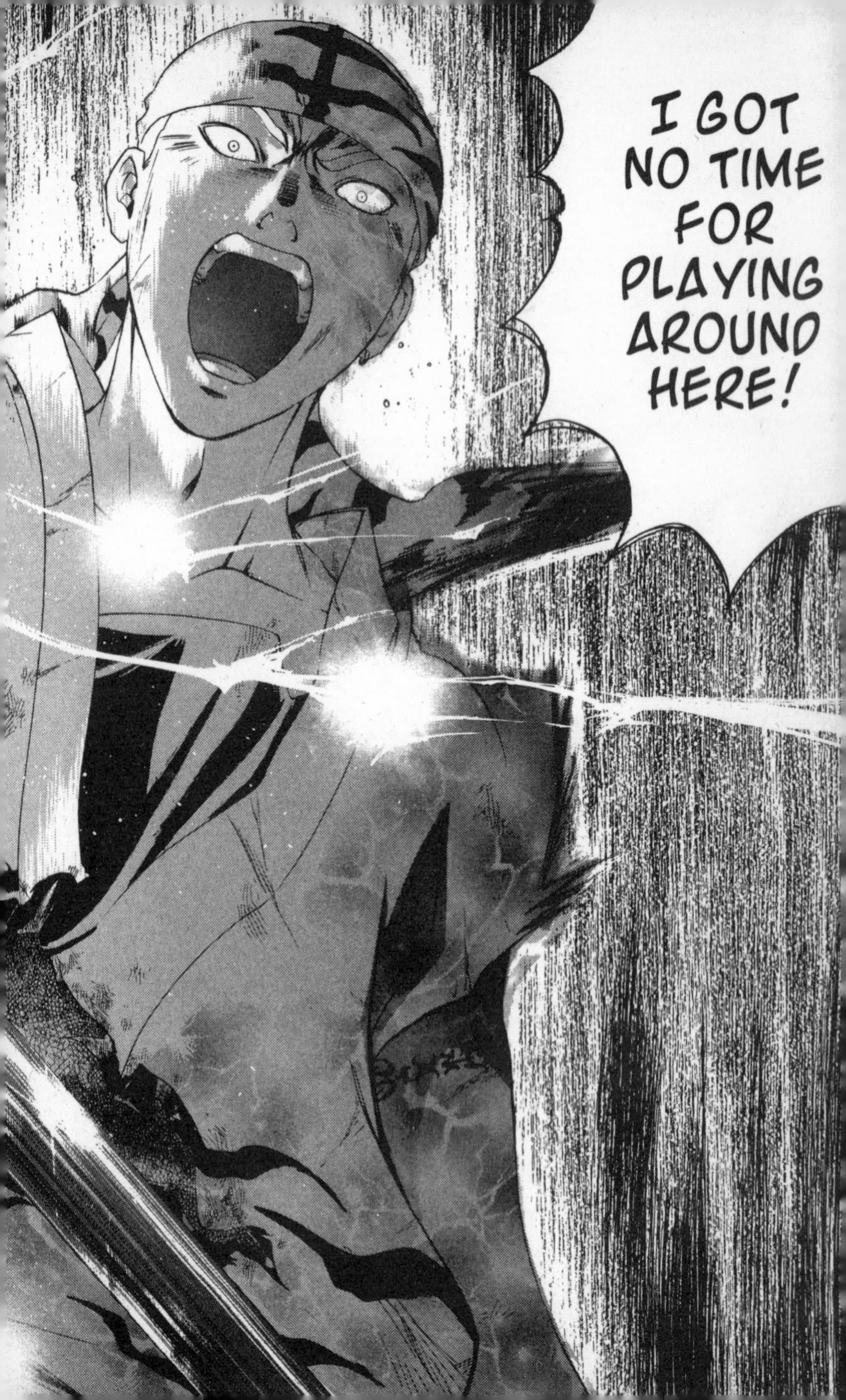
I GOT NO TIME FOR PLAYING AROUND HERE!

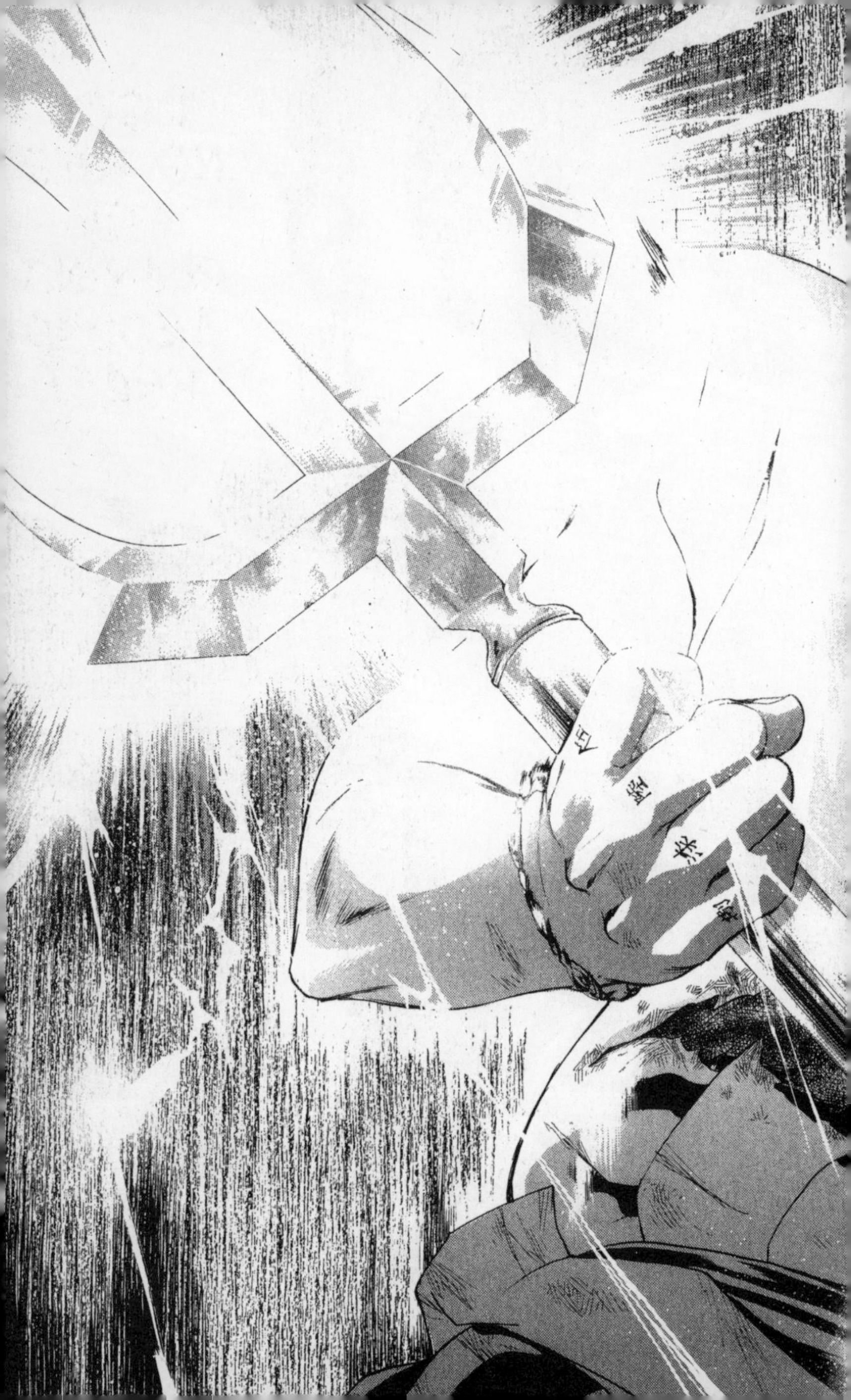

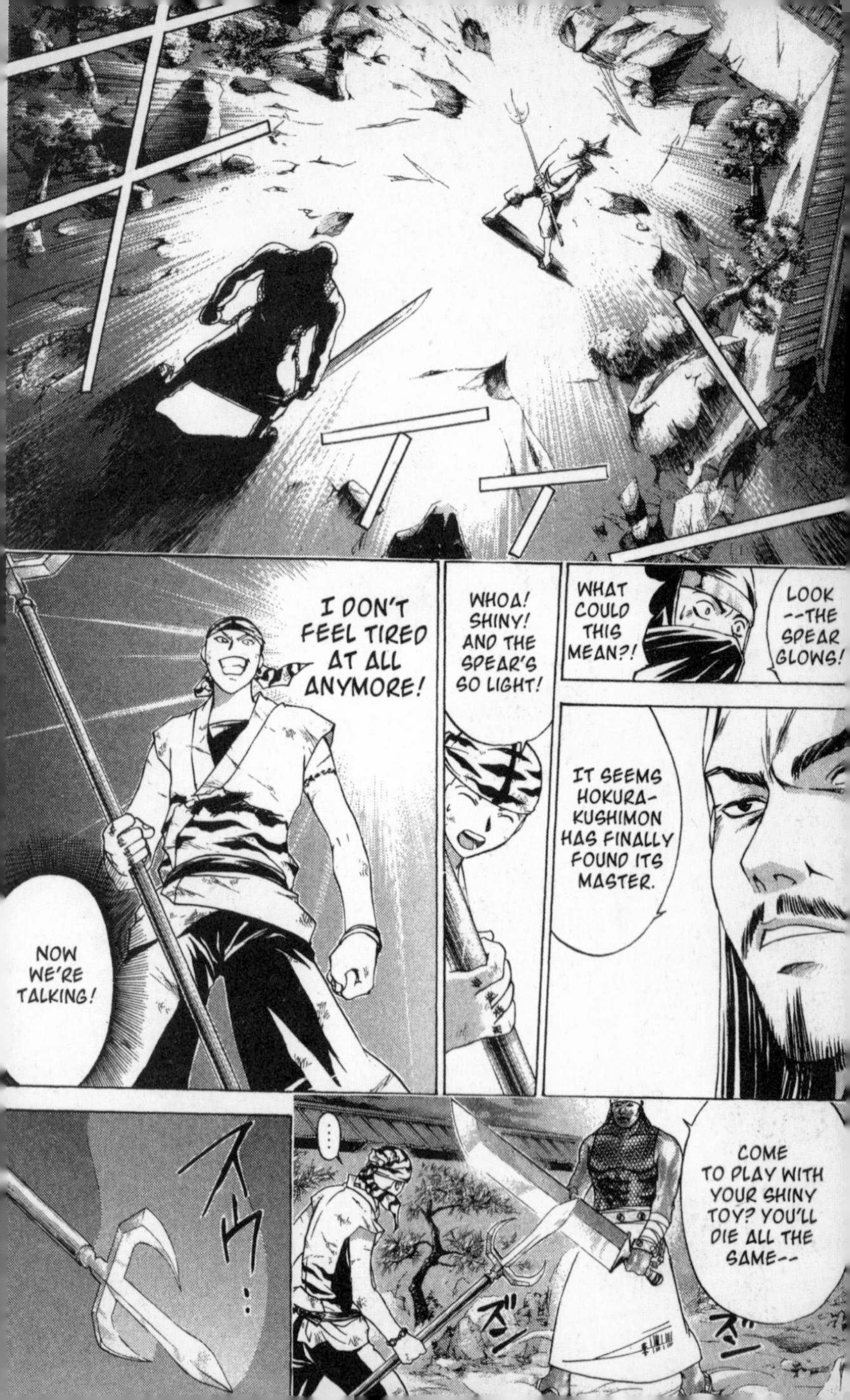
LOOK --THE SPEAR GLOWS!
WHAT COULD THIS MEAN?!
IT SEEMS HOKURA-KUSHIMON HAS FINALLY FOUND ITS MASTER.
WHOA! SHINY! AND THE SPEAR'S SO LIGHT!
I DON'T FEEL TIRED AT ALL ANYMORE!
NOW WE'RE TALKING!
COME TO PLAY WITH YOUR SHINY TOY? YOU'LL DIE ALL THE SAME--
...

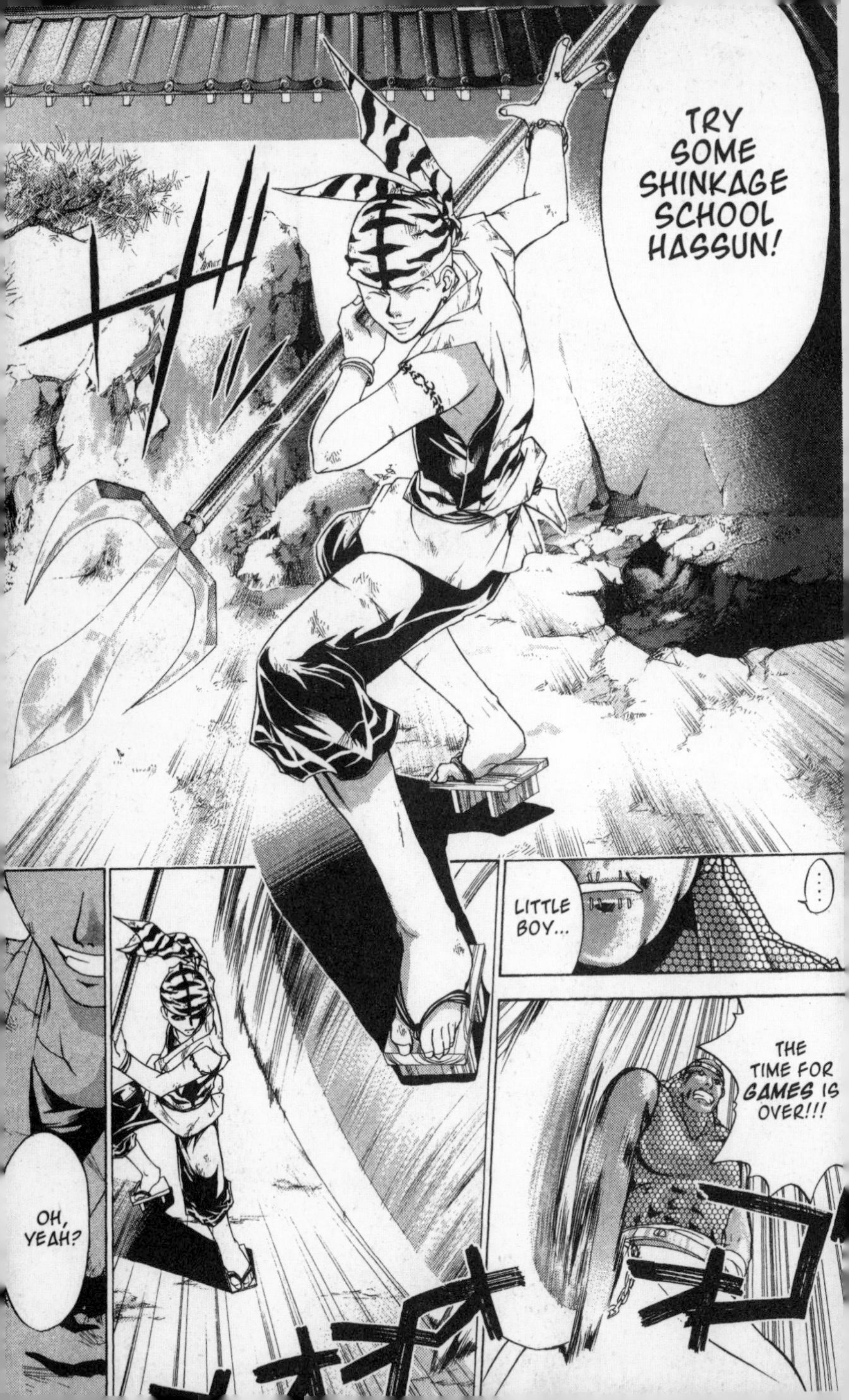
TRY SOME SHINKAGE SCHOOL HASSUN!
...
LITTLE BOY...
THE TIME FOR GAMES IS OVER!!!
OH, YEAH?

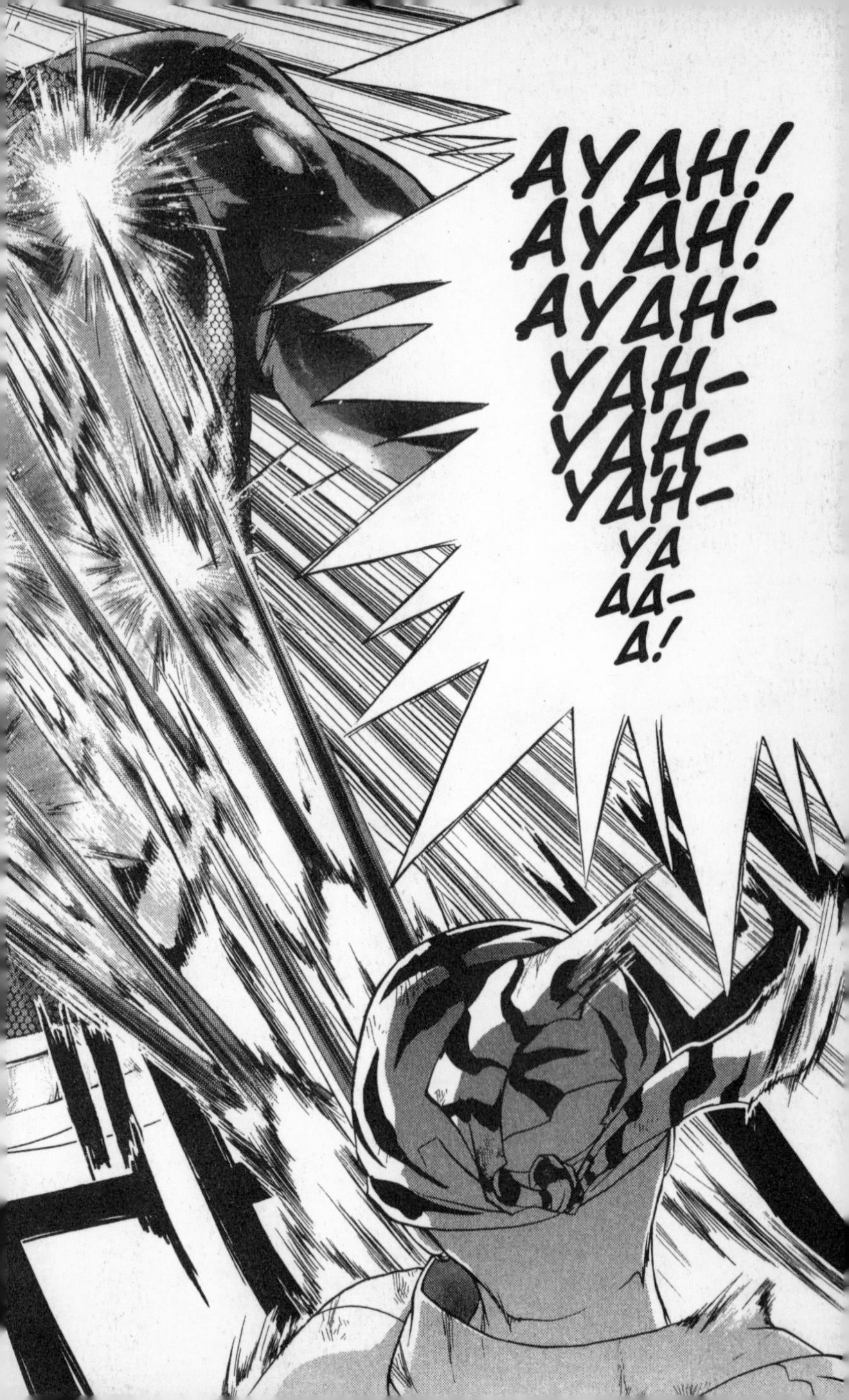
AYAH! AYAH! AYAH-YAH-YAH-YAH-YAAA-A!

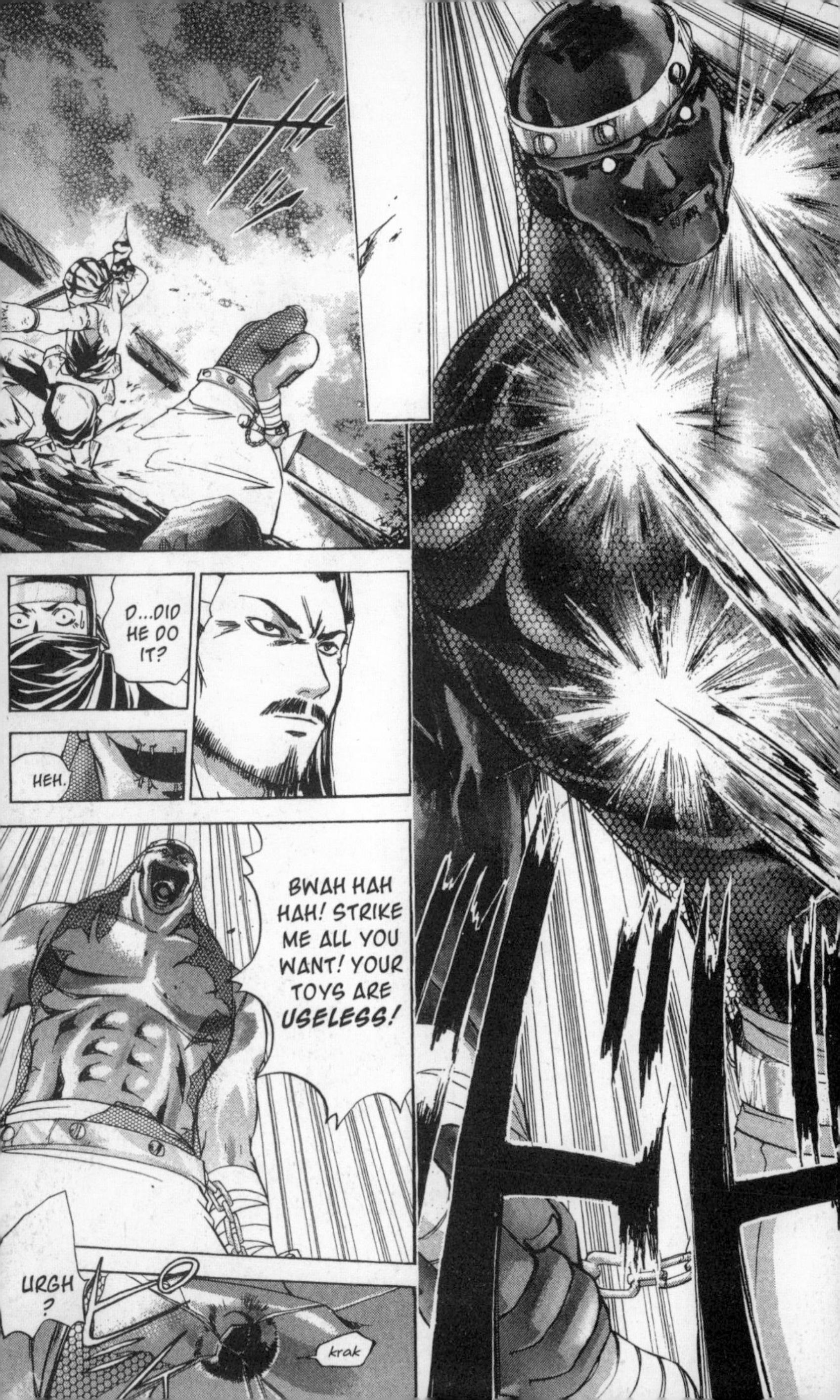
D...DID HE DO IT?
HEH.
BWAH HAH HAH! STRIKE ME ALL YOU WANT! YOUR TOYS ARE USELESS!
URGH?
krak

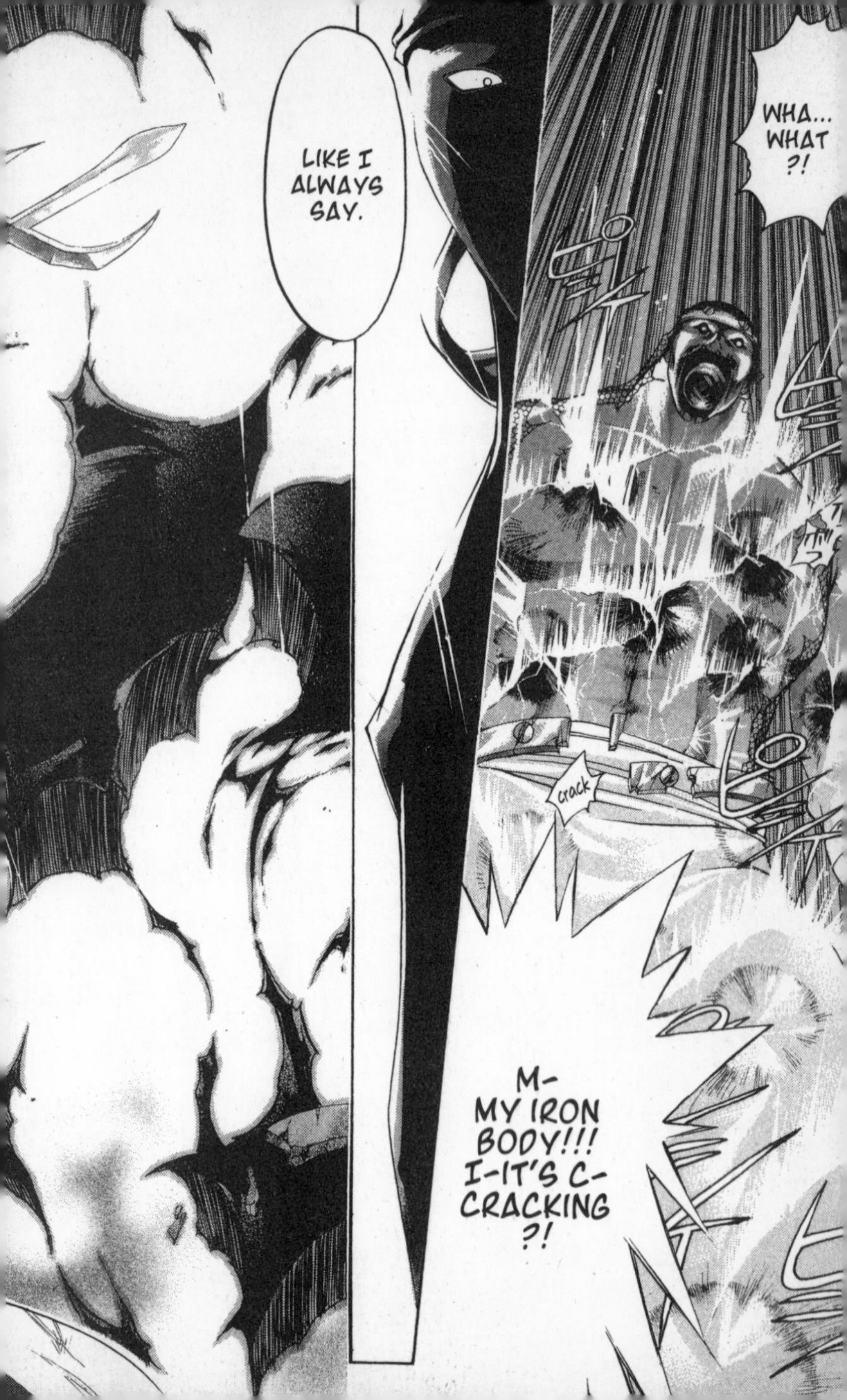
WHA... WHAT ?!
crack
M- MY IRON BODY!!! I-IT'S C-CRACKING ?!
LIKE I ALWAYS SAY.

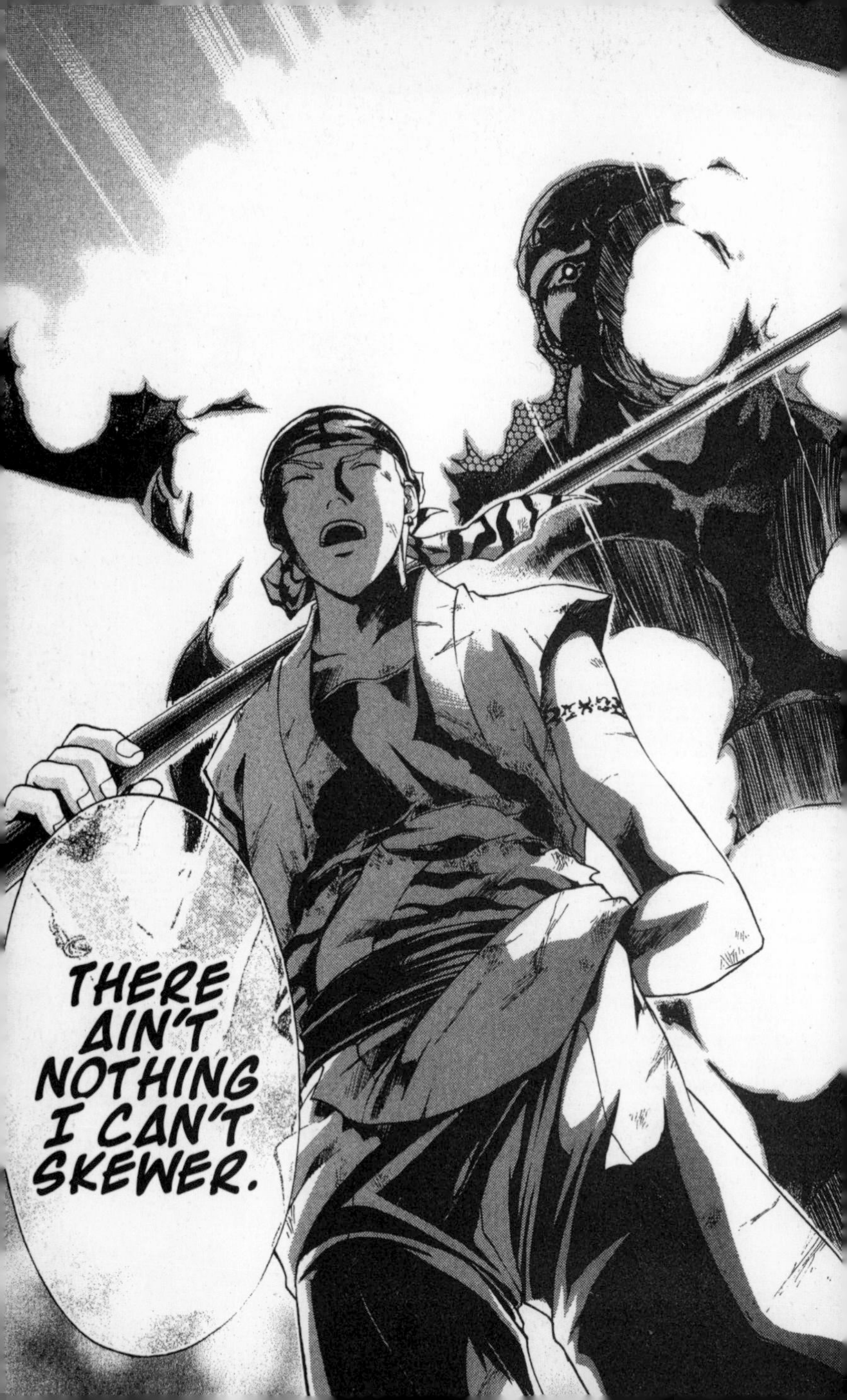
THERE AIN'T NOTHING I CAN'T SKEWER.

"Nagao's World" by Assistant Nagao

Or: The Insidious Brain Invasion

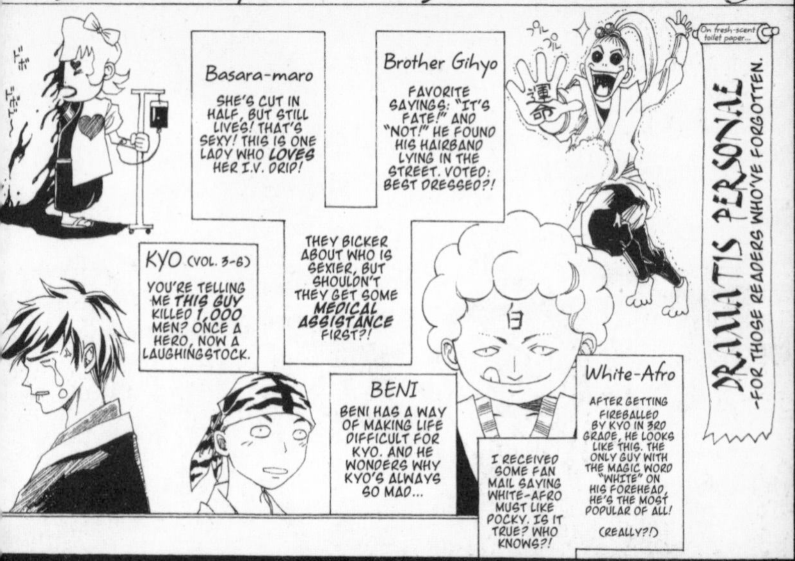
On fresh-scent toilet paper...
DRAMATIS PERSONAE
-FOR THOSE READERS WHO'VE FORGOTTEN.
Brother Gihyo
FAVORITE SAYINGS: "IT'S FATE!" AND "NOT!" HE FOUND HIS HAIRBAND LYING IN THE STREET. VOTED: BEST DRESSED?!
Basara-maro
SHE'S CUT IN HALF, BUT STILL LIVES! THAT'S SEXY! THIS IS ONE LADY WHO LOVES HER I.V. DRIP!
THEY BICKER ABOUT WHO IS SEXIER, BUT SHOULDN'T THEY GET SOME MEDICAL ASSISTANCE FIRST?!
KYO (VOL. 3-6)
YOU'RE TELLING ME THIS GUY KILLED 1,000 MEN? ONCE A HERO, NOW A LAUGHINGSTOCK.
White-Afro
AFTER GETTING FIREBALLED BY KYO IN 3RD GRADE, HE LOOKS LIKE THIS. THE ONLY GUY WITH THE MAGIC WORD "WHITE" ON HIS FOREHEAD, HE'S THE MOST POPULAR OF ALL!
(REALLY?!)
I RECEIVED SOME FAN MAIL SAYING WHITE-AFRO MUST LIKE POCKY. IS IT TRUE? WHO KNOWS?!
BENI
BENI HAS A WAY OF MAKING LIFE DIFFICULT FOR KYO. AND HE WONDERS WHY KYO'S ALWAYS SO MAD...

↑ TAKAYA NAGAO

↓ KEN'ICHI SUETAKE

IT'S BEEN 2 1/2 YEARS SINCE I JOINED KAMIJYO-SENSEI'S TEAM, AND NOW IT'S TIME TO LEAVE. THINKING BACK ON IT, IT SEEMS LIKE JUST YESTERDAY THAT I CAME HERE. I DON'T THINK I EVER REALLY GOT ANY BETTER... SORRY, SENSEI! STILL, I LEARNED A LOT, AND I WAS ALWAYS IMPRESSED WITH HOW EVEN-HANDED AND GOOD NATURED KAMIJYO-SENSEI WAS. GOOD LUCK, SENSEI, AND GOOD LUCK, KYO! CIAO!

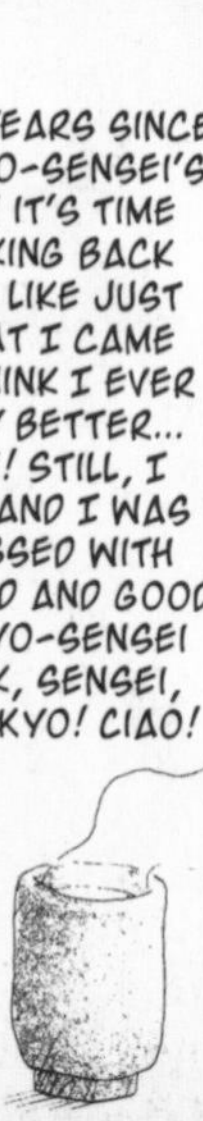

(LIVE) Martial Arts Practice is Dangerous

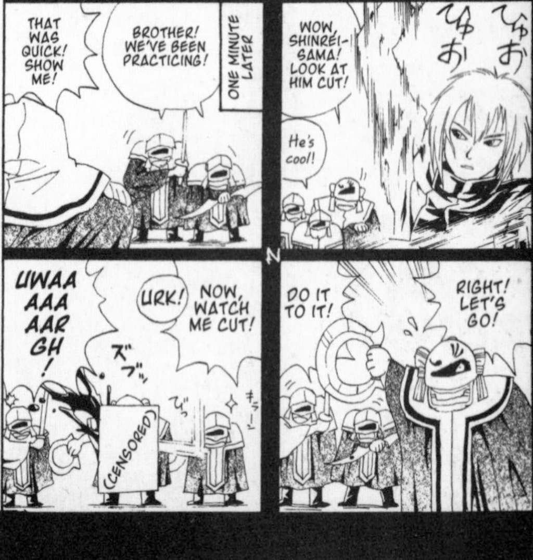
ひゅお ひゅお
WOW, SHINREI-SAMA! LOOK AT HIM CUT!
He's cool!
RIGHT! LET'S GO!
DO IT TO IT!
ONE MINUTE LATER
BROTHER! WE'VE BEEN PRACTICING!
THAT WAS QUICK! SHOW ME!
NOW, WATCH ME CUT!
URK!
UWAAAAAAARGH!
(CENSORED)

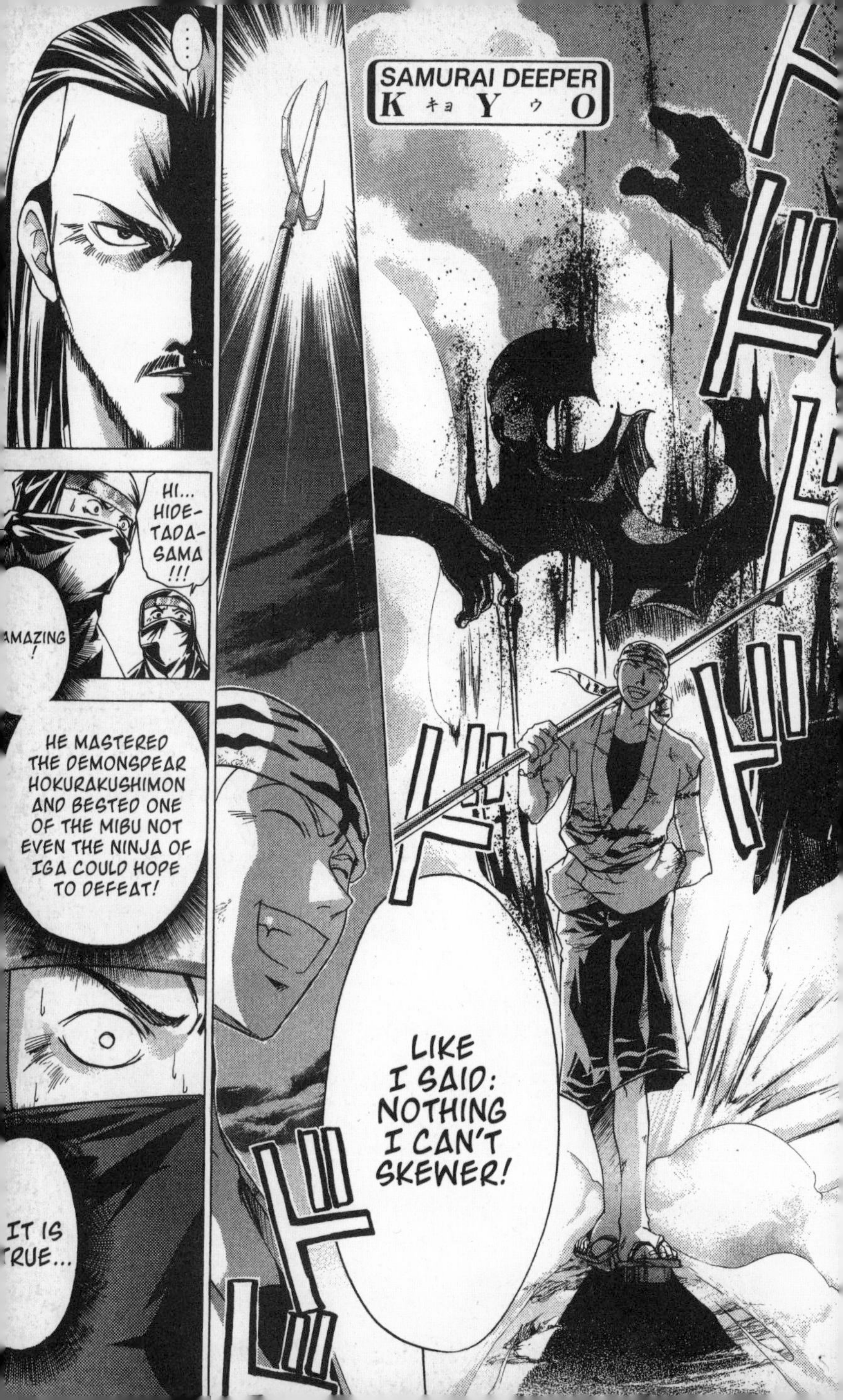
SAMURAI DEEPER
KYO
LIKE I SAID: NOTHING I CAN'T SKEWER!
...
HI... HIDE-TADA-SAMA!!!
AMAZING!
HE MASTERED THE DEMONSPEAR HOKURAKUSHIMON AND BESTED ONE OF THE MIBU NOT EVEN THE NINJA OF IGA COULD HOPE TO DEFEAT!
IT IS TRUE...

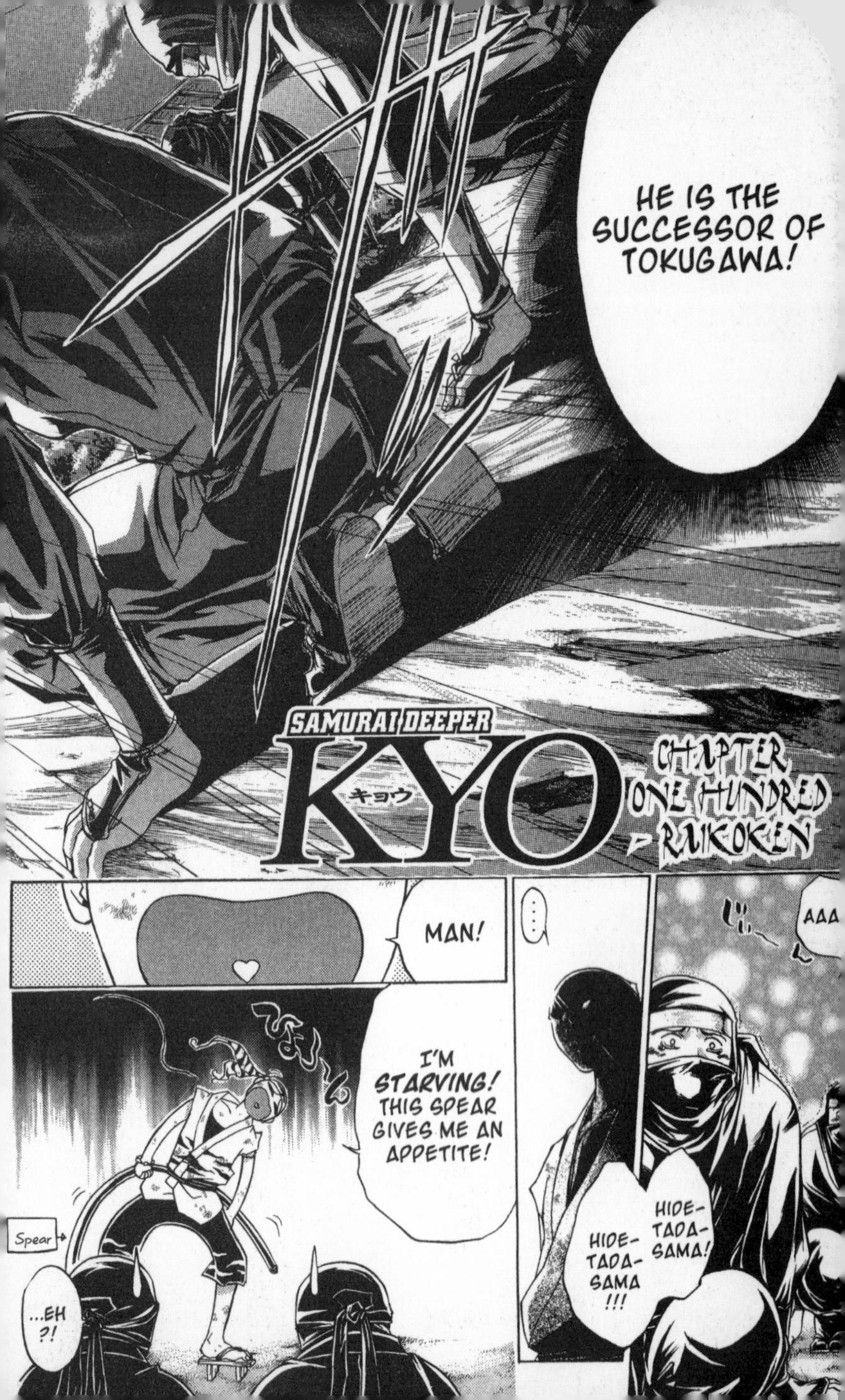
HE IS THE SUCCESSOR OF TOKUGAWA!
SAMURAI DEEPER
KYO
キョウ
CHAPTER ONE HUNDRED - RAIKOKEN
AAA
...
HIDE-TADA-SAMA!
HIDE-TADA-SAMA!!!
MAN!
I'M STARVING! THIS SPEAR GIVES ME AN APPETITE!
Spear
...EH ?!

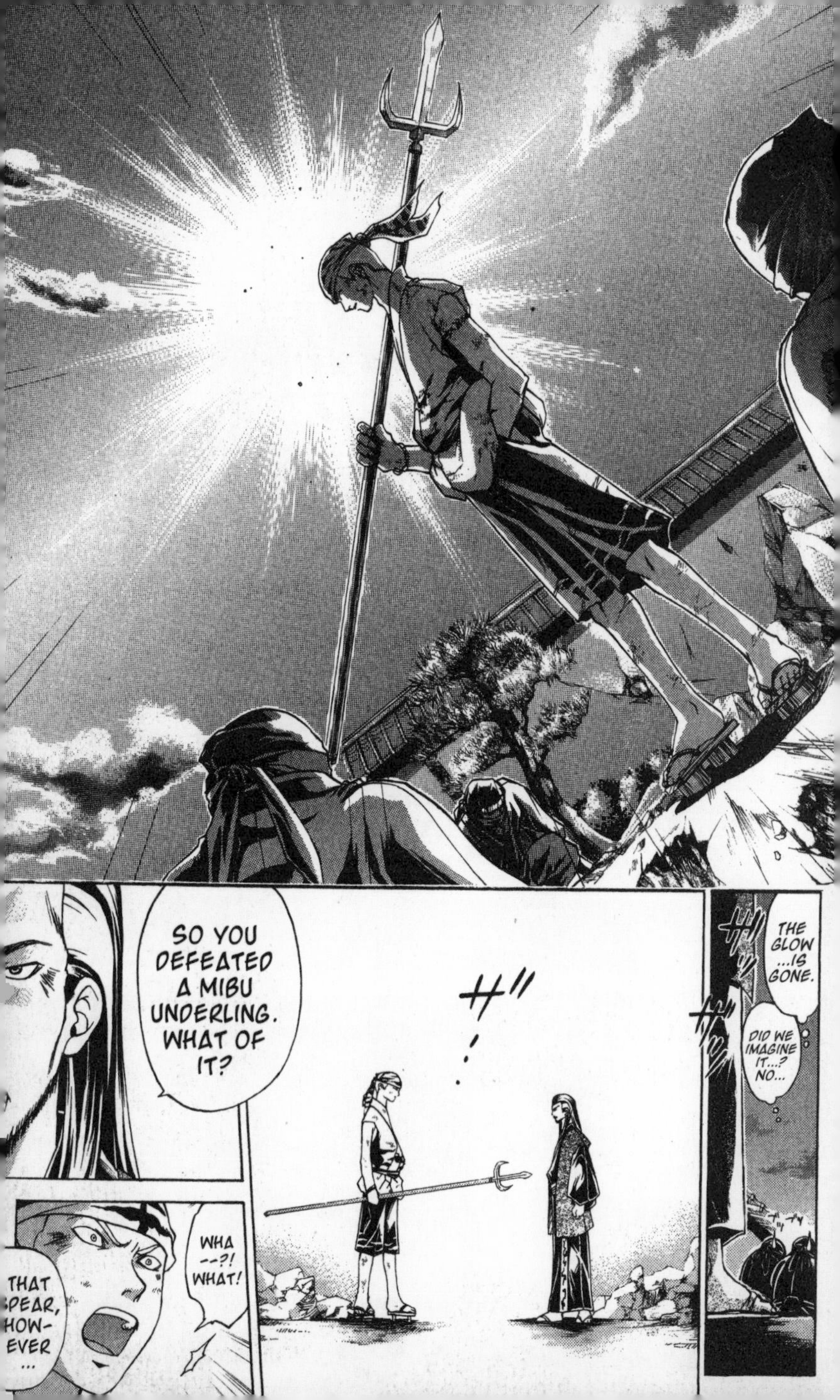
THE GLOW ...IS GONE.
DID WE IMAGINE IT...? NO...
SO YOU DEFEATED A MIBU UNDERLING. WHAT OF IT?
WHA--?! WHAT!
THAT SPEAR, HOWEVER ...

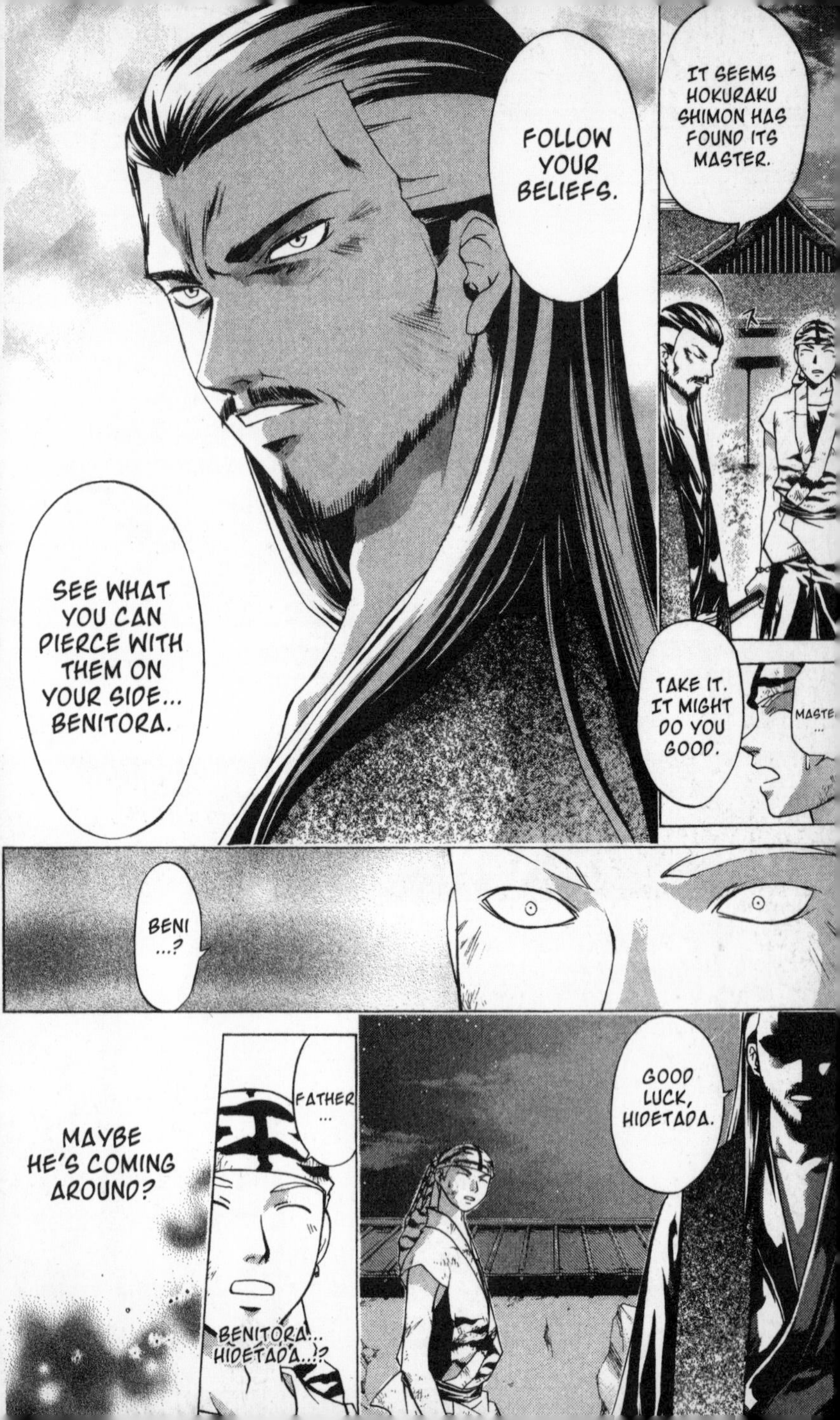
IT SEEMS HOKURAKU SHIMON HAS FOUND ITS MASTER.
TAKE IT. IT MIGHT DO YOU GOOD.
MASTE...
FOLLOW YOUR BELIEFS.
SEE WHAT YOU CAN PIERCE WITH THEM ON YOUR SIDE... BENITORA.
BENI ...?
GOOD LUCK, HIDETADA.
FATHER ...
MAYBE HE'S COMING AROUND?
BENITORA... HIDETADA...!?

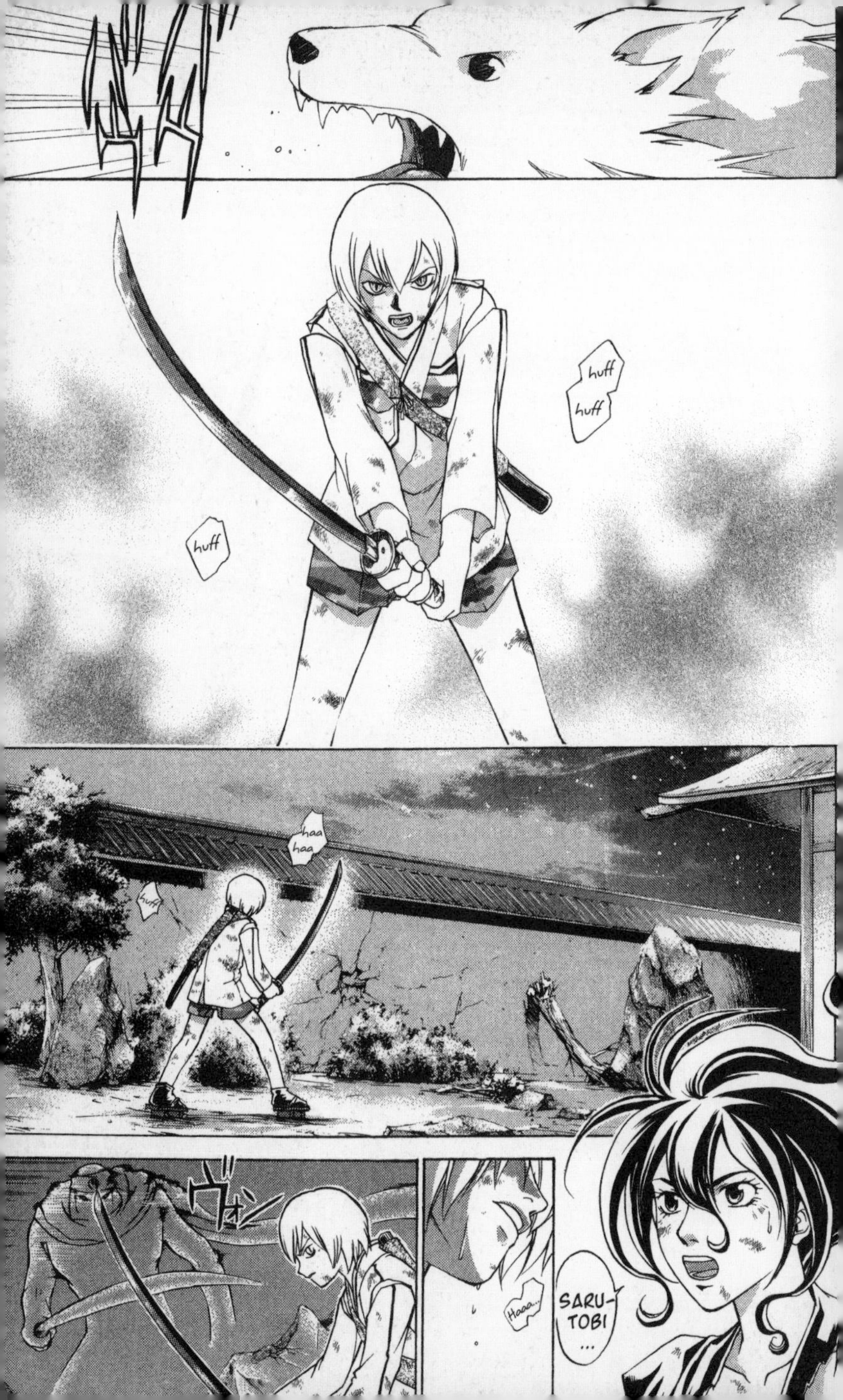
huff
huff
huff
haa
haa
huff
SARU-TOBI ...
Haaa...

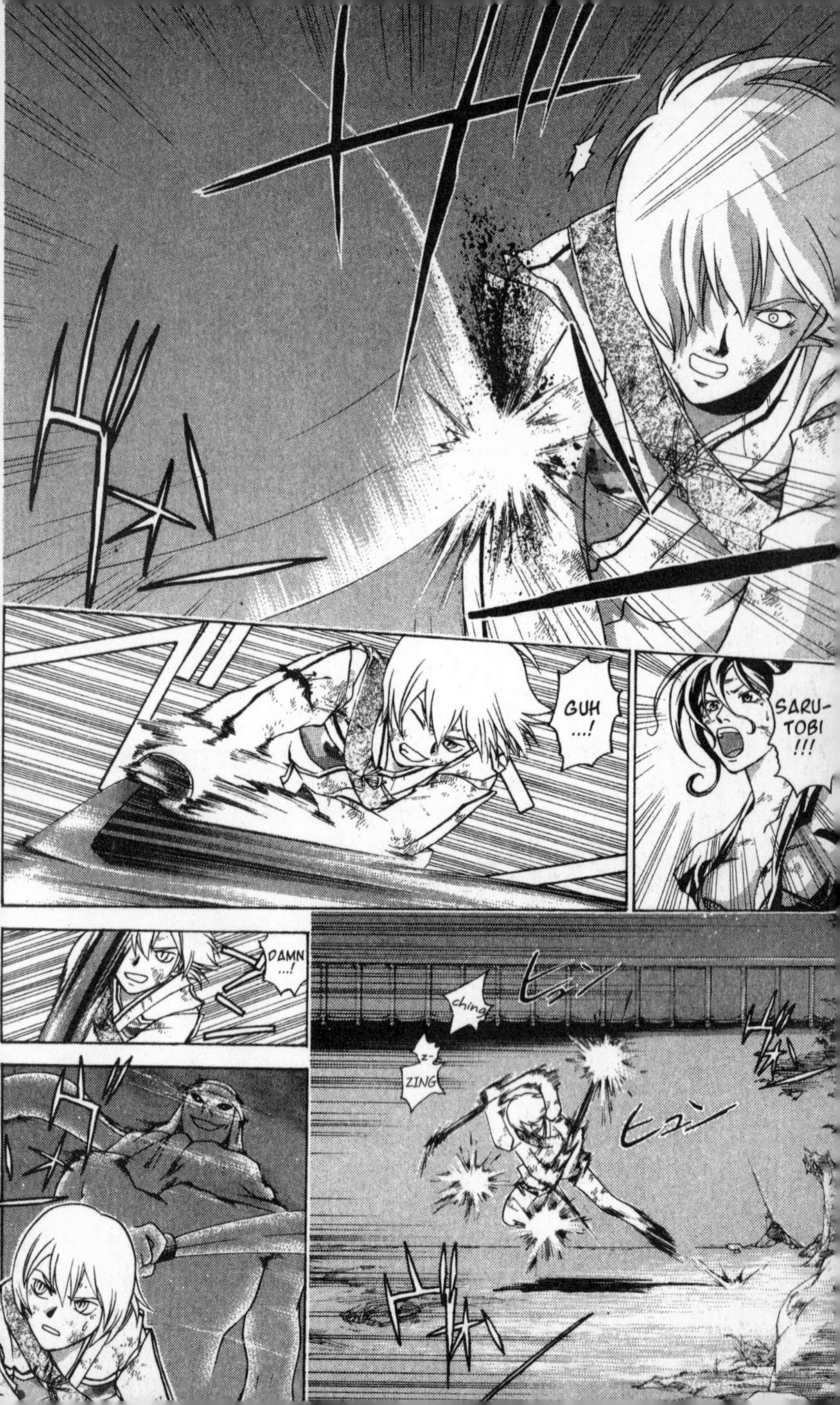
SARU-TOBI !!!
GUH ...!
DAMN ...!
ching
Z-ZING

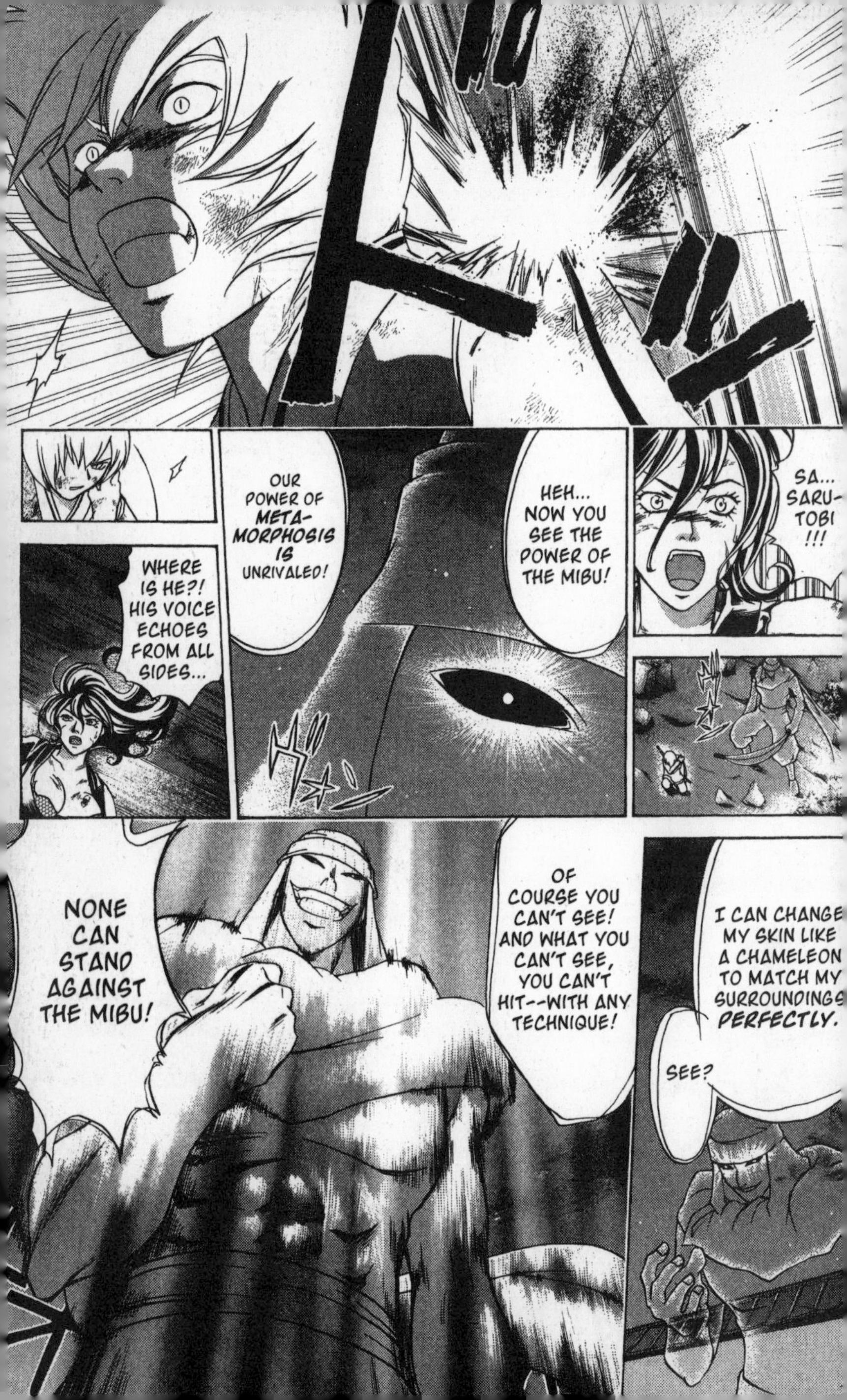
SA... SARU-TOBI!!!
HEH... NOW YOU SEE THE POWER OF THE MIBU!
OUR POWER OF METAMORPHOSIS IS UNRIVALED!
WHERE IS HE?! HIS VOICE ECHOES FROM ALL SIDES...
I CAN CHANGE MY SKIN LIKE A CHAMELEON TO MATCH MY SURROUNDINGS PERFECTLY.
SEE?
OF COURSE YOU CAN'T SEE! AND WHAT YOU CAN'T SEE, YOU CAN'T HIT--WITH ANY TECHNIQUE!
NONE CAN STAND AGAINST THE MIBU!

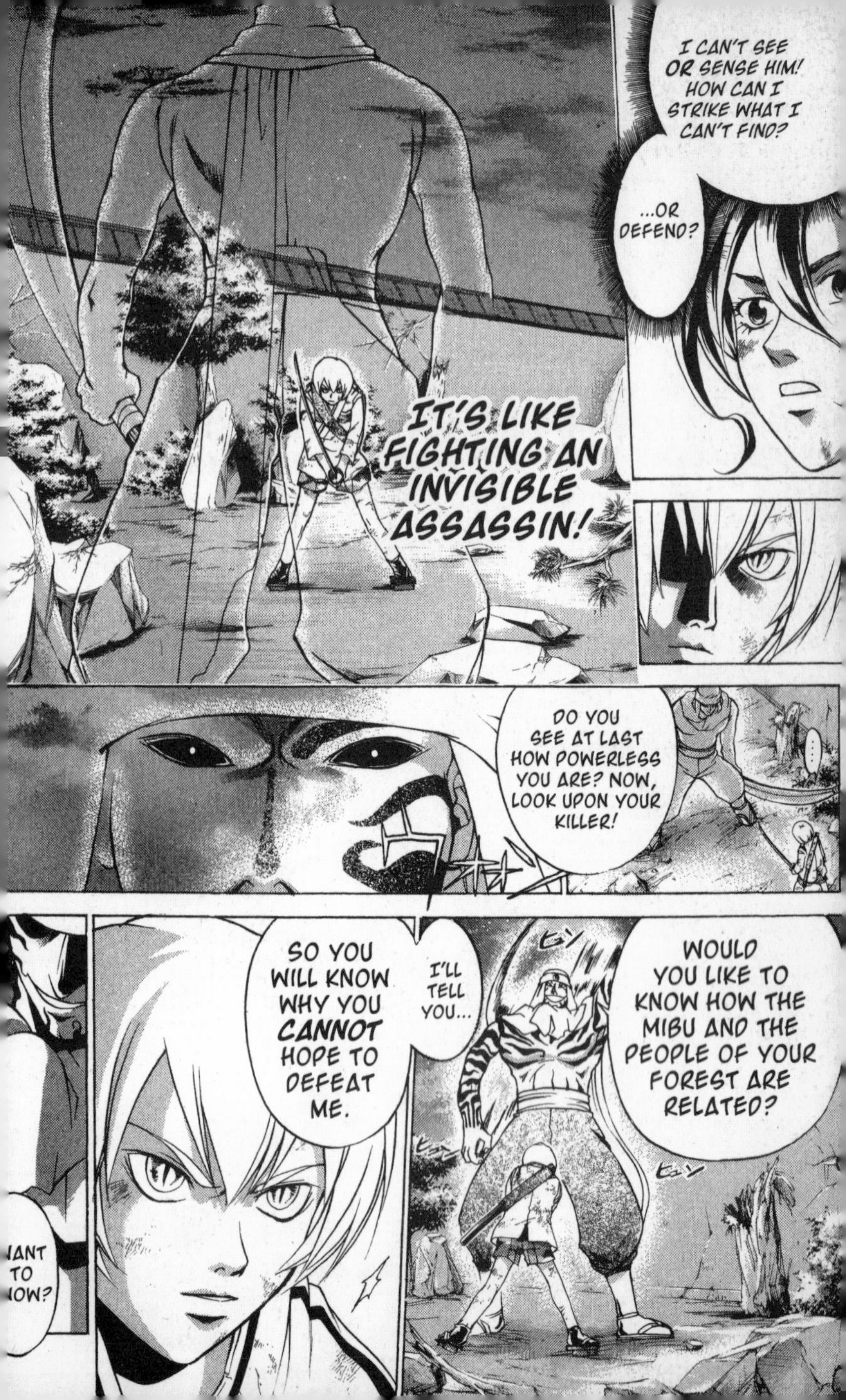

I CAN'T SEE OR SENSE HIM! HOW CAN I STRIKE WHAT I CAN'T FIND?
...OR DEFEND?
IT'S LIKE FIGHTING AN INVISIBLE ASSASSIN!
DO YOU SEE AT LAST HOW POWERLESS YOU ARE? NOW, LOOK UPON YOUR KILLER!
...
WOULD YOU LIKE TO KNOW HOW THE MIBU AND THE PEOPLE OF YOUR FOREST ARE RELATED?
I'LL TELL YOU...
SO YOU WILL KNOW WHY YOU **CANNOT** HOPE TO DEFEAT ME.
ANT TO OW?

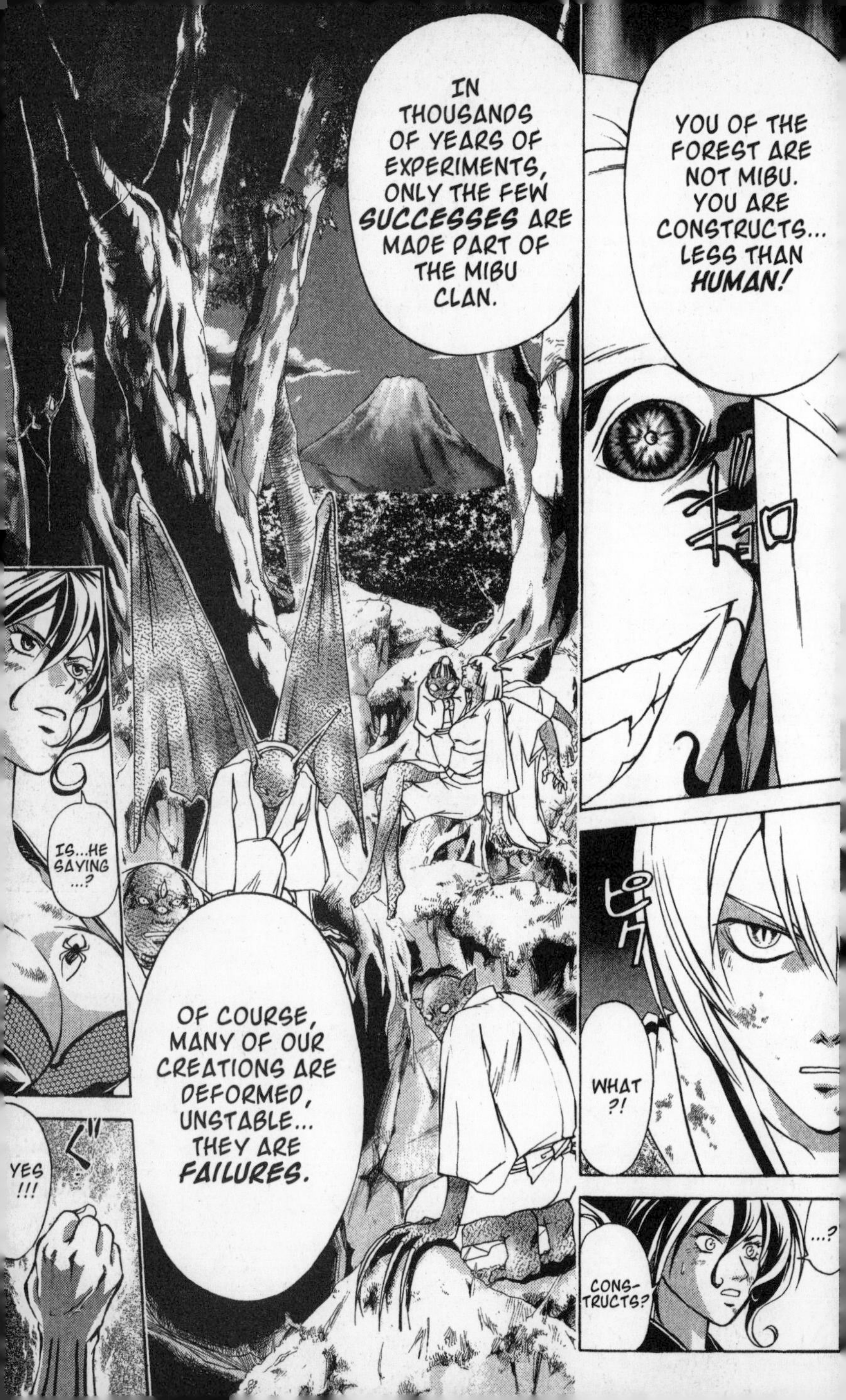
YOU OF THE FOREST ARE NOT MIBU. YOU ARE CONSTRUCTS... LESS THAN *HUMAN!*
キョロ
ピク
WHAT ?!
...?
CONS-TRUCTS?
IN THOUSANDS OF YEARS OF EXPERIMENTS, ONLY THE FEW *SUCCESSES* ARE MADE PART OF THE MIBU CLAN.
IS...HE SAYING ...?
OF COURSE, MANY OF OUR CREATIONS ARE DEFORMED, UNSTABLE... THEY ARE *FAILURES.*
ぐ
YES !!!

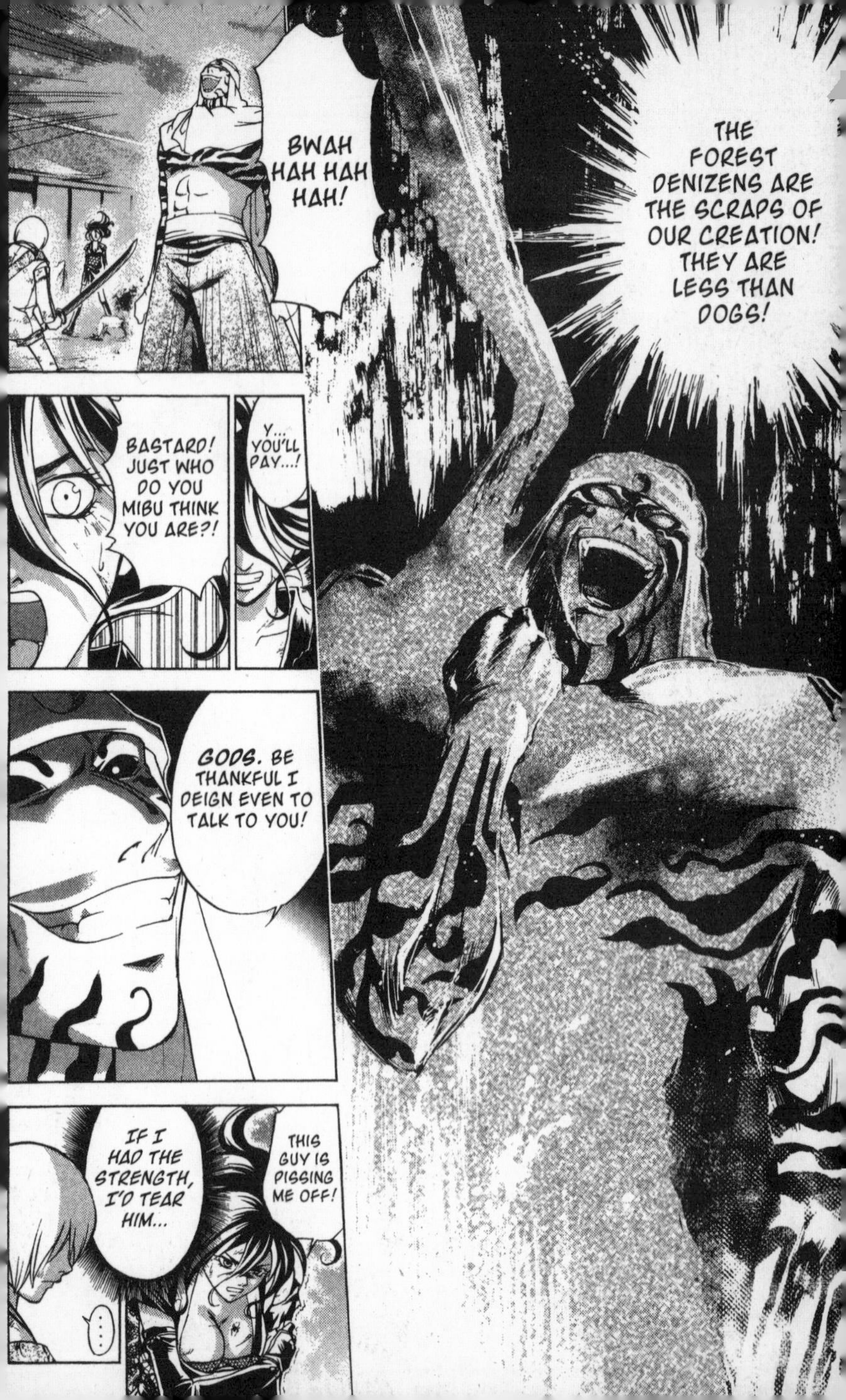
THE FOREST DENIZENS ARE THE SCRAPS OF OUR CREATION! THEY ARE LESS THAN DOGS!
BWAH HAH HAH HAH!
Y... YOU'LL PAY...!
BASTARD! JUST WHO DO YOU MIBU THINK YOU ARE?!
GODS. BE THANKFUL I DEIGN EVEN TO TALK TO YOU!
THIS GUY IS PISSING ME OFF!
IF I HAD THE STRENGTH, I'D TEAR HIM...
...

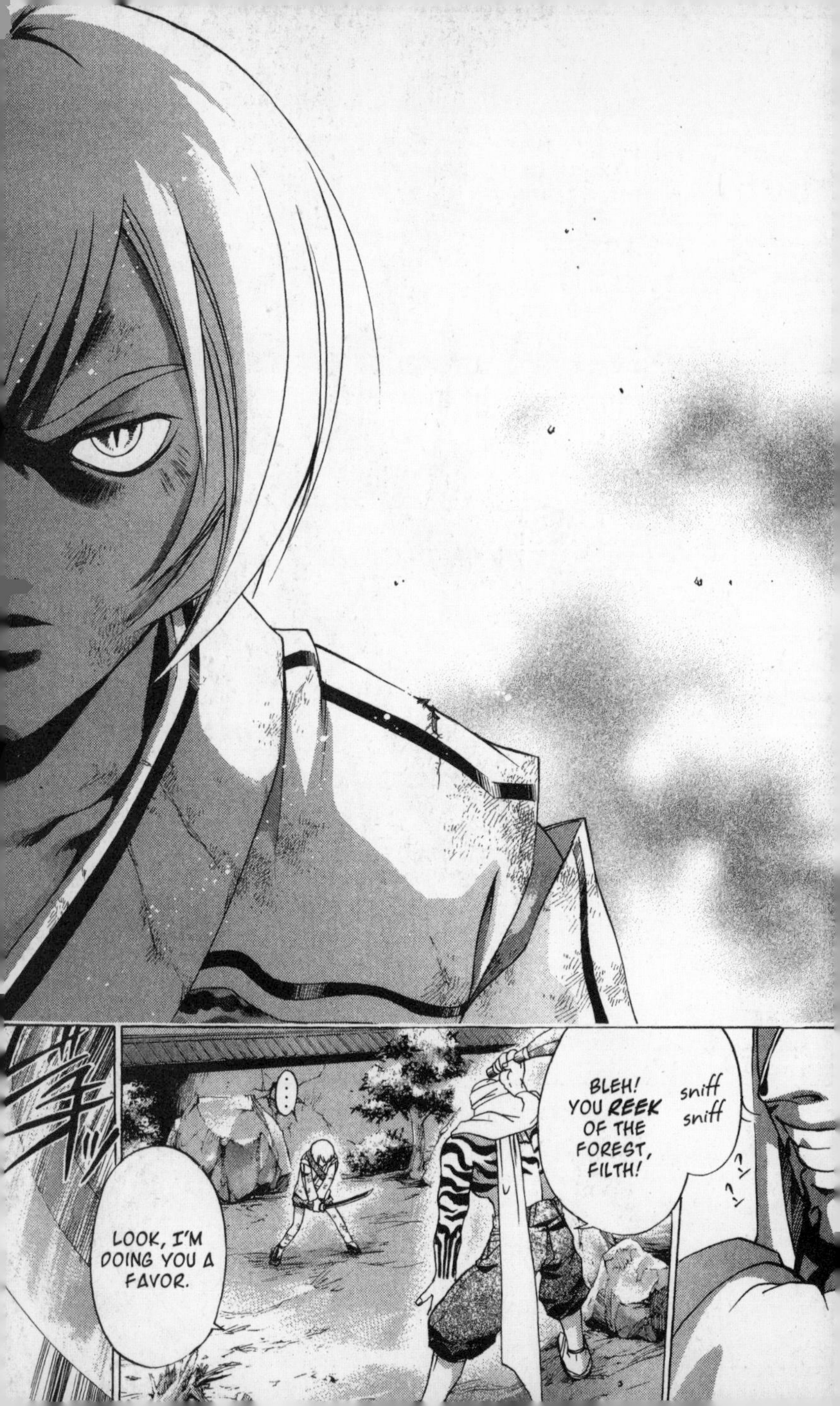
BLEH! YOU **REEK** OF THE FOREST, FILTH!
sniff sniff
?!
?!
...
LOOK, I'M DOING YOU A FAVOR.

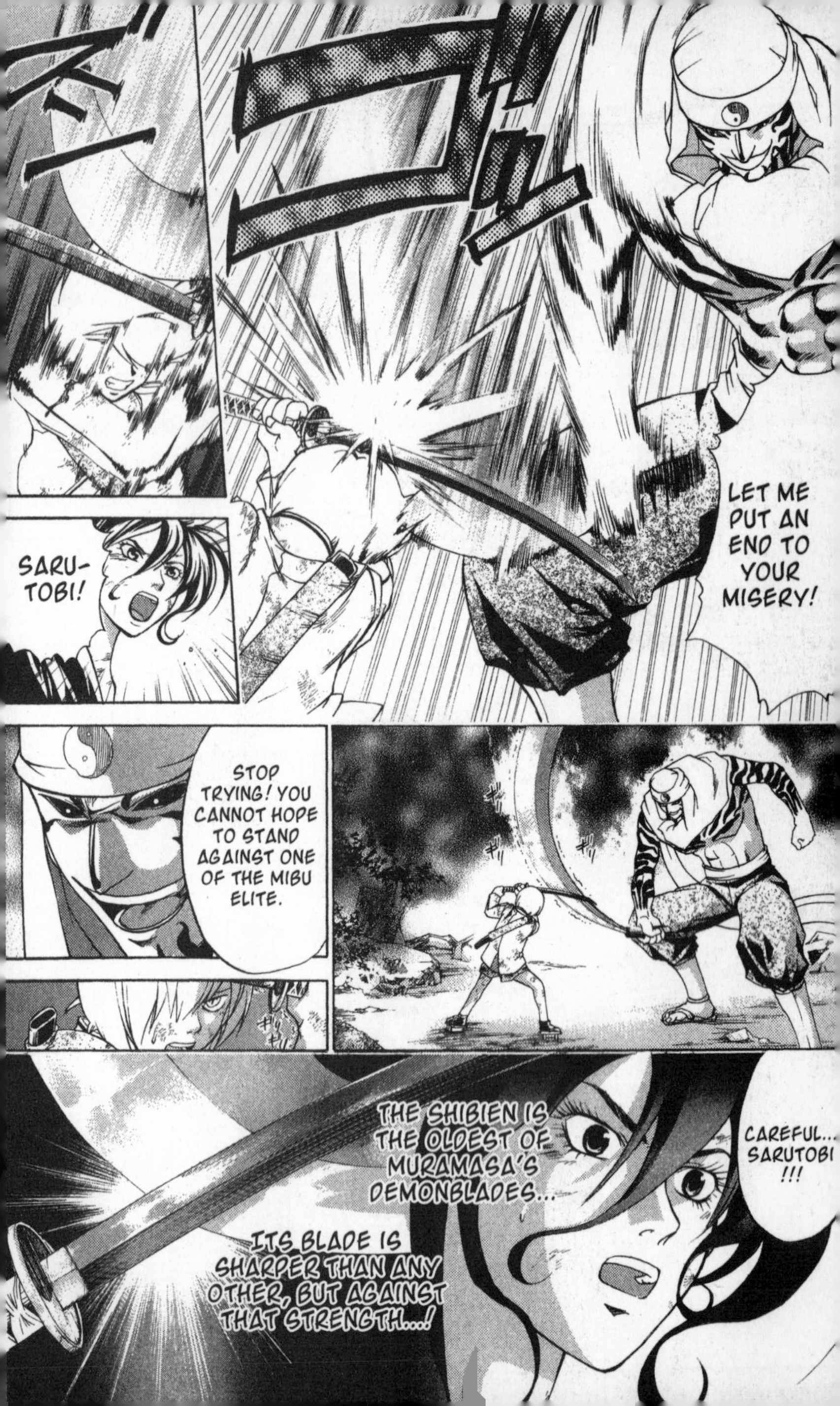
LET ME PUT AN END TO YOUR MISERY!
SARU-TOBI!
STOP TRYING! YOU CANNOT HOPE TO STAND AGAINST ONE OF THE MIBU ELITE.
CAREFUL... SARUTOBI !!!
THE SHIBIEN IS THE OLDEST OF MURAMASA'S DEMONBLADES...
ITS BLADE IS SHARPER THAN ANY OTHER, BUT AGAINST THAT STRENGTH...!

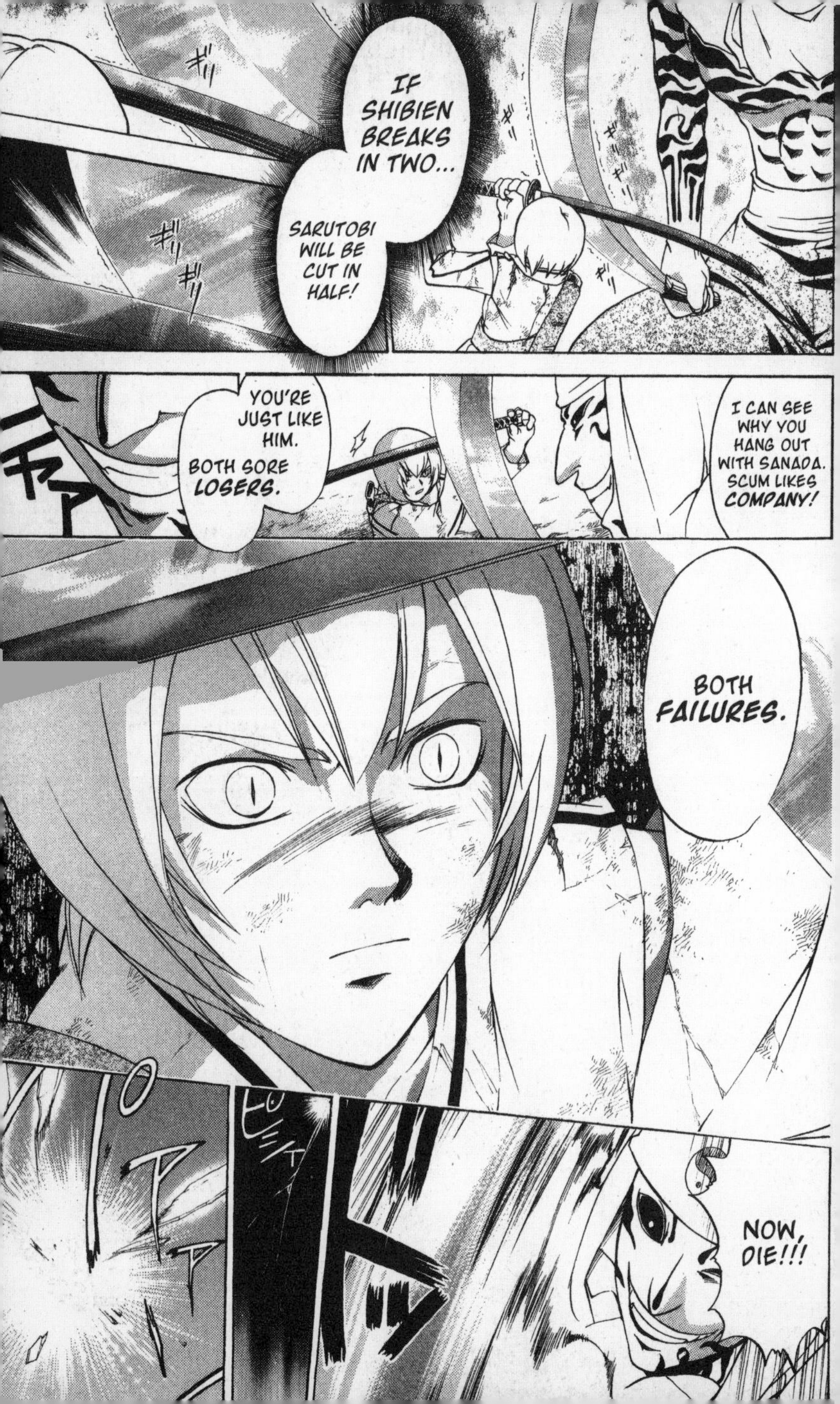
IF SHIBIEN BREAKS IN TWO...
SARUTOBI WILL BE CUT IN HALF!
I CAN SEE WHY YOU HANG OUT WITH SANADA. SCUM LIKES COMPANY!
YOU'RE JUST LIKE HIM.
BOTH SORE LOSERS.
BOTH FAILURES.
NOW, DIE!!!

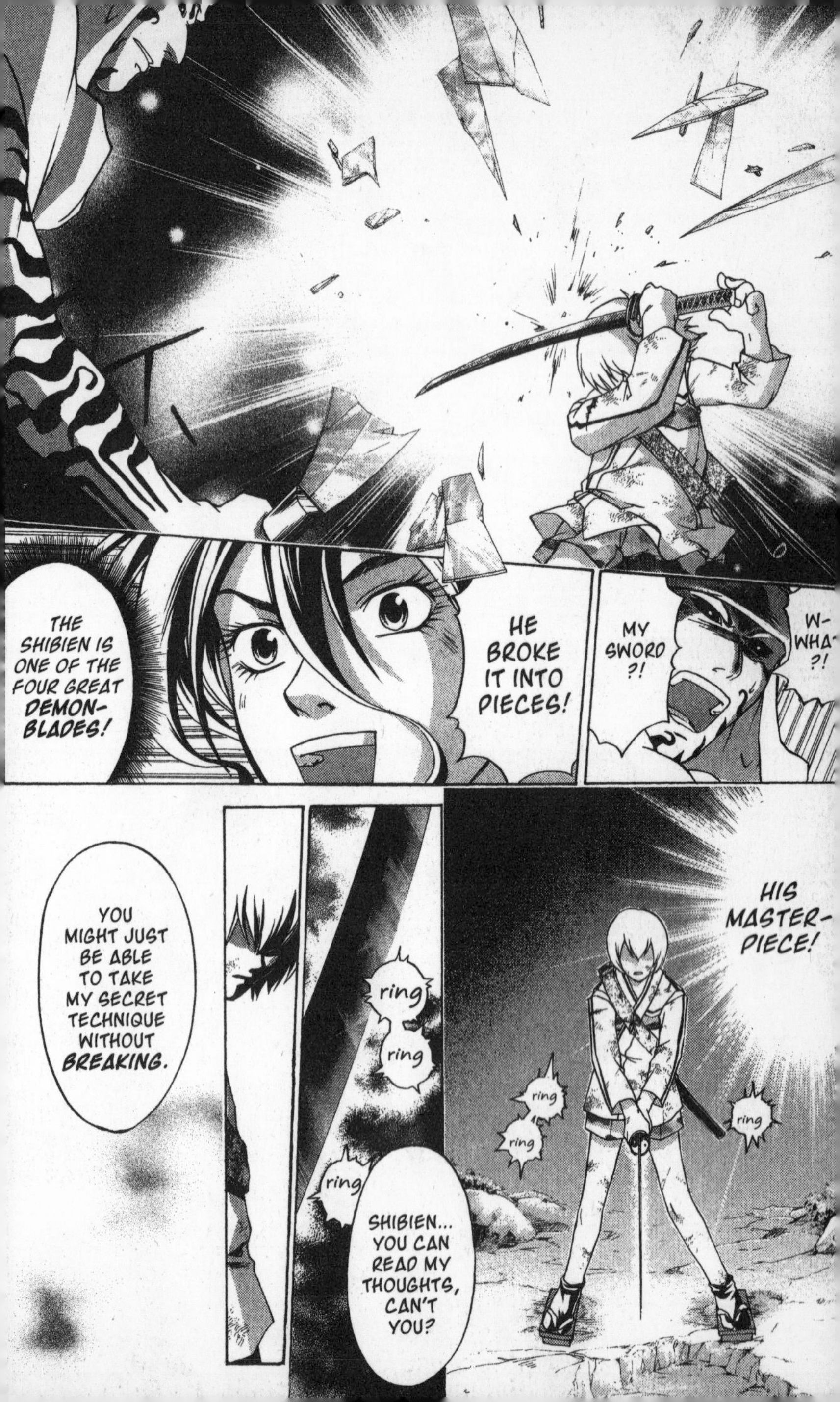
W-WHA?!
MY SWORD?!
HE BROKE IT INTO PIECES!
THE SHIBIEN IS ONE OF THE FOUR GREAT DEMON-BLADES!
HIS MASTER-PIECE!
ring
ring
ring
ring
ring
ring
SHIBIEN... YOU CAN READ MY THOUGHTS, CAN'T YOU?
YOU MIGHT JUST BE ABLE TO TAKE MY SECRET TECHNIQUE WITHOUT BREAKING.

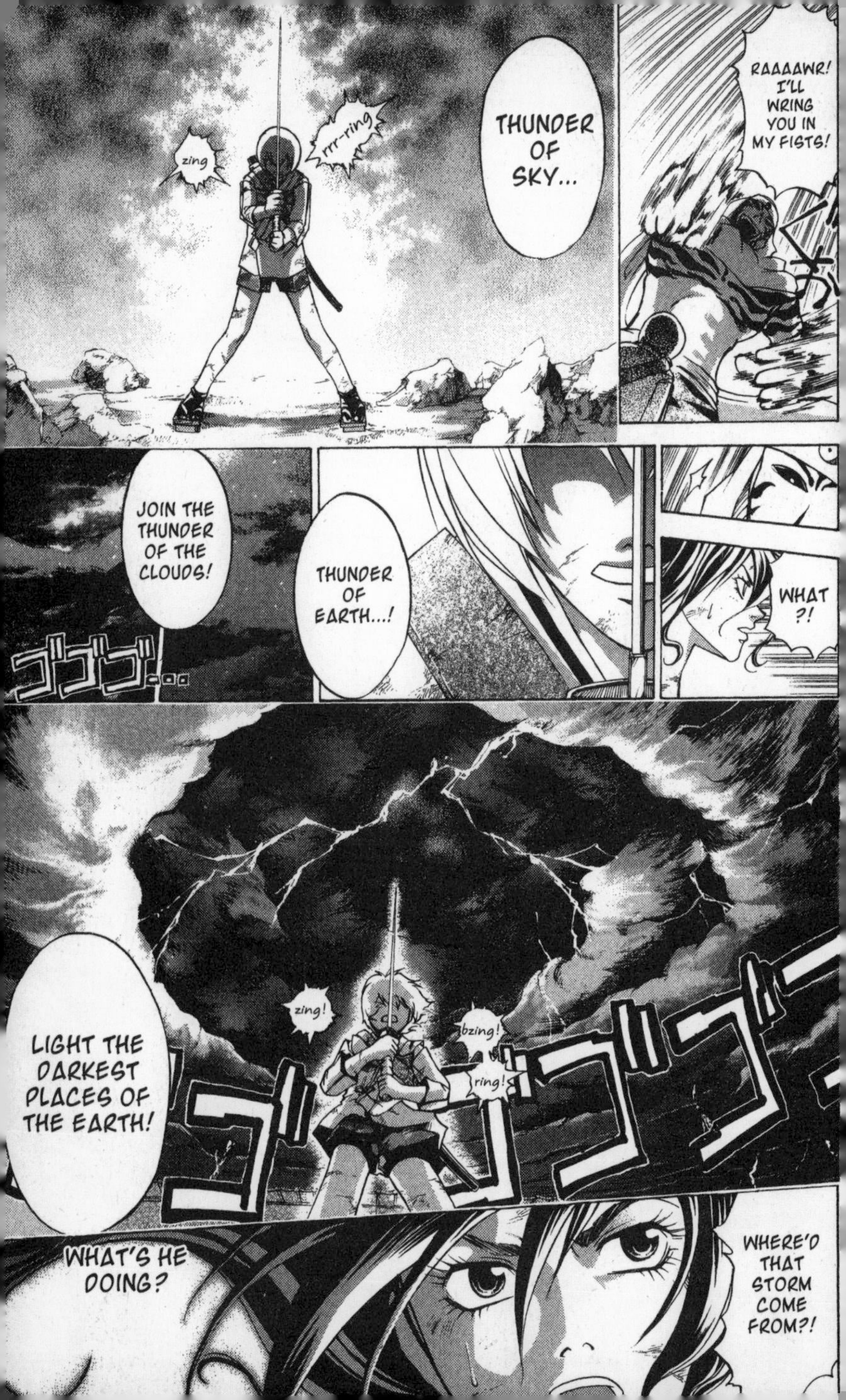
RAAAAWR! I'LL WRING YOU IN MY FISTS!
THUNDER OF SKY...
rrr-ring
zing
WHAT ?!
THUNDER OF EARTH...!
JOIN THE THUNDER OF THE CLOUDS!
ゴゴゴ...
ゴゴゴ
bzing!
ring!
zing!
LIGHT THE DARKEST PLACES OF THE EARTH!
WHERE'D THAT STORM COME FROM?!
WHAT'S HE DOING?

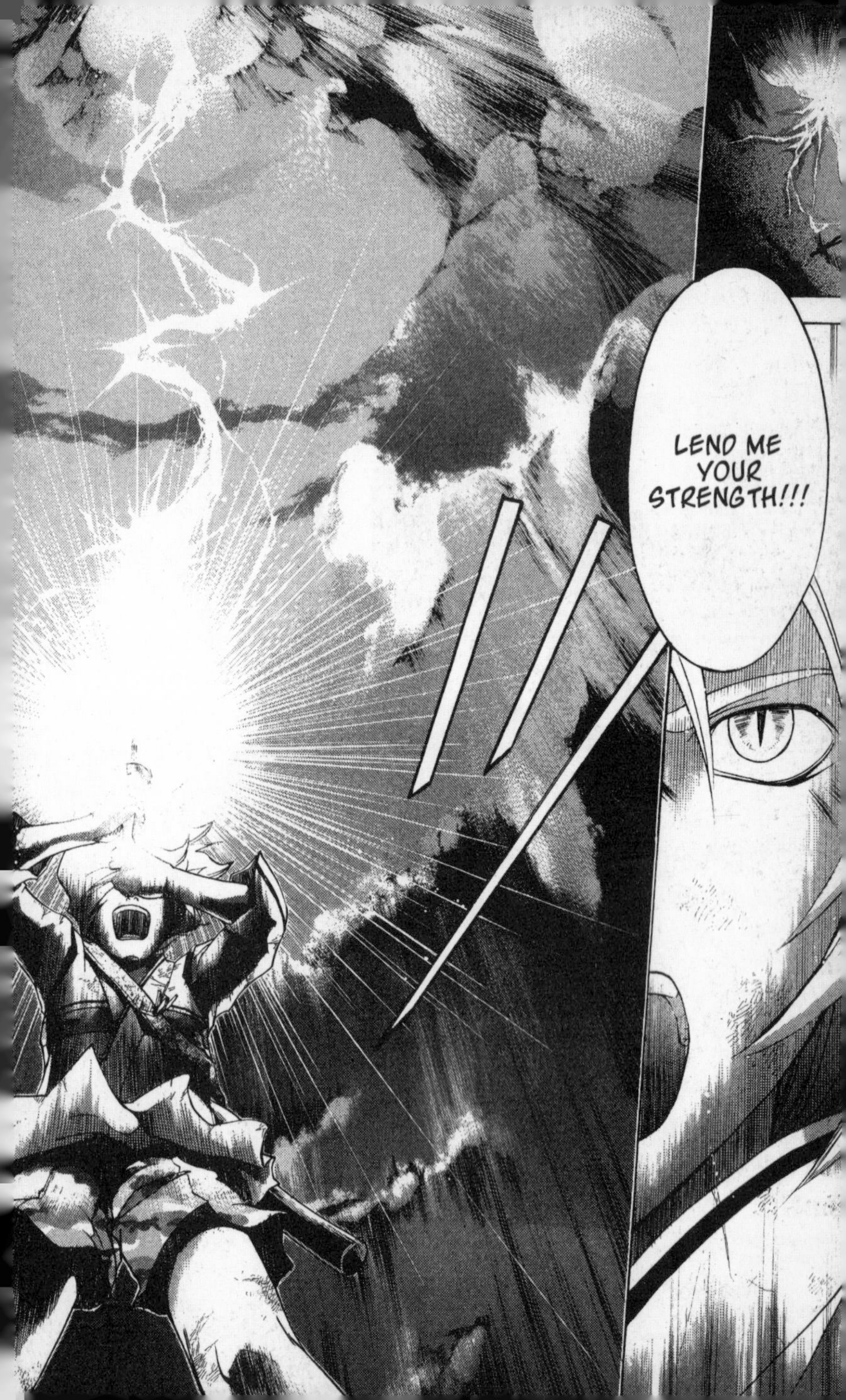
LEND ME YOUR STRENGTH!!!

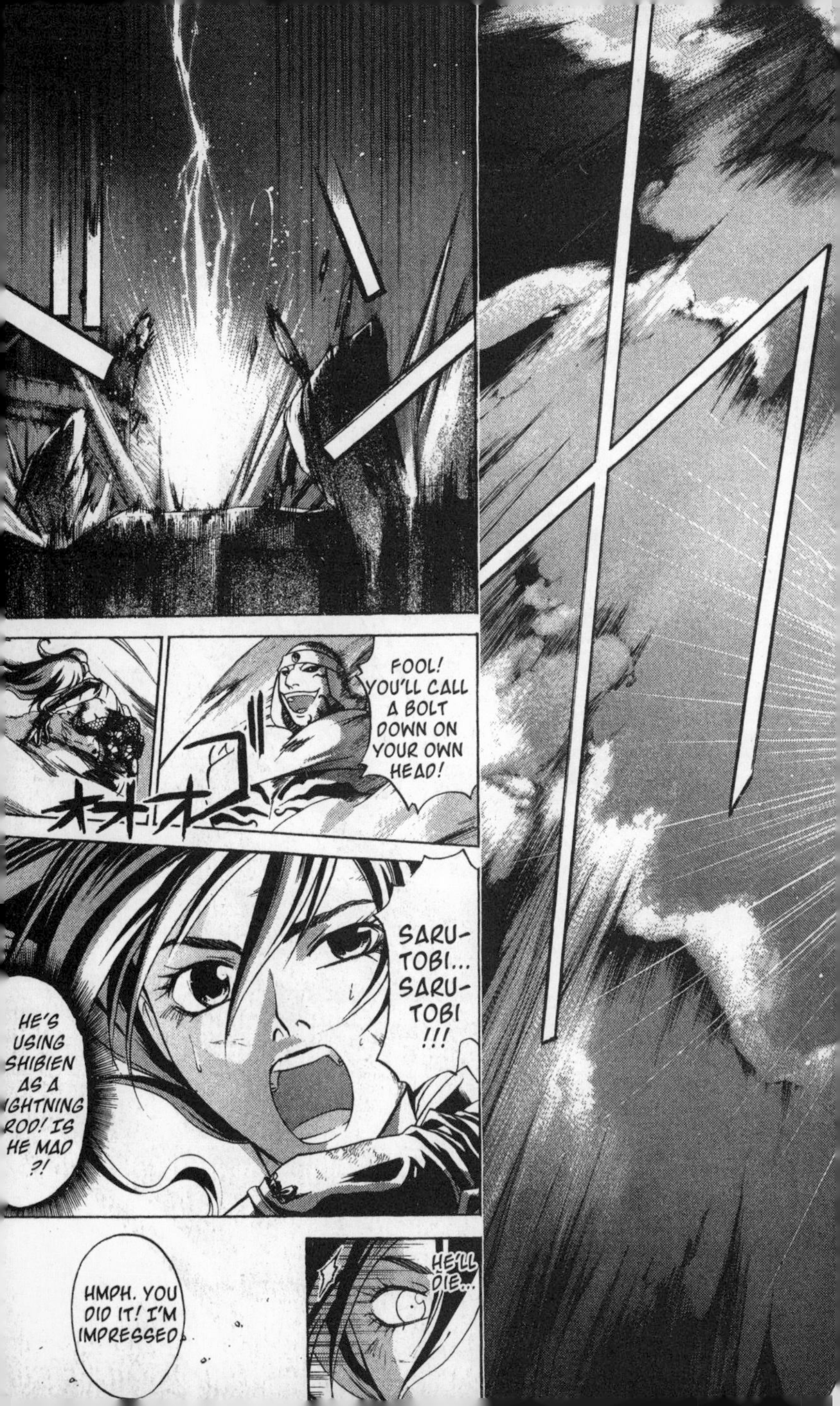
FOOL! YOU'LL CALL A BOLT DOWN ON YOUR OWN HEAD!
SARU-TOBI... SARU-TOBI !!!
HE'S USING SHIBIEN AS A IGHTNING ROD! IS HE MAD ?!
HE'LL DIE...
HMPH. YOU DID IT! I'M IMPRESSED.

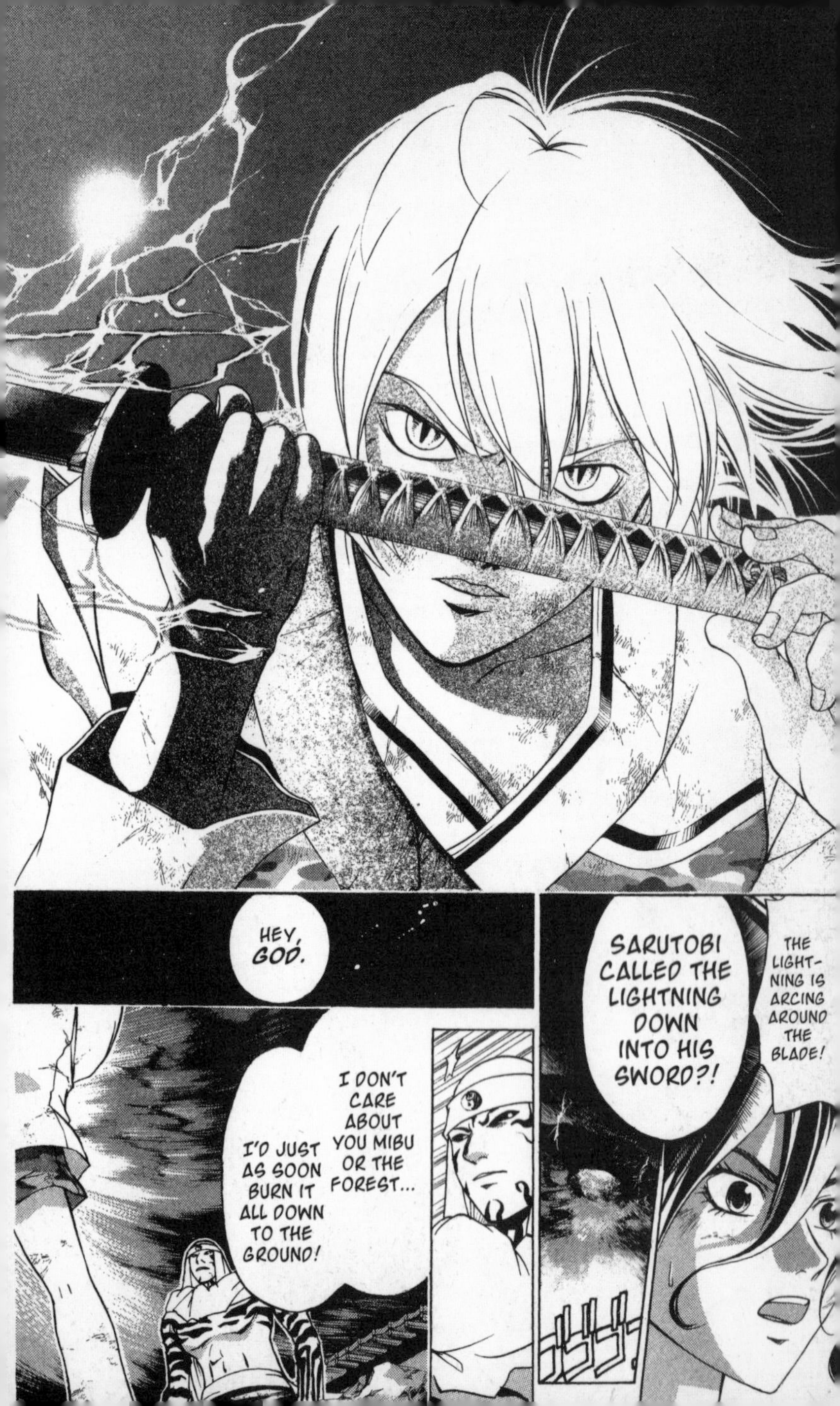
THE LIGHT-NING IS ARCING AROUND THE BLADE!
SARUTOBI CALLED THE LIGHTNING DOWN INTO HIS SWORD?!
HEY, GOD.
I DON'T CARE ABOUT YOU MIBU OR THE FOREST...
I'D JUST AS SOON BURN IT ALL DOWN TO THE GROUND!

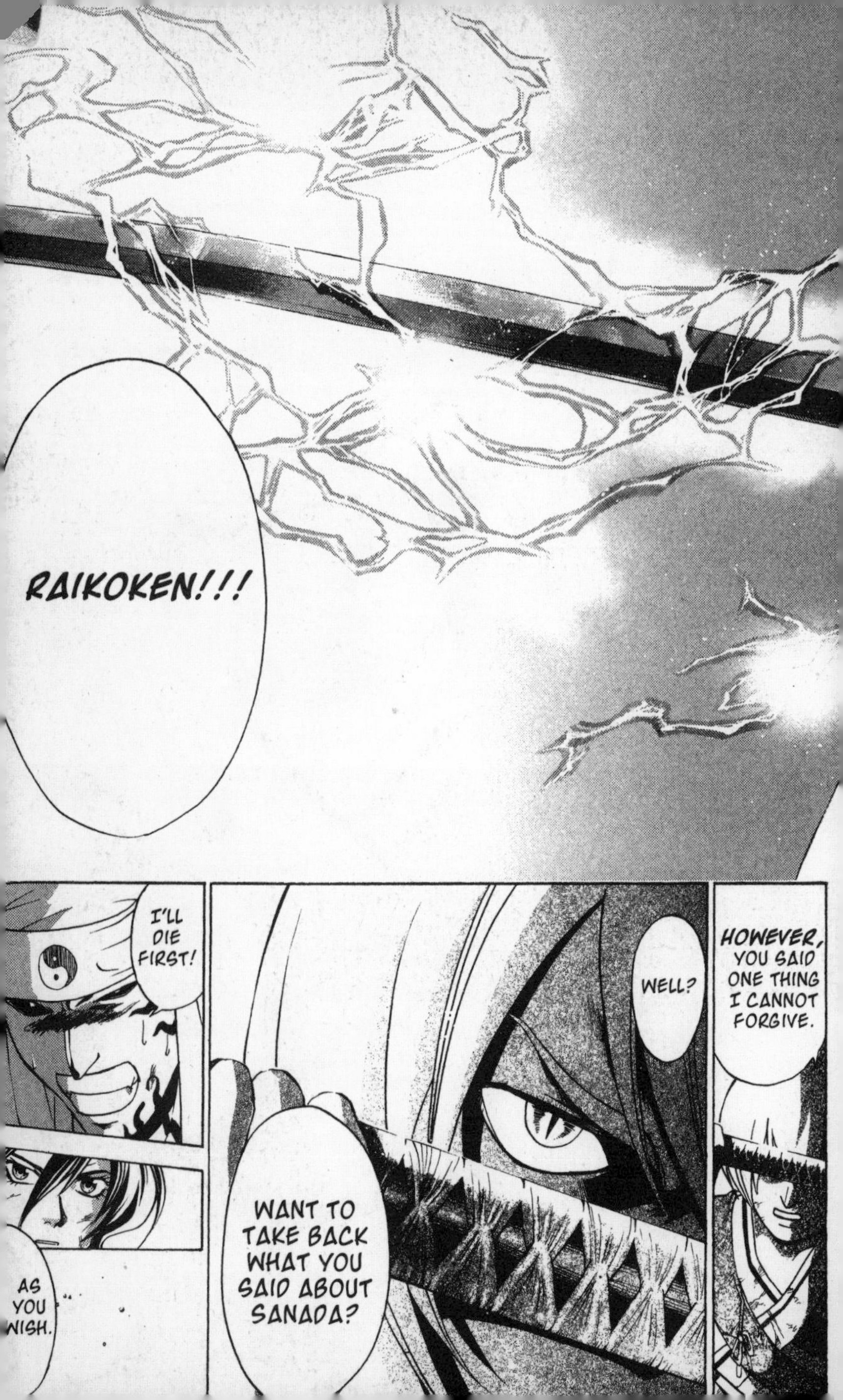
RAIKOKEN!!!
HOWEVER, YOU SAID ONE THING I CANNOT FORGIVE.
WELL?
WANT TO TAKE BACK WHAT YOU SAID ABOUT SANADA?
I'LL DIE FIRST!
AS YOU WISH.

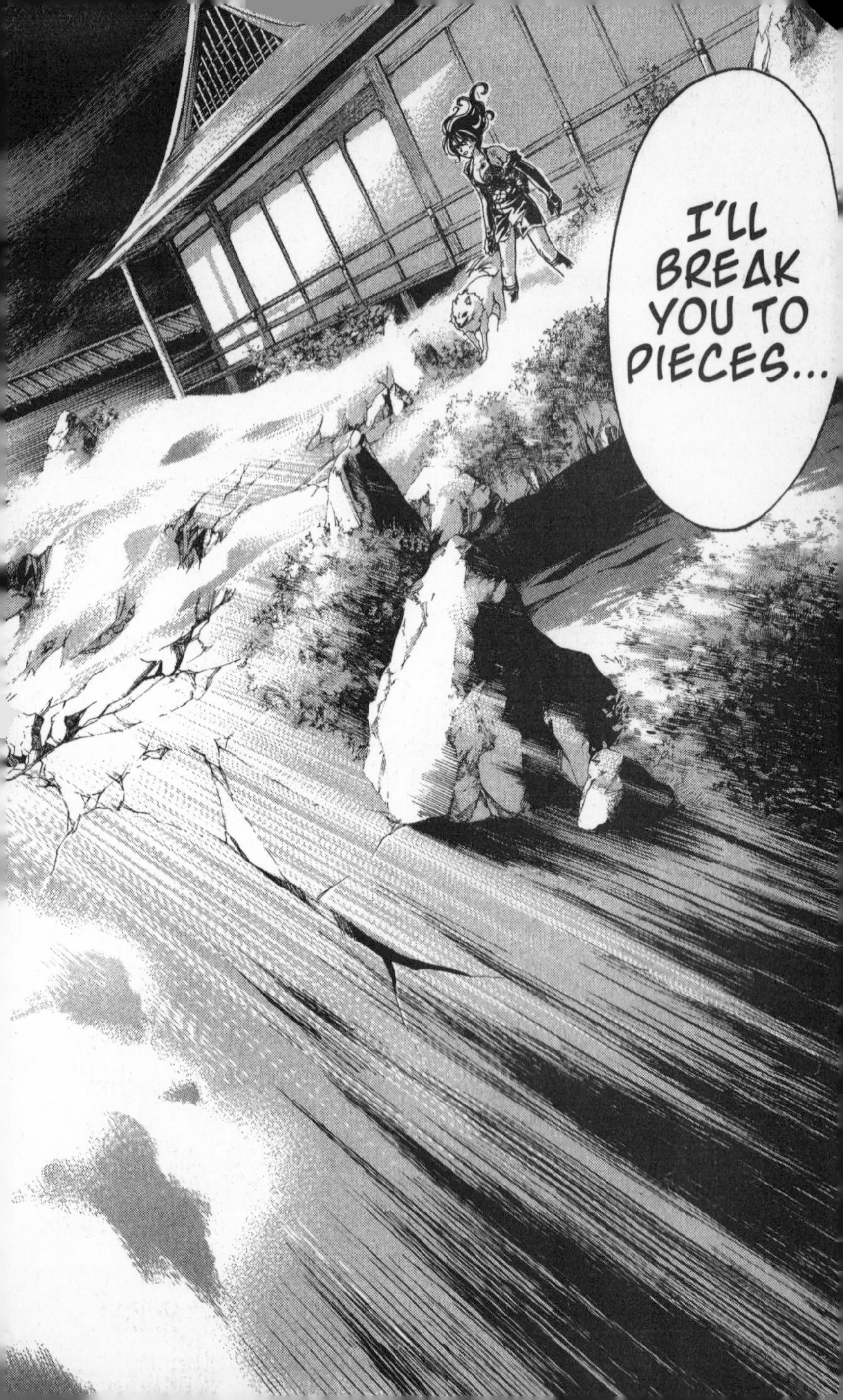
I'LL BREAK YOU TO PIECES...

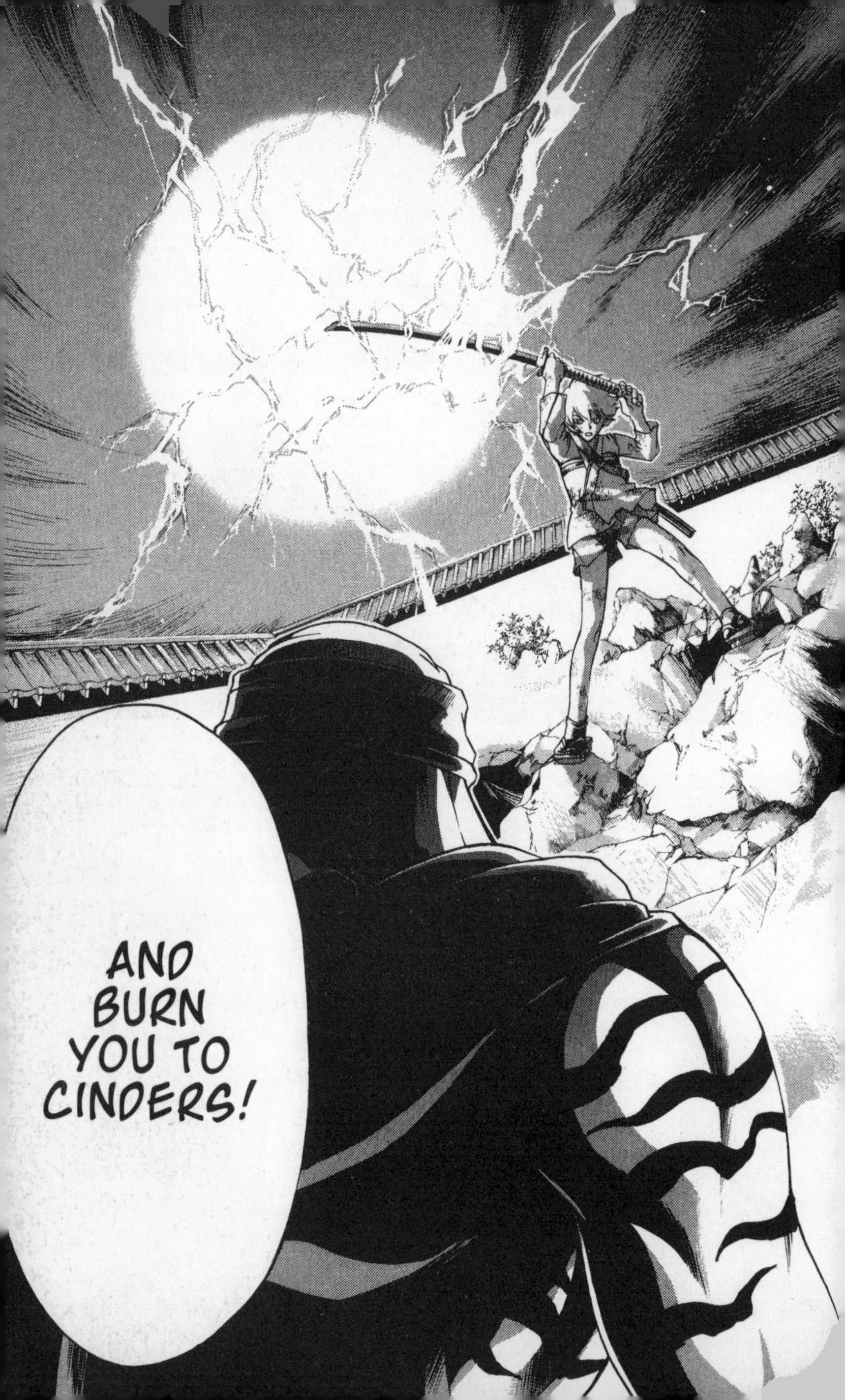
AND BURN YOU TO CINDERS!

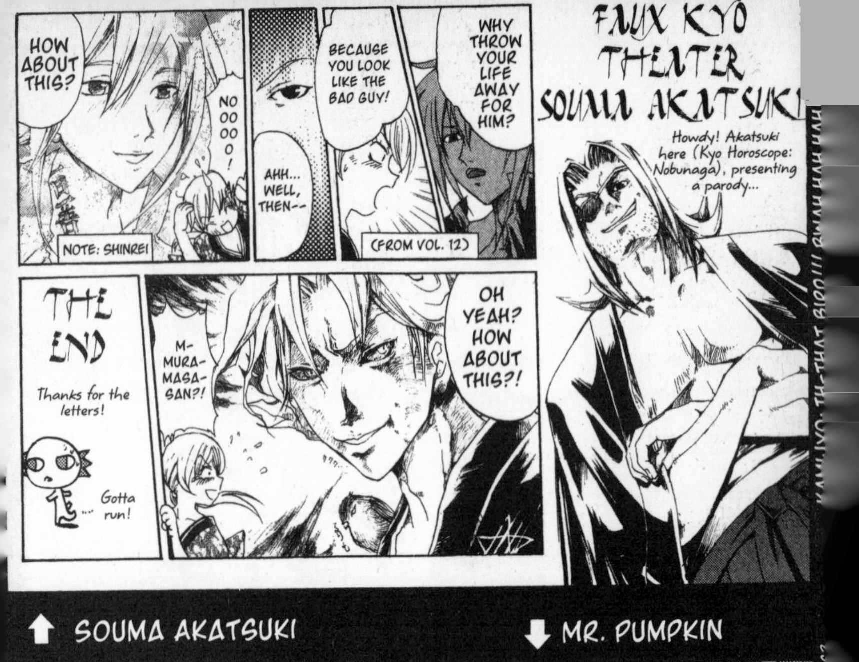
FAUX KYO THEATER
SOUMA AKATSUKI
Howdy! Akatsuki here (Kyo Horoscope: Nobunaga), presenting a parody...
WHY THROW YOUR LIFE AWAY FOR HIM?
BECAUSE YOU LOOK LIKE THE BAD GUY!
AHH... WELL, THEN--
(FROM VOL. 12)
HOW ABOUT THIS?
NOOOOOO!
NOTE: SHINREI
OH YEAH? HOW ABOUT THIS?!
M-MURAMASA-SAN?!
THE END
Thanks for the letters!
Gotta run!

↑ SOUMA AKATSUKI ↓ MR. PUMPKIN

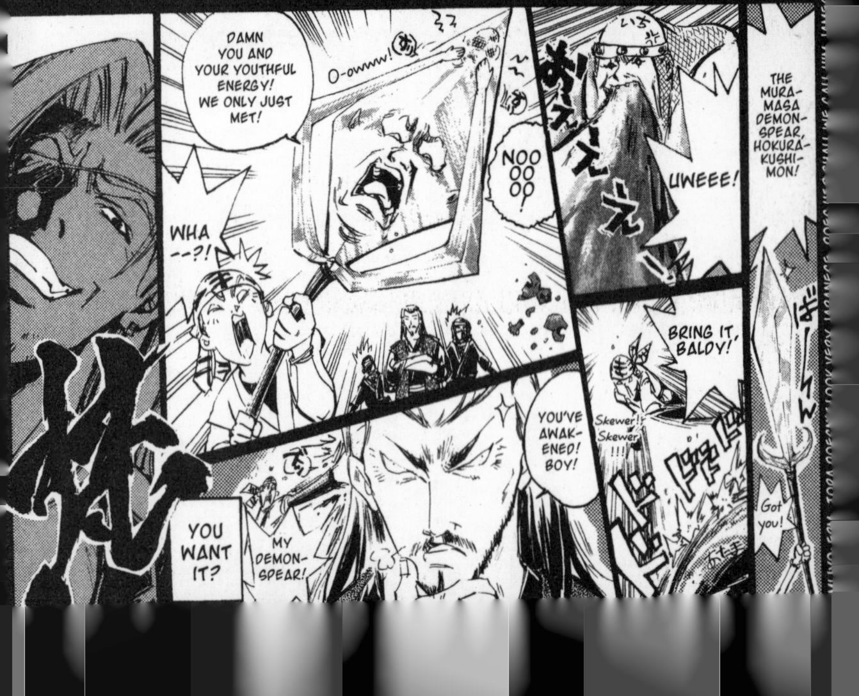
THE MURAMASA DEMON-SPEAR, HOKURAKUSHIMON!
Got you!
UWEEE!
NOOOOOP!
O-owww!
DAMN YOU AND YOUR YOUTHFUL ENERGY! WE ONLY JUST MET!
WHA--?!
BRING IT, BALDY!
Skewer! Skewer!!!!
YOU'VE AWAKENED! BOY!
MY DEMON-SPEAR!
YOU WANT IT?

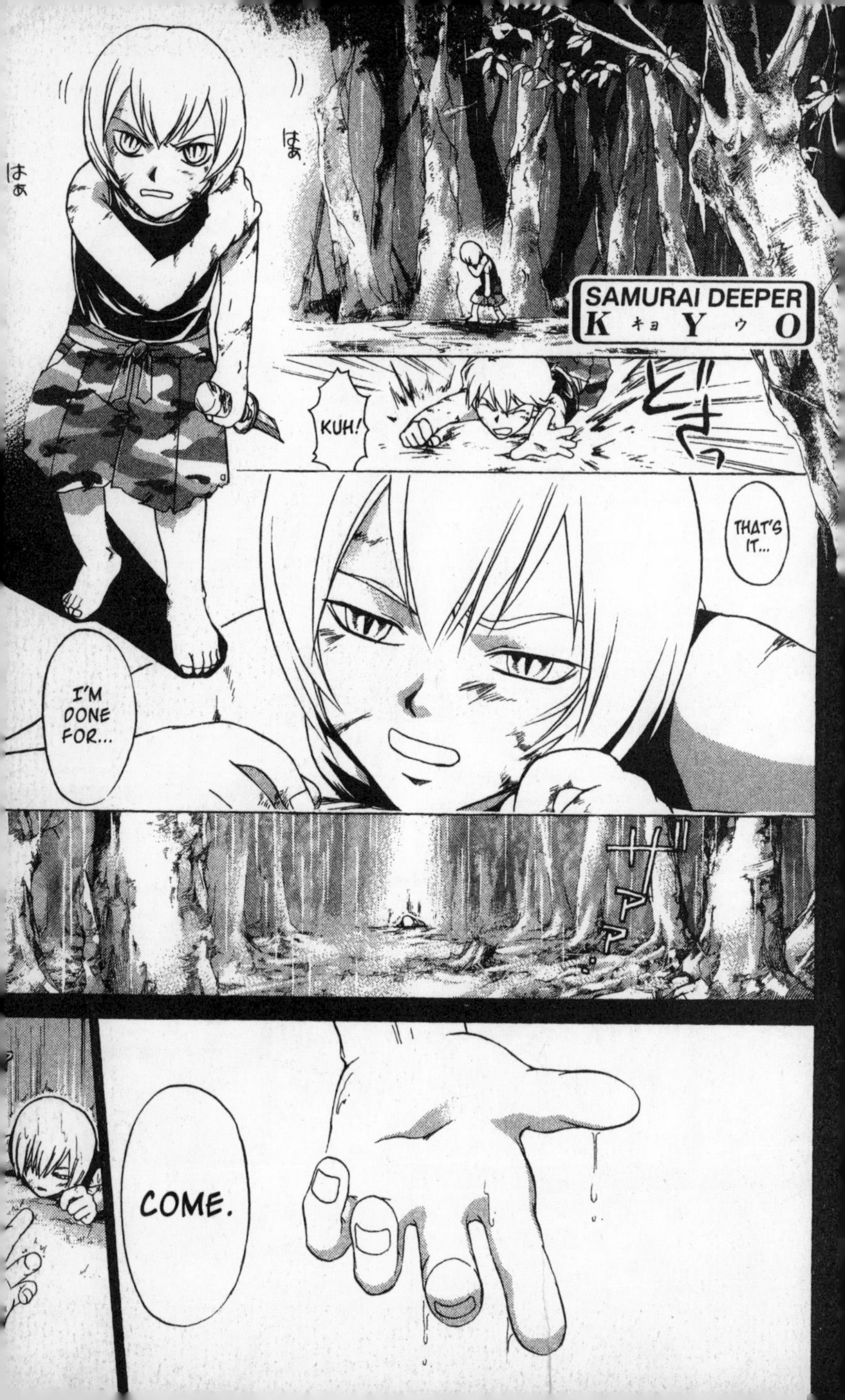
SAMURAI DEEPER
K キョ Y ウ O
KUH!
どさっ
THAT'S IT...
I'M DONE FOR...
はあ
はあ
ザアアア
COME.

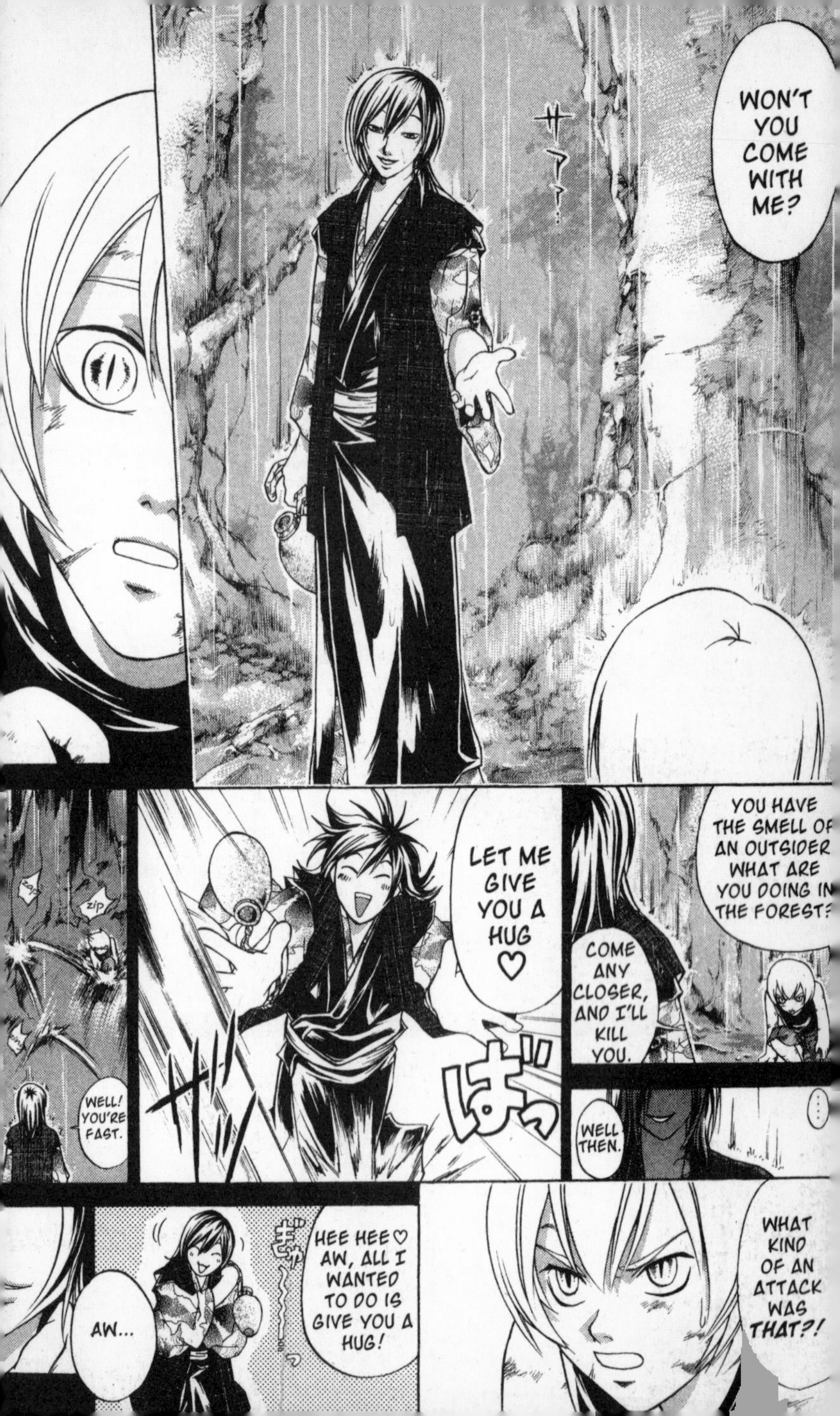
WON'T YOU COME WITH ME?
サァァァ…
YOU HAVE THE SMELL OF AN OUTSIDER. WHAT ARE YOU DOING IN THE FOREST?
COME ANY CLOSER, AND I'LL KILL YOU.
…
WELL THEN.
LET ME GIVE YOU A HUG ♡
ばっ
zap
zip
WELL! YOU'RE FAST.
WHAT KIND OF AN ATTACK WAS THAT?!
HEE HEE ♡ AW, ALL I WANTED TO DO IS GIVE YOU A HUG!
ぎゅ〜〜〜っ
AW...

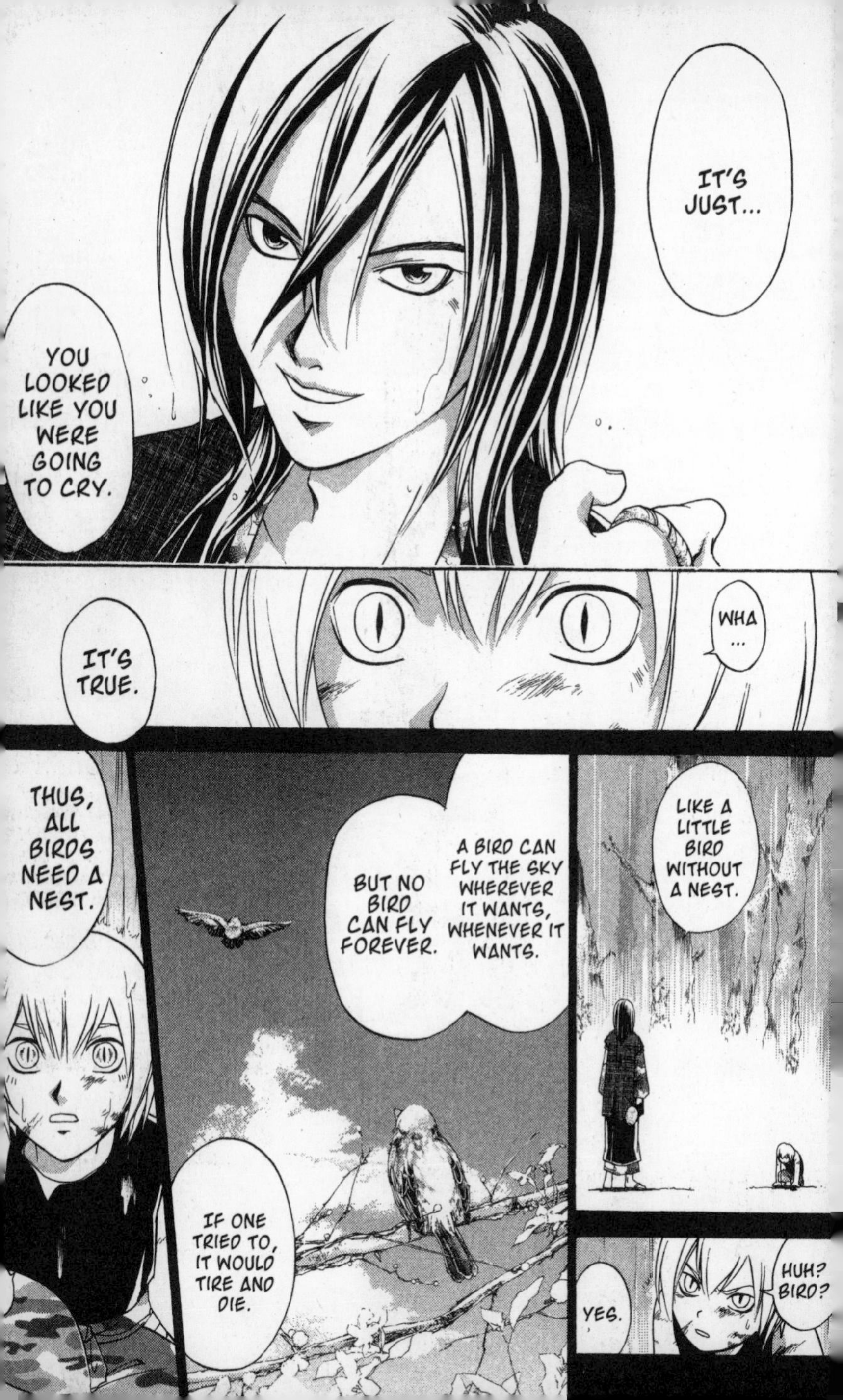
IT'S JUST...
YOU LOOKED LIKE YOU WERE GOING TO CRY.
WHA...
IT'S TRUE.
LIKE A LITTLE BIRD WITHOUT A NEST.
HUH? BIRD?
YES.
A BIRD CAN FLY THE SKY WHEREVER IT WANTS, WHENEVER IT WANTS.
BUT NO BIRD CAN FLY FOREVER.
IF ONE TRIED TO, IT WOULD TIRE AND DIE.
THUS, ALL BIRDS NEED A NEST.

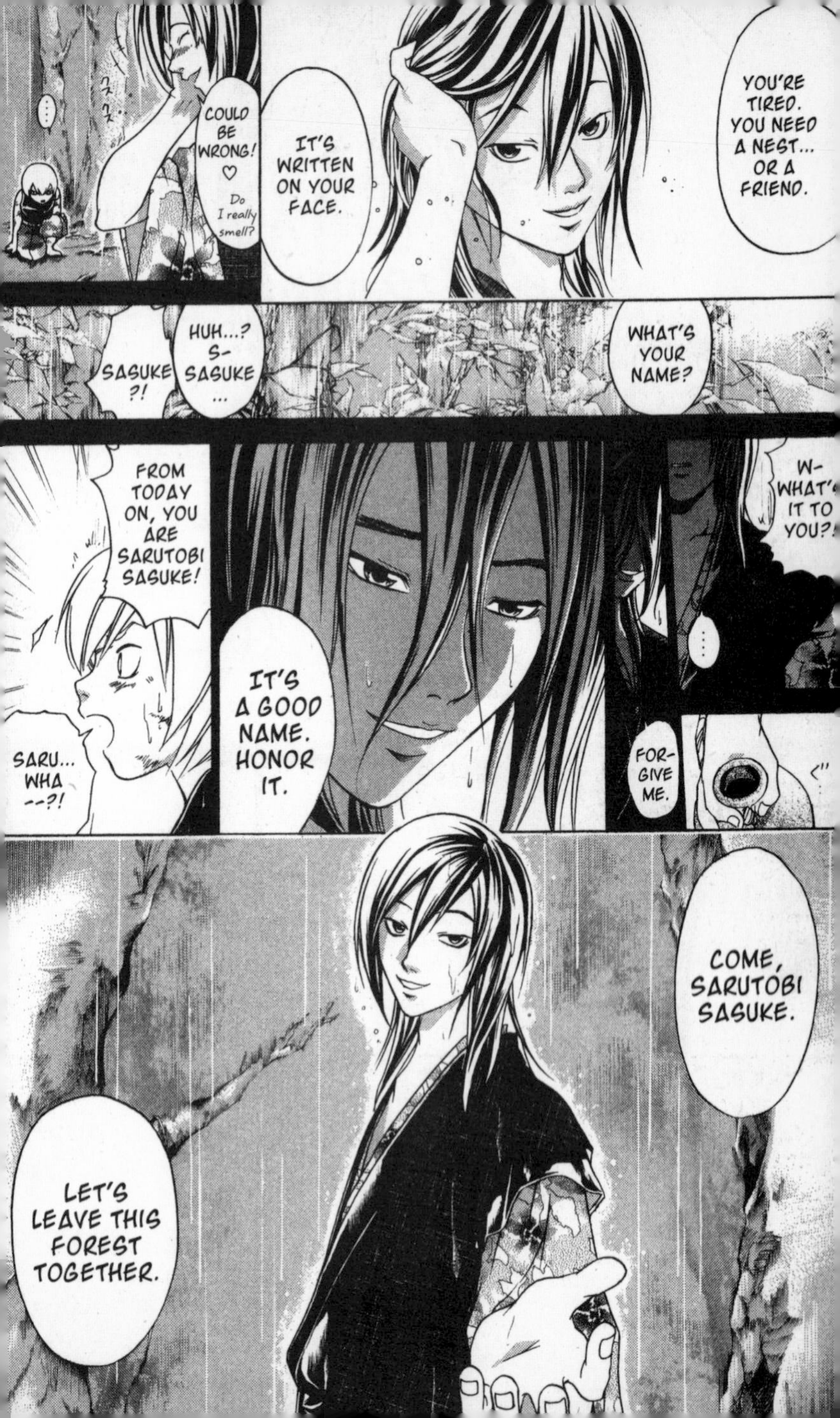
YOU'RE TIRED. YOU NEED A NEST... OR A FRIEND.
IT'S WRITTEN ON YOUR FACE.
COULD BE WRONG! ♡
Do I really smell?
...
WHAT'S YOUR NAME?
HUH...? S-SASUKE...
SASUKE?!
W-WHAT'S IT TO YOU?!
...
FOR-GIVE ME.
IT'S A GOOD NAME. HONOR IT.
FROM TODAY ON, YOU ARE SARUTOBI SASUKE!
SARU... WHA--?!
COME, SARUTOBI SASUKE.
LET'S LEAVE THIS FOREST TOGETHER.

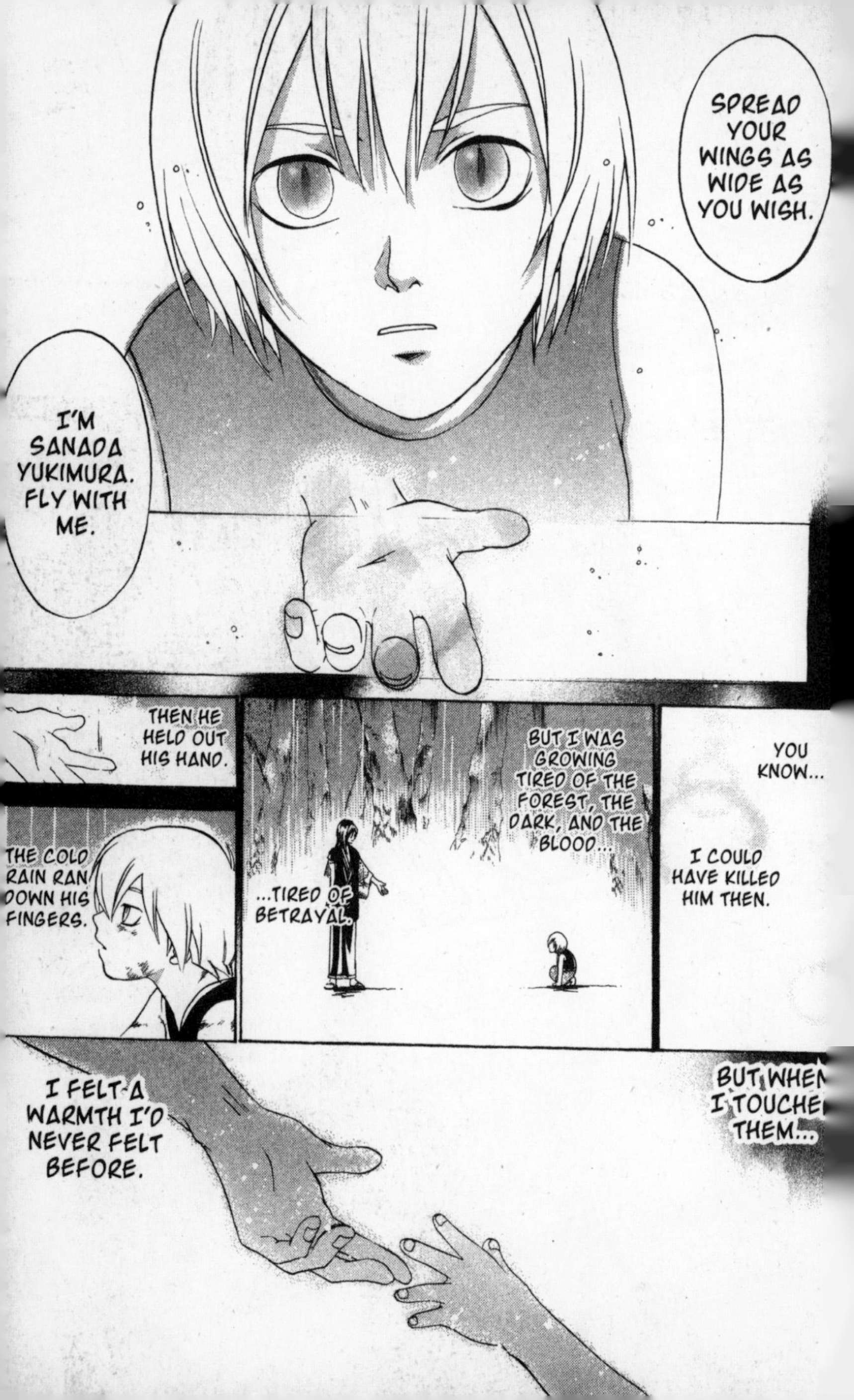
SPREAD YOUR WINGS AS WIDE AS YOU WISH.
I'M SANADA YUKIMURA. FLY WITH ME.
YOU KNOW...
I COULD HAVE KILLED HIM THEN.
BUT I WAS GROWING TIRED OF THE FOREST, THE DARK, AND THE BLOOD...
...TIRED OF BETRAYAL.
THEN HE HELD OUT HIS HAND.
THE COLD RAIN RAN DOWN HIS FINGERS.
BUT WHEN I TOUCHE THEM...
I FELT A WARMTH I'D NEVER FELT BEFORE.

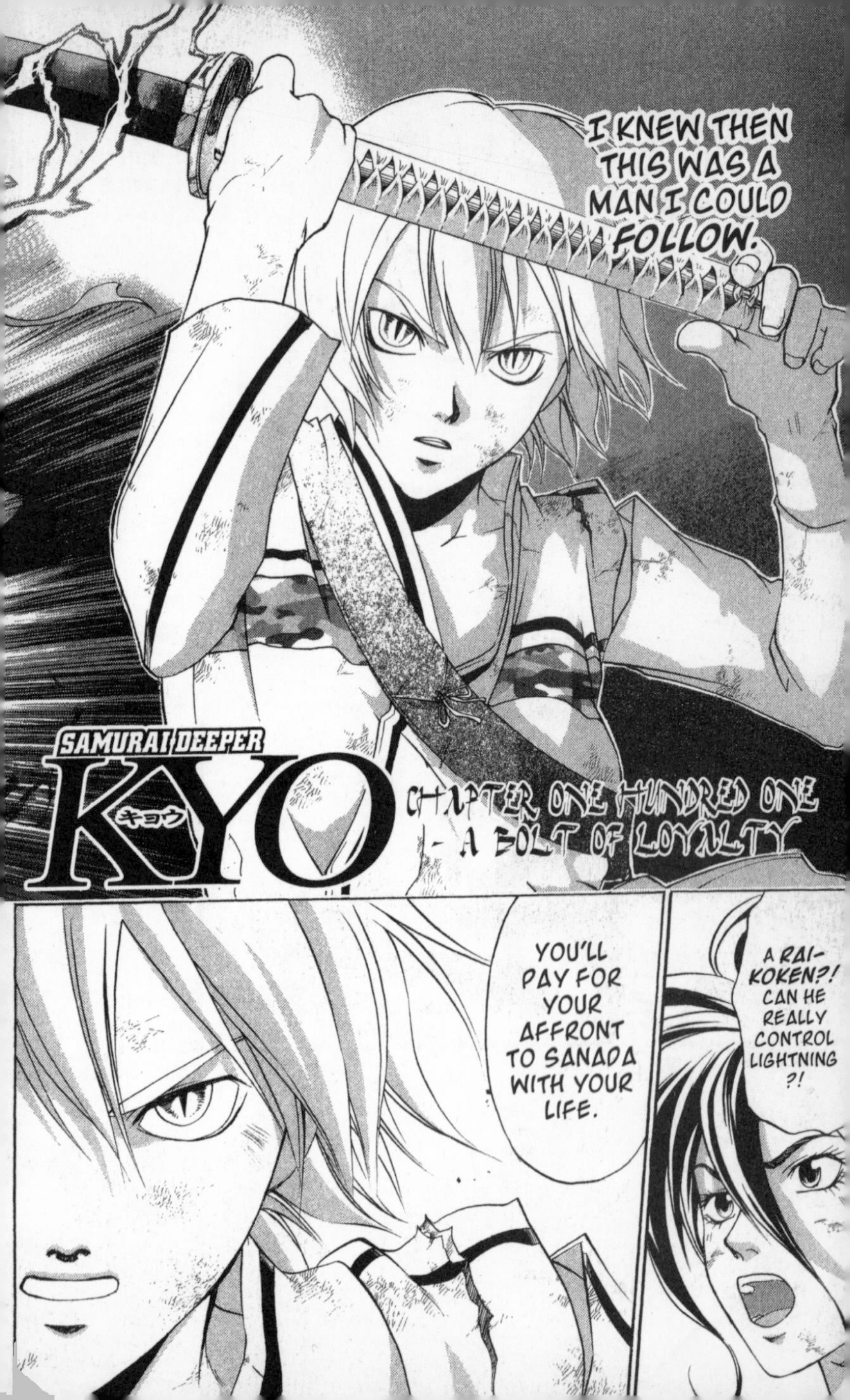
I KNEW THEN THIS WAS A MAN I COULD FOLLOW.
SAMURAI DEEPER KYO キョウ
CHAPTER ONE HUNDRED ONE - A BOLT OF LOYALTY
A RAI-KOKEN?! CAN HE REALLY CONTROL LIGHTNING?!
YOU'LL PAY FOR YOUR AFFRONT TO SANADA WITH YOUR LIFE.

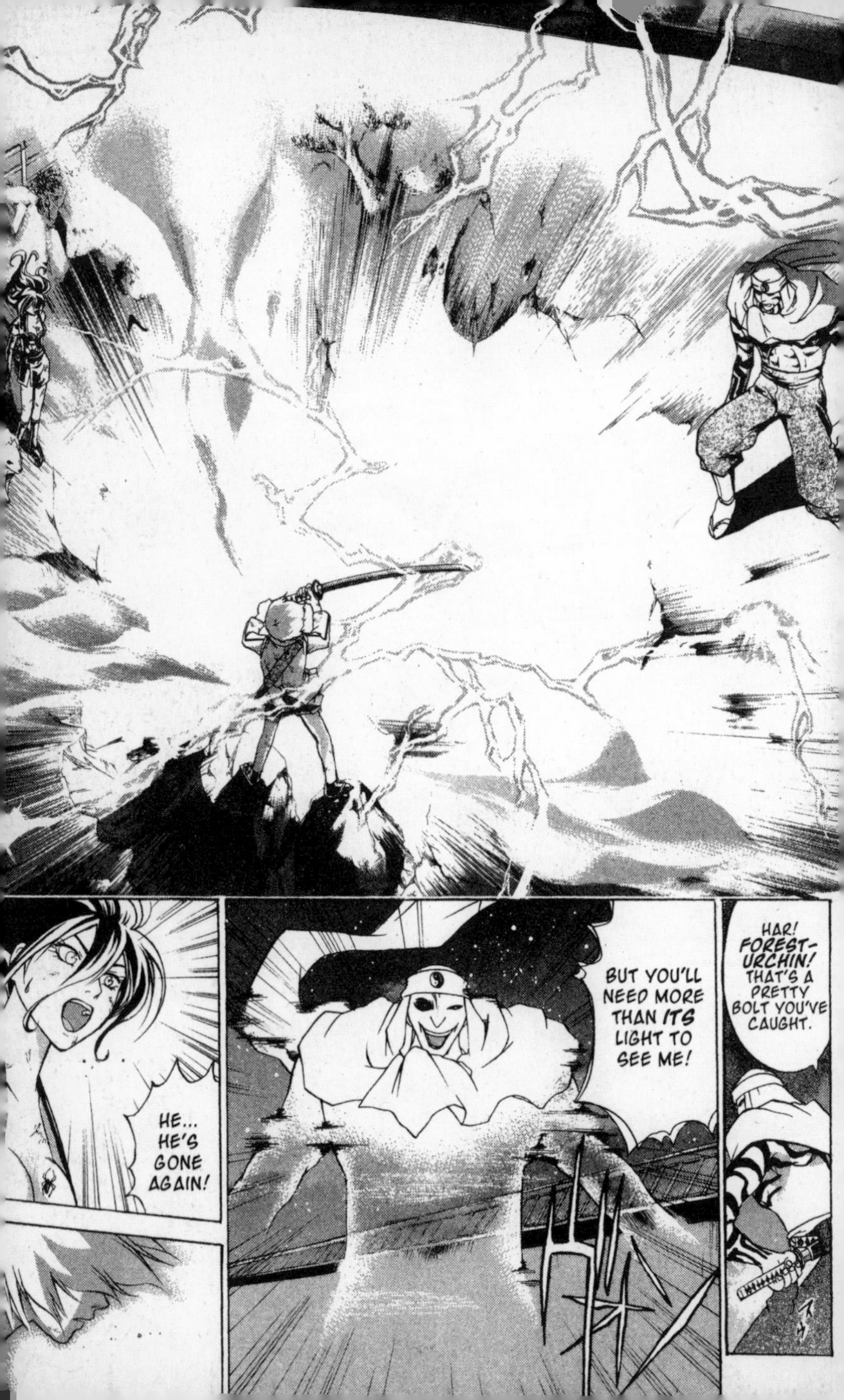
HAR! FOREST-URCHIN! THAT'S A PRETTY BOLT YOU'VE CAUGHT.
BUT YOU'LL NEED MORE THAN ITS LIGHT TO SEE ME!
HE... HE'S GONE AGAIN!
...

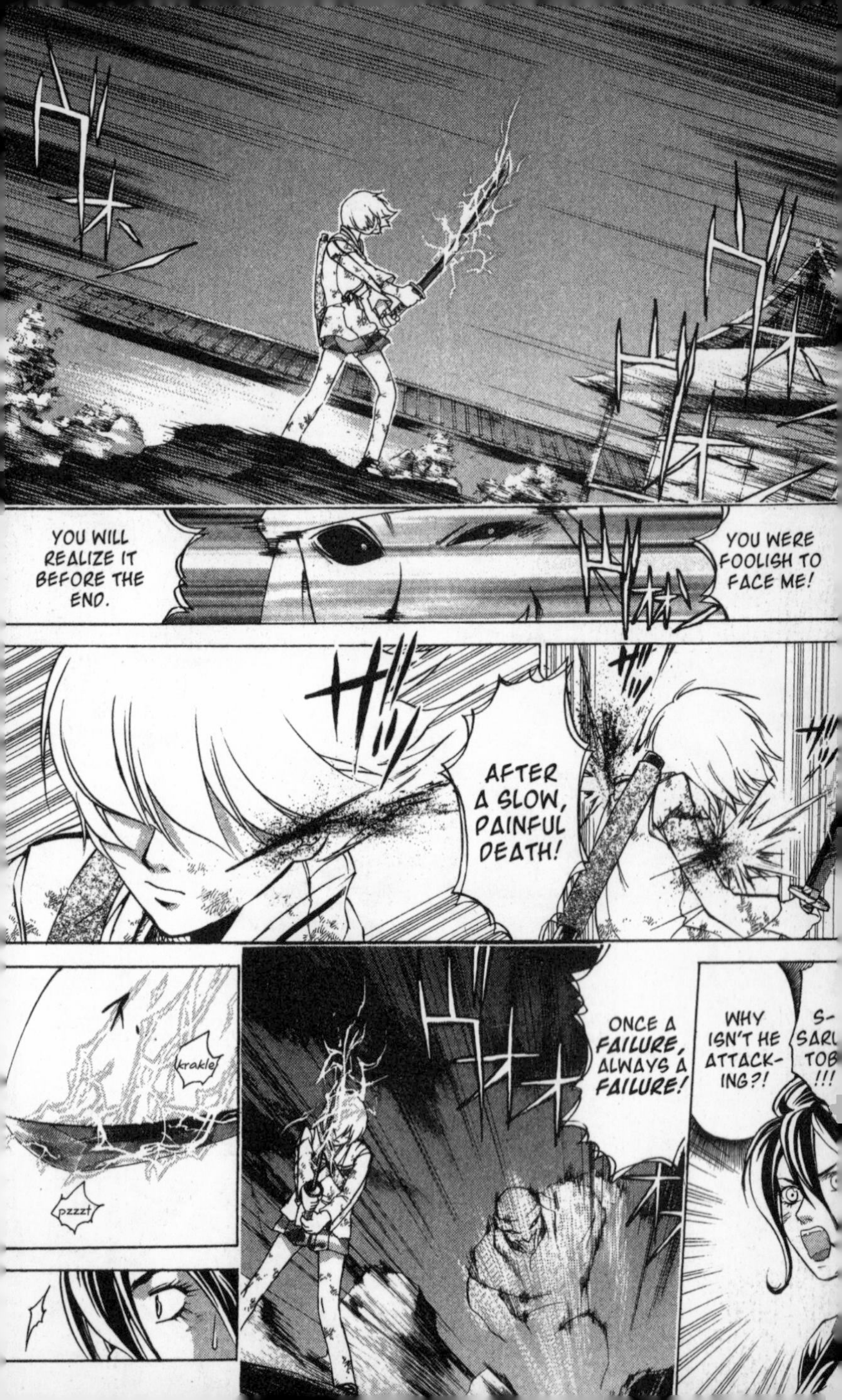
YOU WERE FOOLISH TO FACE ME!
YOU WILL REALIZE IT BEFORE THE END.
AFTER A SLOW, PAINFUL DEATH!
S-SARU TOB !!!
WHY ISN'T HE ATTACKING?!
ONCE A FAILURE, ALWAYS A FAILURE!
krakle
pzzzt

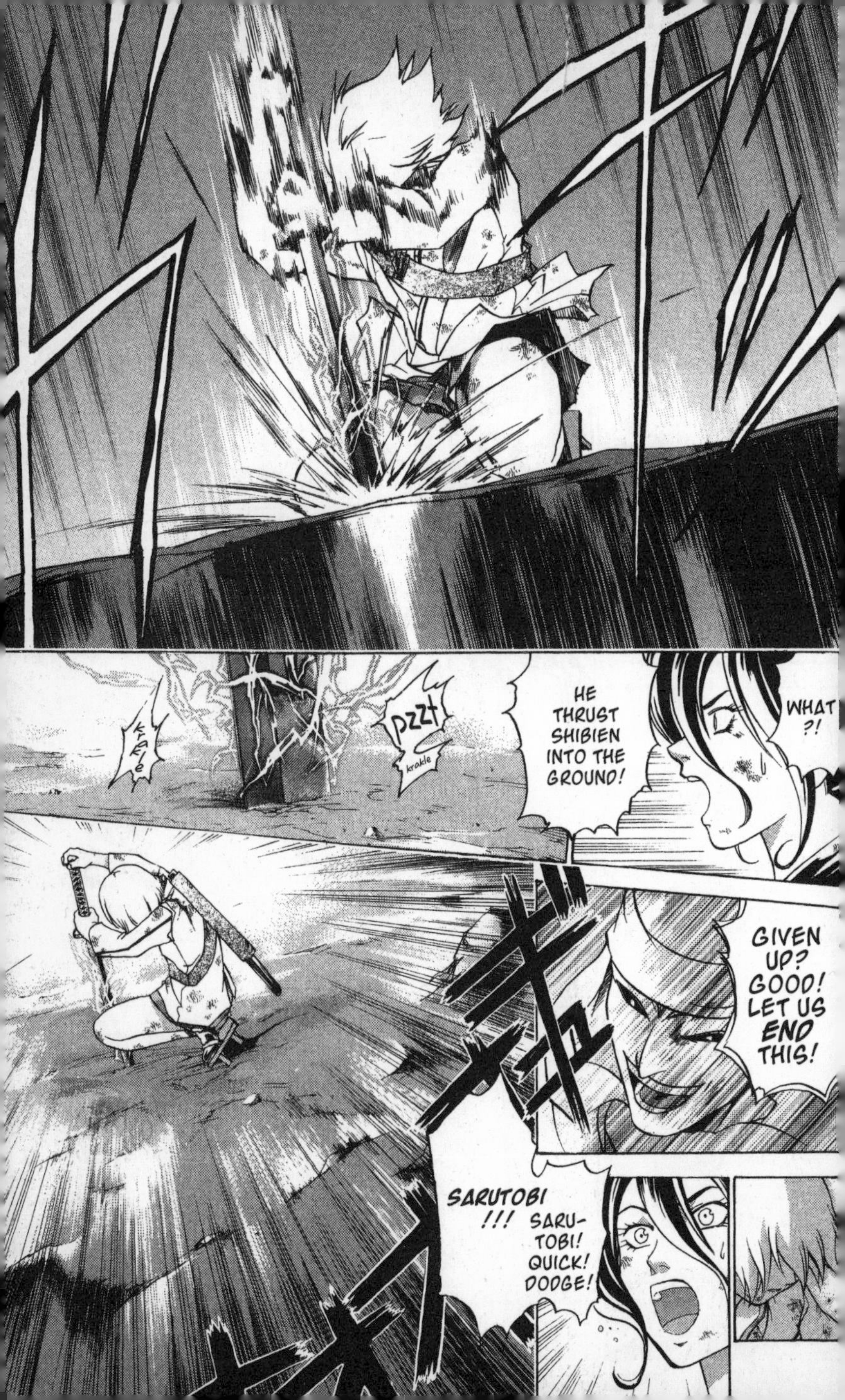
WHAT ?!
HE THRUST SHIBIEN INTO THE GROUND!
pzzt
krakle
krakle
GIVEN UP? GOOD! LET US END THIS!
SARUTOBI!!!
SARU-TOBI! QUICK! DODGE!

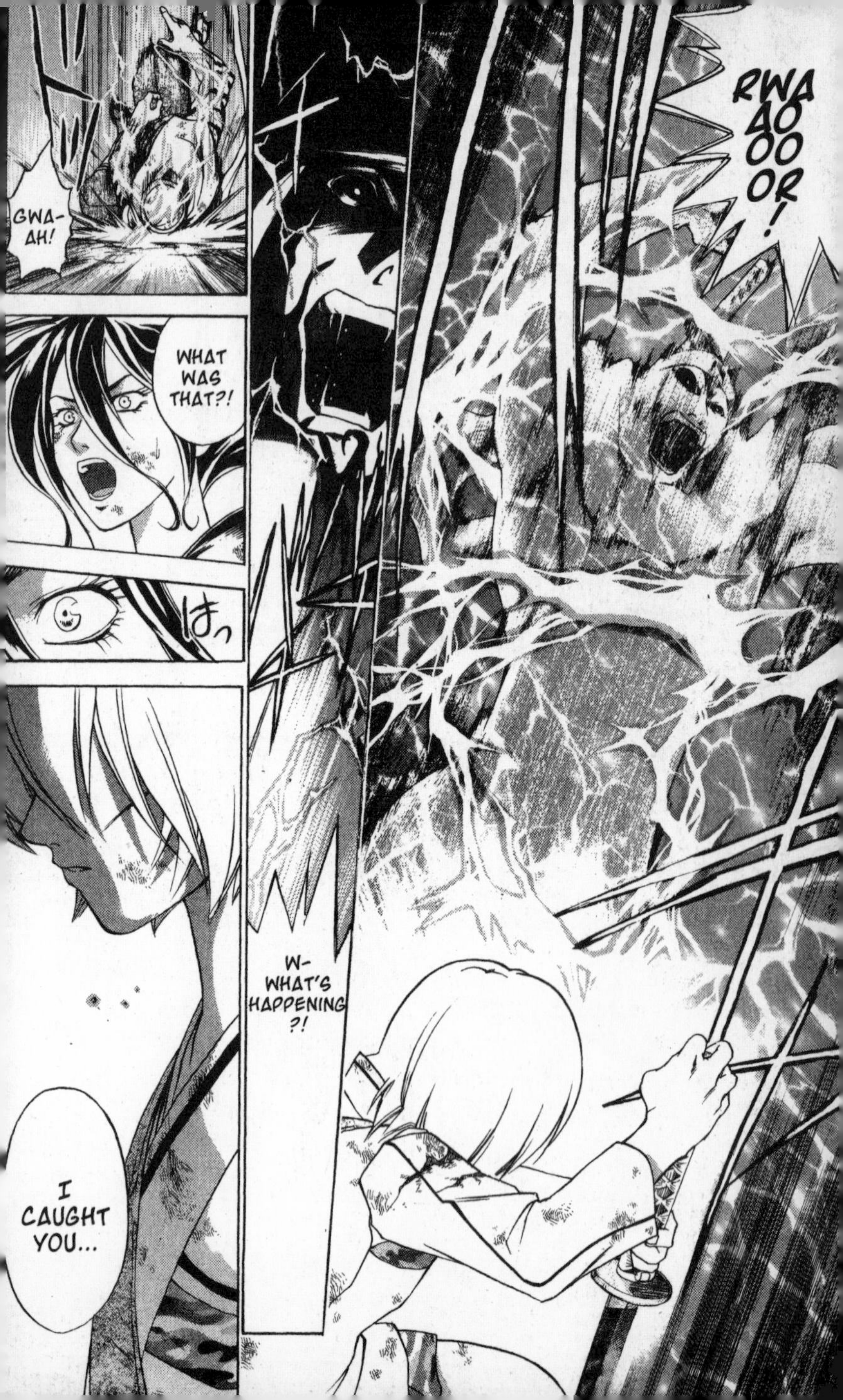

RWAAOOOOR!
W-WHAT'S HAPPENING?!
GWA-AH!
WHAT WAS THAT?!
はっ
I CAUGHT YOU...

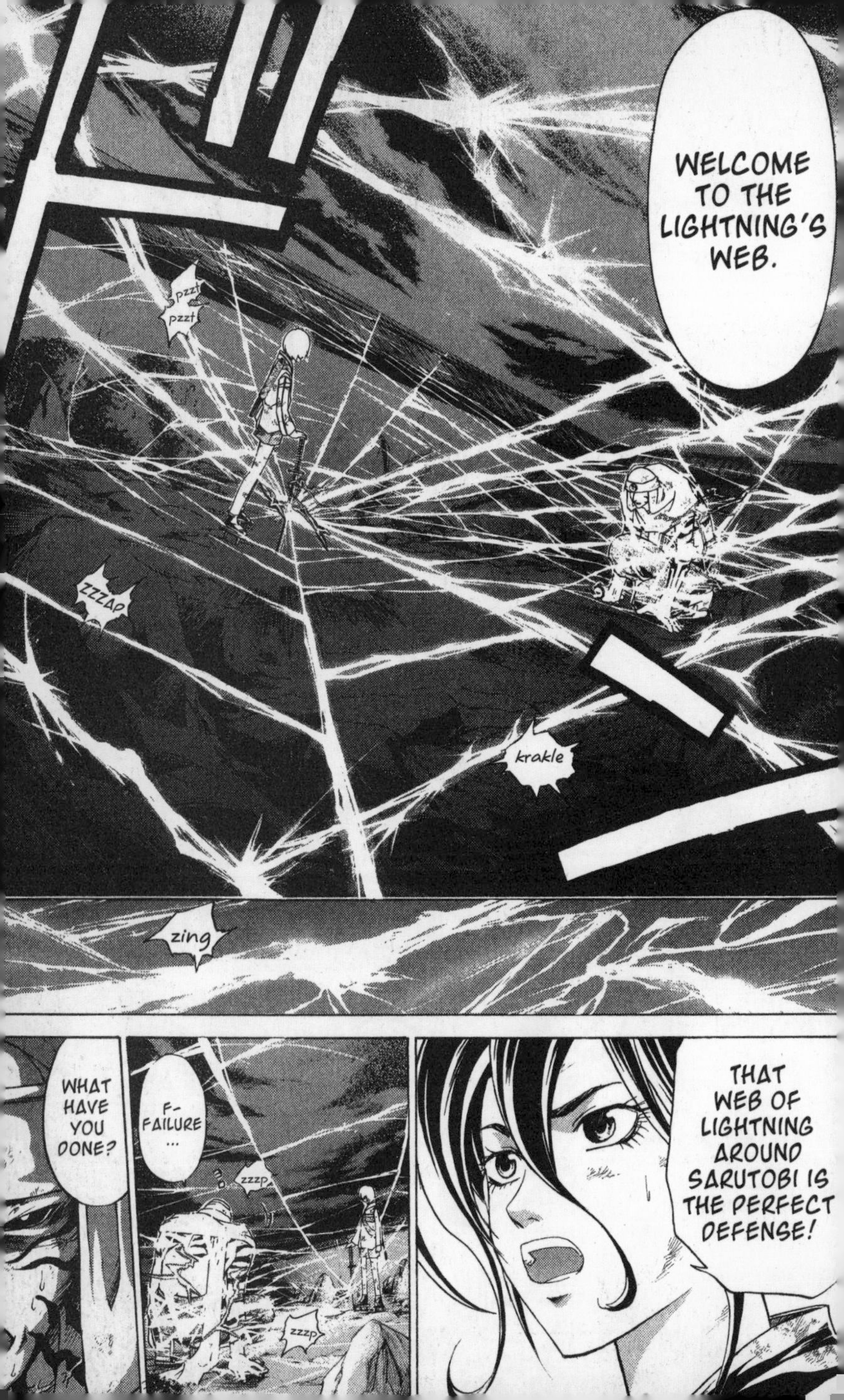
WELCOME TO THE LIGHTNING'S WEB.
pzzt
pzzt
zzzap
krakle
zing
THAT WEB OF LIGHTNING AROUND SARUTOBI IS THE PERFECT DEFENSE!
F- FAILURE ...
zzzp
zzzp
WHAT HAVE YOU DONE?

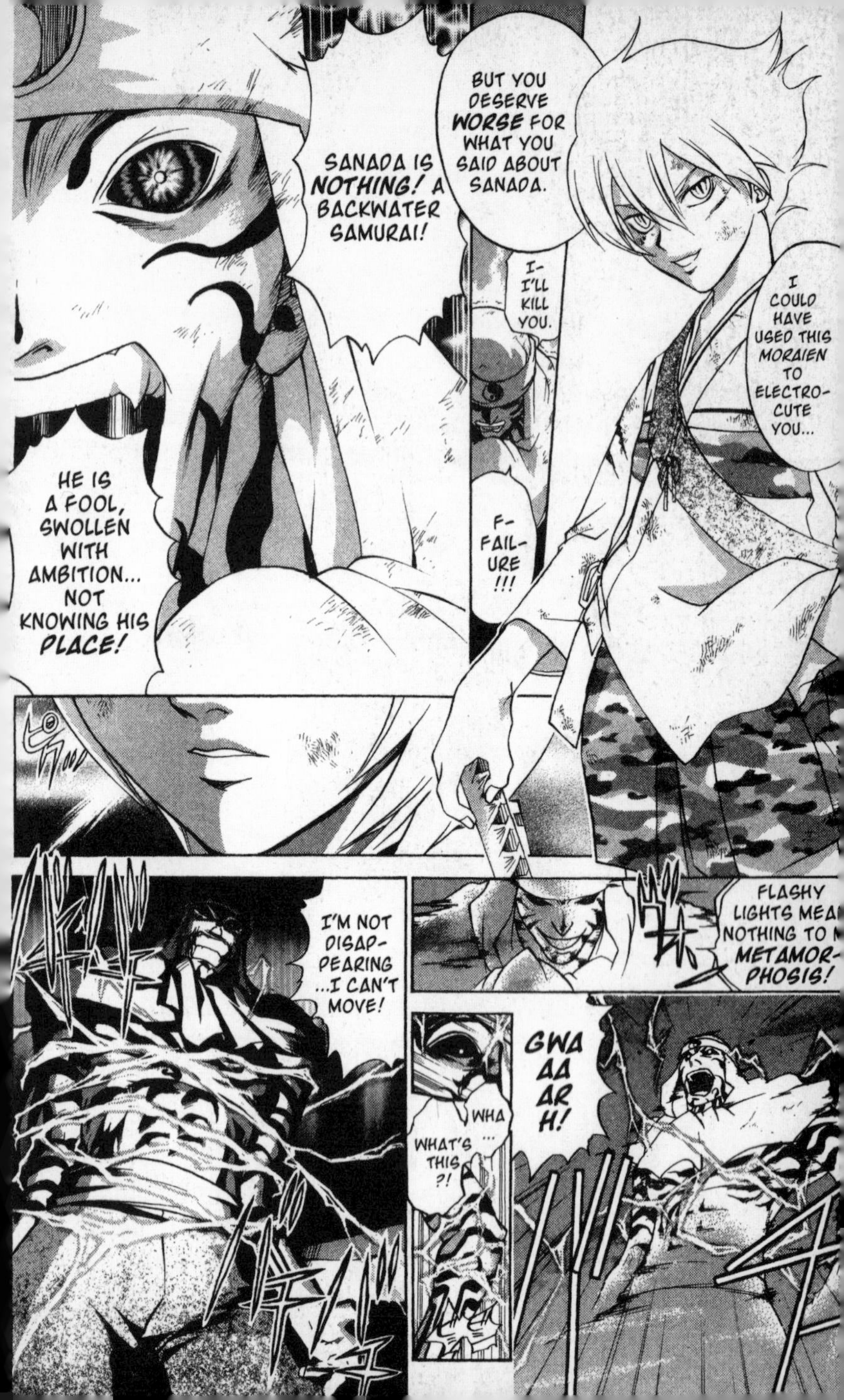

I COULD HAVE USED THIS MORAIEN TO ELECTRO-CUTE YOU...
BUT YOU DESERVE WORSE FOR WHAT YOU SAID ABOUT SANADA.
I-I'LL KILL YOU.
F-FAIL-URE!!!
SANADA IS NOTHING! A BACKWATER SAMURAI!
HE IS A FOOL, SWOLLEN WITH AMBITION... NOT KNOWING HIS PLACE!
FLASHY LIGHTS MEA NOTHING TO M METAMOR-PHOSIS!
GWA AA AR H!
WHA... WHAT'S THIS ?!
I'M NOT DISAP-PEARING ...I CAN'T MOVE!

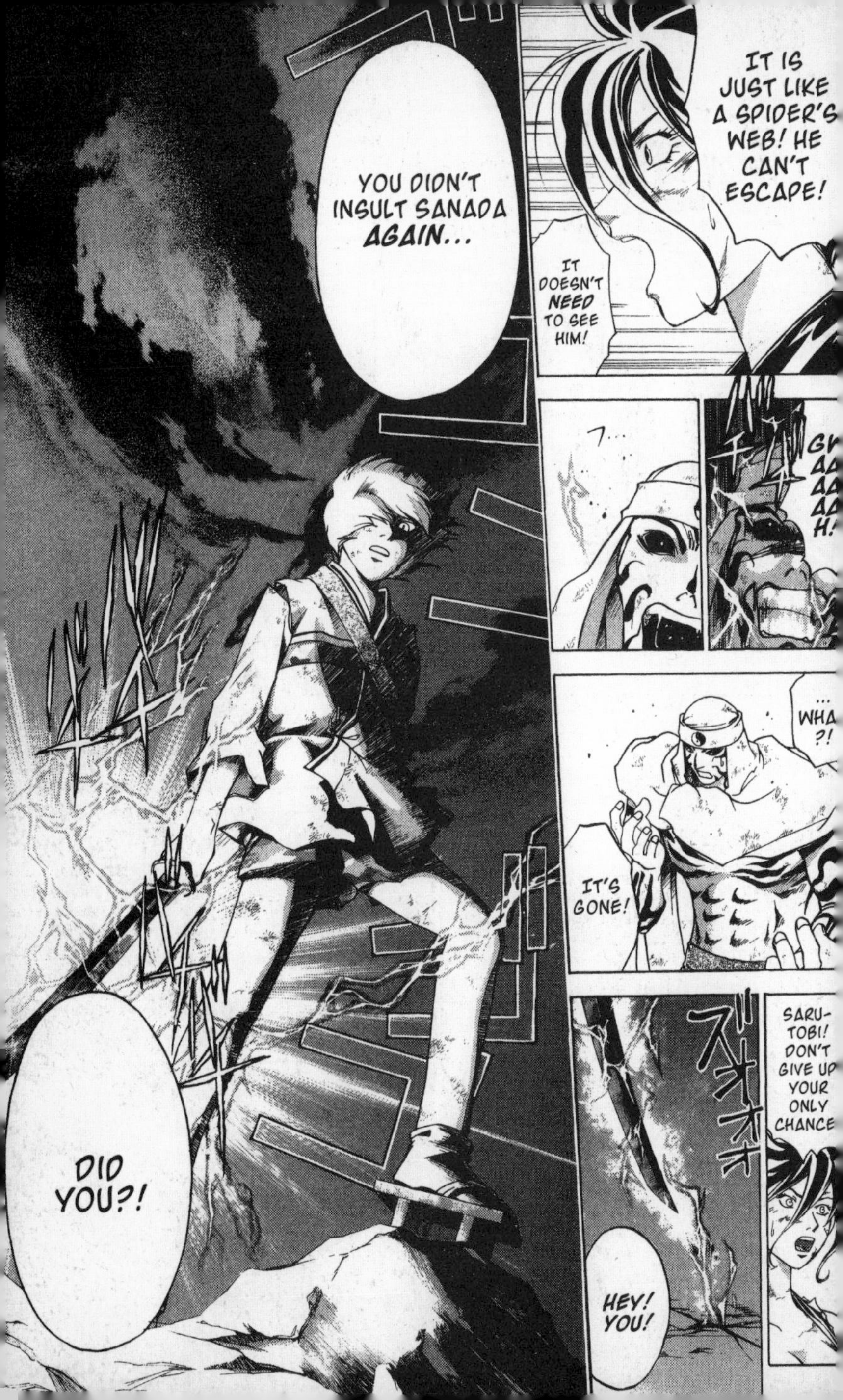

IT IS JUST LIKE A SPIDER'S WEB! HE CAN'T ESCAPE!
IT DOESN'T NEED TO SEE HIM!
GWAAAAAAAAH!
...WHA?!
IT'S GONE!
SARU-TOBI! DON'T GIVE UP YOUR ONLY CHANCE
ズオオオ
HEY! YOU!
YOU DIDN'T INSULT SANADA AGAIN...
DID YOU?!

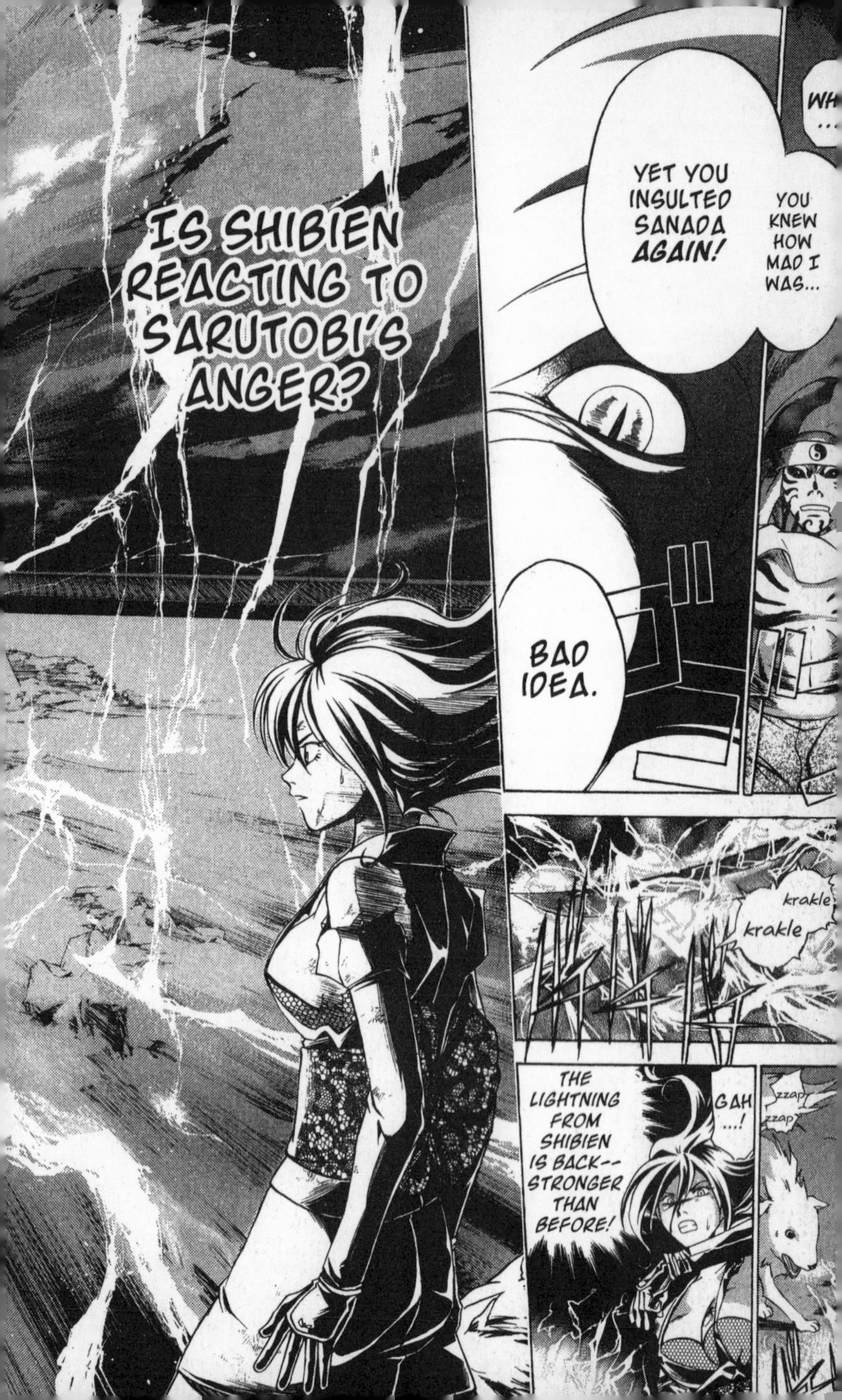
WH...
YOU KNEW HOW MAD I WAS...
YET YOU INSULTED SANADA AGAIN!
BAD IDEA.
krakle
krakle
zzap
zzap
GAH...!
THE LIGHTNING FROM SHIBIEN IS BACK--STRONGER THAN BEFORE!
IS SHIBIEN REACTING TO SARUTOBI'S ANGER?

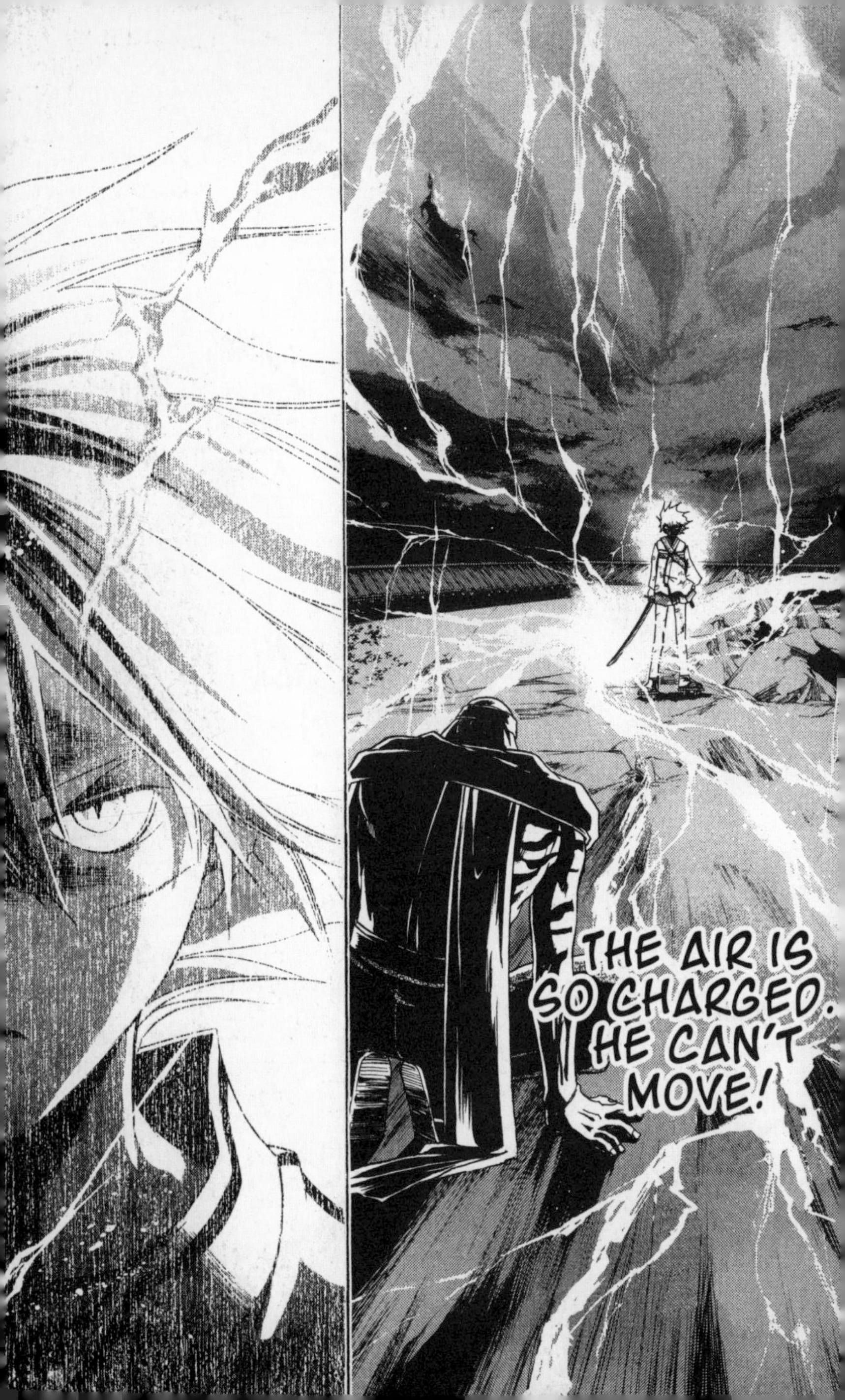
THE AIR IS SO CHARGED. HE CAN'T MOVE!

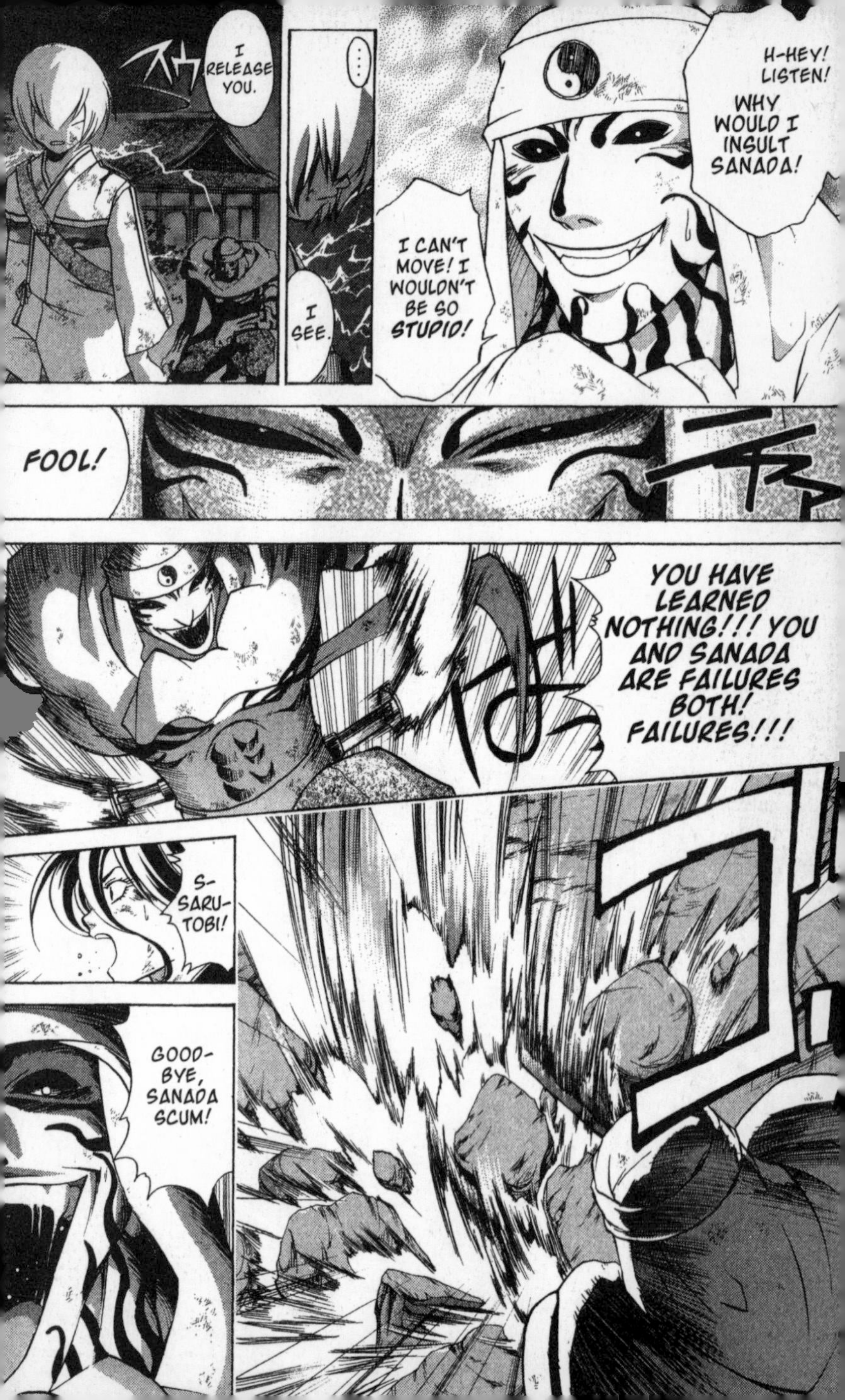
H-HEY! LISTEN! WHY WOULD I INSULT SANADA!
I CAN'T MOVE! I WOULDN'T BE SO STUPID!
...
I SEE.
I RELEASE YOU.
FOOL!
YOU HAVE LEARNED NOTHING!!! YOU AND SANADA ARE FAILURES BOTH! FAILURES!!!
S-SARUTOBI!
GOOD-BYE, SANADA SCUM!

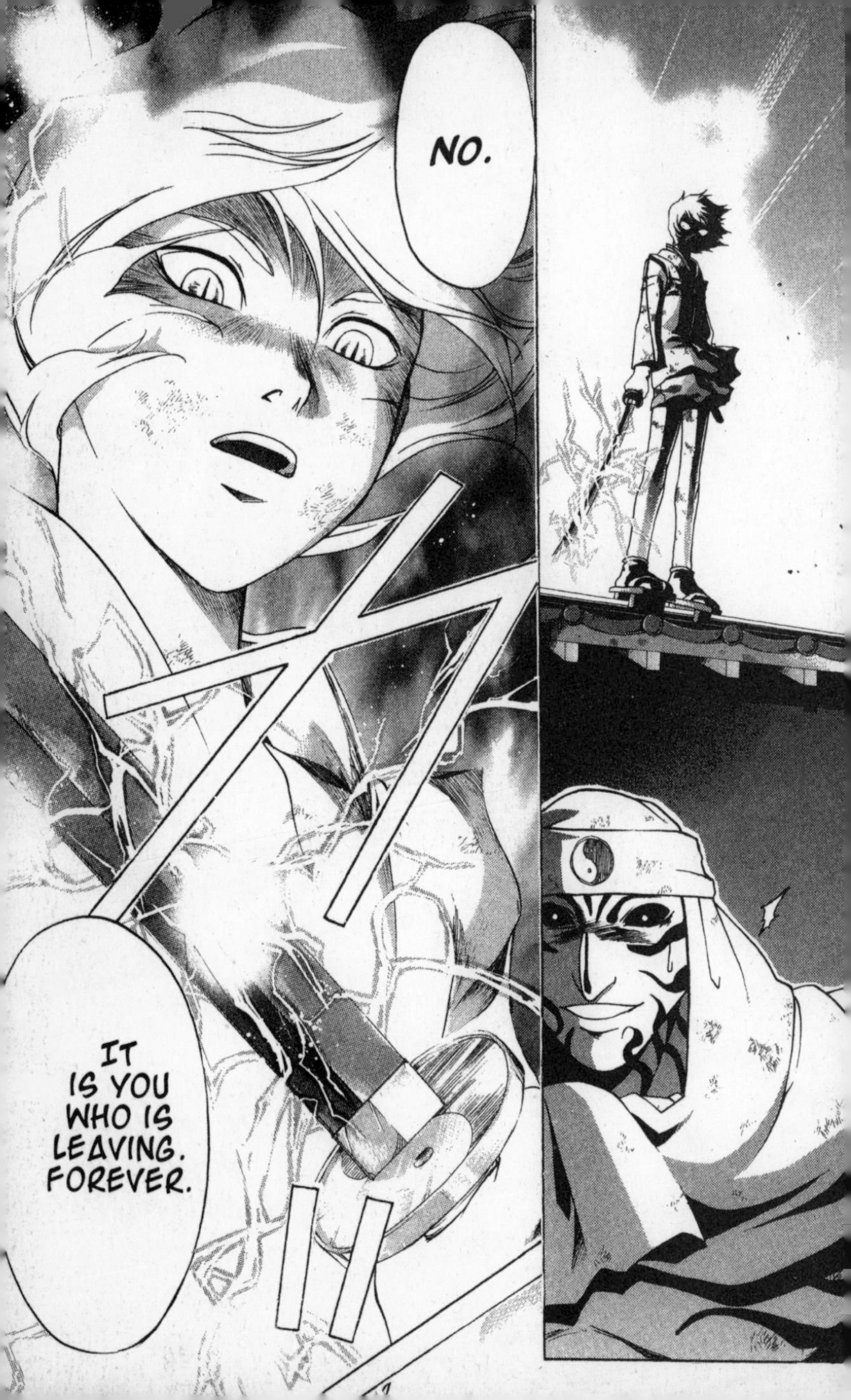
NO.
IT IS YOU WHO IS LEAVING. FOREVER.

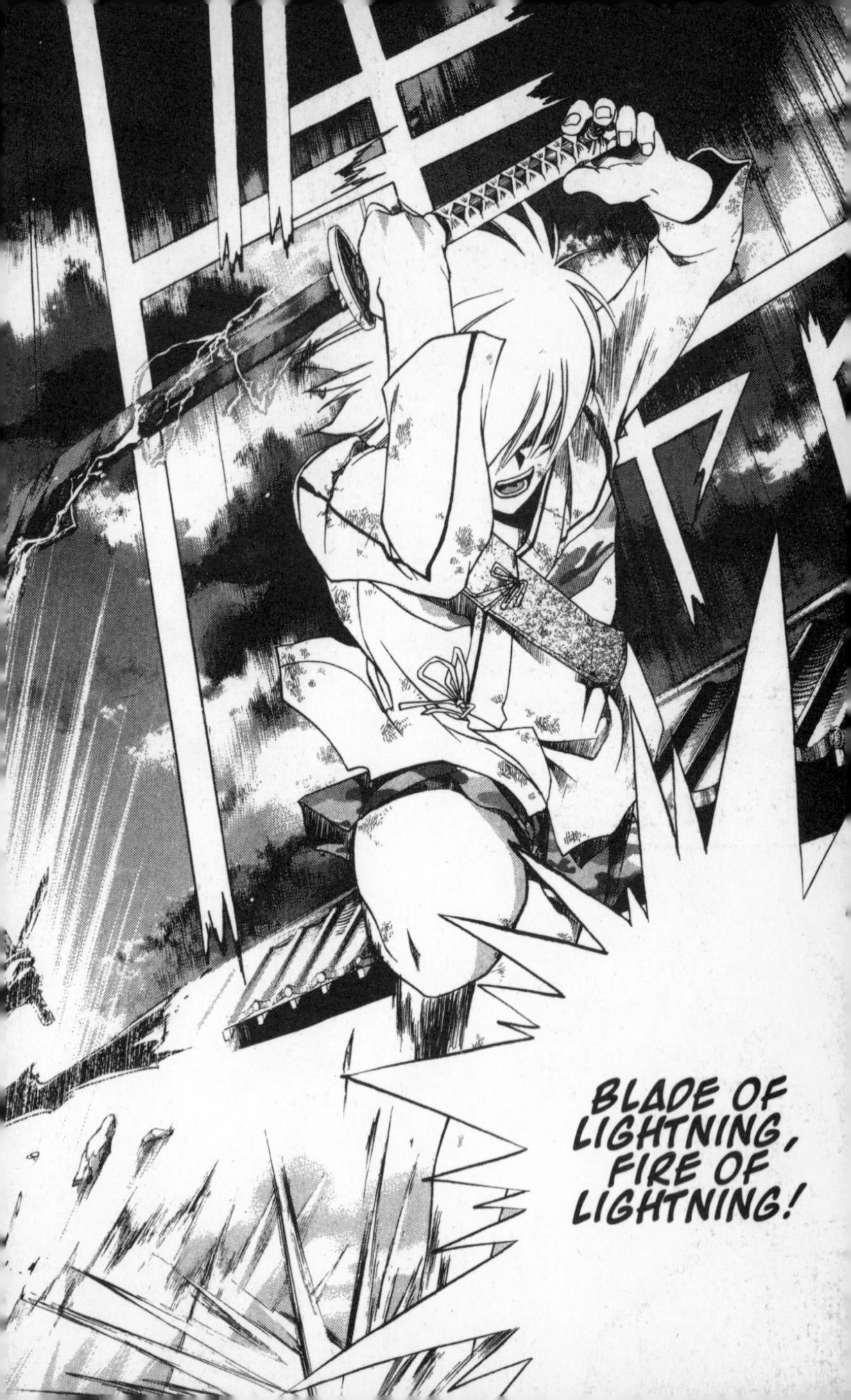
BLADE OF LIGHTNING, FIRE OF LIGHTNING!

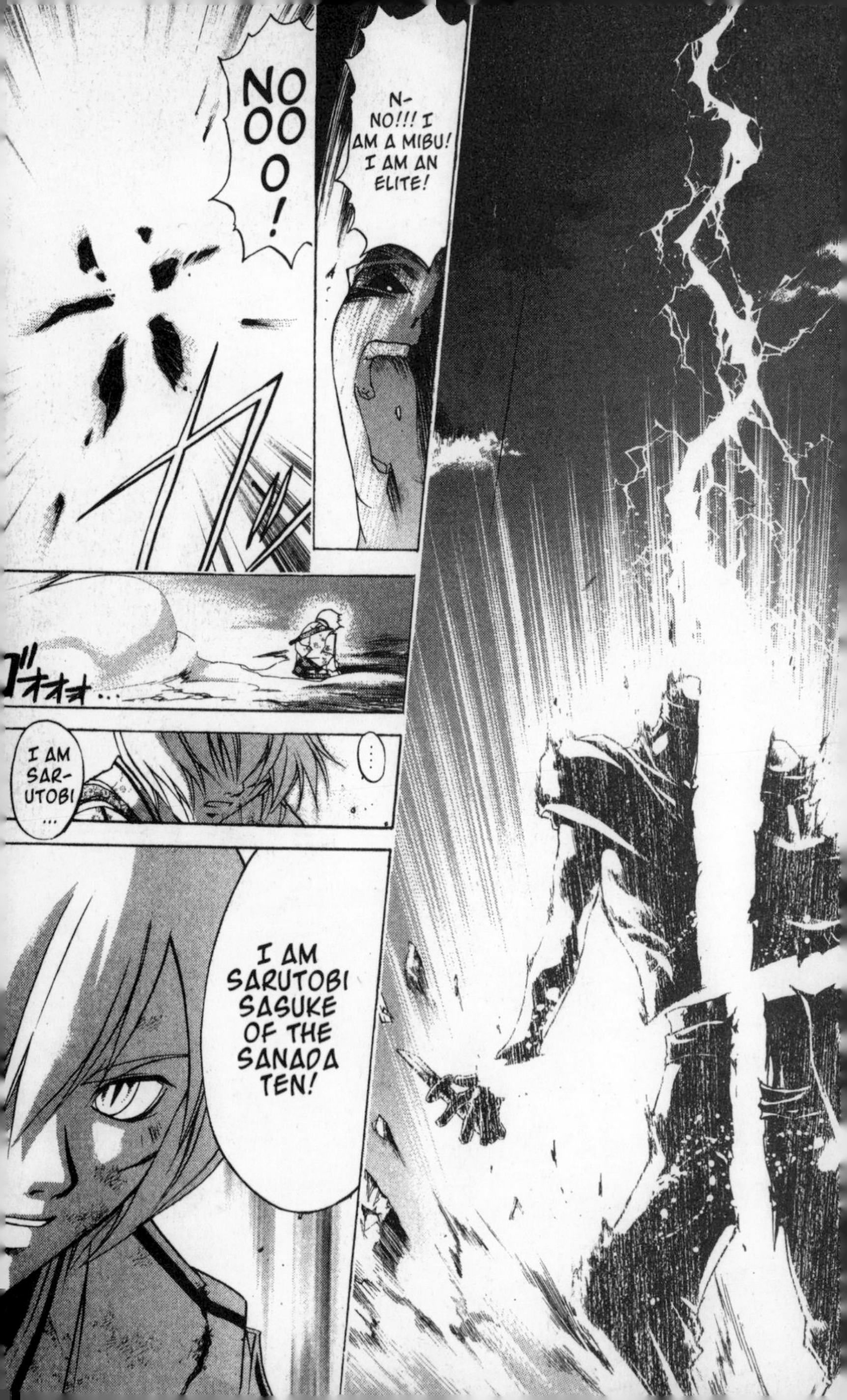
N-NO!!! I AM A MIBU! I AM AN ELITE!
NOOOO!
ゴオオオ…
…
I AM SARUTOBI…
I AM SARUTOBI SASUKE OF THE SANADA TEN!

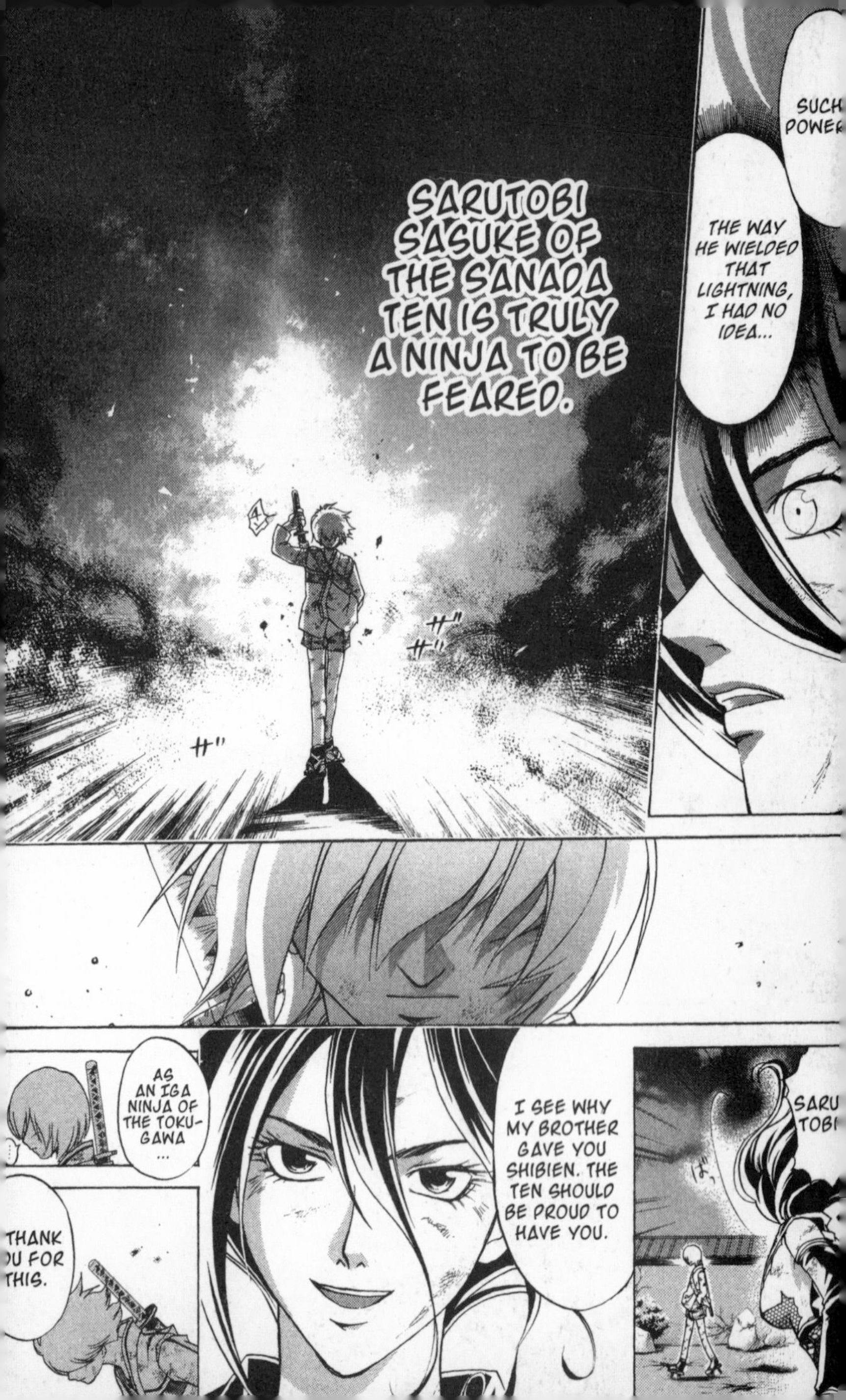
SUCH POWER
THE WAY HE WIELDED THAT LIGHTNING, I HAD NO IDEA...
SARUTOBI SASUKE OF THE SANADA TEN IS TRULY A NINJA TO BE FEARED.
SARUTOBI
ば
I SEE WHY MY BROTHER GAVE YOU SHIBIEN. THE TEN SHOULD BE PROUD TO HAVE YOU.
AS AN IGA NINJA OF THE TOKUGAWA ...
...
THANK YOU FOR THIS.

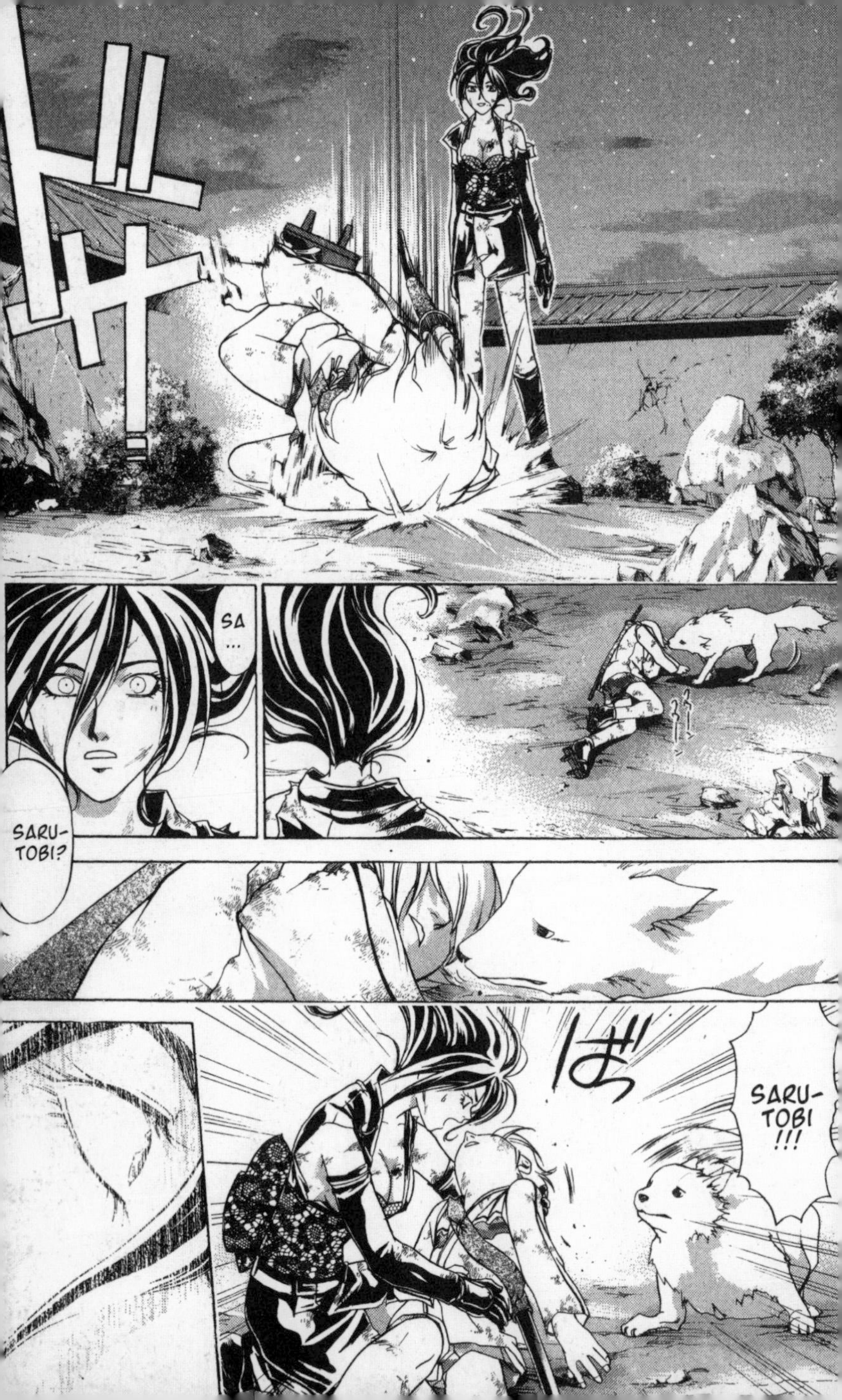
SA ...
SARU-TOBI?
SARU-TOBI !!!

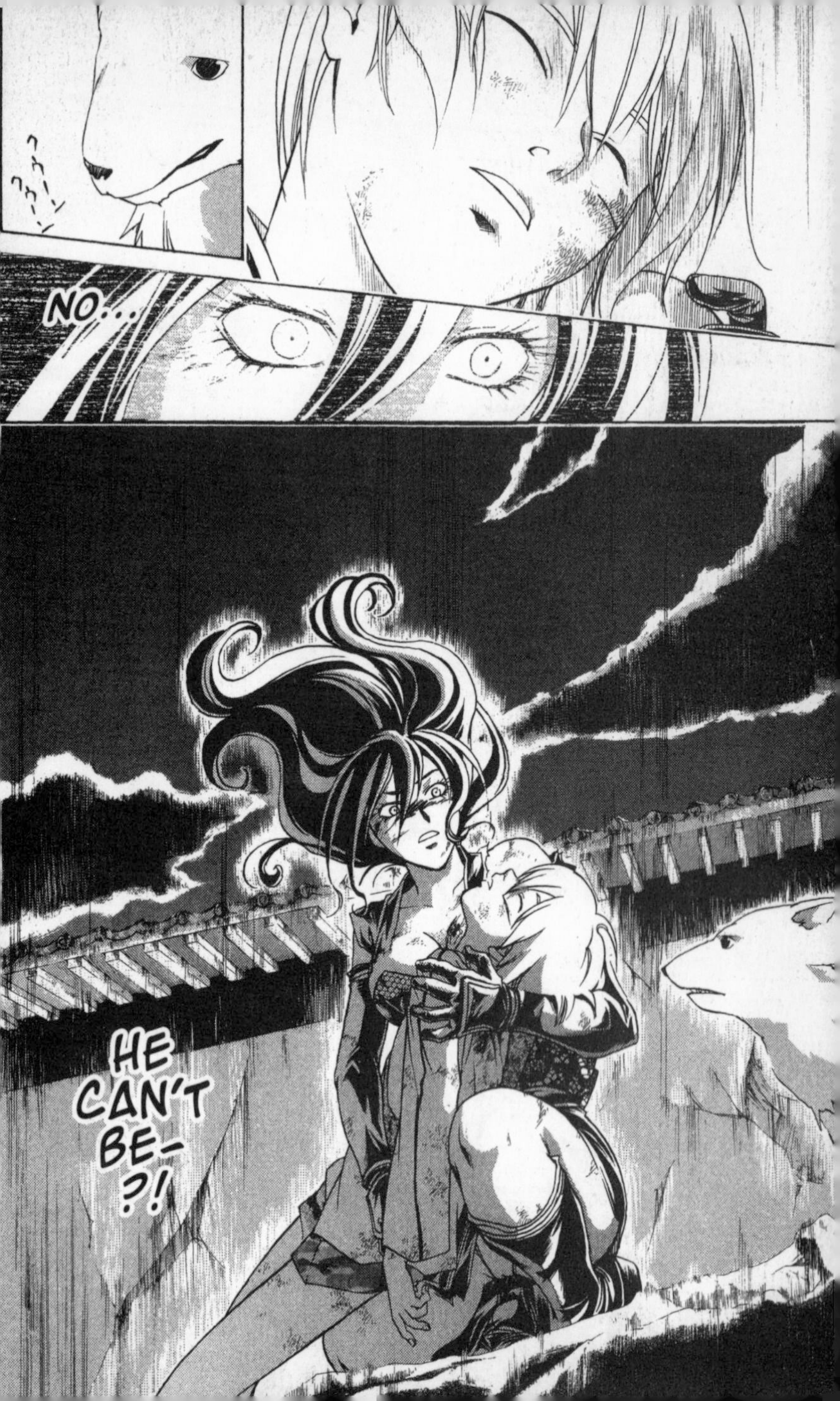
クゥーン
クゥーン
NO...
HE CAN'T BE-?!

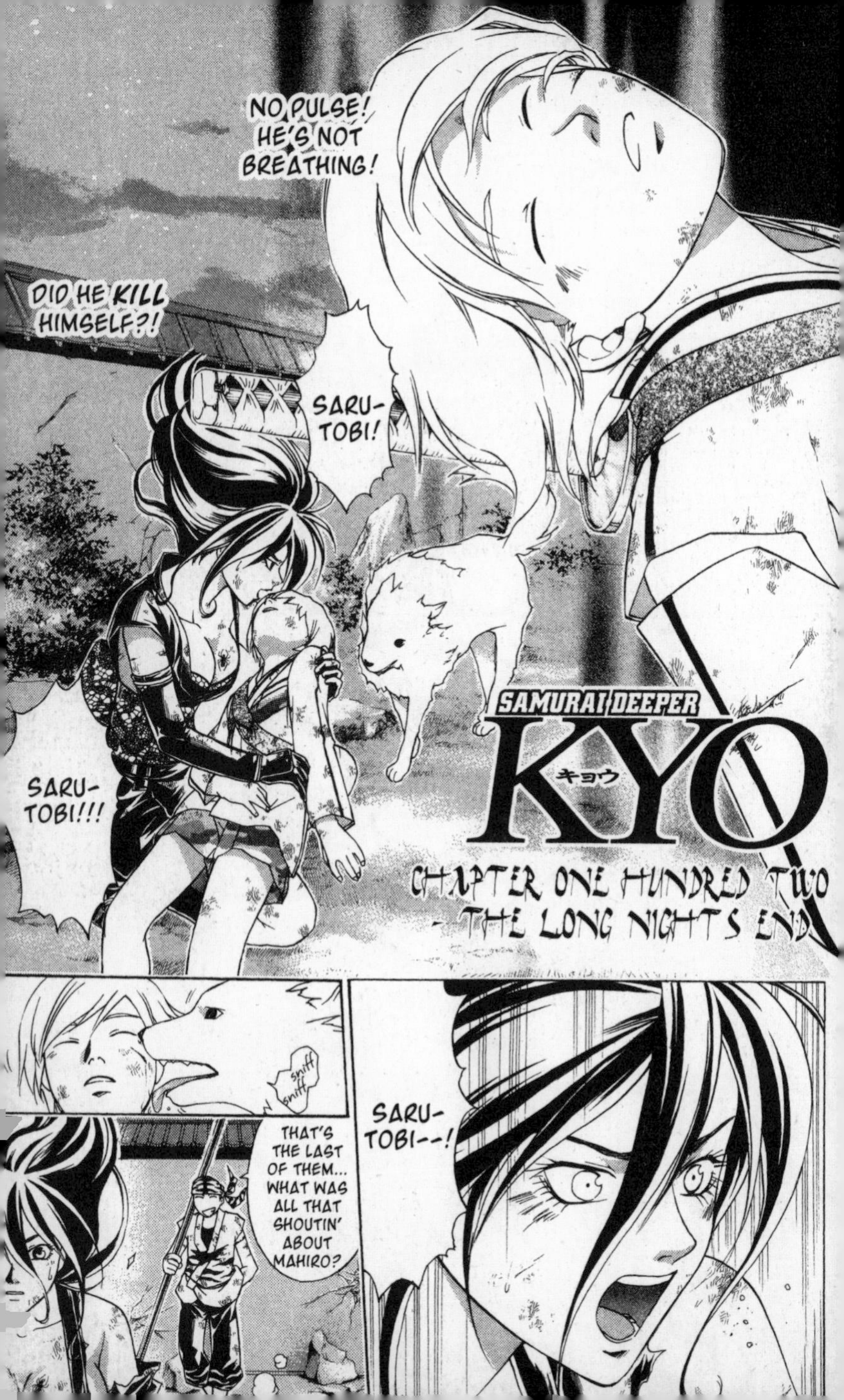
NO PULSE! HE'S NOT BREATHING!
SARU-TOBI!
DID HE **KILL** HIMSELF?!
SAMURAI DEEPER
KYO
キョウ
CHAPTER ONE HUNDRED TWO
- THE LONG NIGHT'S END
SARU-TOBI!!!
SARU-TOBI--!
sniff sniff
THAT'S THE LAST OF THEM... WHAT WAS ALL THAT SHOUTIN' ABOUT MAHIRO?

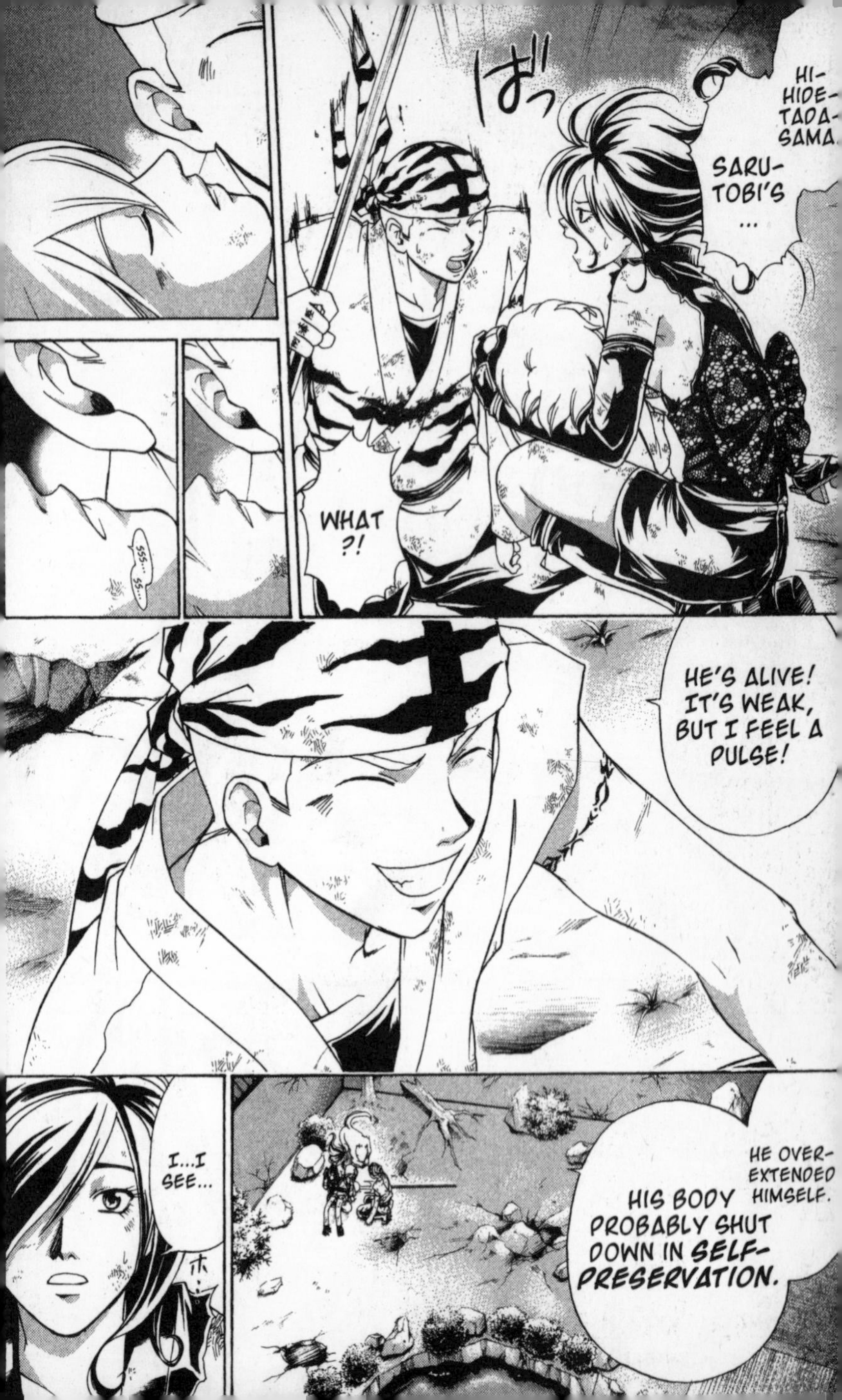
ばっ
HI-HIDE-TADA-SAMA.
SARU-TOBI'S...
WHAT?!
sss... ss...
HE'S ALIVE! IT'S WEAK, BUT I FEEL A PULSE!
HE OVER-EXTENDED HIMSELF.
HIS BODY PROBABLY SHUT DOWN IN SELF-PRESERVATION.
I...I SEE...
ホッ

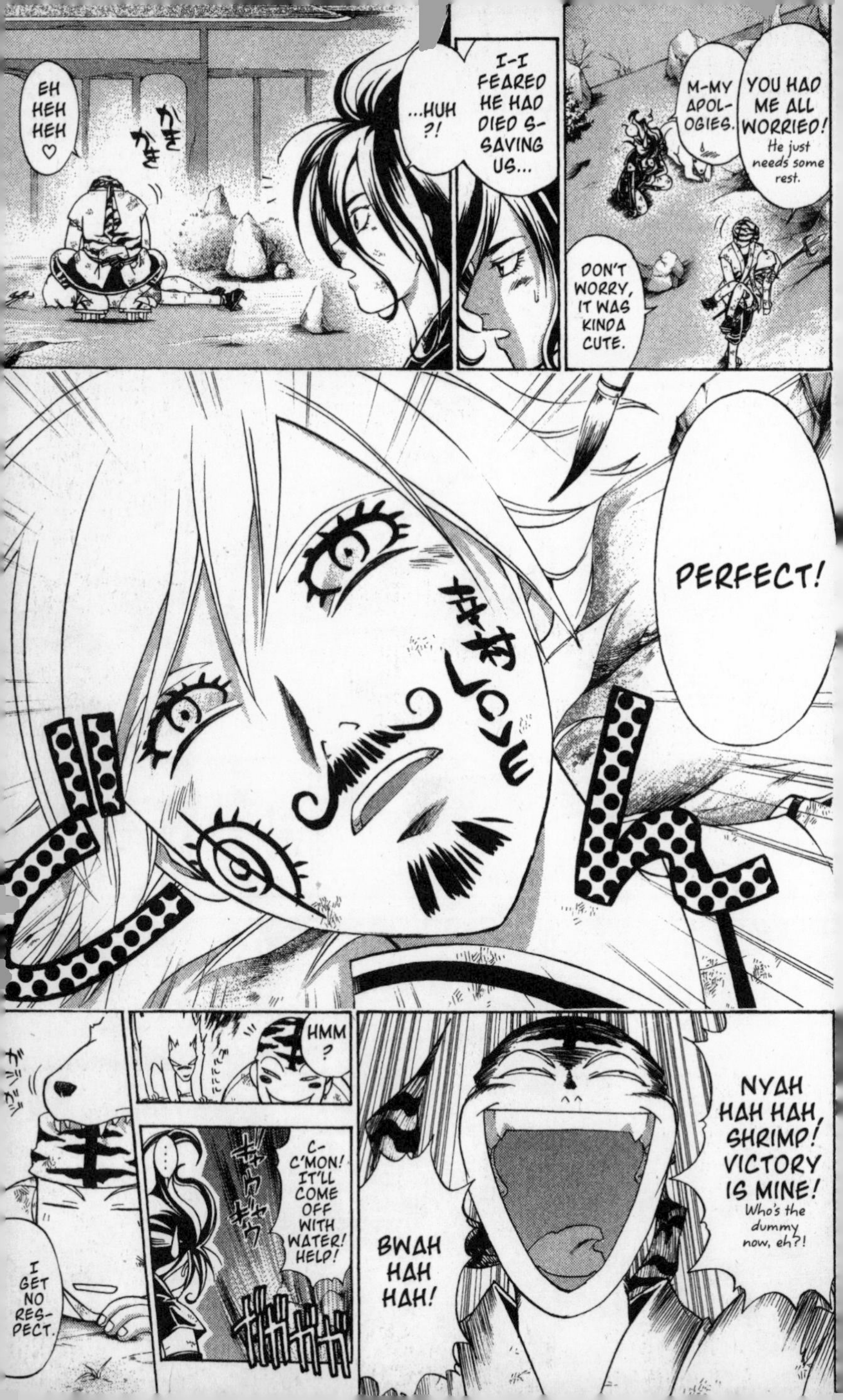
YOU HAD ME ALL WORRIED! He just needs some rest.
M-MY APOLOGIES.
DON'T WORRY, IT WAS KINDA CUTE.
I-I FEARED HE HAD DIED S-SAVING US...
...HUH?!
EH HEH HEH ♡
かき かき
PERFECT!
NYAH HAH HAH, SHRIMP! VICTORY IS MINE! Who's the dummy now, eh?!
BWAH HAH HAH!
HMM?
C-C'MON! IT'LL COME OFF WITH WATER! HELP!
...
I GET NO RESPECT.

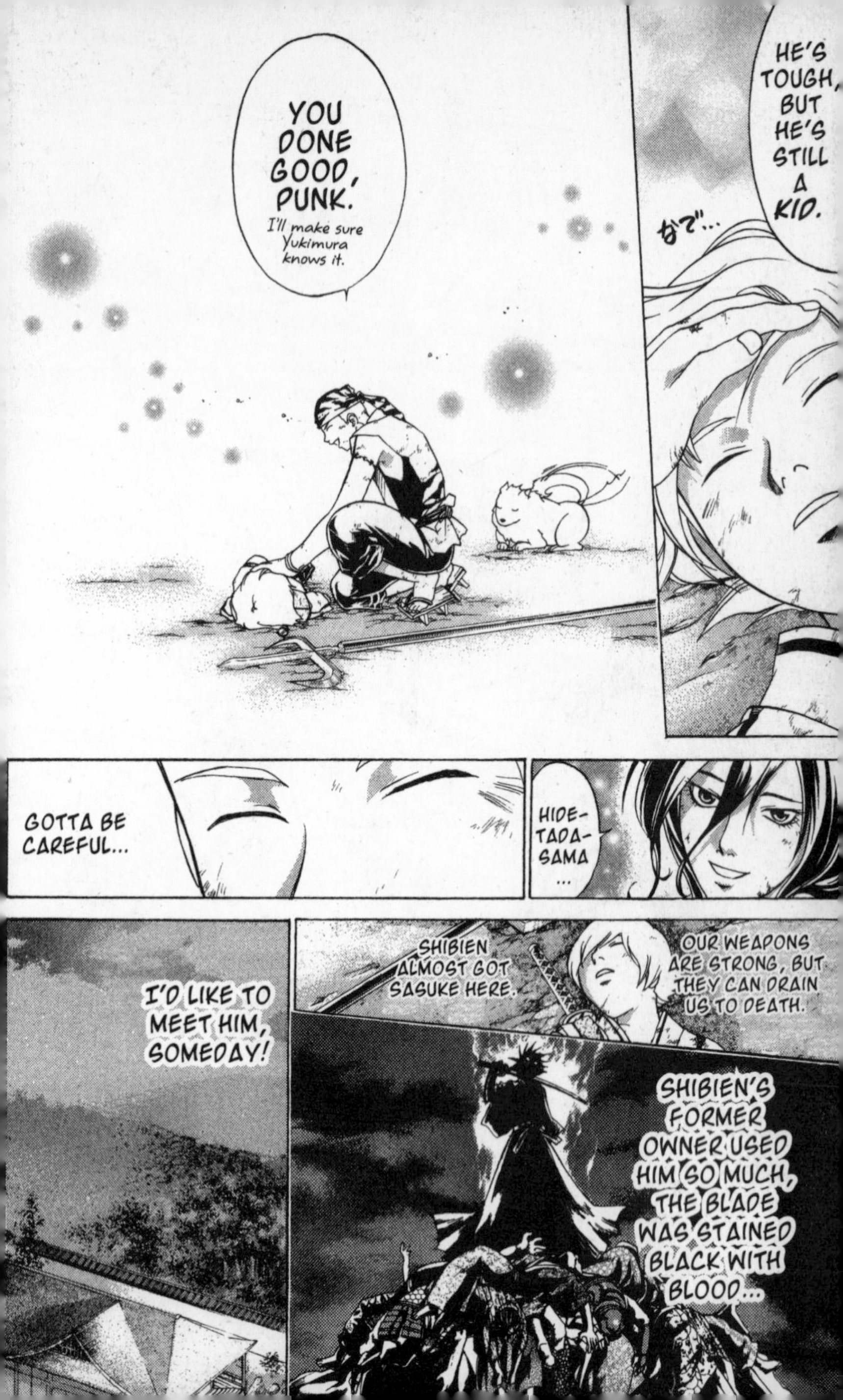
HE'S TOUGH, BUT HE'S STILL A KID.
なで…
YOU DONE GOOD, PUNK.
I'll make sure Yukimura knows it.
HIDE-TADA-SAMA ...
GOTTA BE CAREFUL...
OUR WEAPONS ARE STRONG, BUT THEY CAN DRAIN US TO DEATH.
SHIBIEN ALMOST GOT SASUKE HERE.
SHIBIEN'S FORMER OWNER USED HIM SO MUCH, THE BLADE WAS STAINED BLACK WITH BLOOD...
I'D LIKE TO MEET HIM, SOMEDAY!

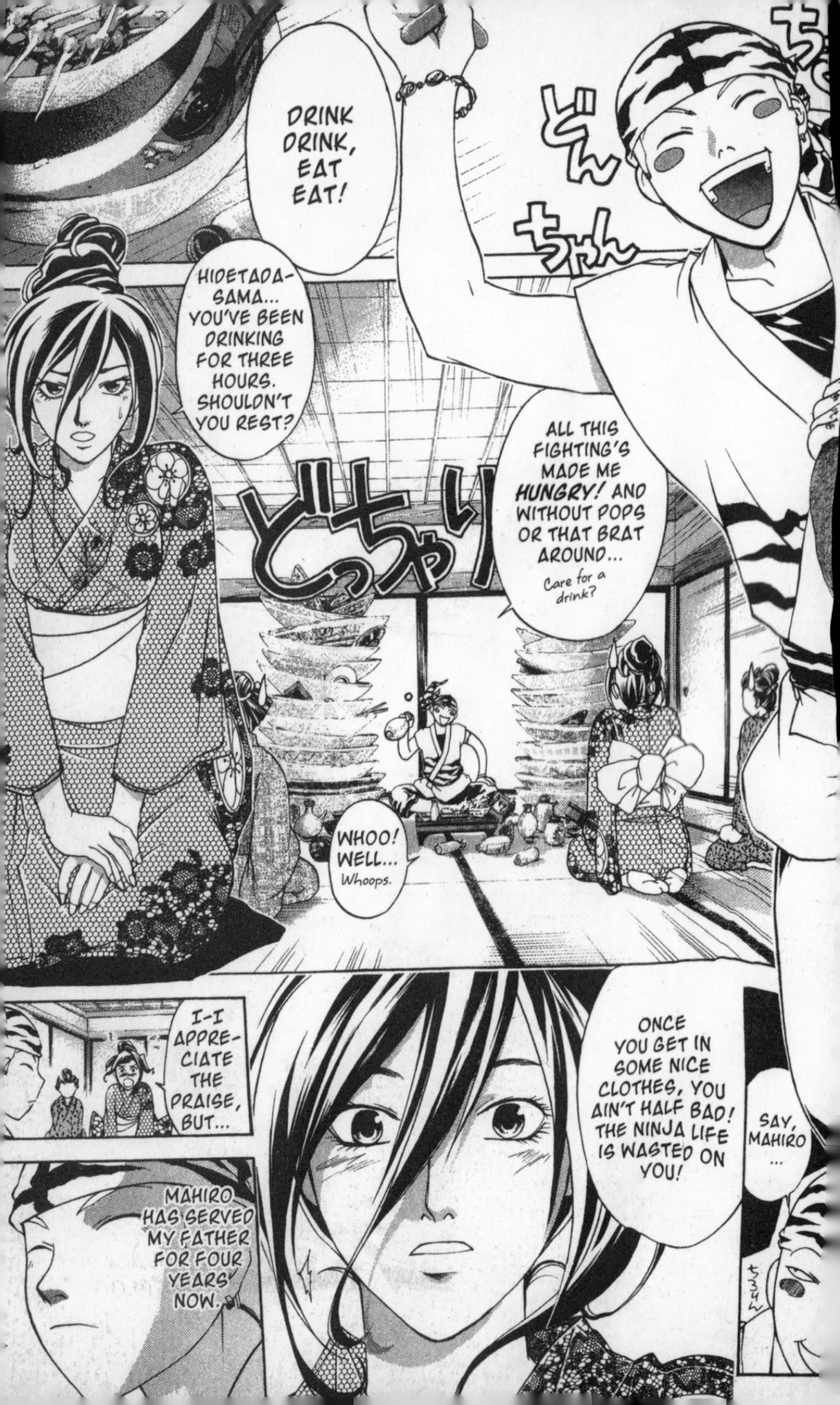
どん
ちゃん
DRINK DRINK, EAT EAT!
ALL THIS FIGHTING'S MADE ME *HUNGRY!* AND WITHOUT POPS OR THAT BRAT AROUND...
Care for a drink?
HIDETADA-SAMA... YOU'VE BEEN DRINKING FOR THREE HOURS. SHOULDN'T YOU REST?
どっちゃり
WHOO! WELL...
Whoops.
SAY, MAHIRO...
ONCE YOU GET IN SOME NICE CLOTHES, YOU AIN'T HALF BAD! THE NINJA LIFE IS WASTED ON YOU!
I-I APPRECIATE THE PRAISE, BUT...
MAHIRO HAS SERVED MY FATHER FOR FOUR YEARS NOW.

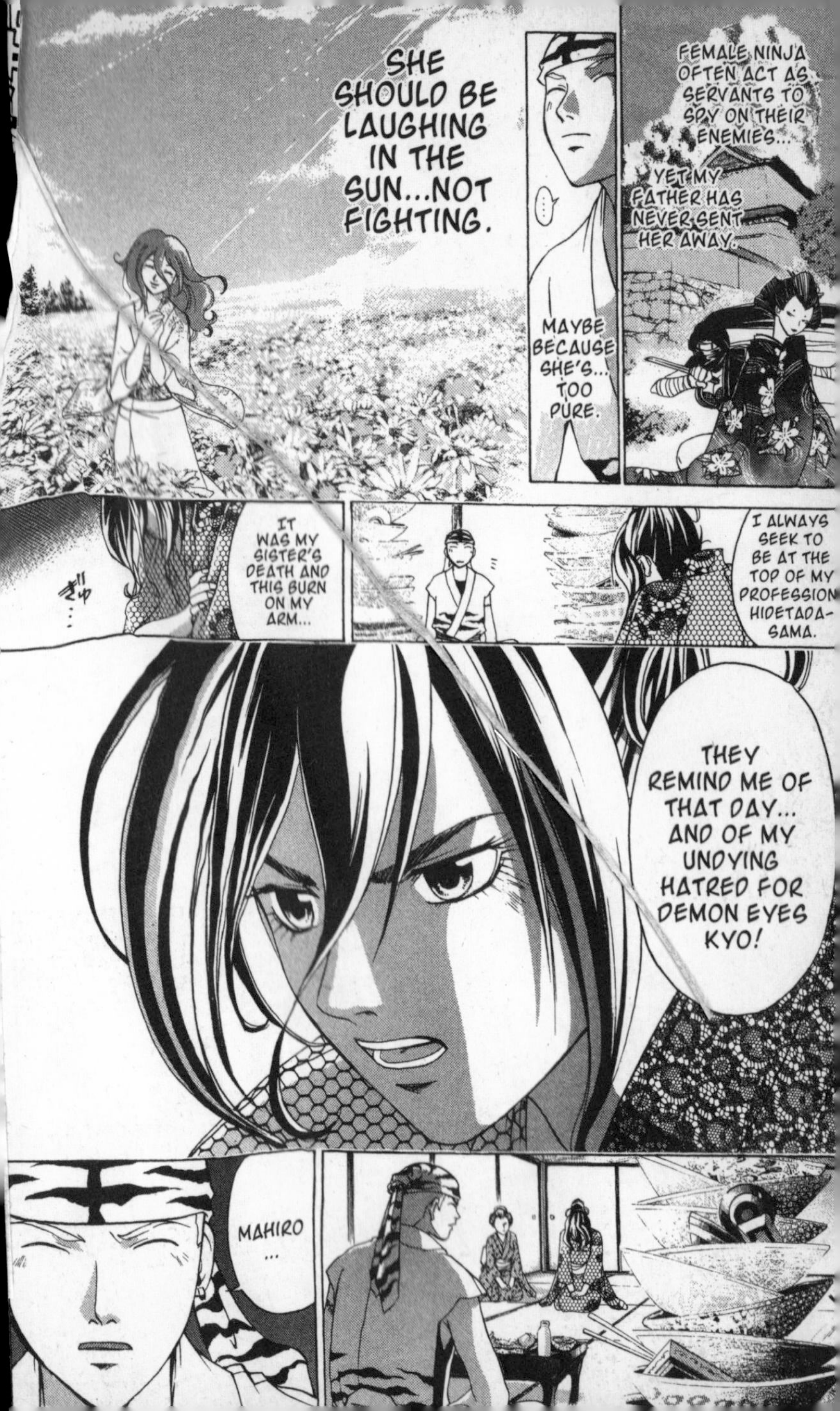
FEMALE NINJA OFTEN ACT AS SERVANTS TO SPY ON THEIR ENEMIES...
YET MY FATHER HAS NEVER SENT HER AWAY.
...
MAYBE BECAUSE SHE'S... TOO PURE.
SHE SHOULD BE LAUGHING IN THE SUN...NOT FIGHTING.
I ALWAYS SEEK TO BE AT THE TOP OF MY PROFESSION HIDETADA-SAMA.
IT WAS MY SISTER'S DEATH AND THIS BURN ON MY ARM...
THEY REMIND ME OF THAT DAY... AND OF MY UNDYING HATRED FOR DEMON EYES KYO!
MAHIRO ...

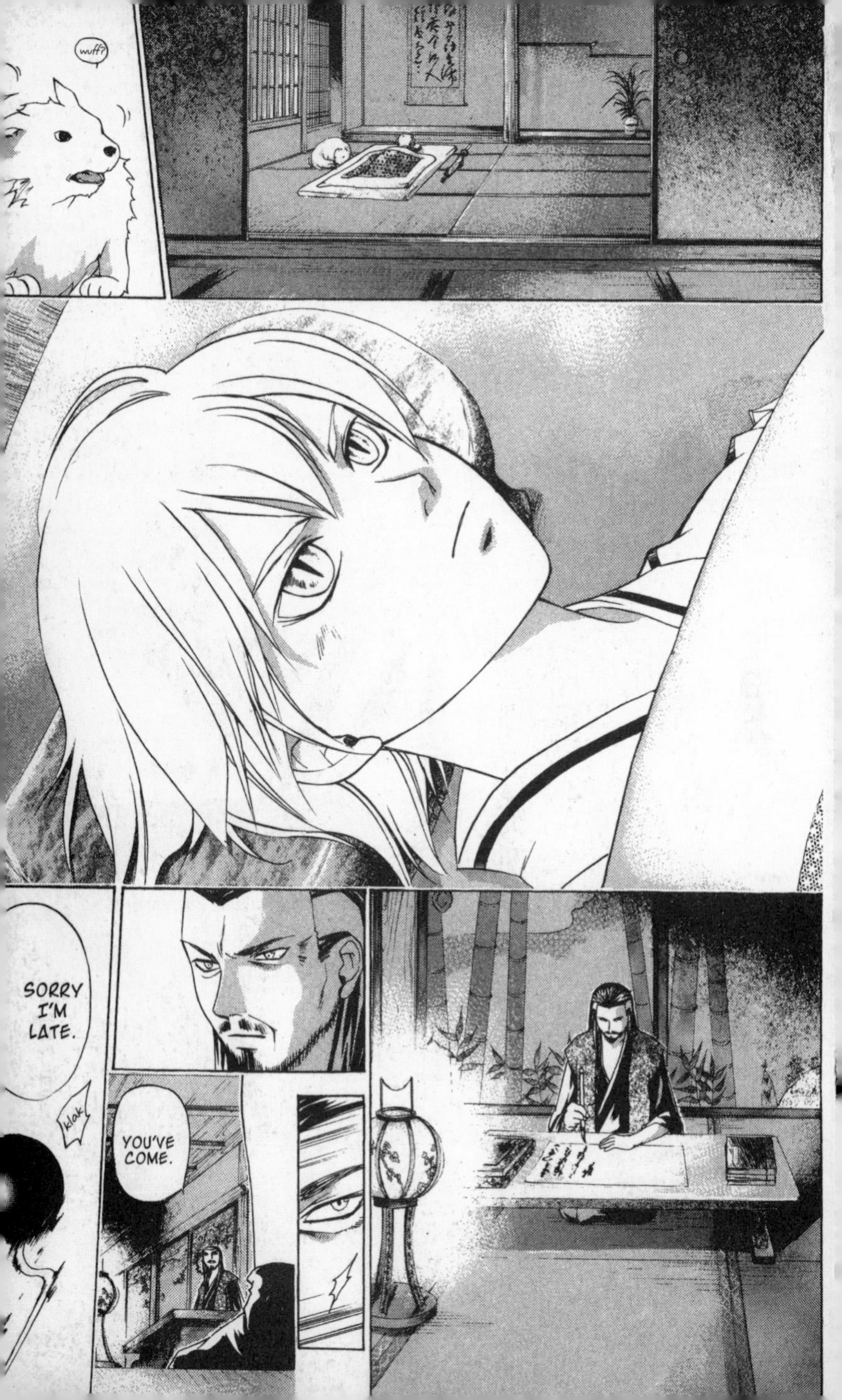
wuff?
SORRY I'M LATE.
klak
YOU'VE COME.

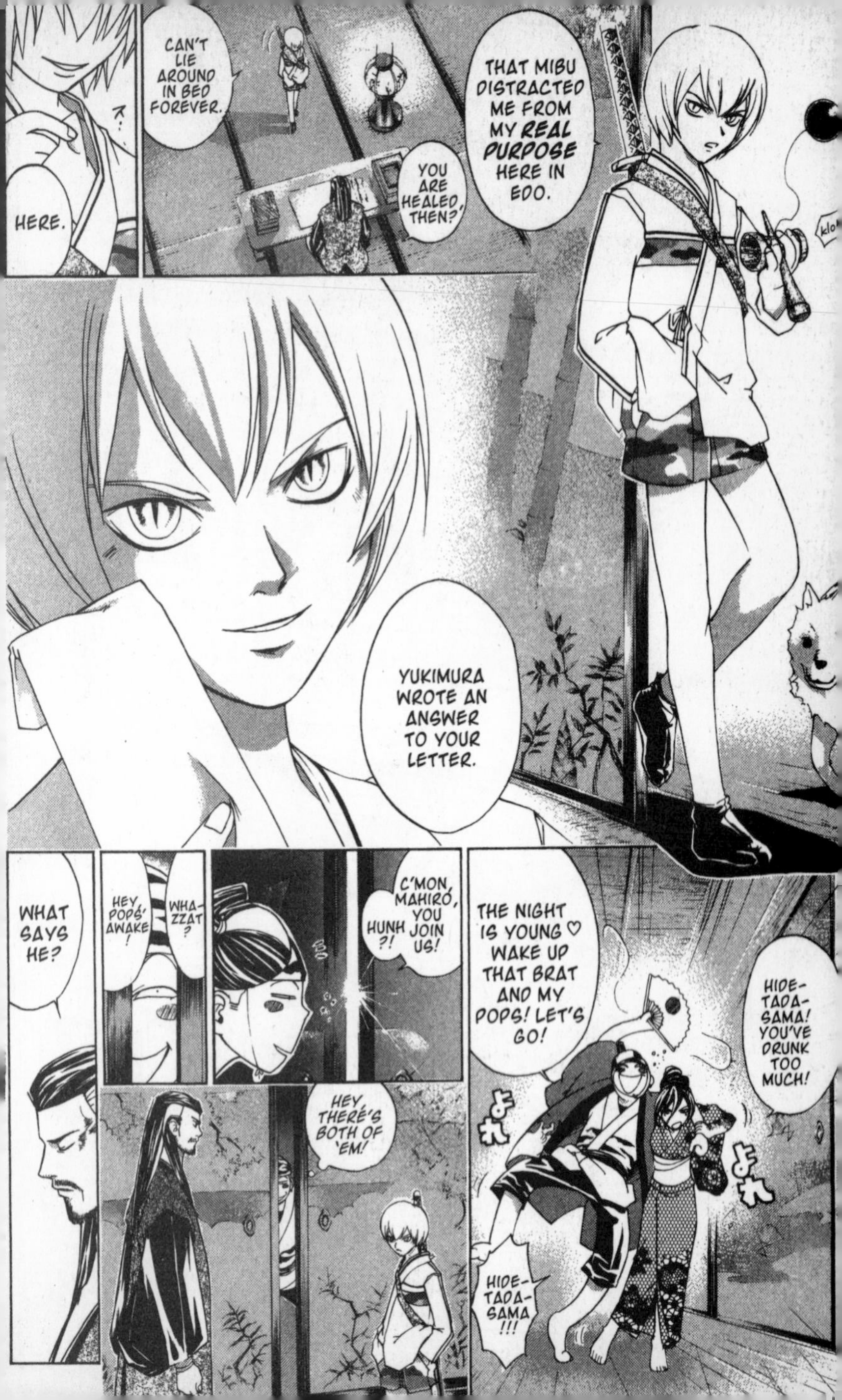

THAT MIBU DISTRACTED ME FROM MY REAL PURPOSE HERE IN EDO.
klo
CAN'T LIE AROUND IN BED FOREVER.
YOU ARE HEALED, THEN?
HERE.
YUKIMURA WROTE AN ANSWER TO YOUR LETTER.
HIDE-TADA-SAMA! YOU'VE DRUNK TOO MUCH!
よれ
THE NIGHT IS YOUNG ♡ WAKE UP THAT BRAT AND MY POPS! LET'S GO!
よれ
HIDE-TADA-SAMA!!!
C'MON, MAHIRO, YOU JOIN US!
HUNH?!
WHAZZAT?
HEY, POPS, AWAKE!
HEY, THERE'S BOTH OF 'EM!
WHAT SAYS HE?

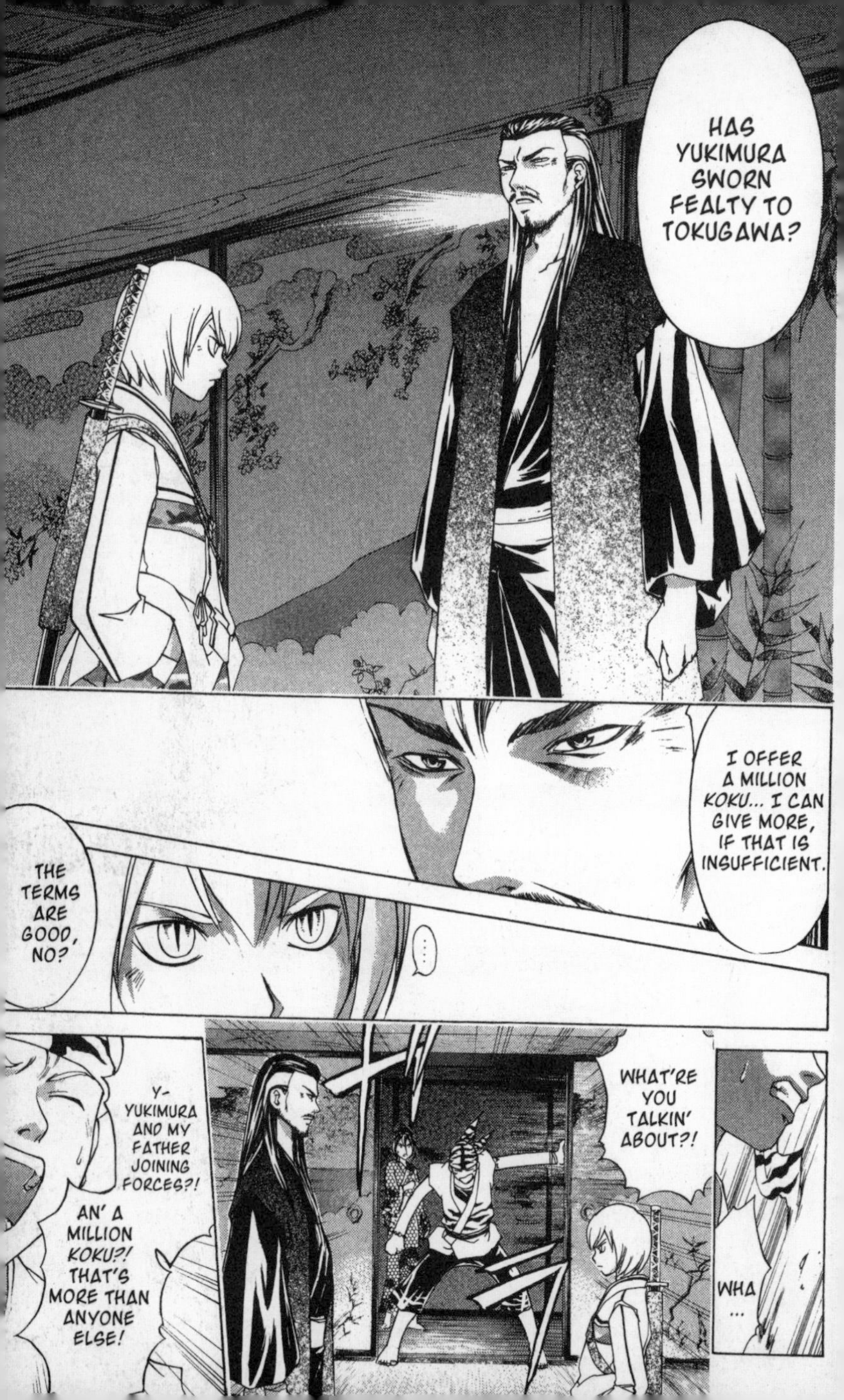
HAS YUKIMURA SWORN FEALTY TO TOKUGAWA?
I OFFER A MILLION KOKU... I CAN GIVE MORE, IF THAT IS INSUFFICIENT.
...
THE TERMS ARE GOOD, NO?
WHA...
WHAT'RE YOU TALKIN' ABOUT?!
Y-YUKIMURA AND MY FATHER JOINING FORCES?!
AN' A MILLION KOKU?! THAT'S MORE THAN ANYONE ELSE!

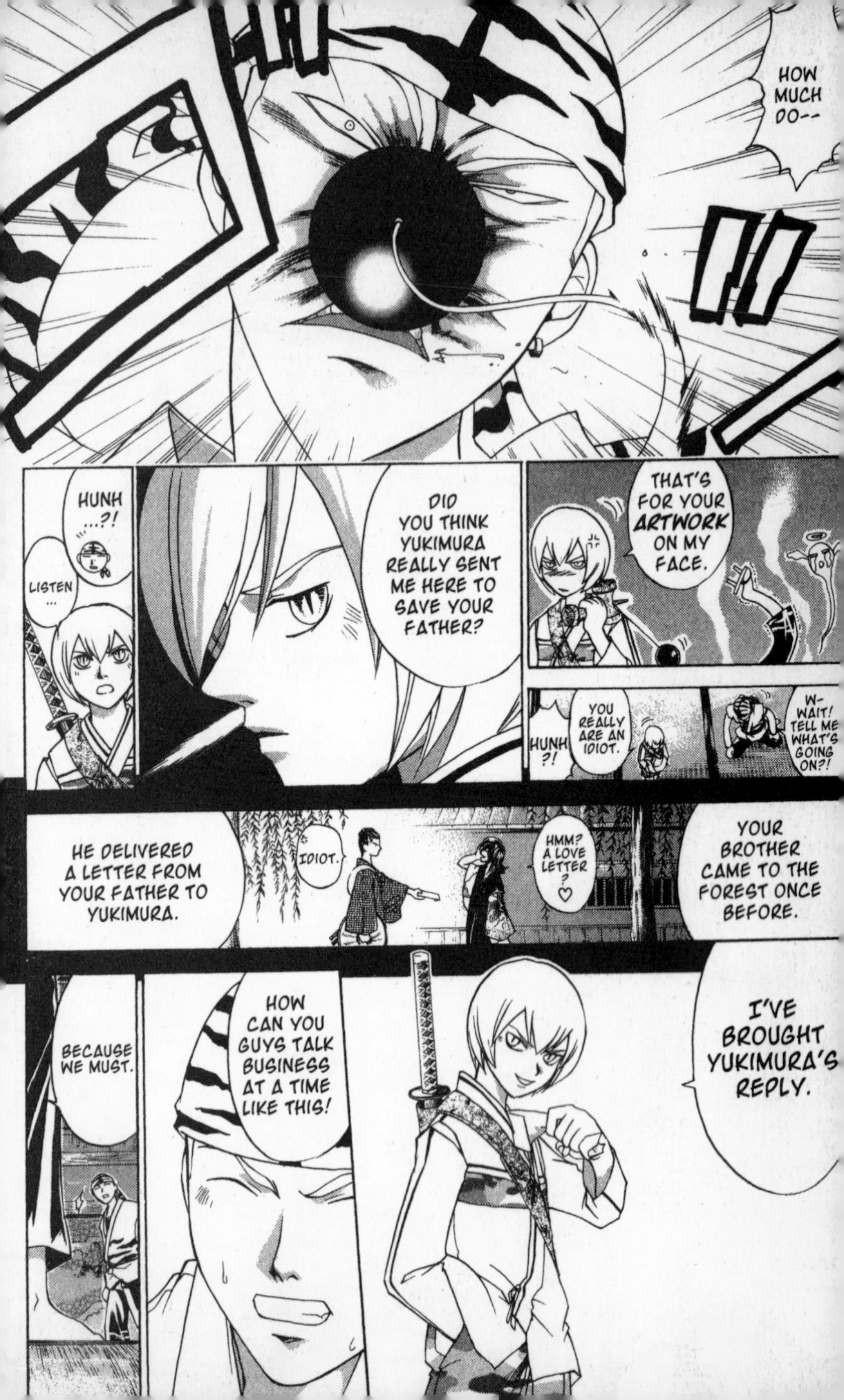
HOW MUCH DO--
THAT'S FOR YOUR **ARTWORK** ON MY FACE.
W-WAIT! TELL ME WHAT'S GOING ON?!
YOU REALLY ARE AN IDIOT.
HUNH ?!
DID YOU THINK YUKIMURA REALLY SENT ME HERE TO SAVE YOUR FATHER?
HUNH ...?!
LISTEN ...
YOUR BROTHER CAME TO THE FOREST ONCE BEFORE.
HMM? A LOVE LETTER ? ♡
IDIOT.
HE DELIVERED A LETTER FROM YOUR FATHER TO YUKIMURA.
I'VE BROUGHT YUKIMURA'S REPLY.
HOW CAN YOU GUYS TALK BUSINESS AT A TIME LIKE THIS!
BECAUSE WE MUST.

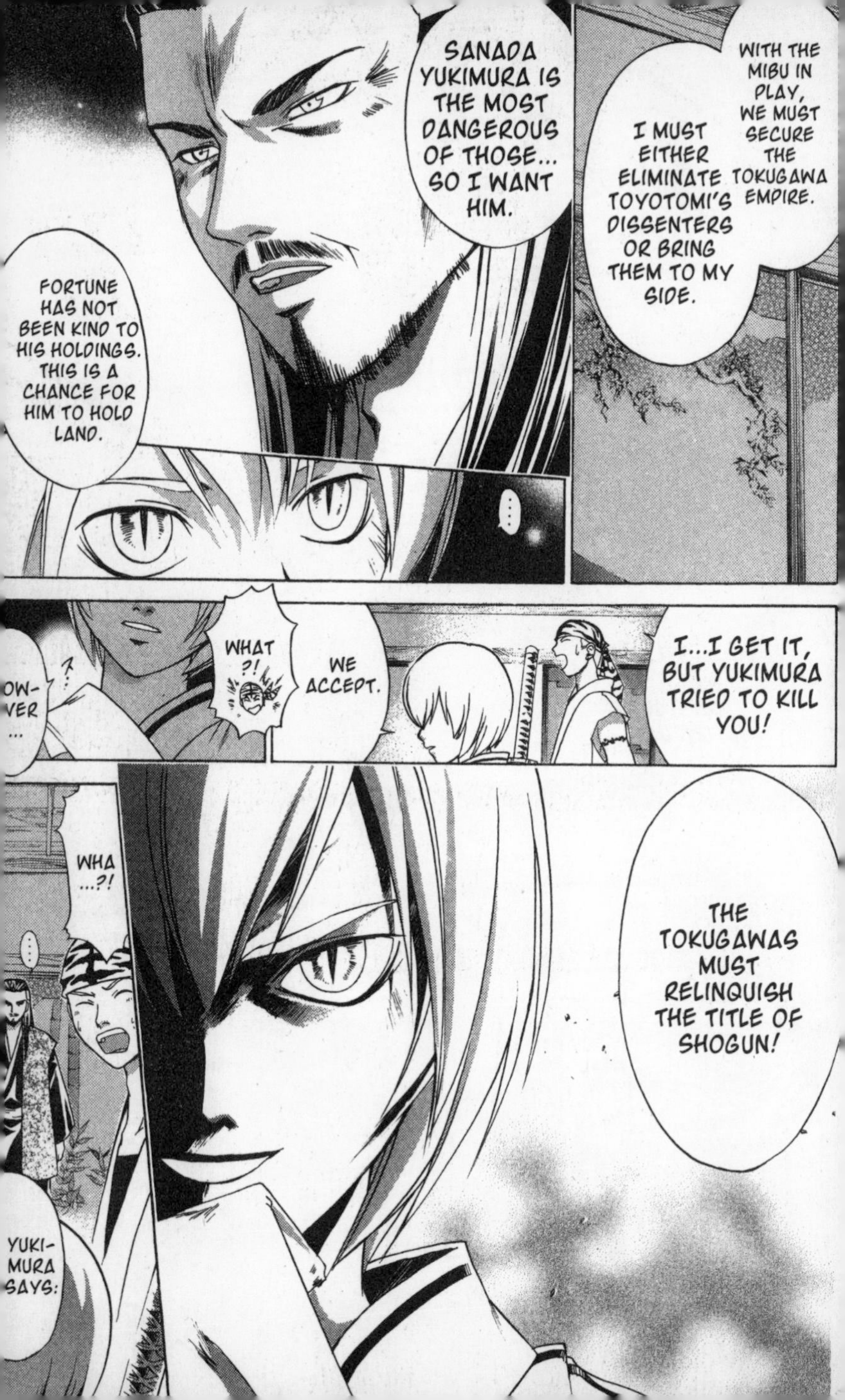
WITH THE MIBU IN PLAY, WE MUST SECURE THE TOKUGAWA EMPIRE.
I MUST EITHER ELIMINATE TOYOTOMI'S DISSENTERS OR BRING THEM TO MY SIDE.
SANADA YUKIMURA IS THE MOST DANGEROUS OF THOSE... SO I WANT HIM.
FORTUNE HAS NOT BEEN KIND TO HIS HOLDINGS. THIS IS A CHANCE FOR HIM TO HOLD LAND.
...
I...I GET IT, BUT YUKIMURA TRIED TO KILL YOU!
WE ACCEPT.
WHAT ?!
?
OW- VER ...
THE TOKUGAWAS MUST RELINQUISH THE TITLE OF SHOGUN!
WHA ...?!
...
YUKI- MURA SAYS:

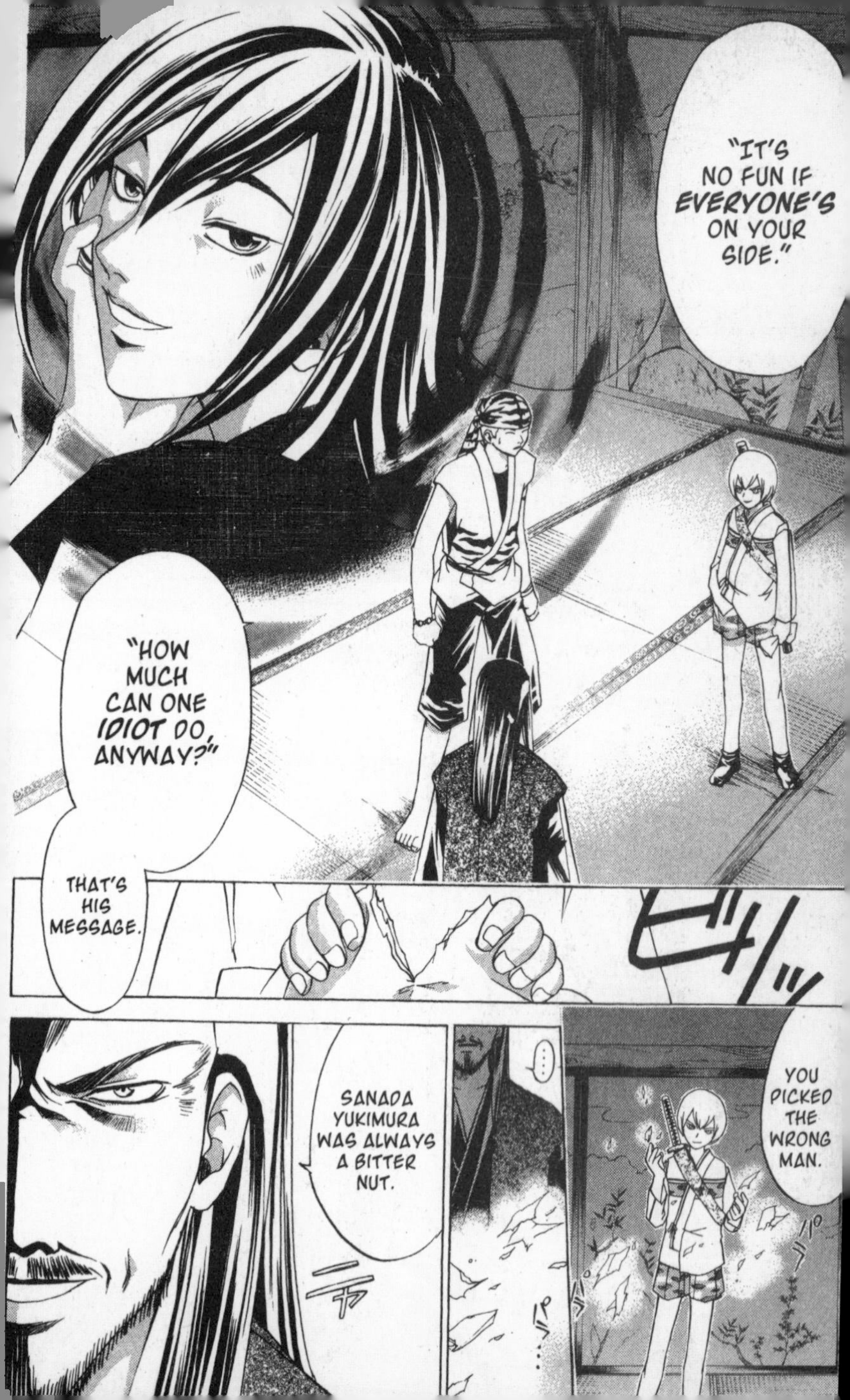
"IT'S NO FUN IF EVERYONE'S ON YOUR SIDE."
"HOW MUCH CAN ONE IDIOT DO, ANYWAY?"
THAT'S HIS MESSAGE.
YOU PICKED THE WRONG MAN.
...
SANADA YUKIMURA WAS ALWAYS A BITTER NUT.

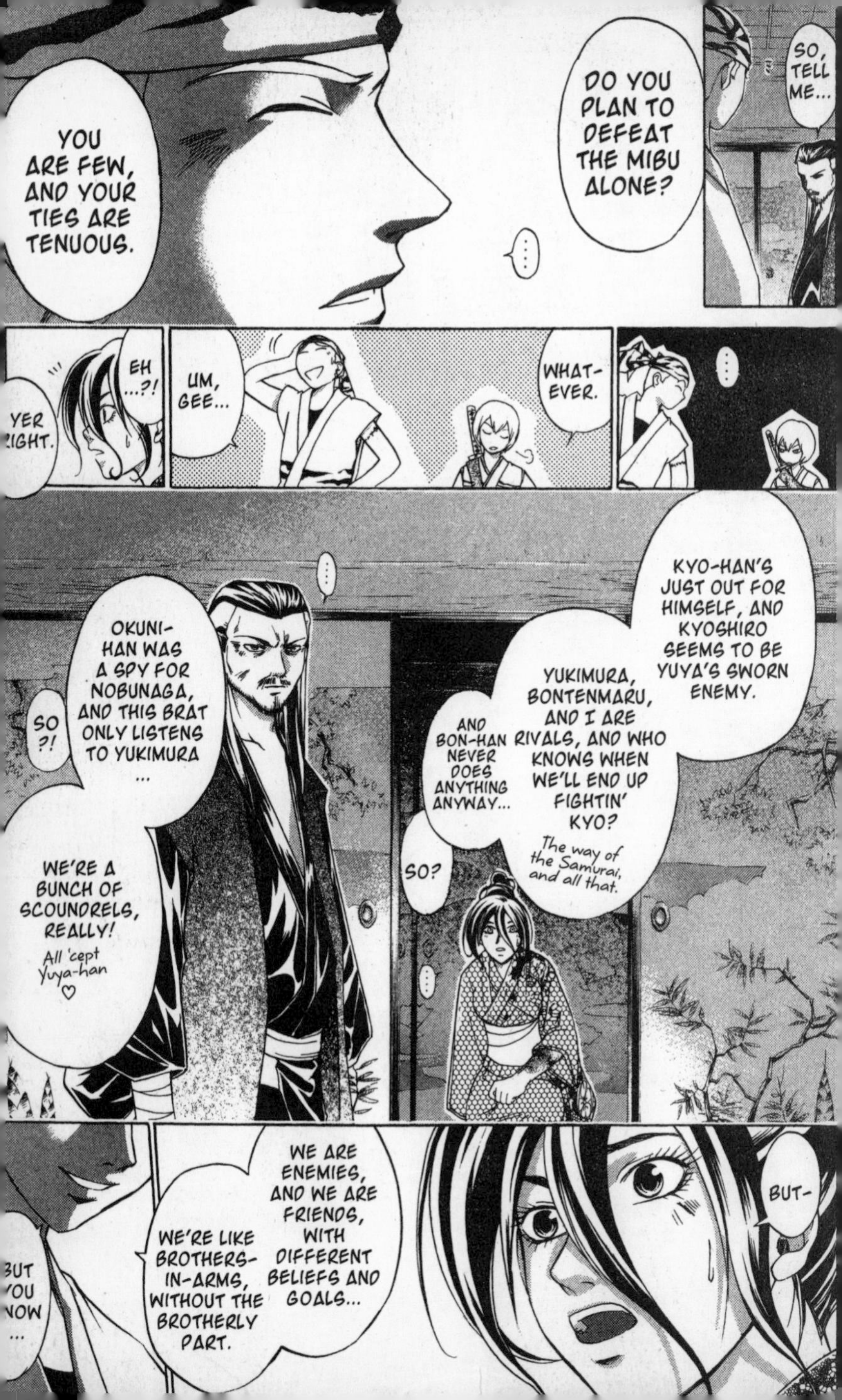

SO, TELL ME...
DO YOU PLAN TO DEFEAT THE MIBU ALONE?
...
YOU ARE FEW, AND YOUR TIES ARE TENUOUS.
...
WHAT-EVER.
UM, GEE...
EH ...?!
YER IGHT.
KYO-HAN'S JUST OUT FOR HIMSELF, AND KYOSHIRO SEEMS TO BE YUYA'S SWORN ENEMY.
YUKIMURA, BONTENMARU, AND I ARE RIVALS, AND WHO KNOWS WHEN WE'LL END UP FIGHTIN' KYO?
The way of the Samurai, and all that.
AND BON-HAN NEVER DOES ANYTHING ANYWAY...
SO?
...
OKUNI-HAN WAS A SPY FOR NOBUNAGA, AND THIS BRAT ONLY LISTENS TO YUKIMURA ...
SO ?!
WE'RE A BUNCH OF SCOUNDRELS, REALLY!
All 'cept Yuya-han ♡
...
BUT-
WE ARE ENEMIES, AND WE ARE FRIENDS, WITH DIFFERENT BELIEFS AND GOALS...
WE'RE LIKE BROTHERS-IN-ARMS, WITHOUT THE BROTHERLY PART.
UT OU NOW ...

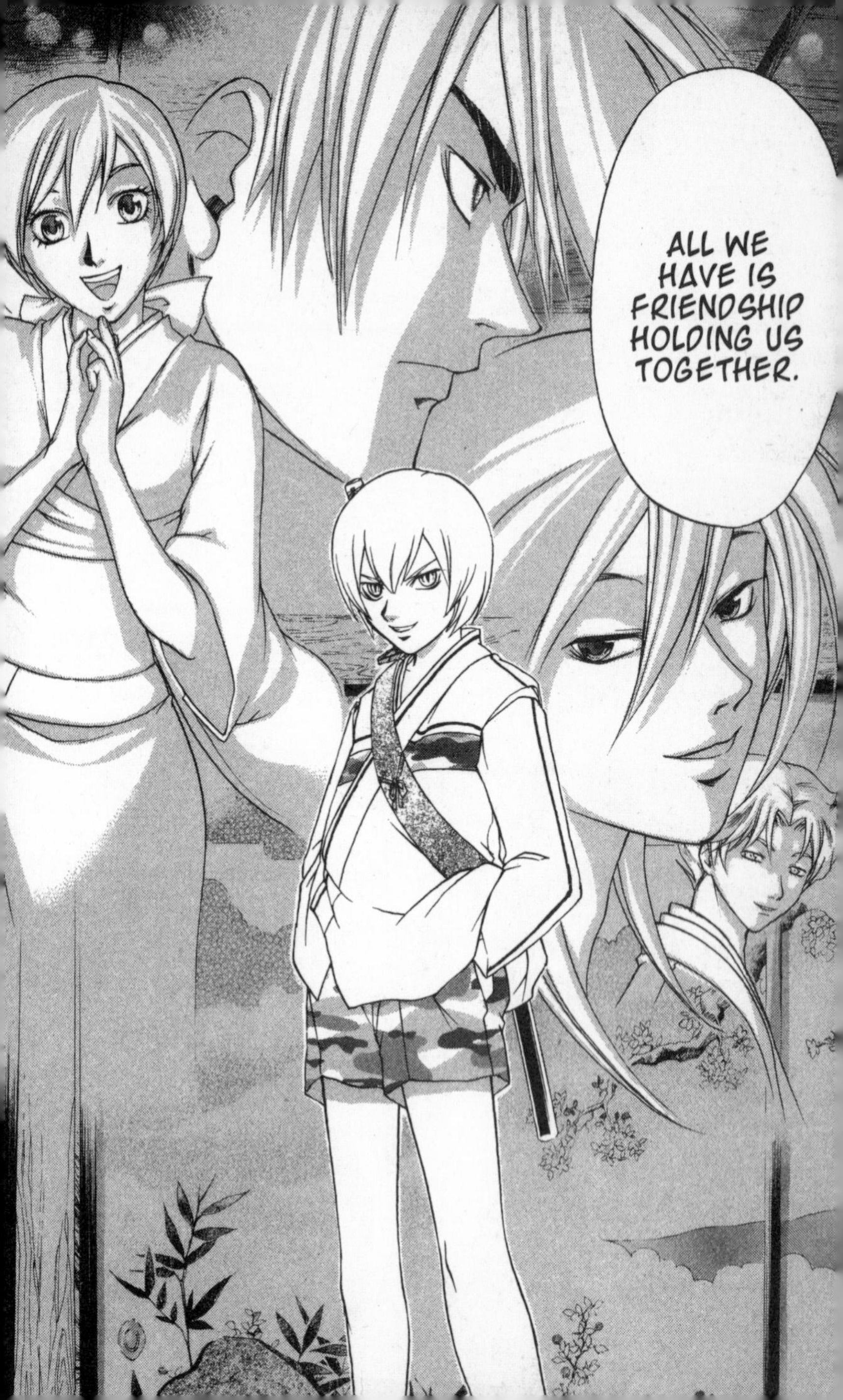
ALL WE HAVE IS FRIENDSHIP HOLDING US TOGETHER.

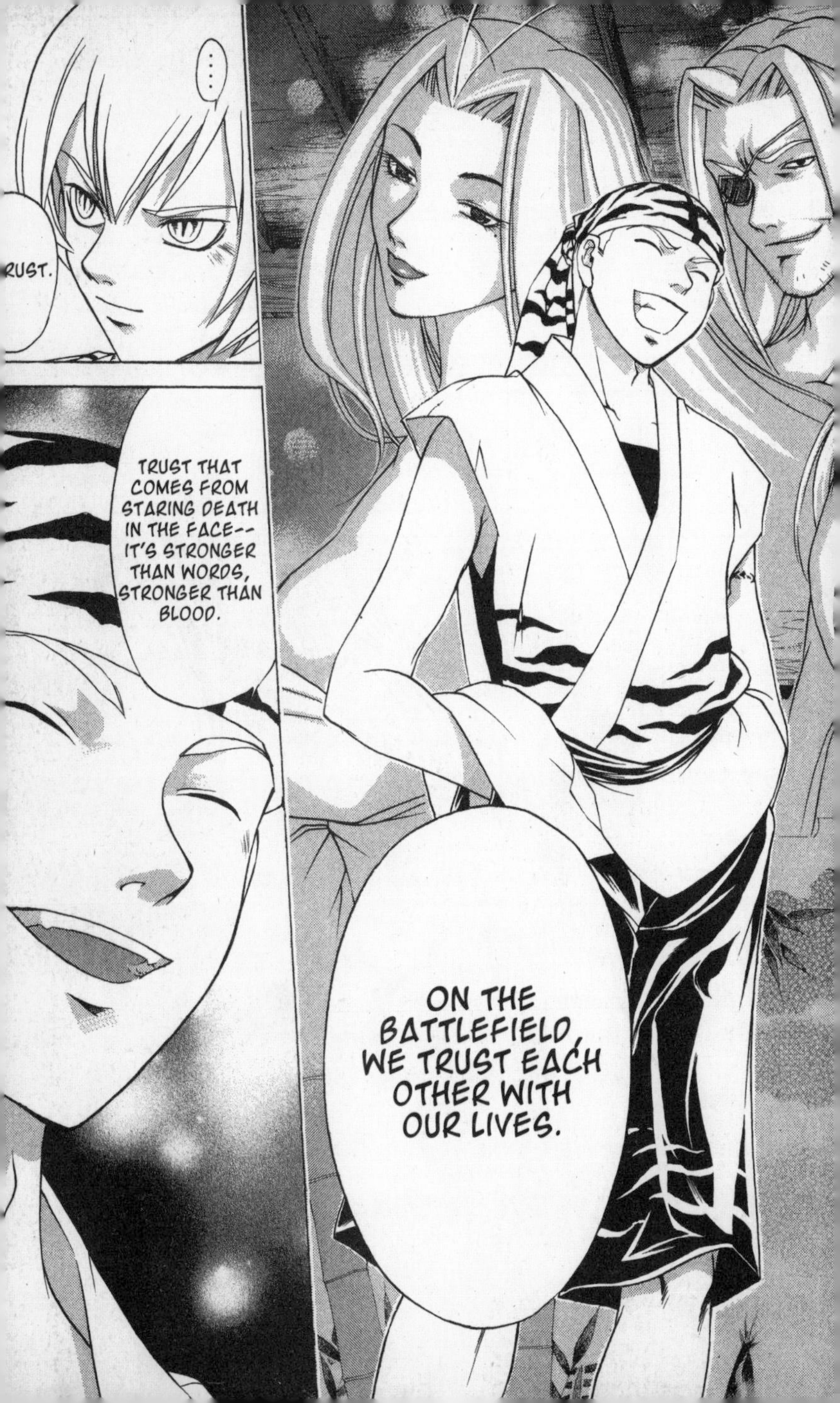
ON THE BATTLEFIELD, WE TRUST EACH OTHER WITH OUR LIVES.
...
RUST.
TRUST THAT COMES FROM STARING DEATH IN THE FACE-- IT'S STRONGER THAN WORDS, STRONGER THAN BLOOD.

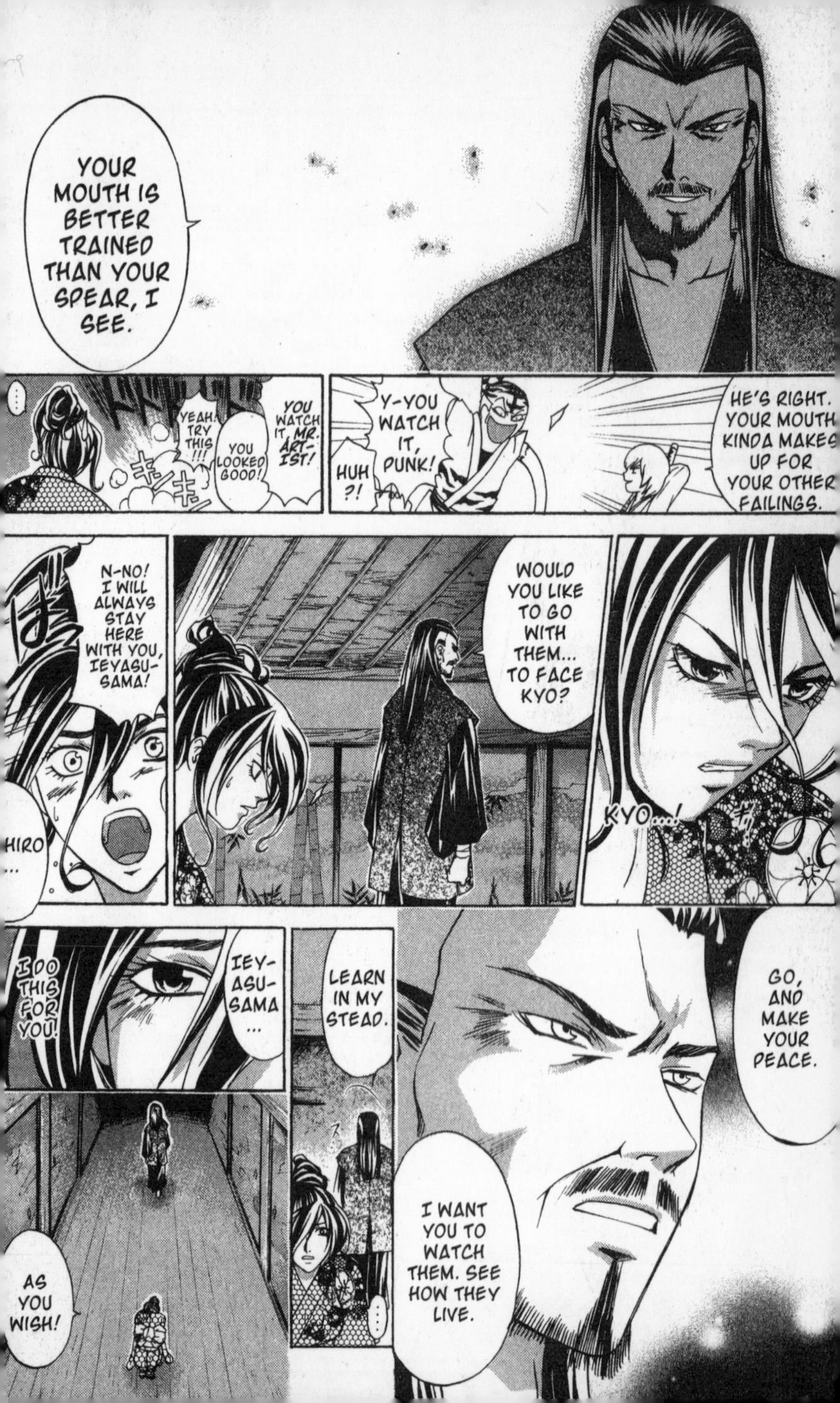
YOUR MOUTH IS BETTER TRAINED THAN YOUR SPEAR, I SEE.
HE'S RIGHT. YOUR MOUTH KINDA MAKES UP FOR YOUR OTHER FAILINGS.
Y-YOU WATCH IT, PUNK!
HUH?!
YOU WATCH IT, MR. ART-IST!
YOU LOOKED GOOD!
YEAH. TRY THIS!!!
...
KYO...!
WOULD YOU LIKE TO GO WITH THEM... TO FACE KYO?
N-NO! I WILL ALWAYS STAY HERE WITH YOU, IEYASU-SAMA!
HIRO...
GO, AND MAKE YOUR PEACE.
I WANT YOU TO WATCH THEM. SEE HOW THEY LIVE.
LEARN IN MY STEAD.
IEY-ASU-SAMA...
...
I DO THIS FOR YOU!
AS YOU WISH!

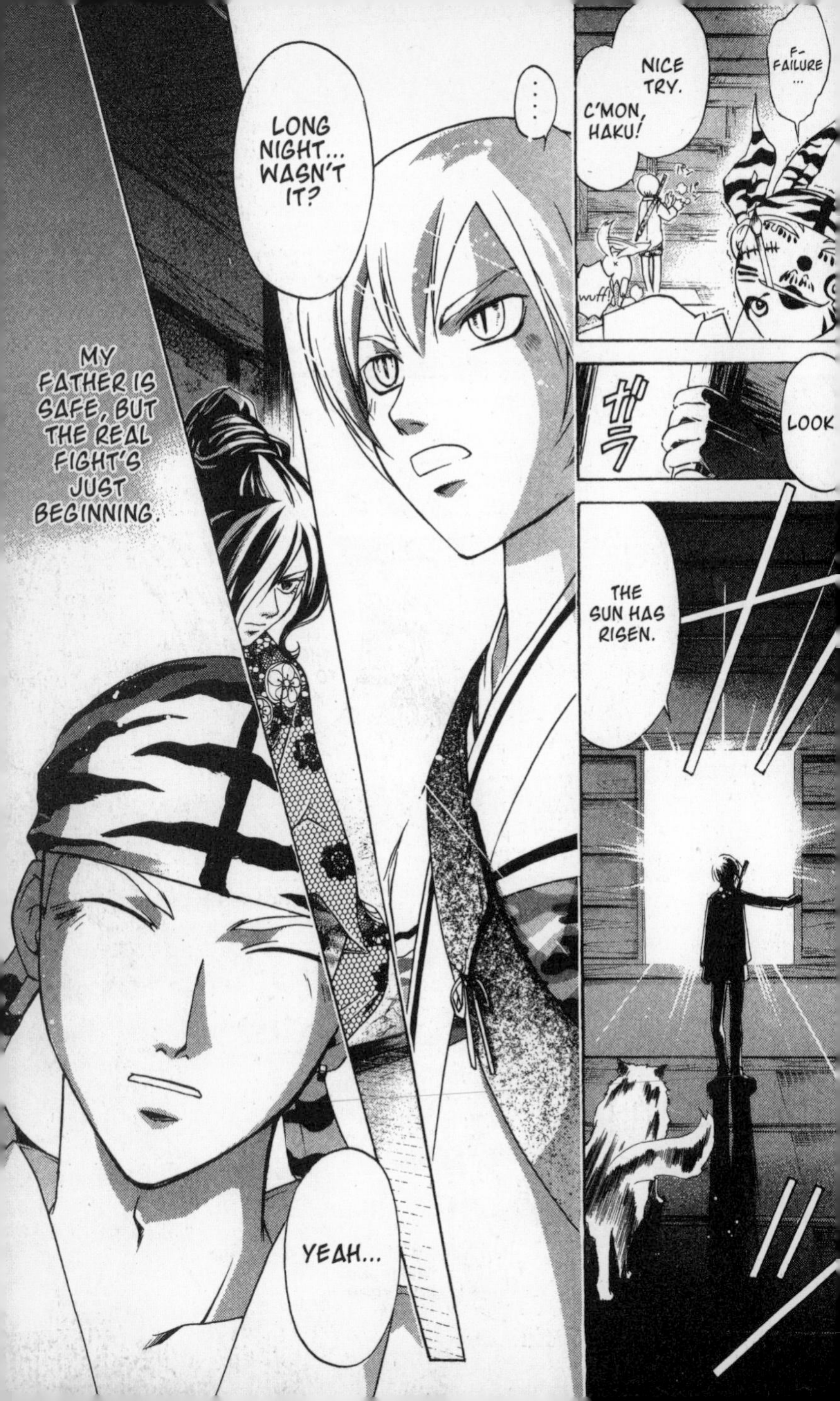
F-FAILURE...
NICE TRY.
C'MON, HAKU!
wuff!
LOOK
THE SUN HAS RISEN.
...
LONG NIGHT... WASN'T IT?
MY FATHER IS SAFE, BUT THE REAL FIGHT'S JUST BEGINNING.
YEAH...

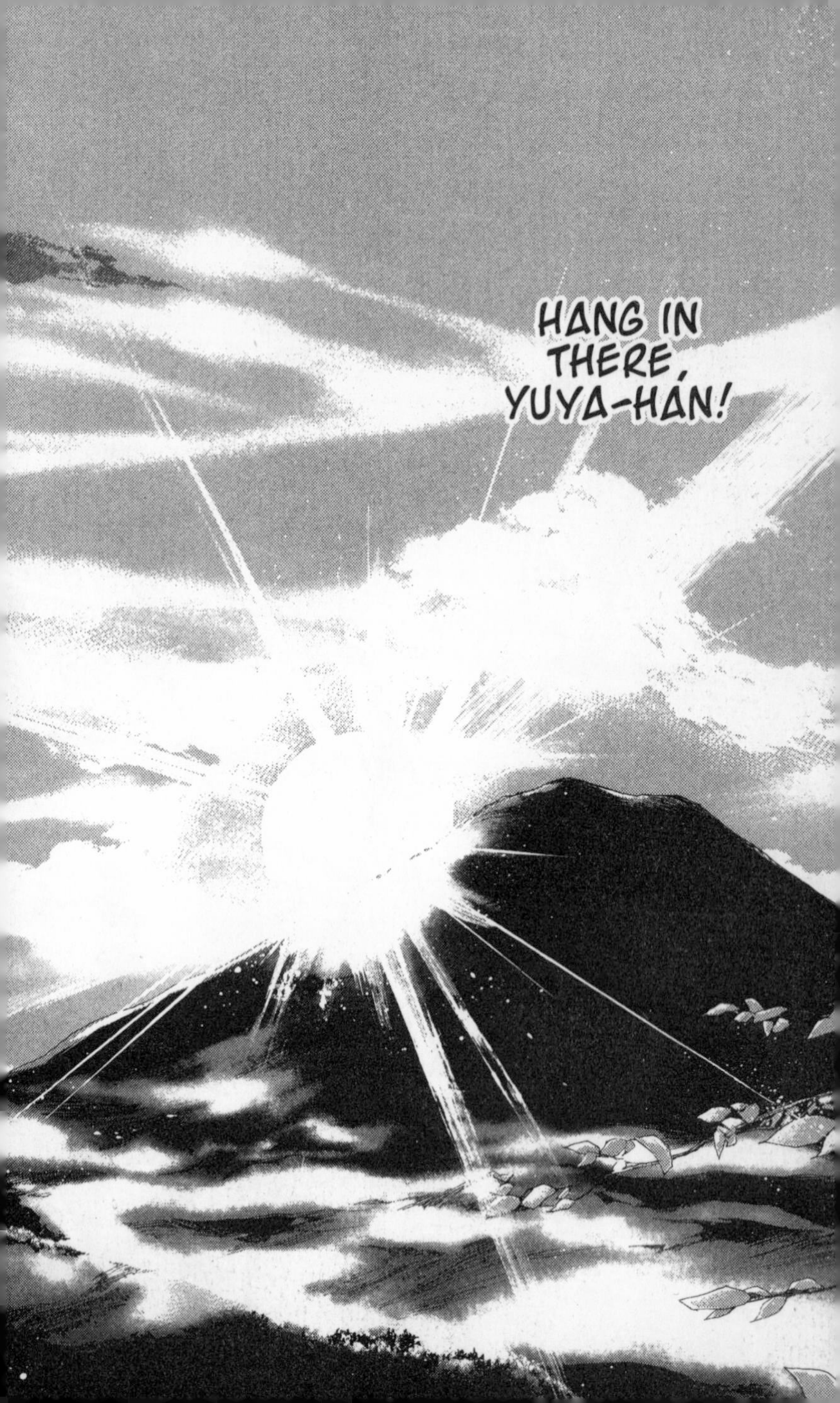
HANG IN THERE, YUYA-HAN!

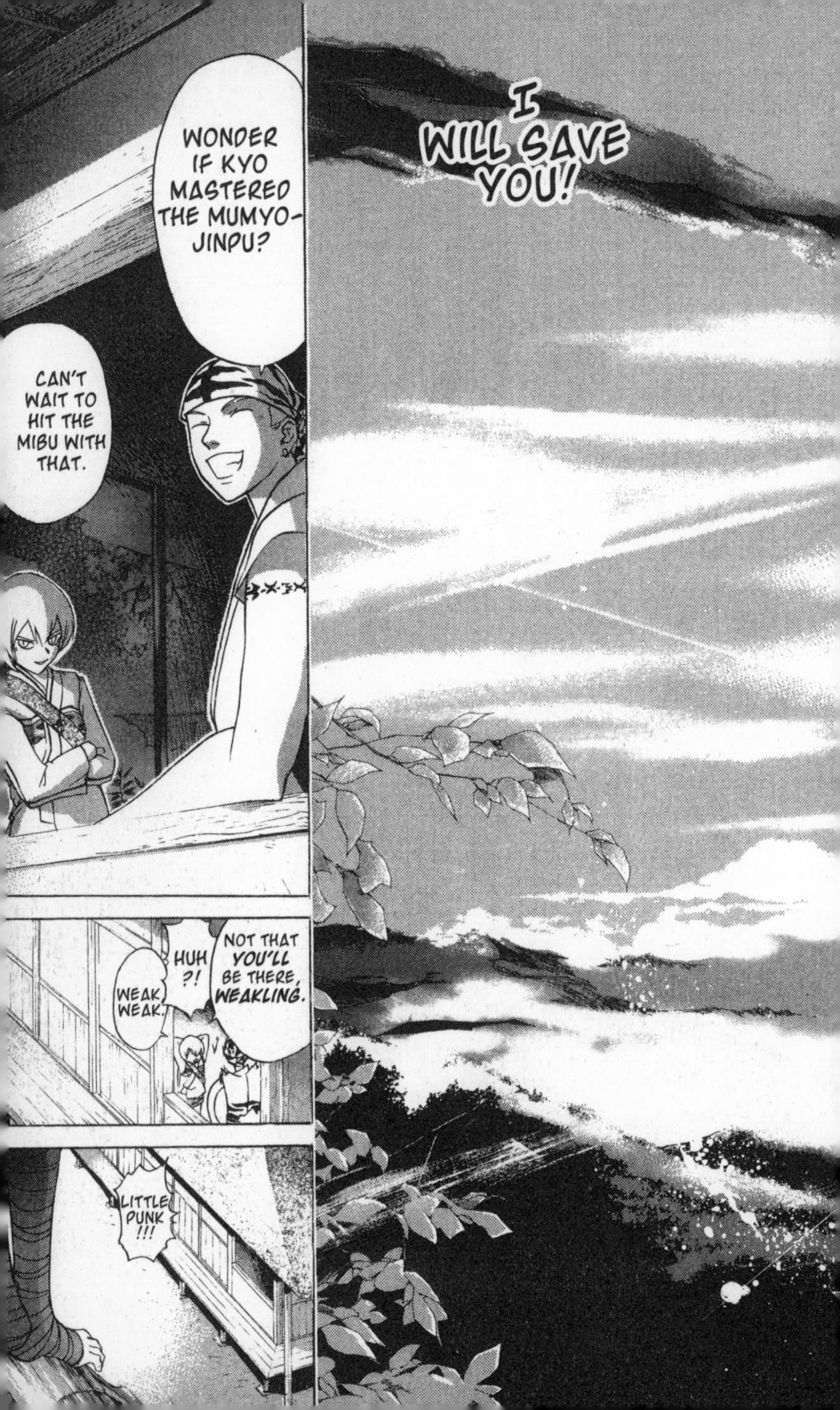
I WILL SAVE YOU!
WONDER IF KYO MASTERED THE MUMYO-JINPU?
CAN'T WAIT TO HIT THE MIBU WITH THAT.
NOT THAT YOU'LL BE THERE, WEAKLING.
HUH ?!
WEAK WEAK.
LITTLE PUNK !!!

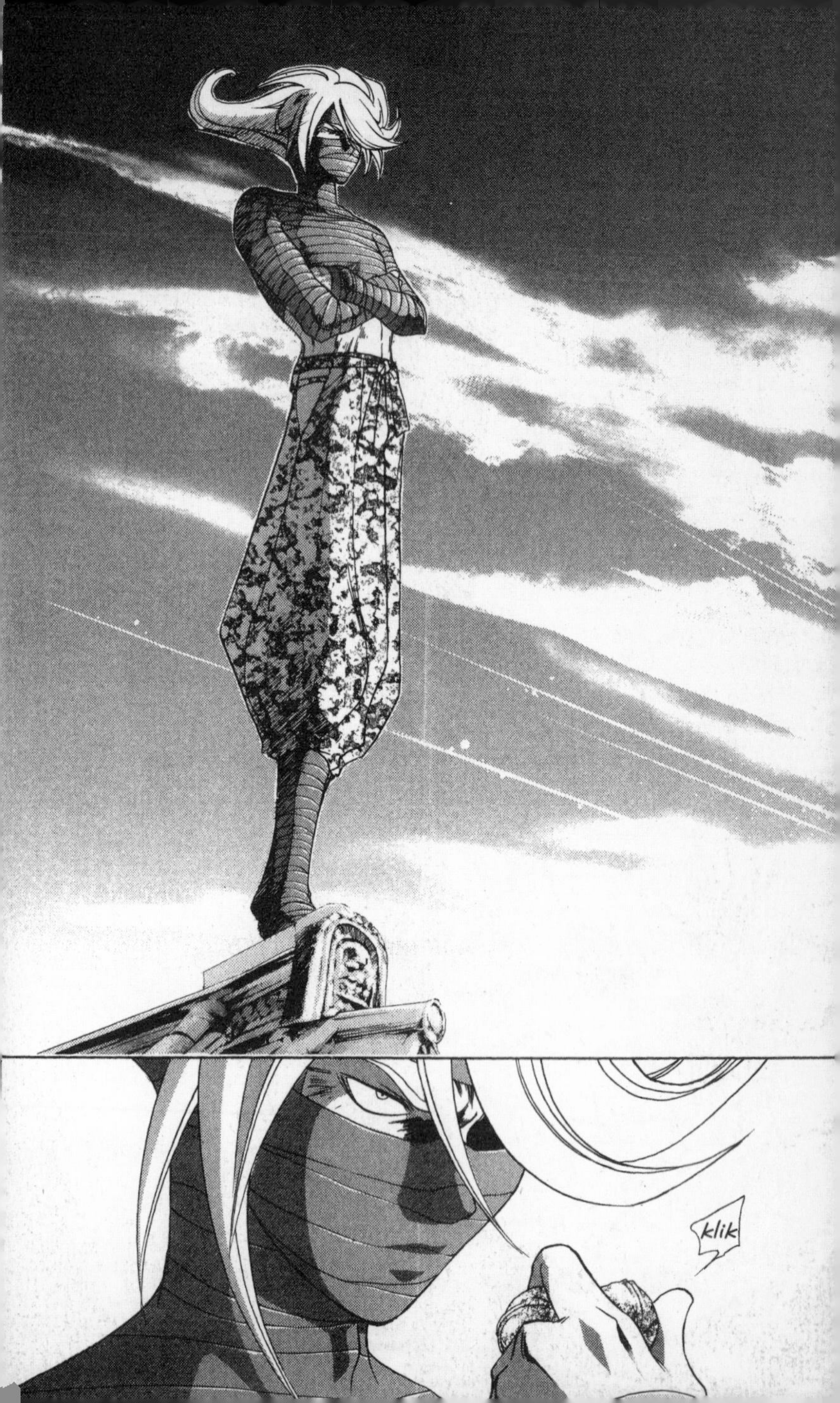
klik

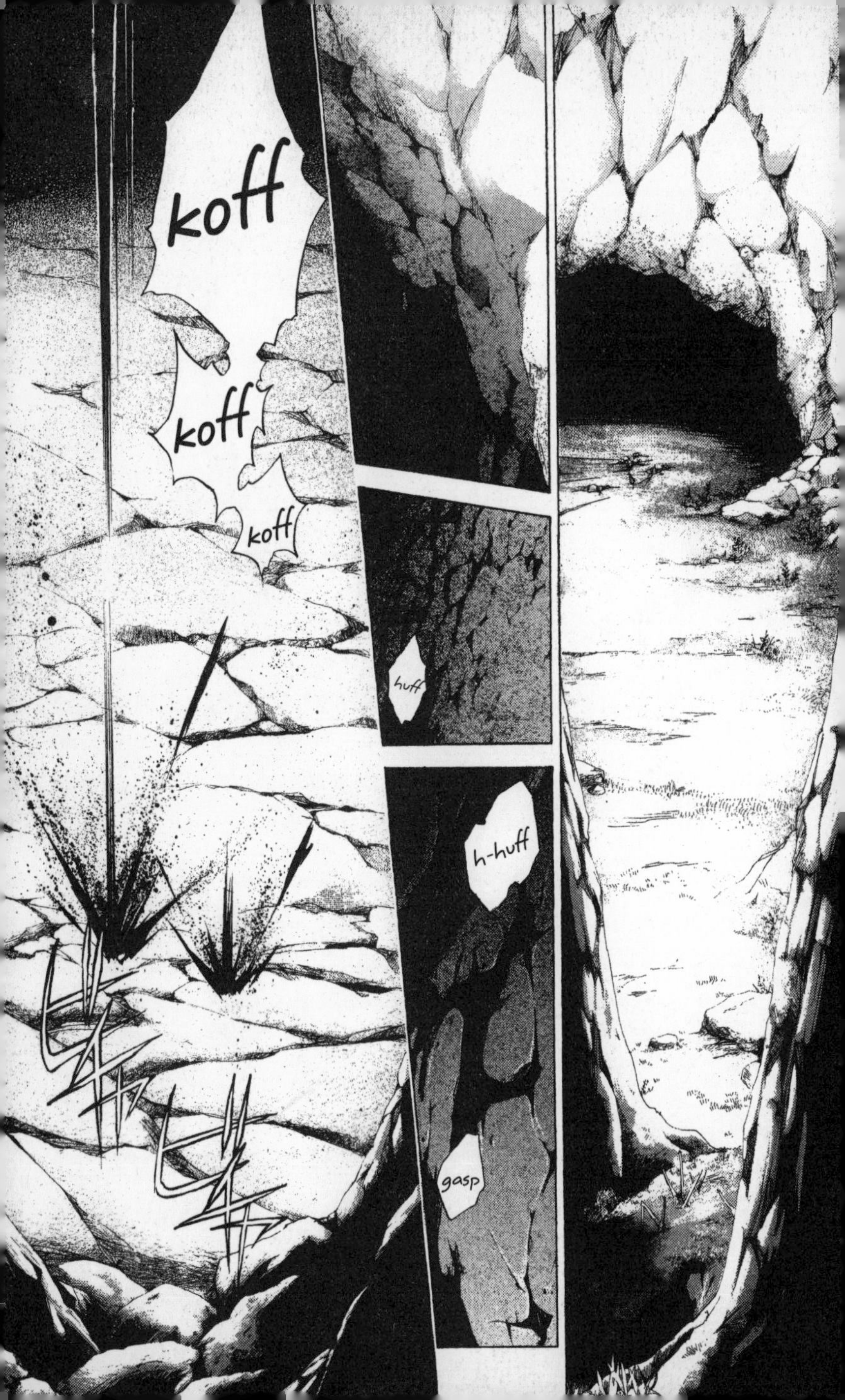
huff
h-huff
gasp
koff
koff
koff

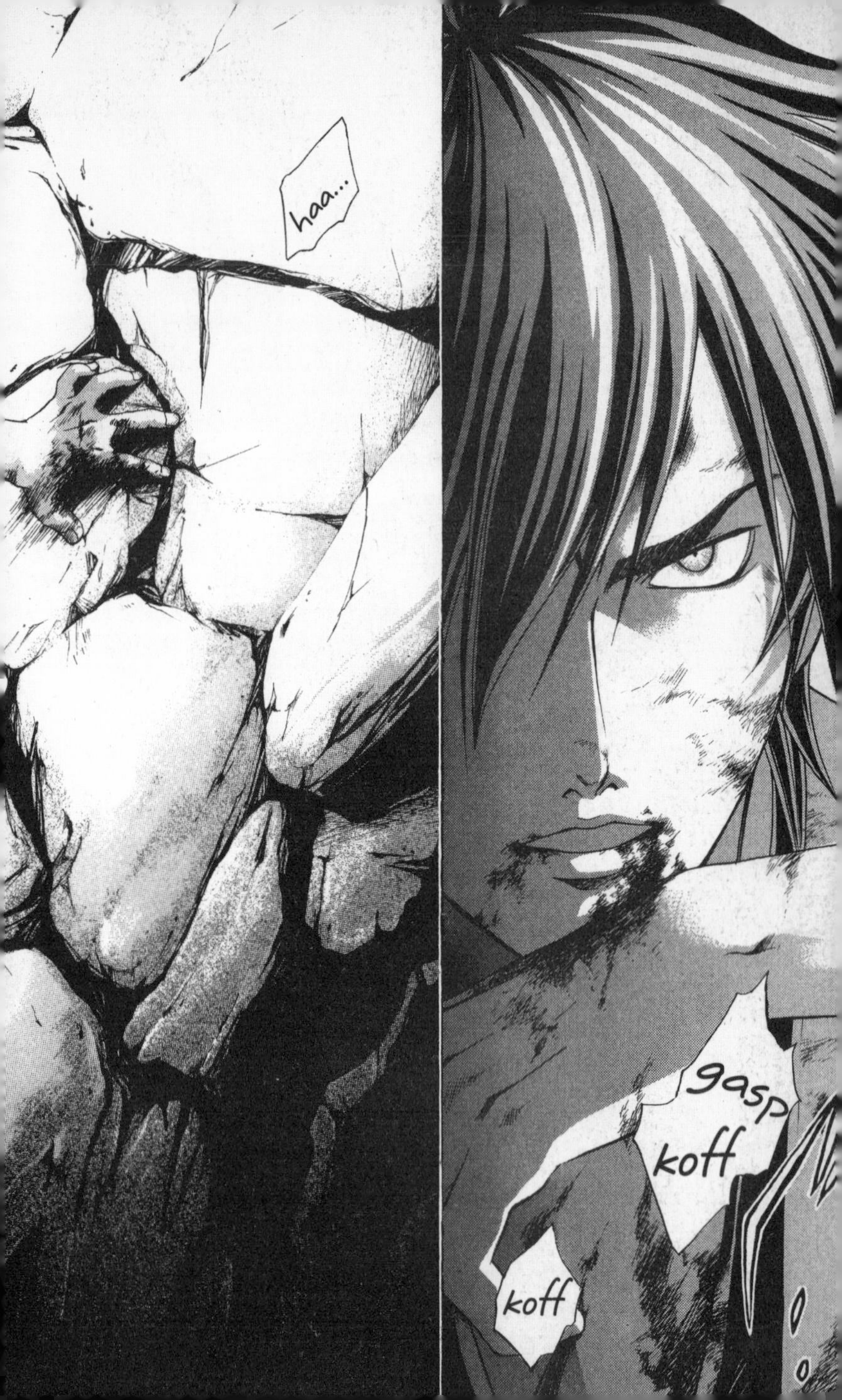
gasp koff
koff
haa...

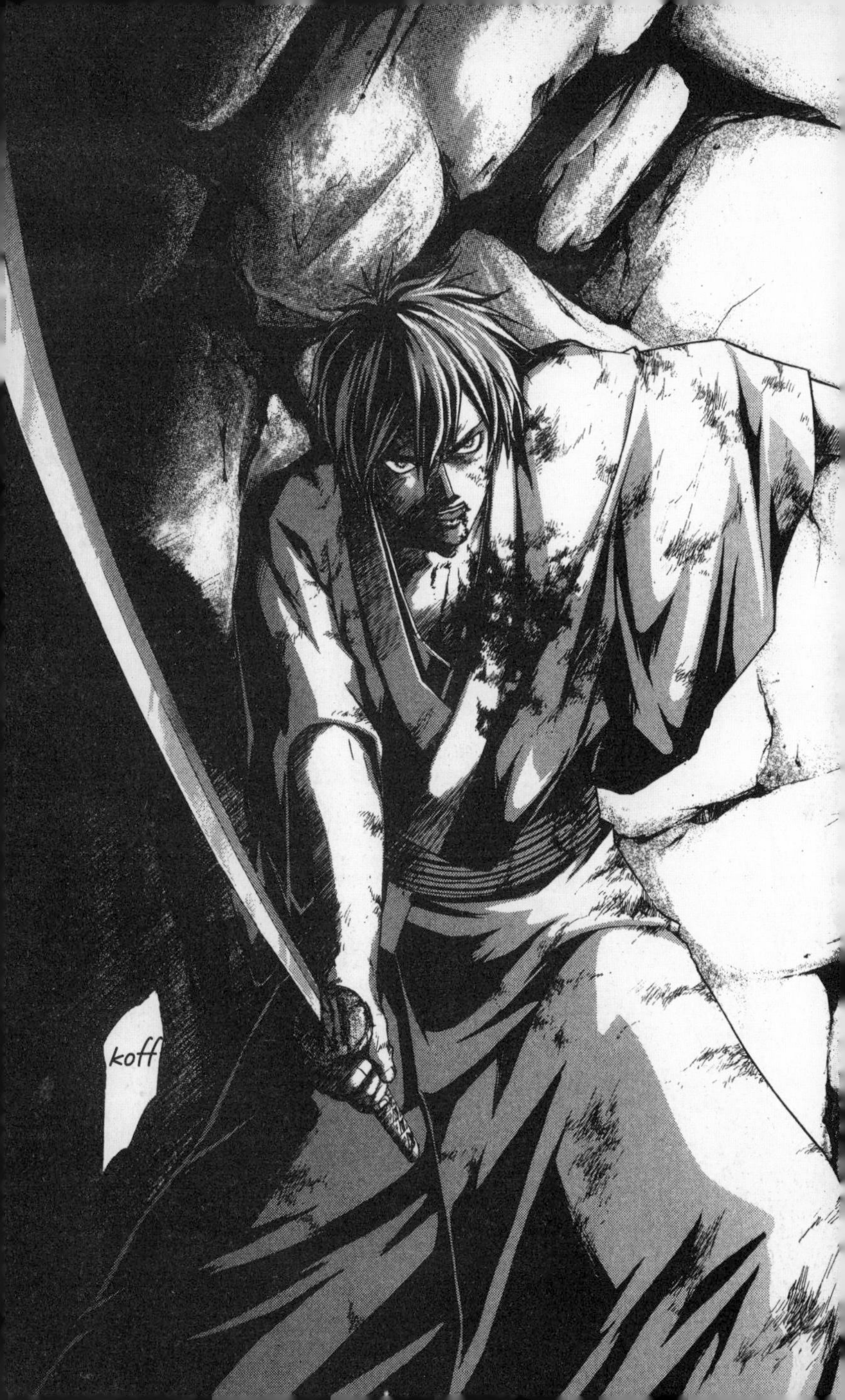
koff

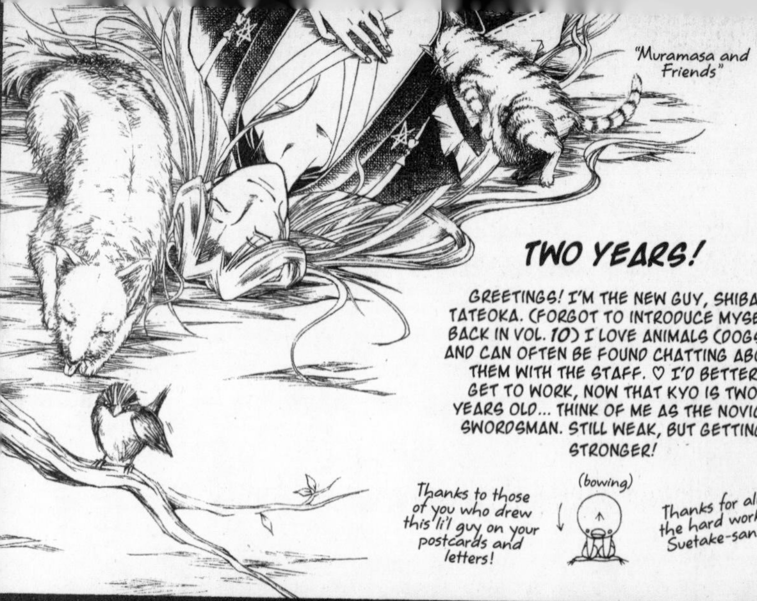

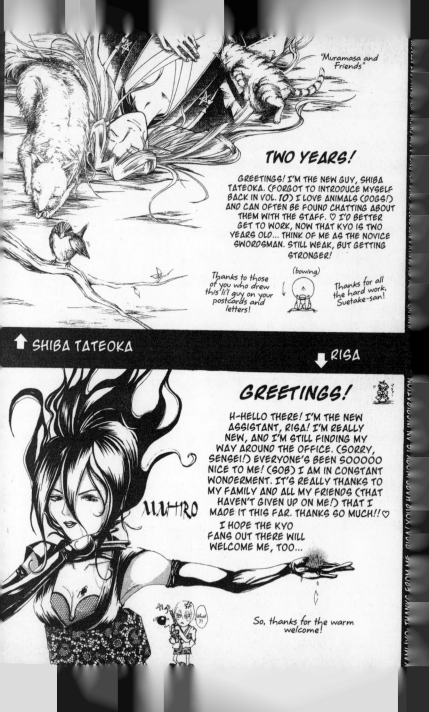

"Muramasa and Friends"

TWO YEARS!

GREETINGS! I'M THE NEW GUY, SHIBA TATEOKA. (FORGOT TO INTRODUCE MYSELF BACK IN VOL. 10) I LOVE ANIMALS (DOGS!) AND CAN OFTEN BE FOUND CHATTING ABOUT THEM WITH THE STAFF. ♡ I'D BETTER GET TO WORK, NOW THAT KYO IS TWO YEARS OLD... THINK OF ME AS THE NOVICE SWORDSMAN. STILL WEAK, BUT GETTING STRONGER!

(bowing)

Thanks to those of you who drew this li'l guy on your postcards and letters!

Thanks for all the hard work, Suetake-san!

↑ SHIBA TATEOKA

↓ RISA

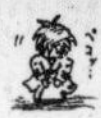

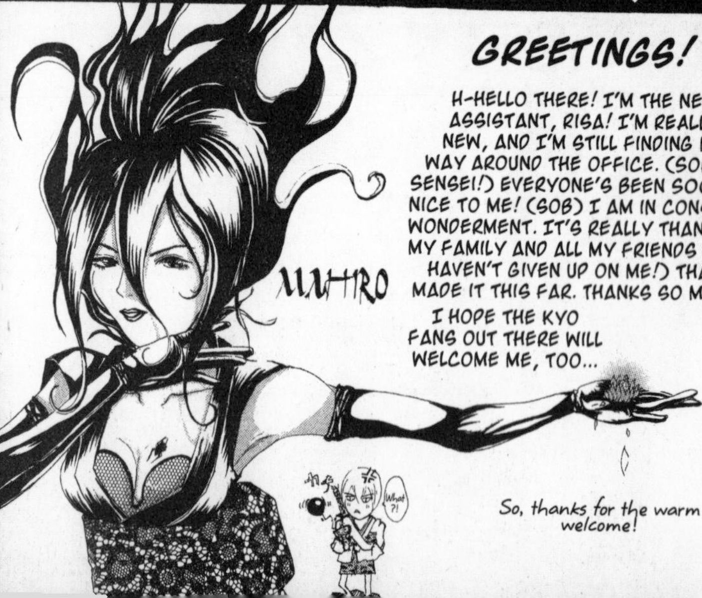

GREETINGS!

H-HELLO THERE! I'M THE NEW ASSISTANT, RISA! I'M REALLY NEW, AND I'M STILL FINDING MY WAY AROUND THE OFFICE. (SORRY, SENSEI!) EVERYONE'S BEEN SOOOOO NICE TO ME! (SOB) I AM IN CONSTANT WONDERMENT. IT'S REALLY THANKS TO MY FAMILY AND ALL MY FRIENDS (THAT HAVEN'T GIVEN UP ON ME!) THAT I MADE IT THIS FAR. THANKS SO MUCH!! ♡

I HOPE THE KYO FANS OUT THERE WILL WELCOME ME, TOO...

So, thanks for the warm welcome!

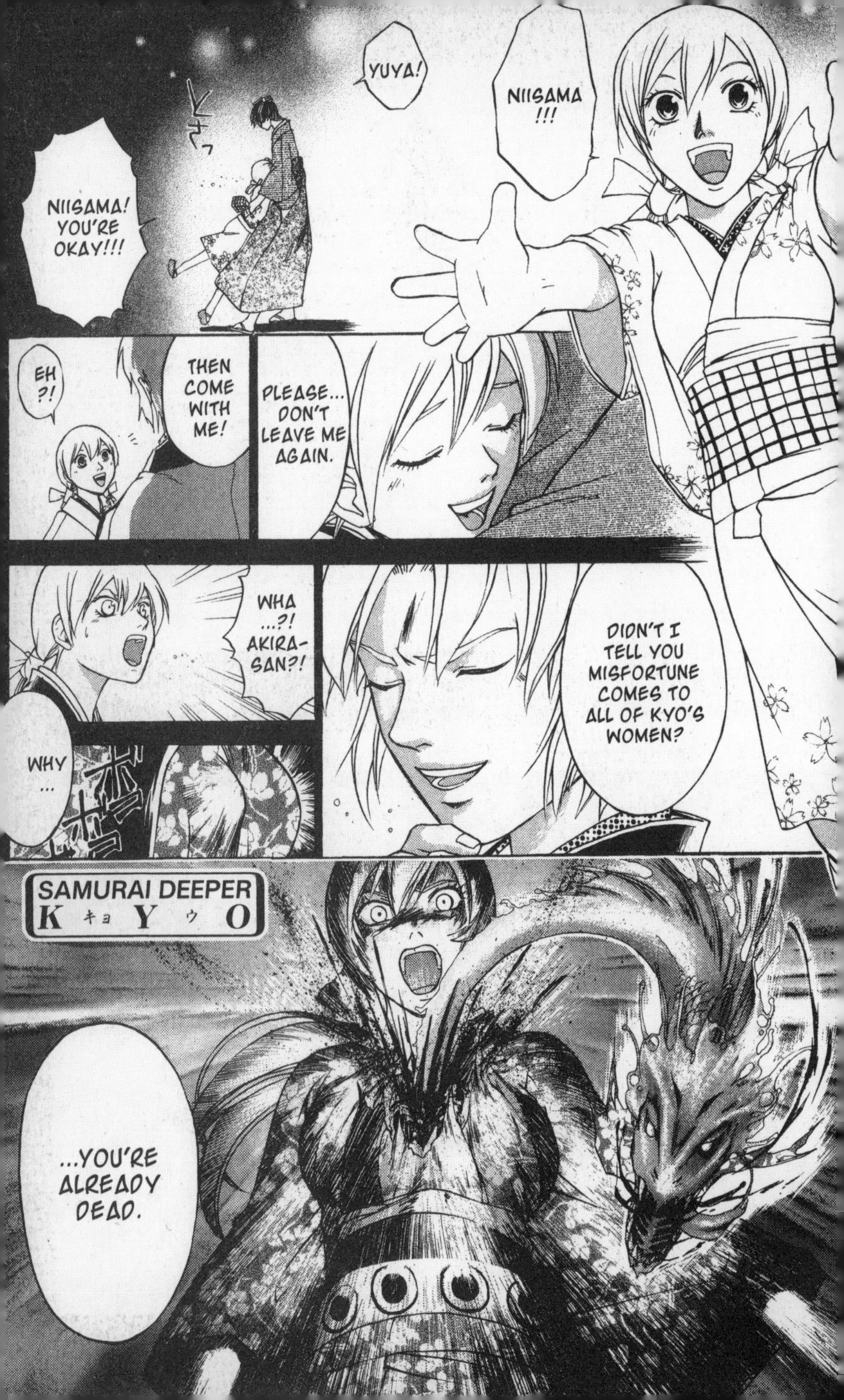
NIISAMA !!!
YUYA!
NIISAMA! YOU'RE OKAY!!!
PLEASE... DON'T LEAVE ME AGAIN.
THEN COME WITH ME!
EH ?!
DIDN'T I TELL YOU MISFORTUNE COMES TO ALL OF KYO'S WOMEN?
WHA ...?! AKIRA-SAN?!
WHY ...
SAMURAI DEEPER KYO
...YOU'RE ALREADY DEAD.

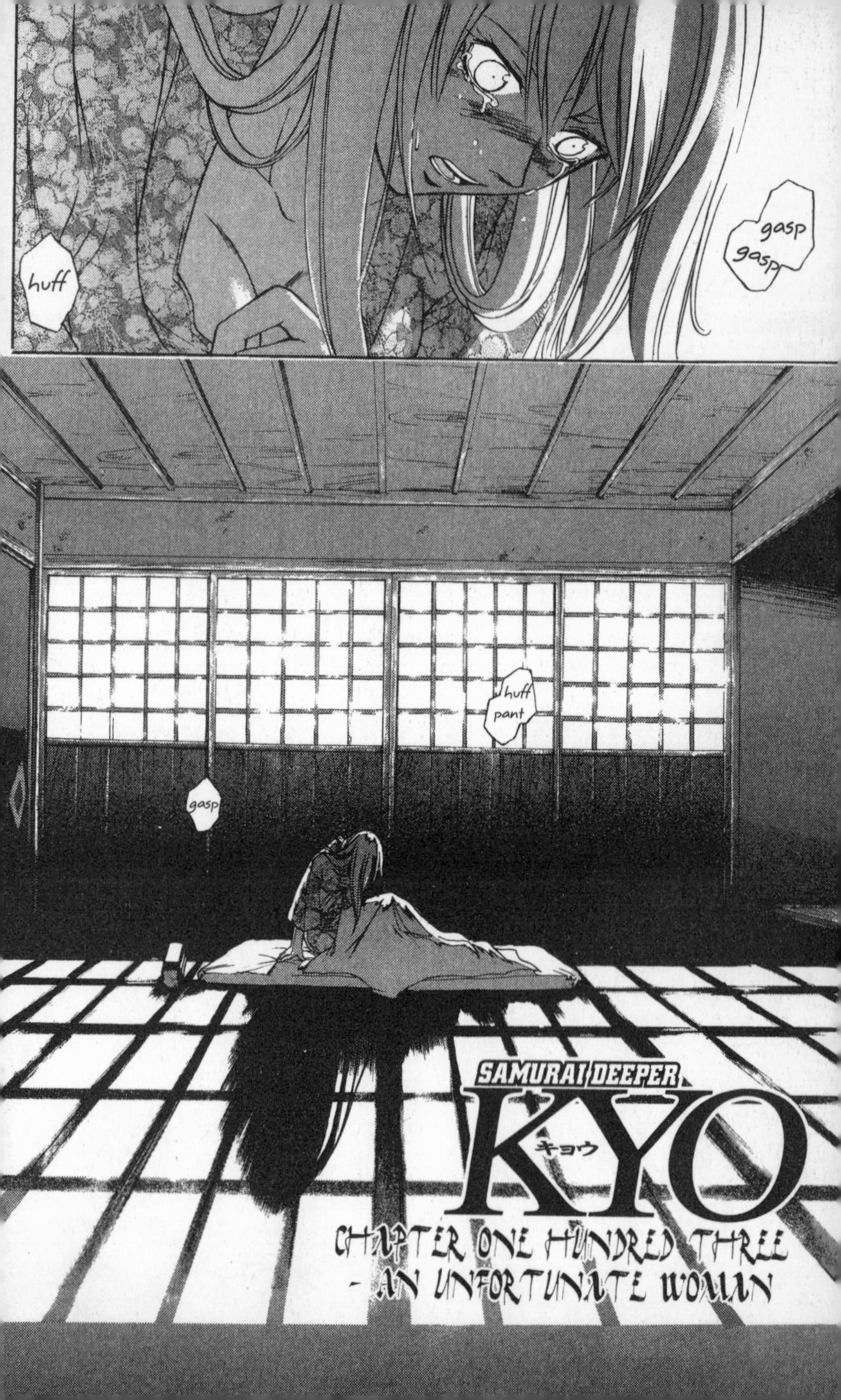
gasp gasp
huff
huff pant
gasp
SAMURAI DEEPER
KYO
キョウ
CHAPTER ONE HUNDRED THREE
- AN UNFORTUNATE WOMAN

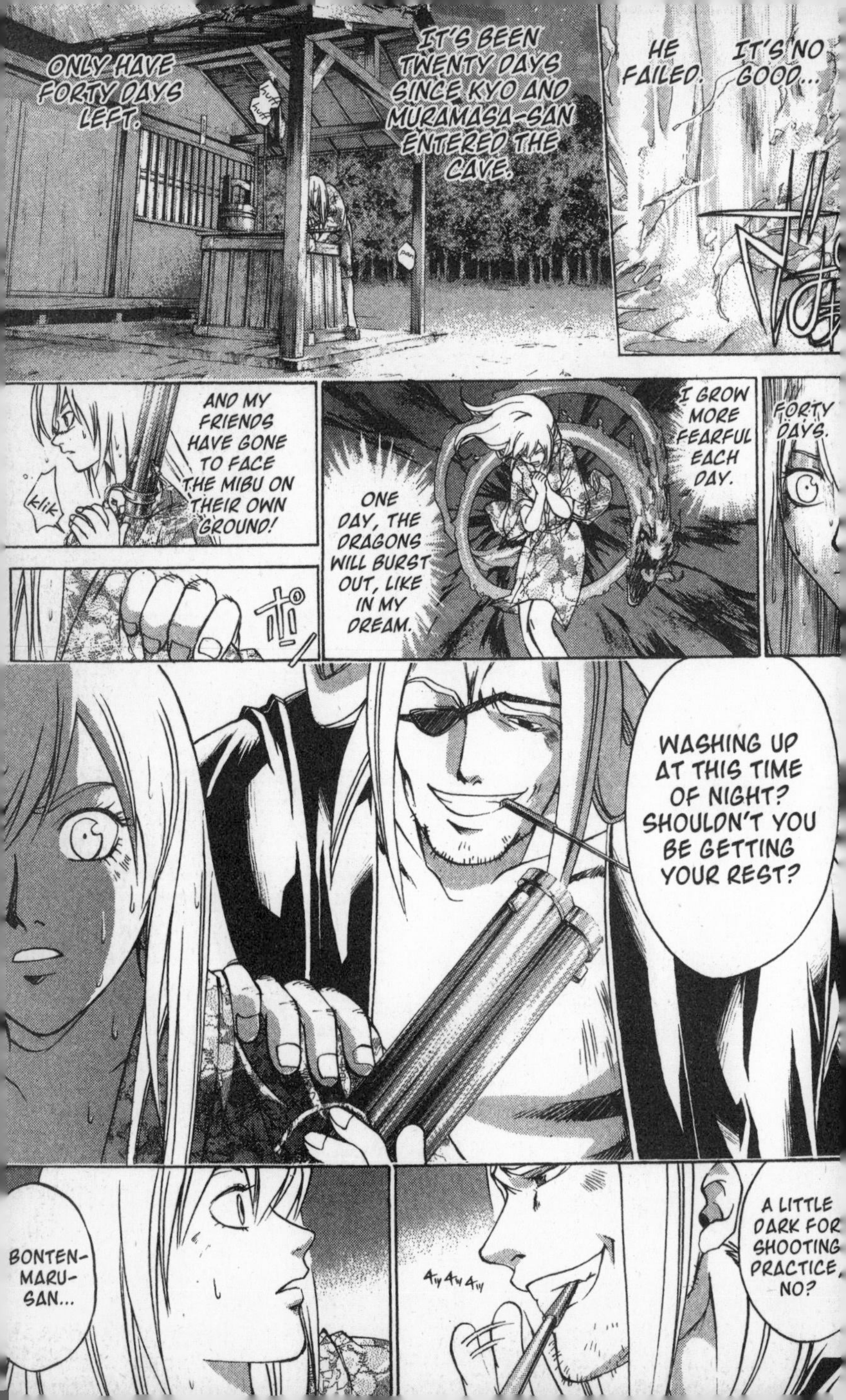
IT'S NO GOOD...
HE FAILED.
IT'S BEEN TWENTY DAYS SINCE KYO AND MURAMASA-SAN ENTERED THE CAVE.
huff huff
ONLY HAVE FORTY DAYS LEFT.
pan
FORTY DAYS.
I GROW MORE FEARFUL EACH DAY.
ONE DAY, THE DRAGONS WILL BURST OUT, LIKE IN MY DREAM.
AND MY FRIENDS HAVE GONE TO FACE THE MIBU ON THEIR OWN GROUND!
klik
WASHING UP AT THIS TIME OF NIGHT? SHOULDN'T YOU BE GETTING YOUR REST?
A LITTLE DARK FOR SHOOTING PRACTICE, NO?
BONTEN-MARU-SAN...

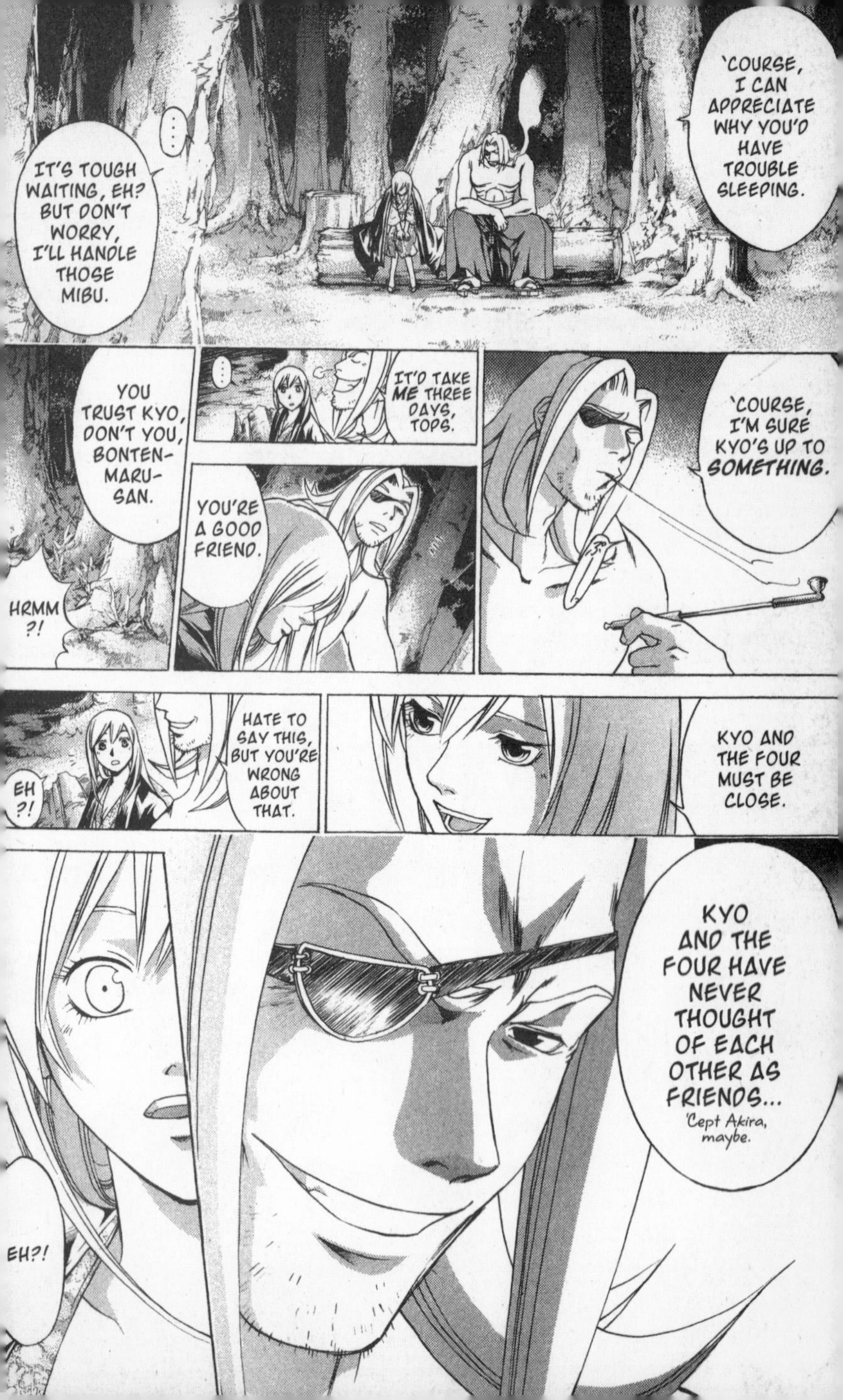

'COURSE, I CAN APPRECIATE WHY YOU'D HAVE TROUBLE SLEEPING.
...
IT'S TOUGH WAITING, EH? BUT DON'T WORRY, I'LL HANDLE THOSE MIBU.
'COURSE, I'M SURE KYO'S UP TO SOMETHING.
IT'D TAKE ME THREE DAYS, TOPS.
...
YOU'RE A GOOD FRIEND.
YOU TRUST KYO, DON'T YOU, BONTEN-MARU-SAN.
HRMM ?!
KYO AND THE FOUR MUST BE CLOSE.
HATE TO SAY THIS, BUT YOU'RE WRONG ABOUT THAT.
EH ?!
KYO AND THE FOUR HAVE NEVER THOUGHT OF EACH OTHER AS FRIENDS...
'Cept Akira, maybe.
EH?!

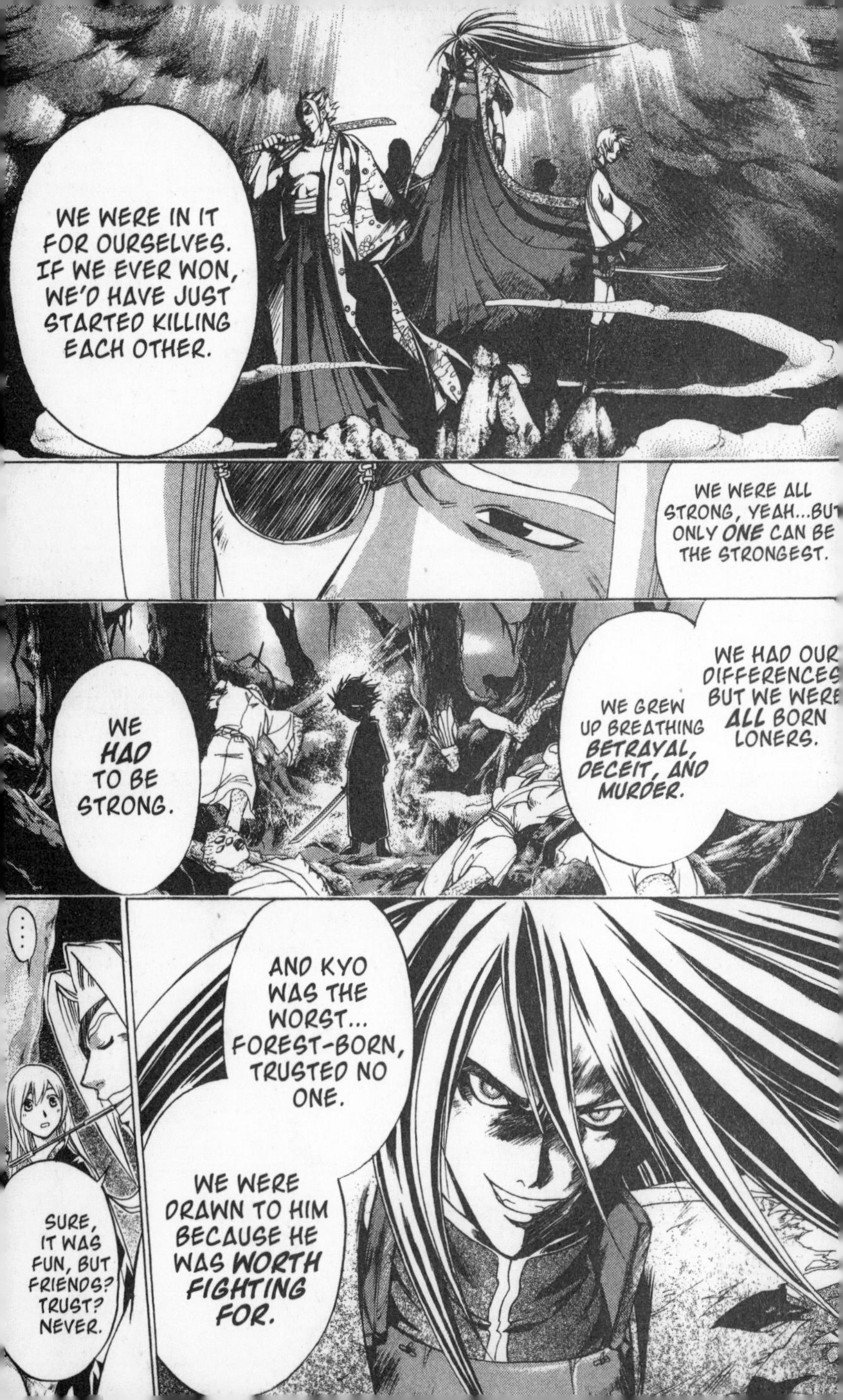
WE WERE IN IT FOR OURSELVES. IF WE EVER WON, WE'D HAVE JUST STARTED KILLING EACH OTHER.
WE WERE ALL STRONG, YEAH...BUT ONLY ONE CAN BE THE STRONGEST.
WE HAD OUR DIFFERENCES BUT WE WERE ALL BORN LONERS.
WE GREW UP BREATHING BETRAYAL, DECEIT, AND MURDER.
WE HAD TO BE STRONG.
AND KYO WAS THE WORST... FOREST-BORN, TRUSTED NO ONE.
WE WERE DRAWN TO HIM BECAUSE HE WAS WORTH FIGHTING FOR.
....
SURE, IT WAS FUN, BUT FRIENDS? TRUST? NEVER.

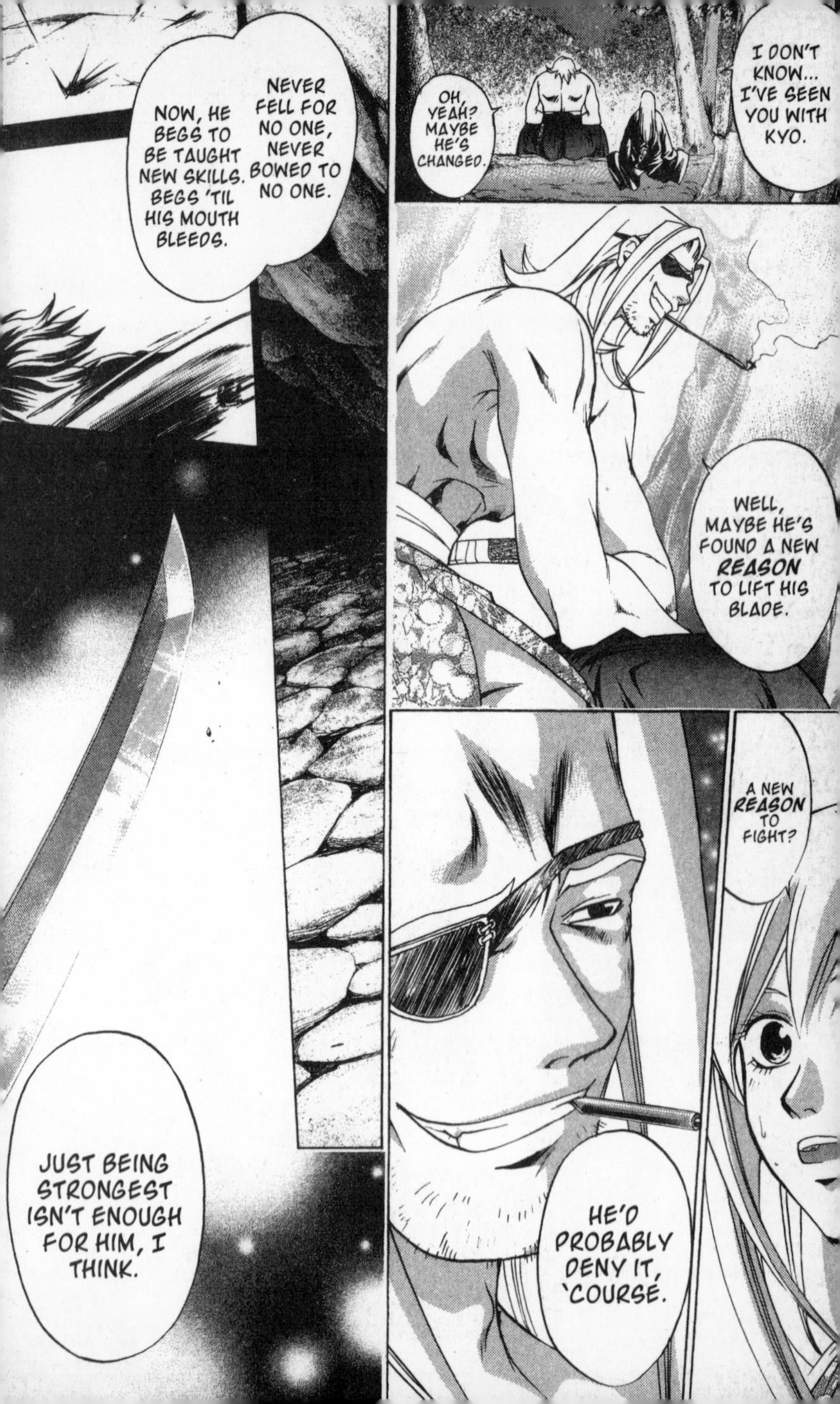
I DON'T KNOW... I'VE SEEN YOU WITH KYO.
OH, YEAH? MAYBE HE'S CHANGED.
WELL, MAYBE HE'S FOUND A NEW **REASON** TO LIFT HIS BLADE.
A NEW **REASON** TO FIGHT?
HE'D PROBABLY DENY IT, 'COURSE.
NEVER FELL FOR NO ONE, NEVER BOWED TO NO ONE.
NOW, HE BEGS TO BE TAUGHT NEW SKILLS. BEGS 'TIL HIS MOUTH BLEEDS.
JUST BEING STRONGEST ISN'T ENOUGH FOR HIM, I THINK.

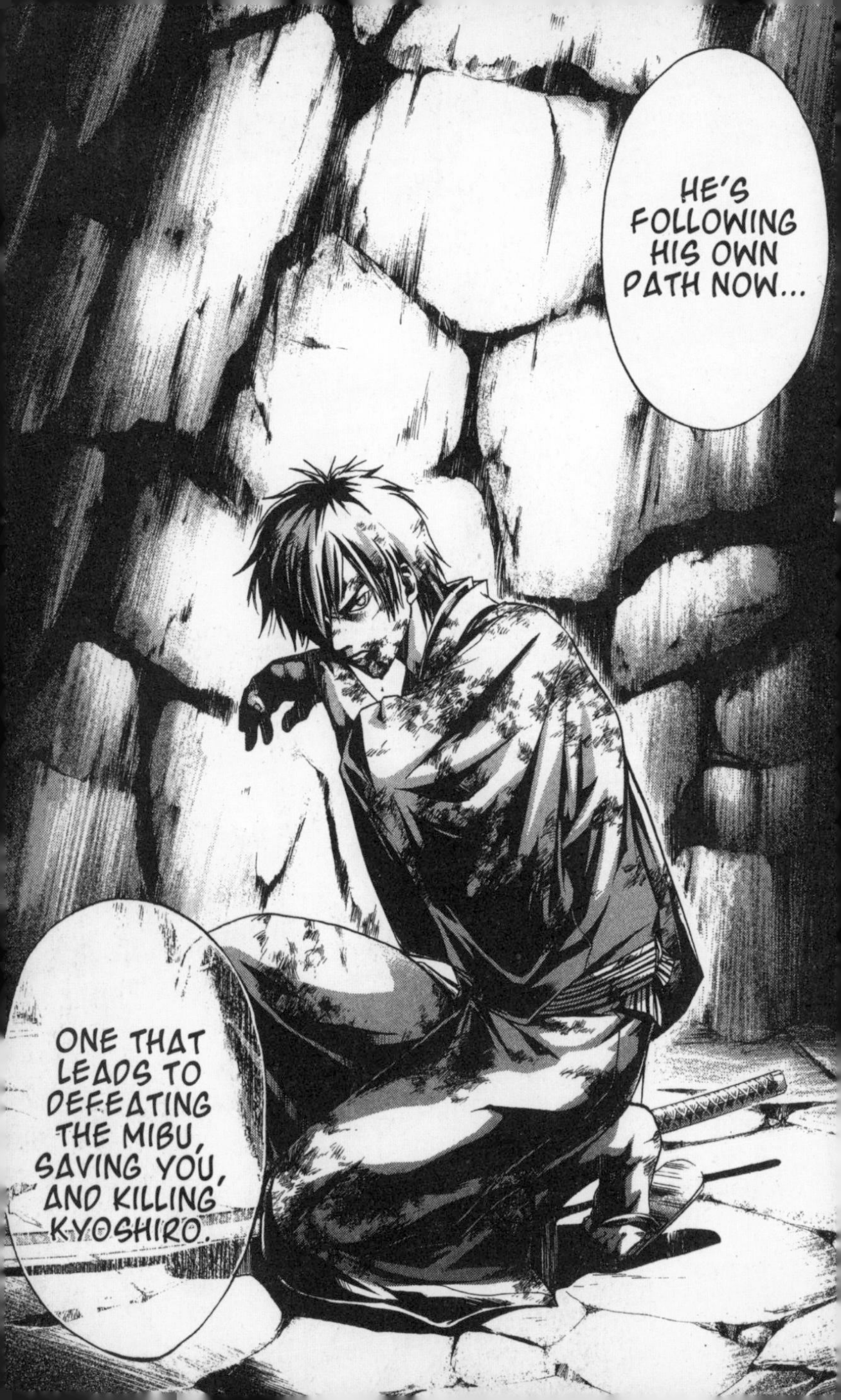
HE'S FOLLOWING HIS OWN PATH NOW...
ONE THAT LEADS TO DEFEATING THE MIBU, SAVING YOU, AND KILLING KYOSHIRO.

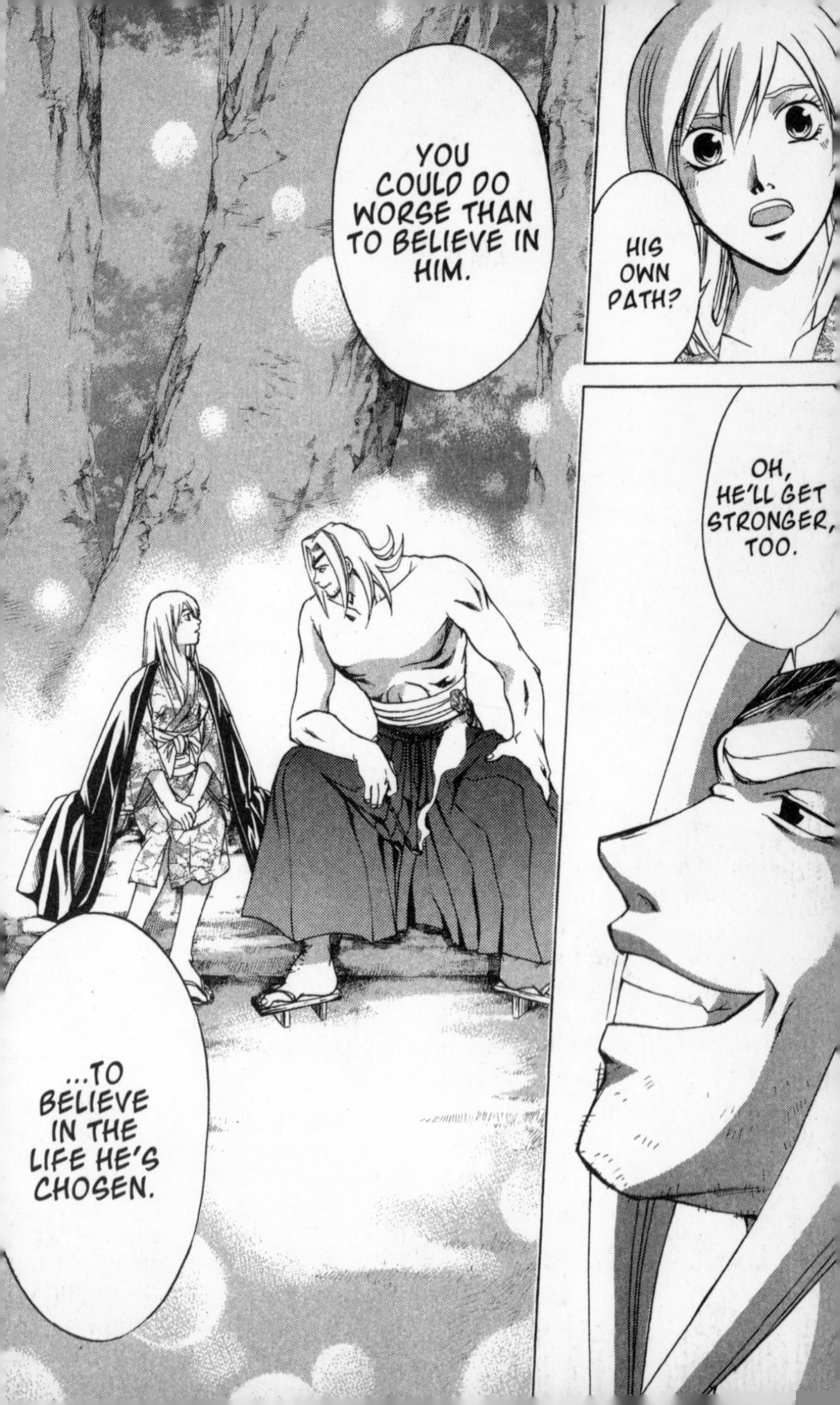
HIS OWN PATH?
OH, HE'LL GET STRONGER, TOO.
YOU COULD DO WORSE THAN TO BELIEVE IN HIM.
...TO BELIEVE IN THE LIFE HE'S CHOSEN.

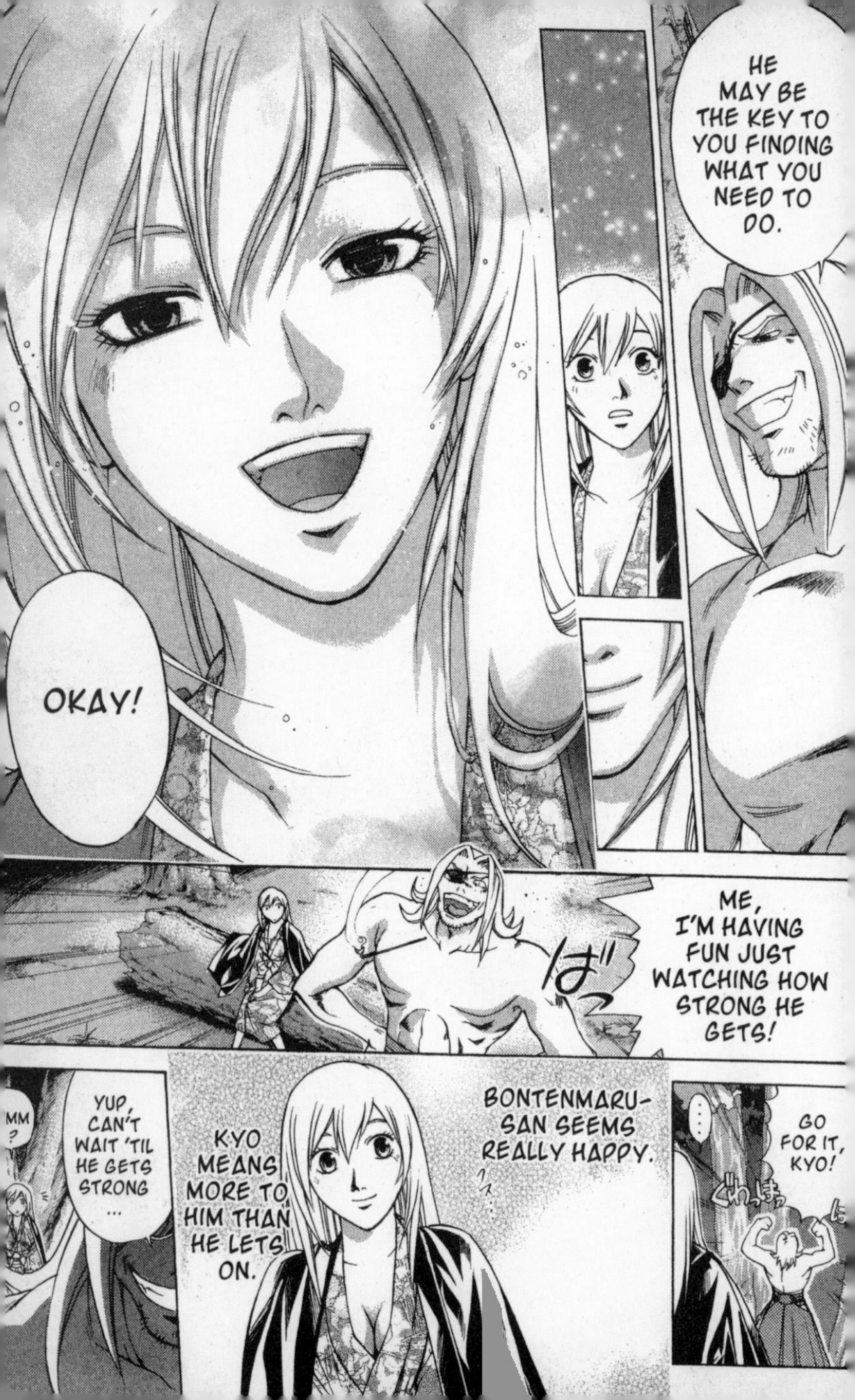
HE MAY BE THE KEY TO YOU FINDING WHAT YOU NEED TO DO.
OKAY!
ME, I'M HAVING FUN JUST WATCHING HOW STRONG HE GETS!
ばっ
...
GO FOR IT, KYO!
BONTENMARU-SAN SEEMS REALLY HAPPY.
KYO MEANS MORE TO HIM THAN HE LETS ON.
YUP, CAN'T WAIT 'TIL HE GETS STRONG ...
MM ?

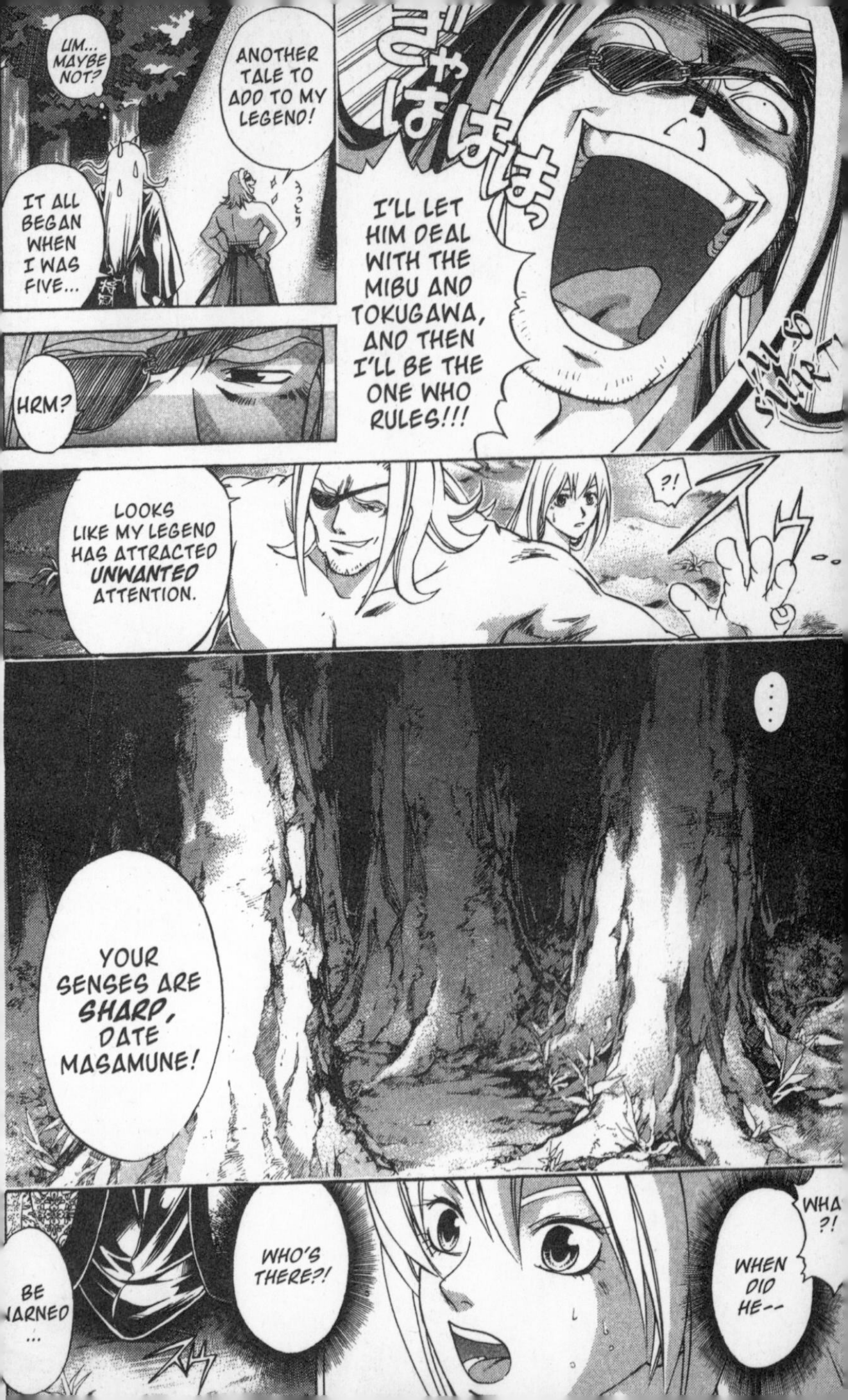
ぎゃははは
I'LL LET HIM DEAL WITH THE MIBU AND TOKUGAWA, AND THEN I'LL BE THE ONE WHO RULES!!!
ANOTHER TALE TO ADD TO MY LEGEND!
UM... MAYBE NOT?
IT ALL BEGAN WHEN I WAS FIVE...
HRM?
?!
LOOKS LIKE MY LEGEND HAS ATTRACTED UNWANTED ATTENTION.
...
YOUR SENSES ARE SHARP, DATE MASAMUNE!
WHA?!
WHEN DID HE--
WHO'S THERE?!
BE WARNED...

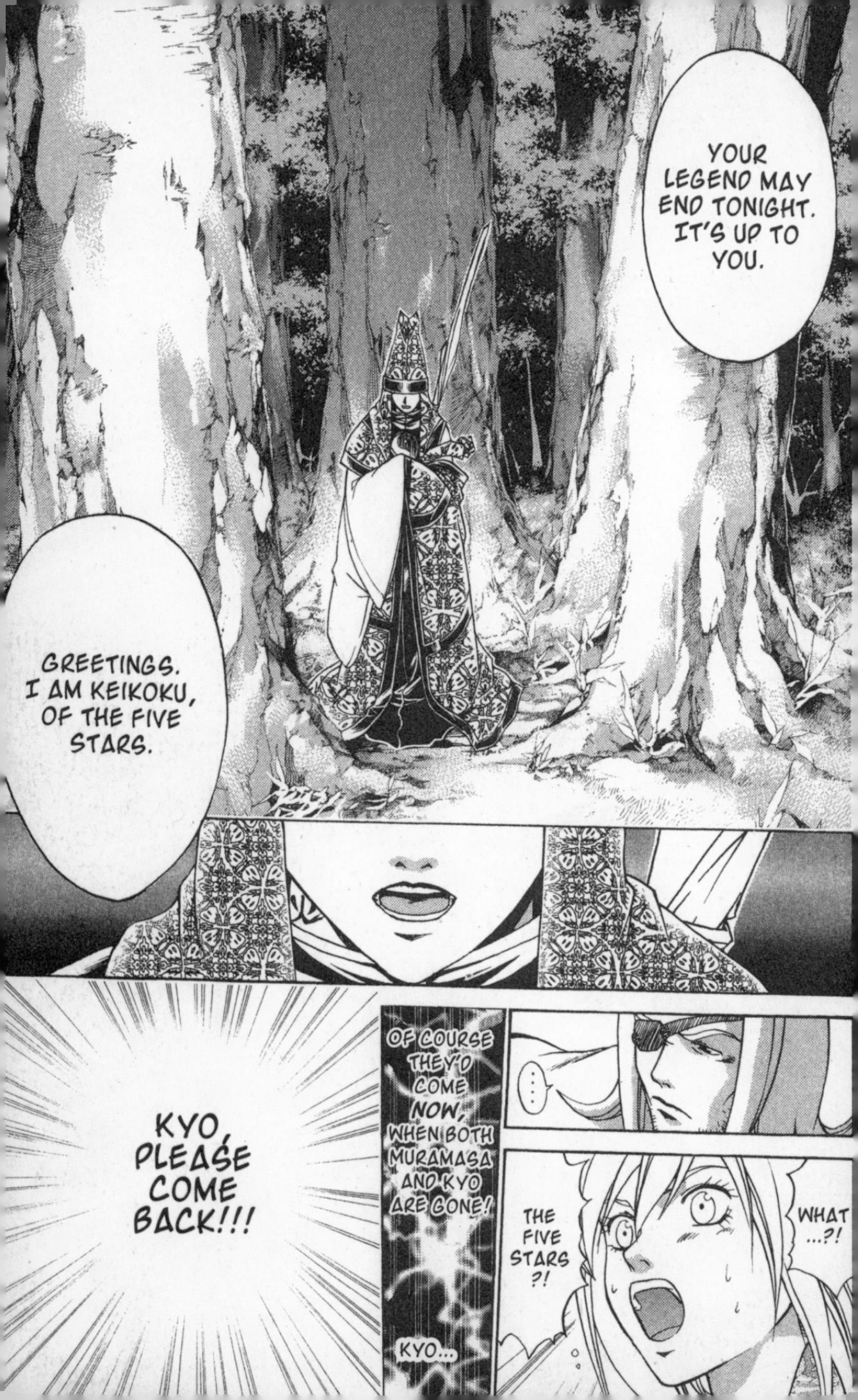
YOUR LEGEND MAY END TONIGHT. IT'S UP TO YOU.
GREETINGS. I AM KEIKOKU, OF THE FIVE STARS.
...
WHAT ...?!
THE FIVE STARS ?!
OF COURSE THEY'D COME NOW, WHEN BOTH MURAMASA AND KYO ARE GONE!
KYO...
KYO, PLEASE COME BACK!!!

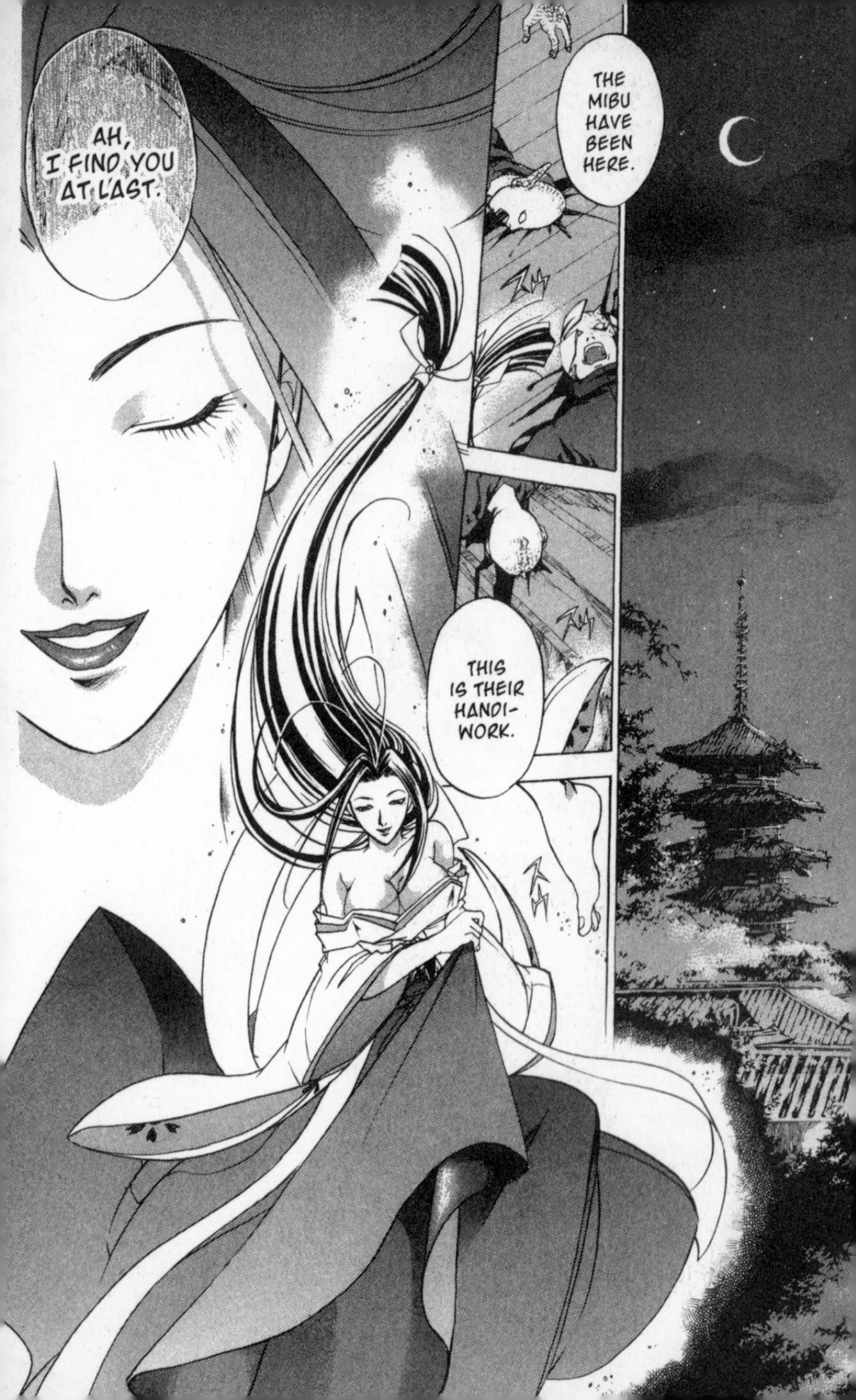
THE MIBU HAVE BEEN HERE.
THIS IS THEIR HANDI-WORK.
AH, I FIND YOU AT LAST.

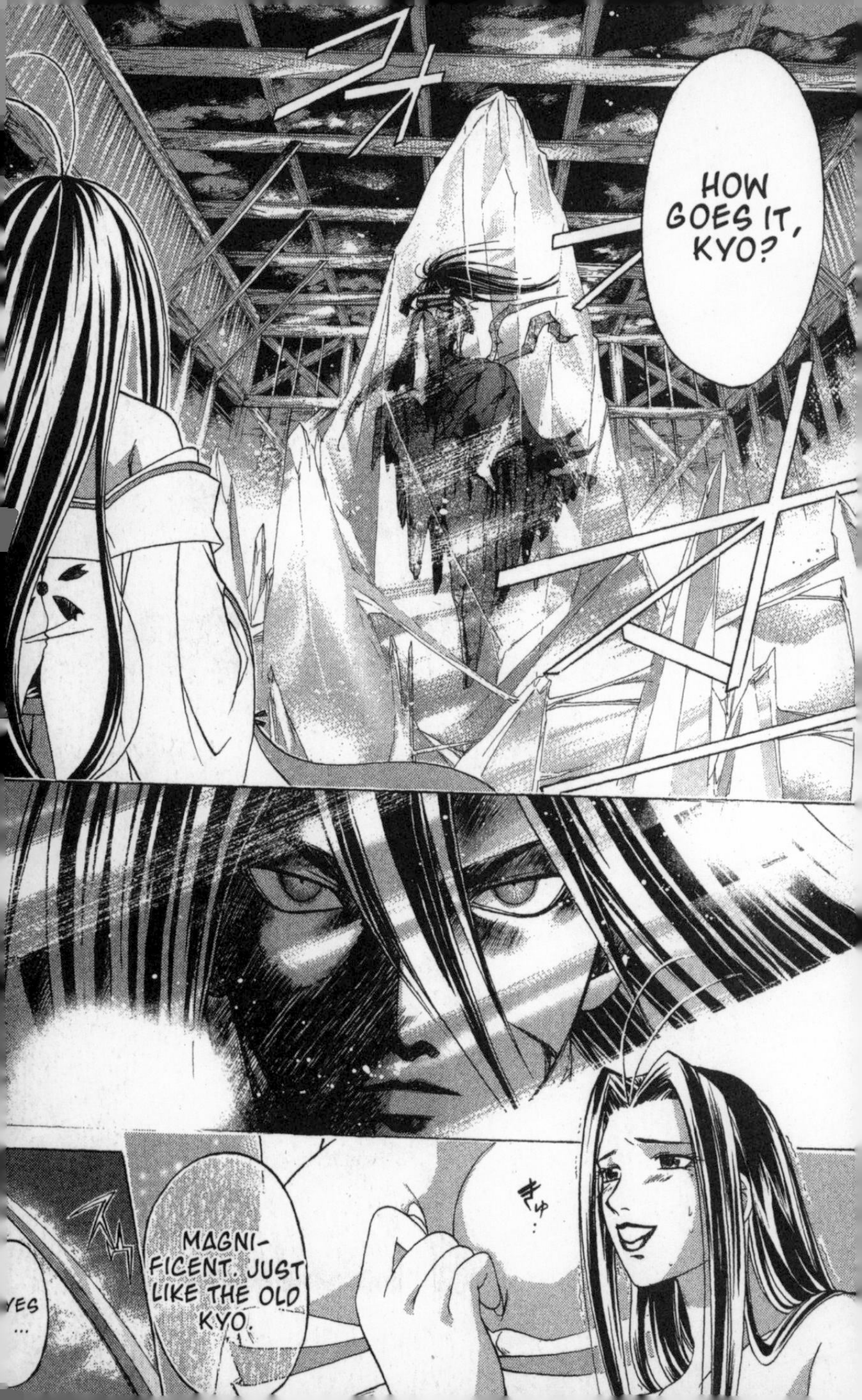
HOW GOES IT, KYO?
きゅ…
MAGNI-FICENT. JUST LIKE THE OLD KYO.
YES ...

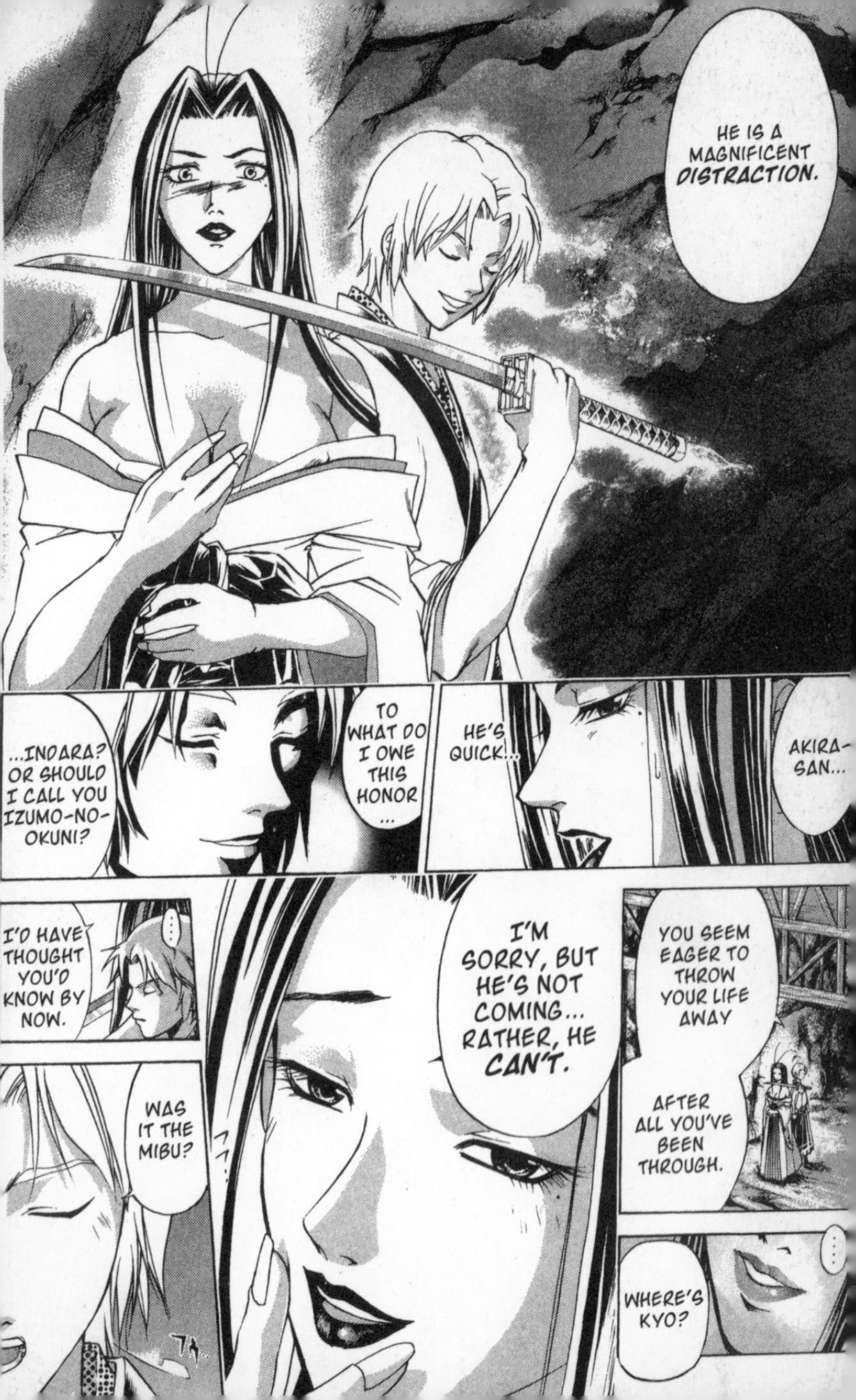
HE IS A MAGNIFICENT DISTRACTION.
AKIRA-SAN...
HE'S QUICK...
TO WHAT DO I OWE THIS HONOR ...
...INDARA? OR SHOULD I CALL YOU IZUMO-NO-OKUNI?
YOU SEEM EAGER TO THROW YOUR LIFE AWAY
AFTER ALL YOU'VE BEEN THROUGH.
...
WHERE'S KYO?
I'M SORRY, BUT HE'S NOT COMING... RATHER, HE CAN'T.
...
I'D HAVE THOUGHT YOU'D KNOW BY NOW.
WAS IT THE MIBU?

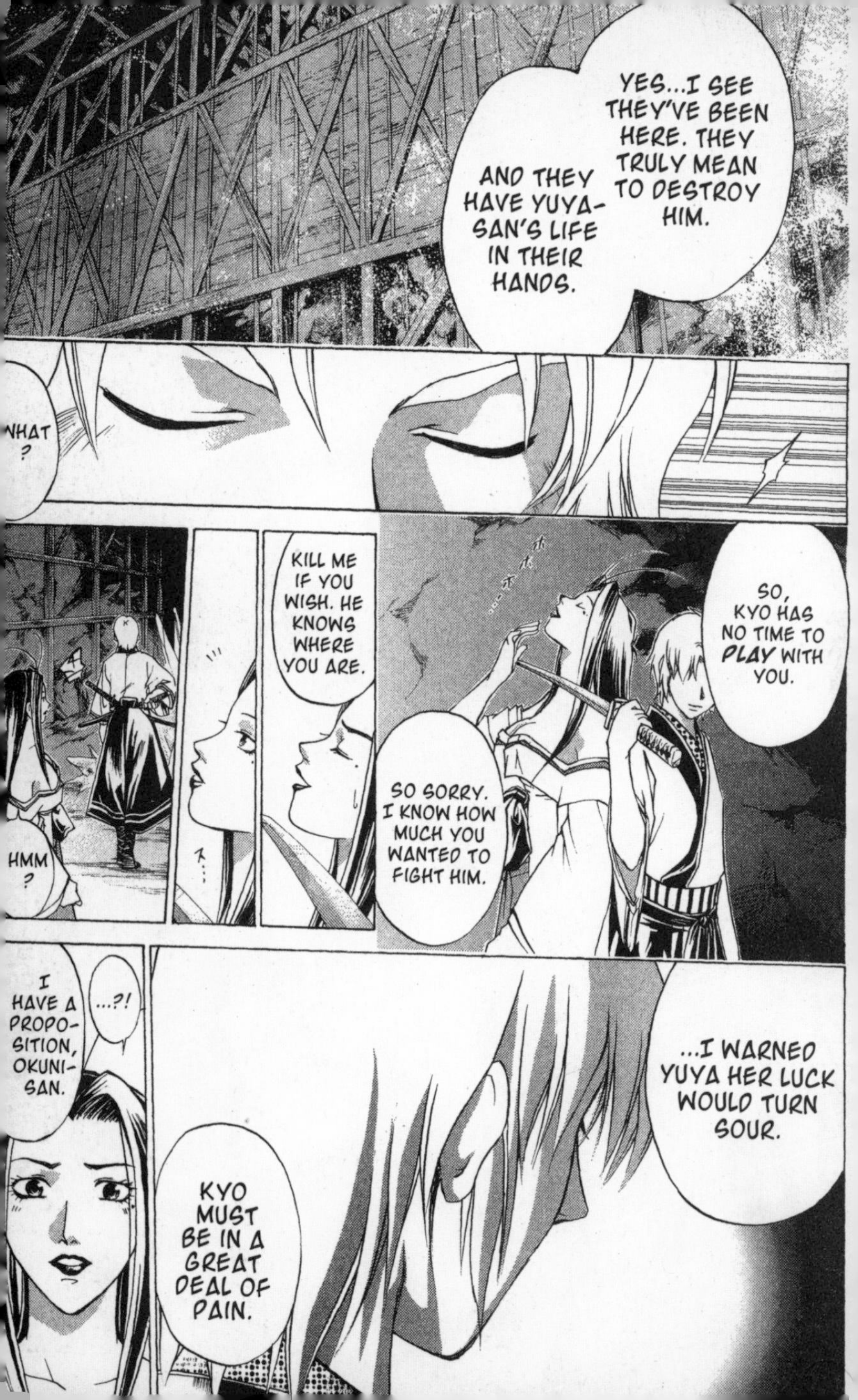
YES...I SEE THEY'VE BEEN HERE. THEY TRULY MEAN TO DESTROY HIM.
AND THEY HAVE YUYA-SAN'S LIFE IN THEIR HANDS.
WHAT?
SO, KYO HAS NO TIME TO PLAY WITH YOU.
SO SORRY. I KNOW HOW MUCH YOU WANTED TO FIGHT HIM.
KILL ME IF YOU WISH. HE KNOWS WHERE YOU ARE.
HMM?
...I WARNED YUYA HER LUCK WOULD TURN SOUR.
KYO MUST BE IN A GREAT DEAL OF PAIN.
...?!
I HAVE A PROPOSITION, OKUNI-SAN.

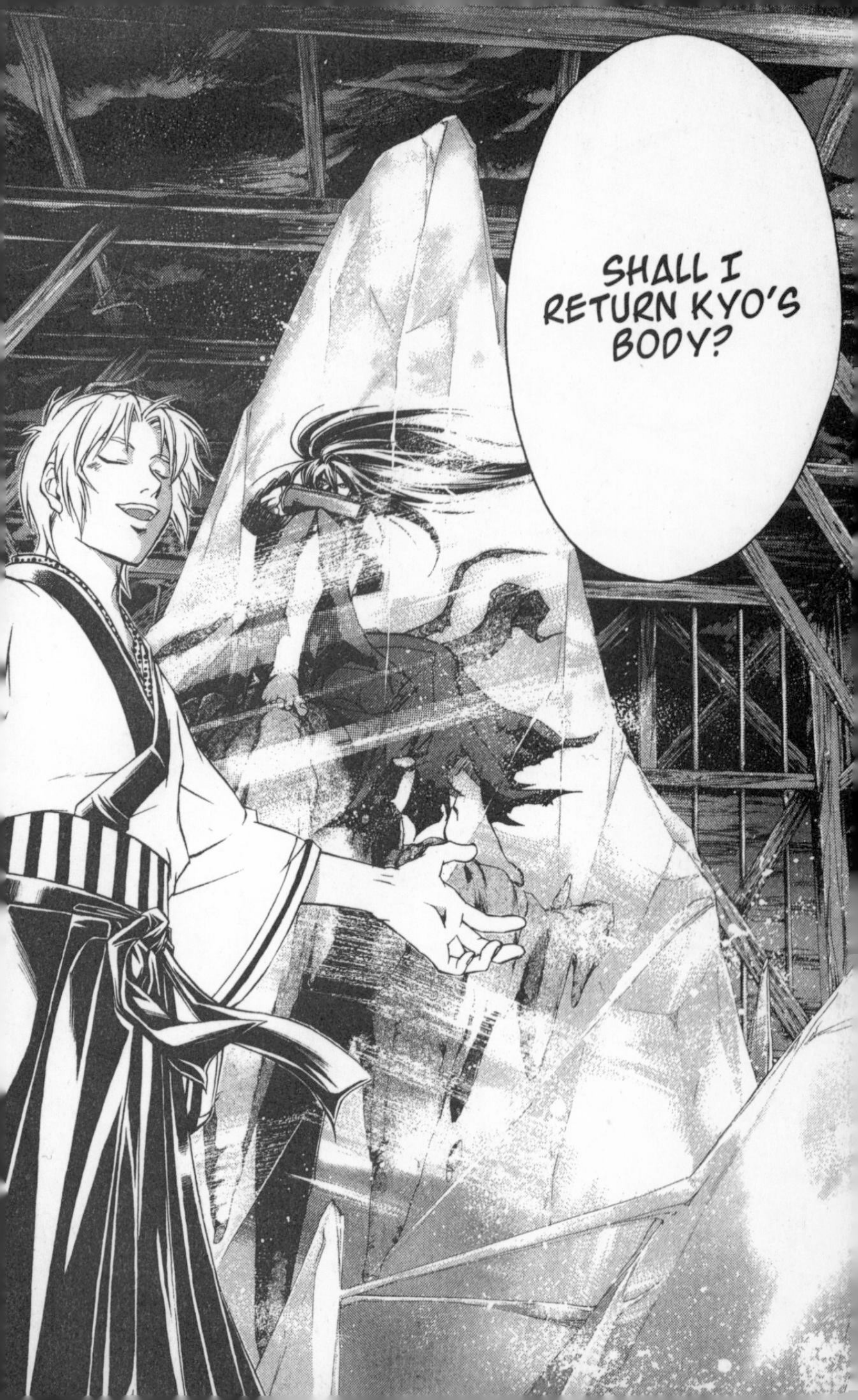
SHALL I RETURN KYO'S BODY?

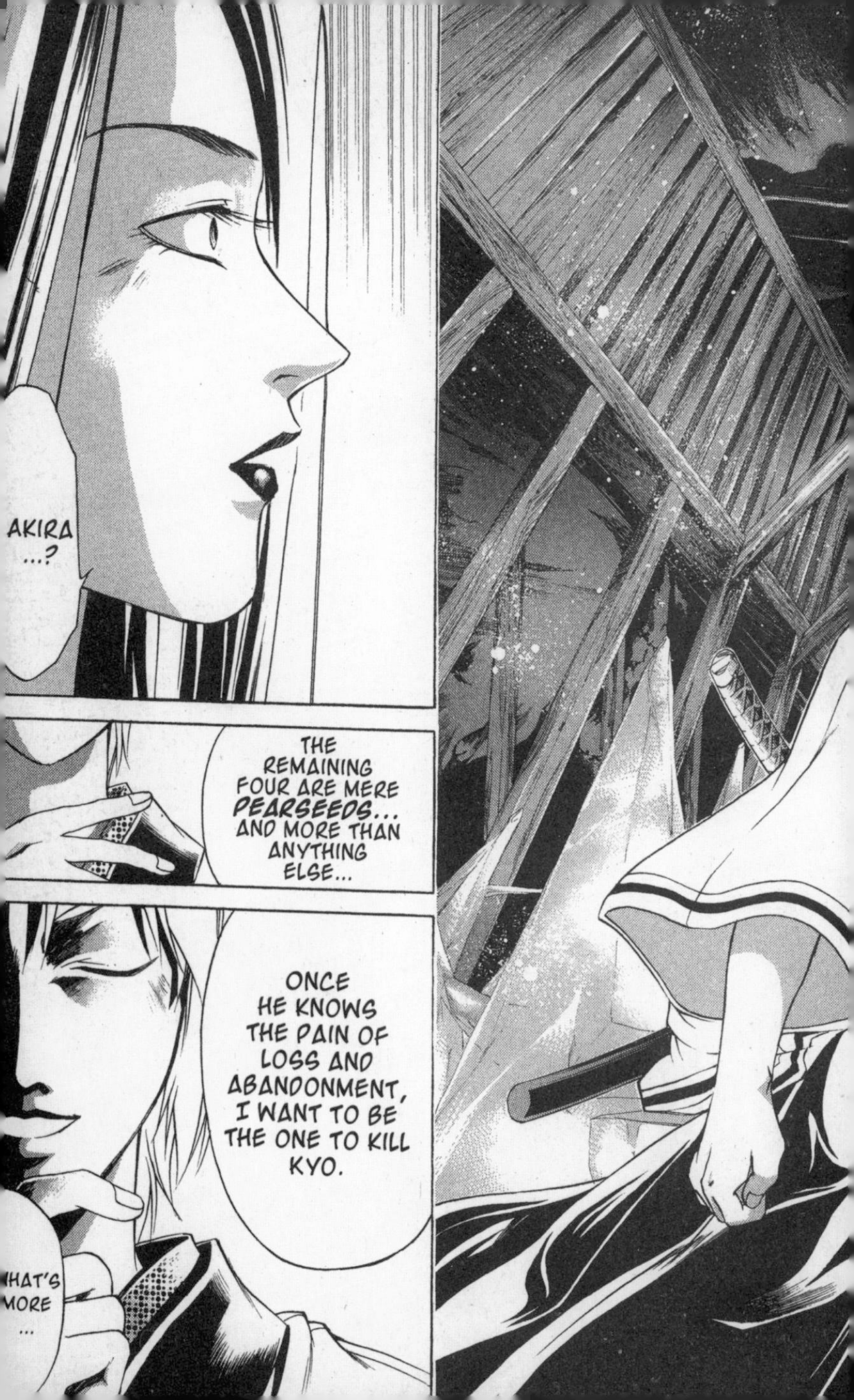
AKIRA ...?
THE REMAINING FOUR ARE MERE PEARSEEDS... AND MORE THAN ANYTHING ELSE...
ONCE HE KNOWS THE PAIN OF LOSS AND ABANDONMENT, I WANT TO BE THE ONE TO KILL KYO.
HAT'S MORE ...

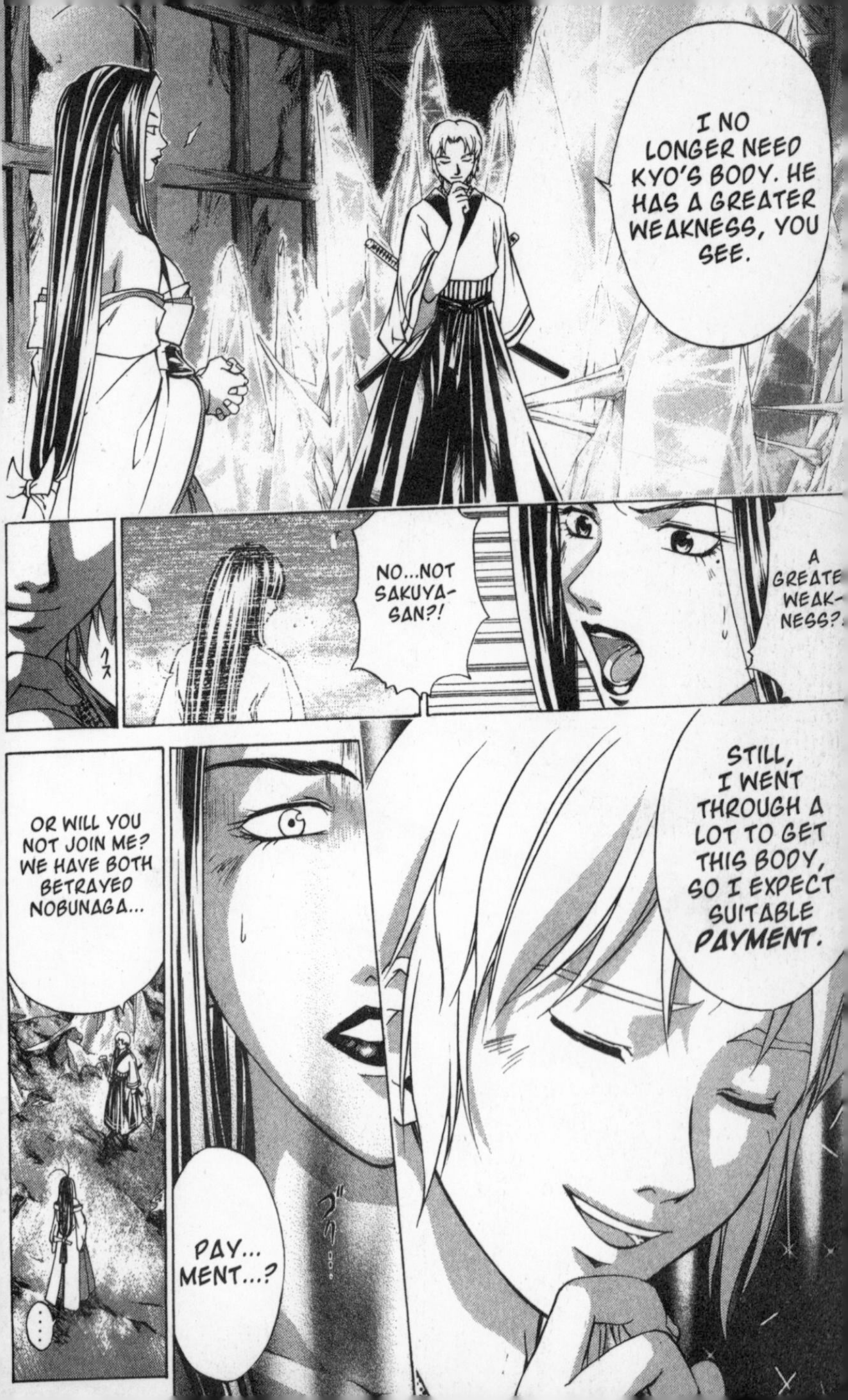
I NO LONGER NEED KYO'S BODY. HE HAS A GREATER WEAKNESS, YOU SEE.
A GREATE WEAK-NESS?
NO...NOT SAKUYA-SAN?!
STILL, I WENT THROUGH A LOT TO GET THIS BODY, SO I EXPECT SUITABLE PAYMENT.
PAY... MENT...?
OR WILL YOU NOT JOIN ME? WE HAVE BOTH BETRAYED NOBUNAGA...
...

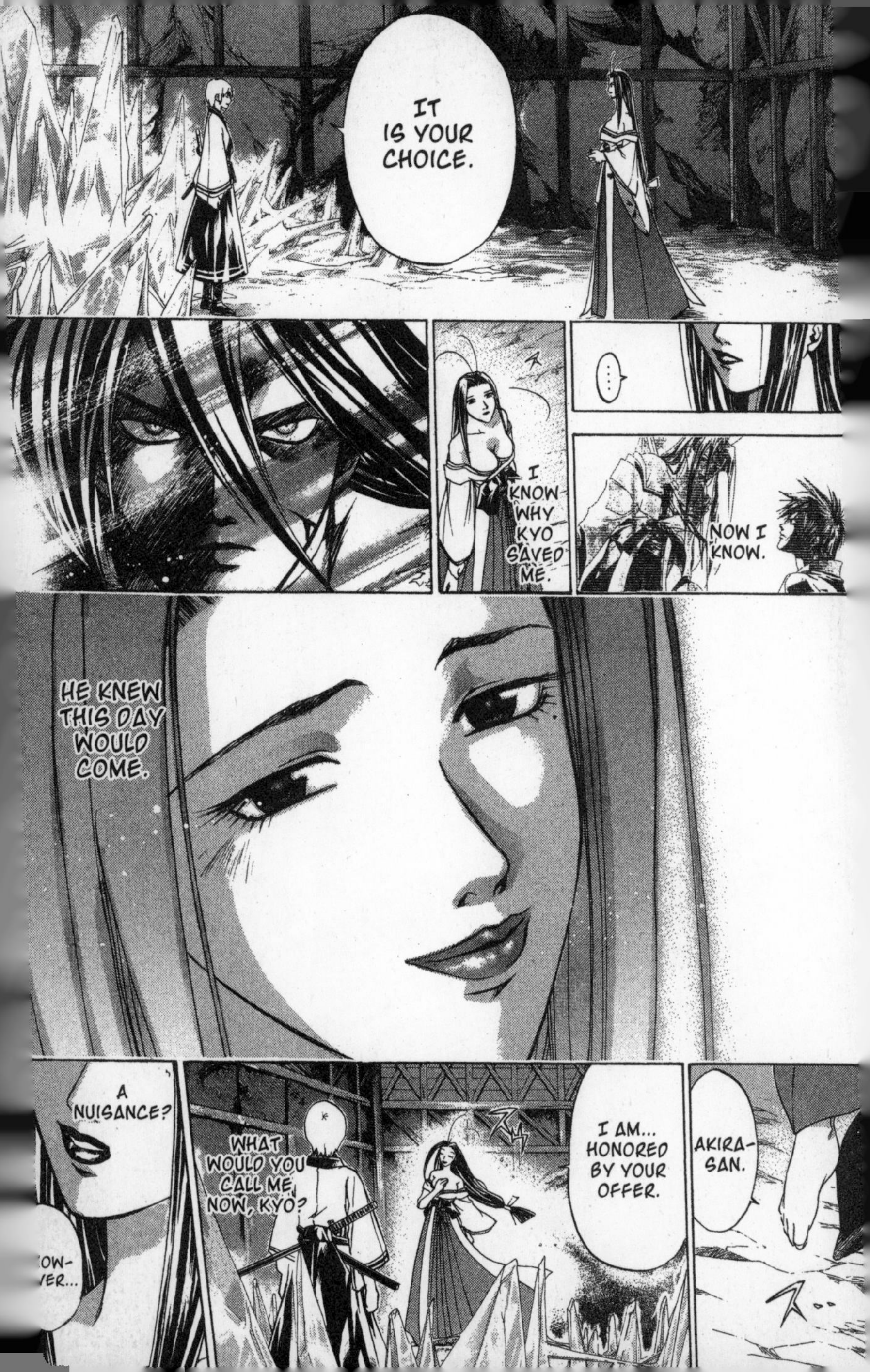
IT IS YOUR CHOICE.
...
NOW I KNOW.
I KNOW WHY KYO SAVED ME.
HE KNEW THIS DAY WOULD COME.
AKIRA-SAN.
I AM... HONORED BY YOUR OFFER.
WHAT WOULD YOU CALL ME NOW, KYO?
A NUISANCE?

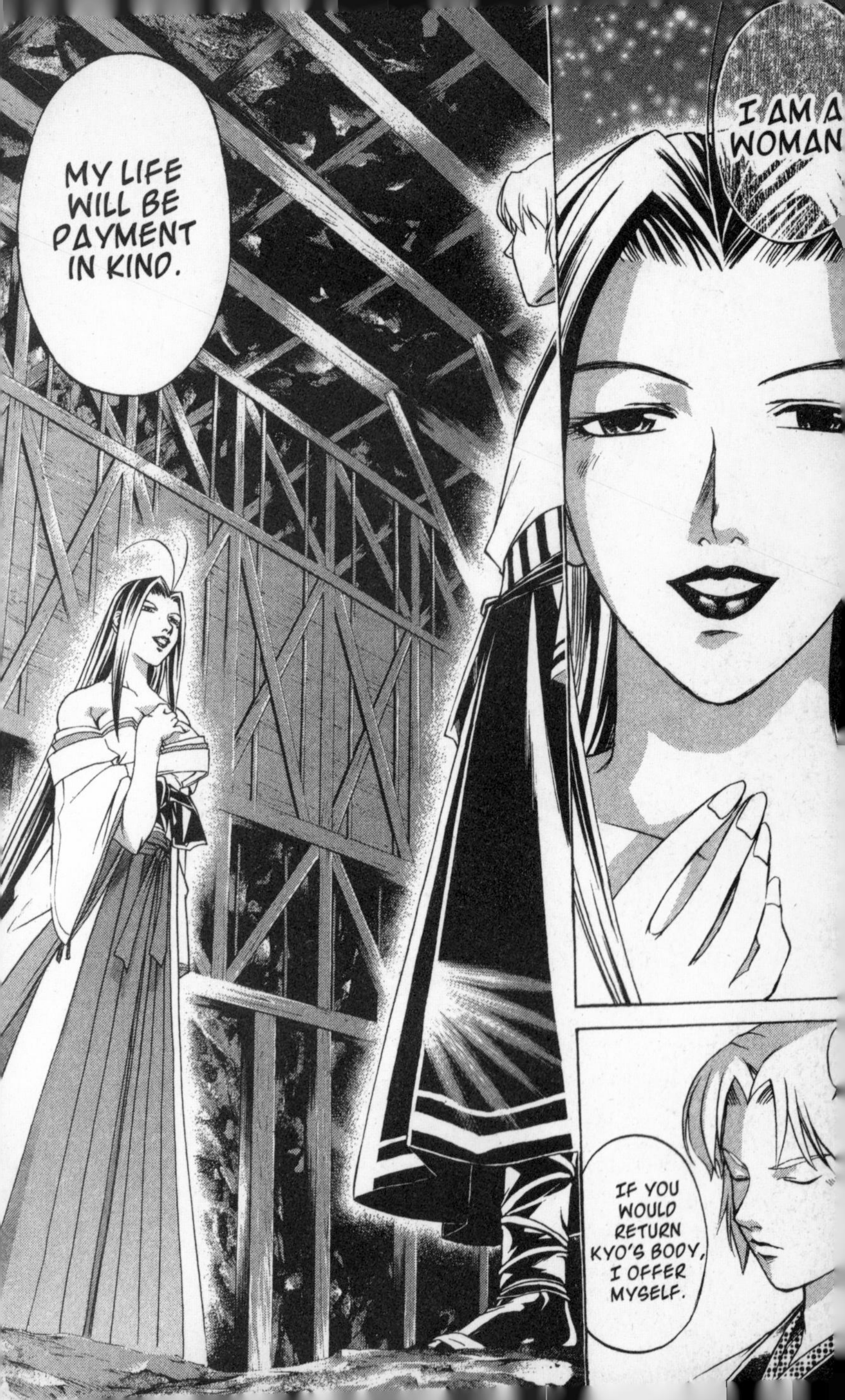
I AM A WOMAN
IF YOU WOULD RETURN KYO'S BODY, I OFFER MYSELF.
MY LIFE WILL BE PAYMENT IN KIND.

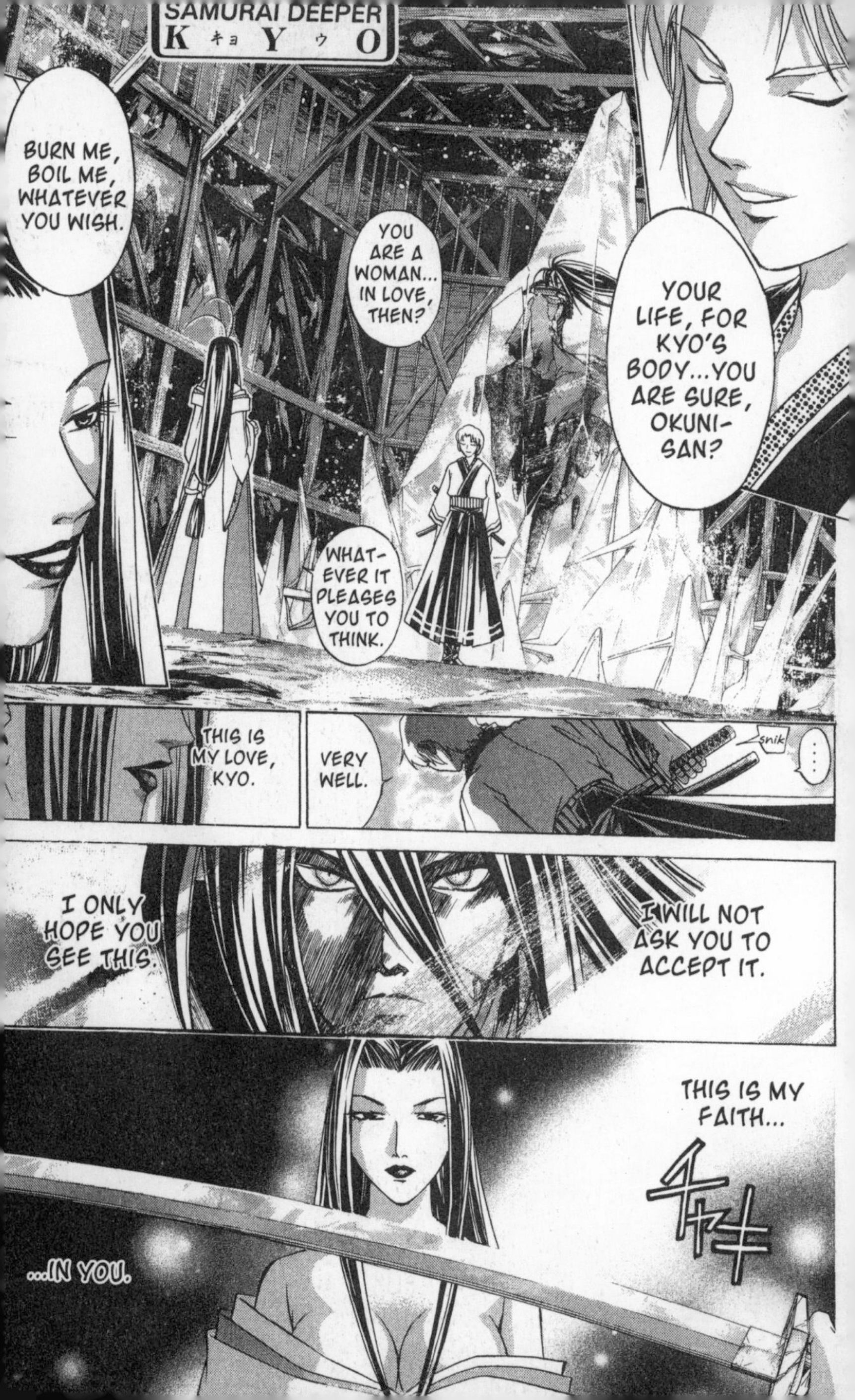
SAMURAI DEEPER KYO キョウ
YOUR LIFE, FOR KYO'S BODY...YOU ARE SURE, OKUNI-SAN?
BURN ME, BOIL ME, WHATEVER YOU WISH.
YOU ARE A WOMAN... IN LOVE, THEN?
WHATEVER IT PLEASES YOU TO THINK.
snik
....
VERY WELL.
THIS IS MY LOVE, KYO.
I WILL NOT ASK YOU TO ACCEPT IT.
I ONLY HOPE YOU SEE THIS.
THIS IS MY FAITH...
チャキ
...IN YOU.

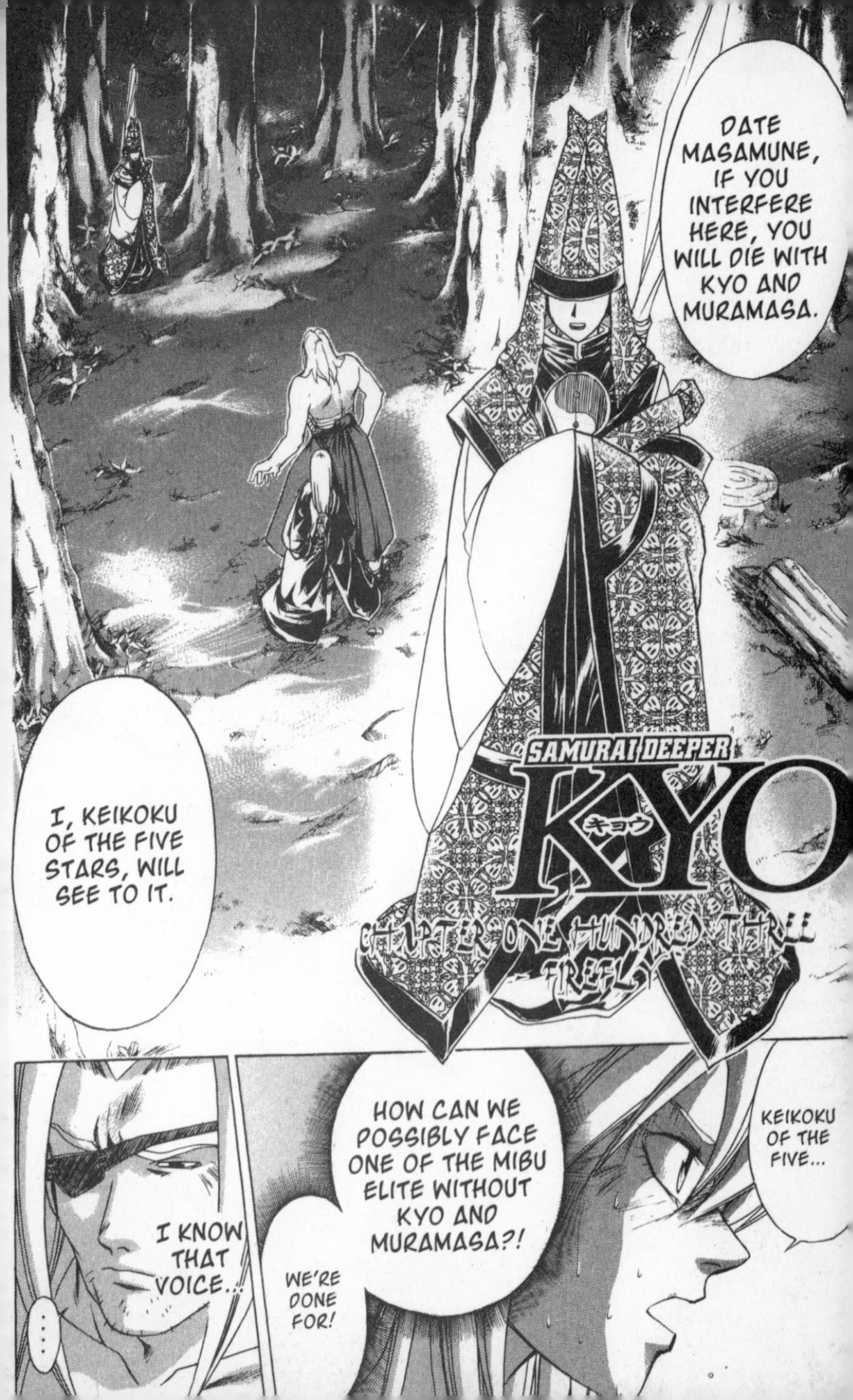

DATE MASAMUNE, IF YOU INTERFERE HERE, YOU WILL DIE WITH KYO AND MURAMASA.
SAMURAI DEEPER
KYO
キョウ
CHAPTER ONE HUNDRED THREE
FIREFLY
I, KEIKOKU OF THE FIVE STARS, WILL SEE TO IT.
KEIKOKU OF THE FIVE...
HOW CAN WE POSSIBLY FACE ONE OF THE MIBU ELITE WITHOUT KYO AND MURAMASA?!
WE'RE DONE FOR!
I KNOW THAT VOICE...
....

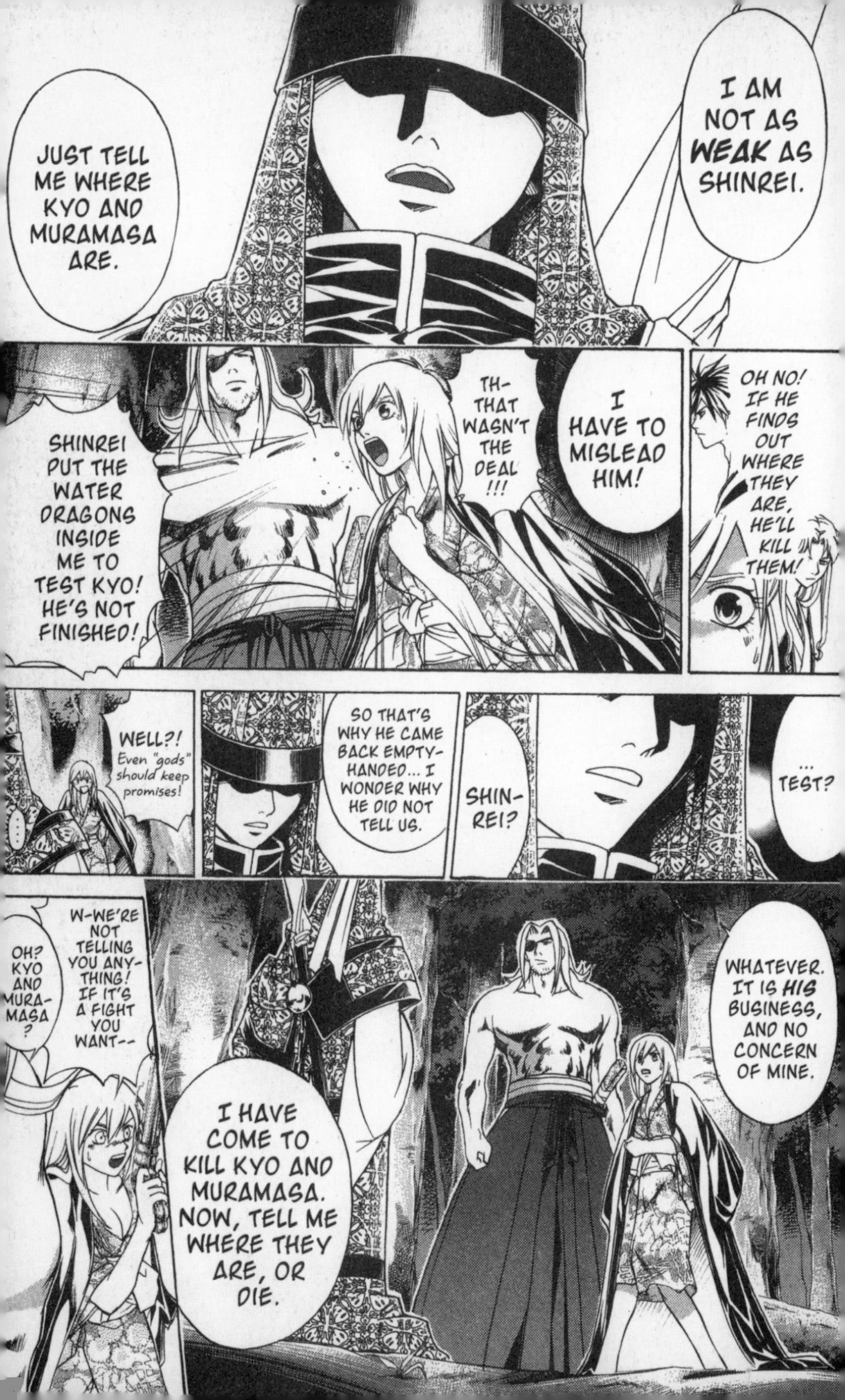
I AM NOT AS WEAK AS SHINREI.
JUST TELL ME WHERE KYO AND MURAMASA ARE.
OH NO! IF HE FINDS OUT WHERE THEY ARE, HE'LL KILL THEM!
I HAVE TO MISLEAD HIM!
TH-THAT WASN'T THE DEAL!!!
SHINREI PUT THE WATER DRAGONS INSIDE ME TO TEST KYO! HE'S NOT FINISHED!
... TEST?
SHIN-REI?
SO THAT'S WHY HE CAME BACK EMPTY-HANDED... I WONDER WHY HE DID NOT TELL US.
WELL?!
Even "gods" should keep promises!
...
WHATEVER. IT IS HIS BUSINESS, AND NO CONCERN OF MINE.
I HAVE COME TO KILL KYO AND MURAMASA. NOW, TELL ME WHERE THEY ARE, OR DIE.
W-WE'RE NOT TELLING YOU ANYTHING! IF IT'S A FIGHT YOU WANT--
OH? KYO AND MURA-MASA?

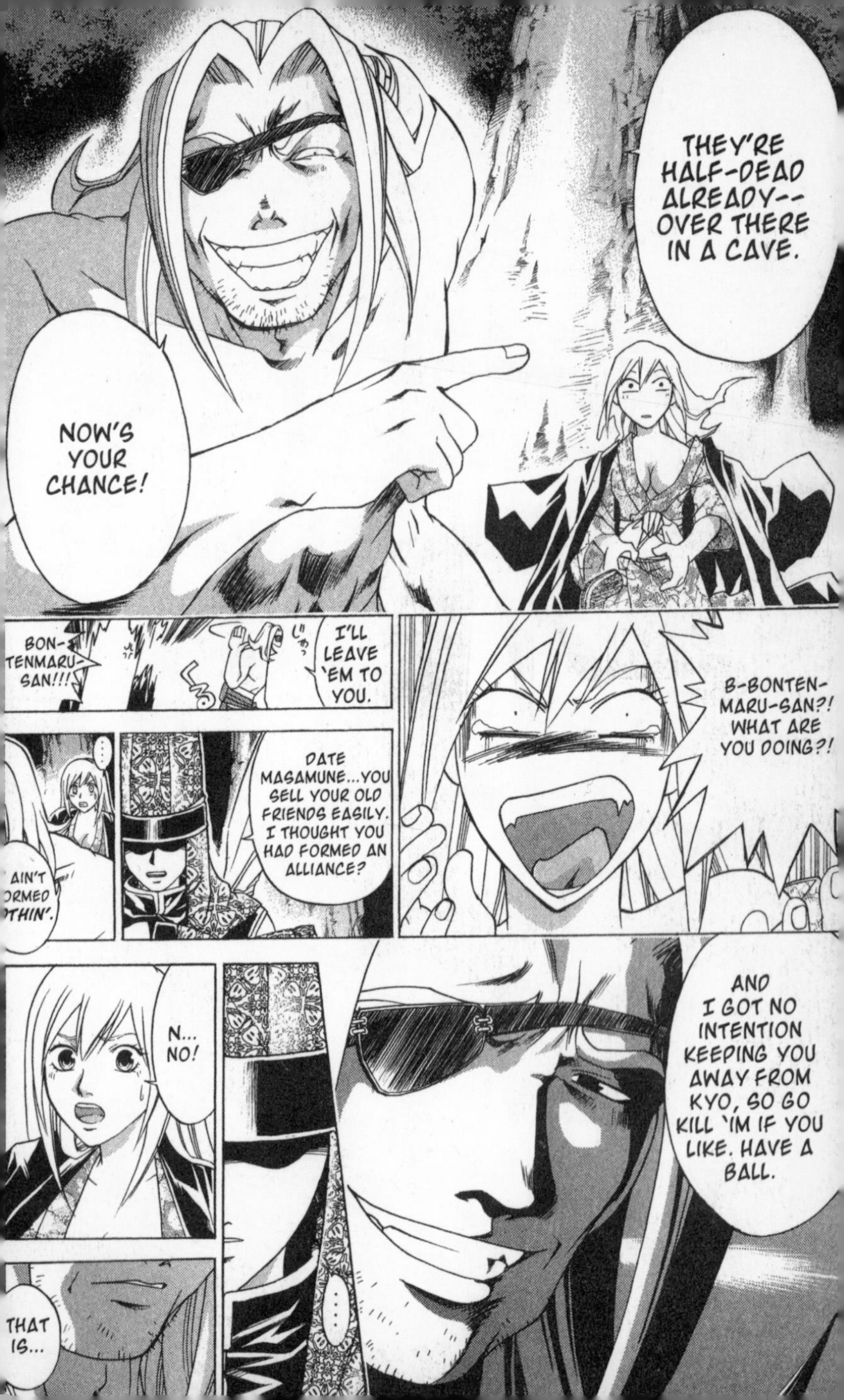
THEY'RE HALF-DEAD ALREADY-- OVER THERE IN A CAVE.
NOW'S YOUR CHANCE!
B-BONTEN-MARU-SAN?! WHAT ARE YOU DOING?!
I'LL LEAVE 'EM TO YOU.
BON-TENMARU-SAN!!!
DATE MASAMUNE...YOU SELL YOUR OLD FRIENDS EASILY. I THOUGHT YOU HAD FORMED AN ALLIANCE?
...
AIN'T ORMED OTHIN'.
AND I GOT NO INTENTION KEEPING YOU AWAY FROM KYO, SO GO KILL 'IM IF YOU LIKE. HAVE A BALL.
N... NO!
....
THAT IS...

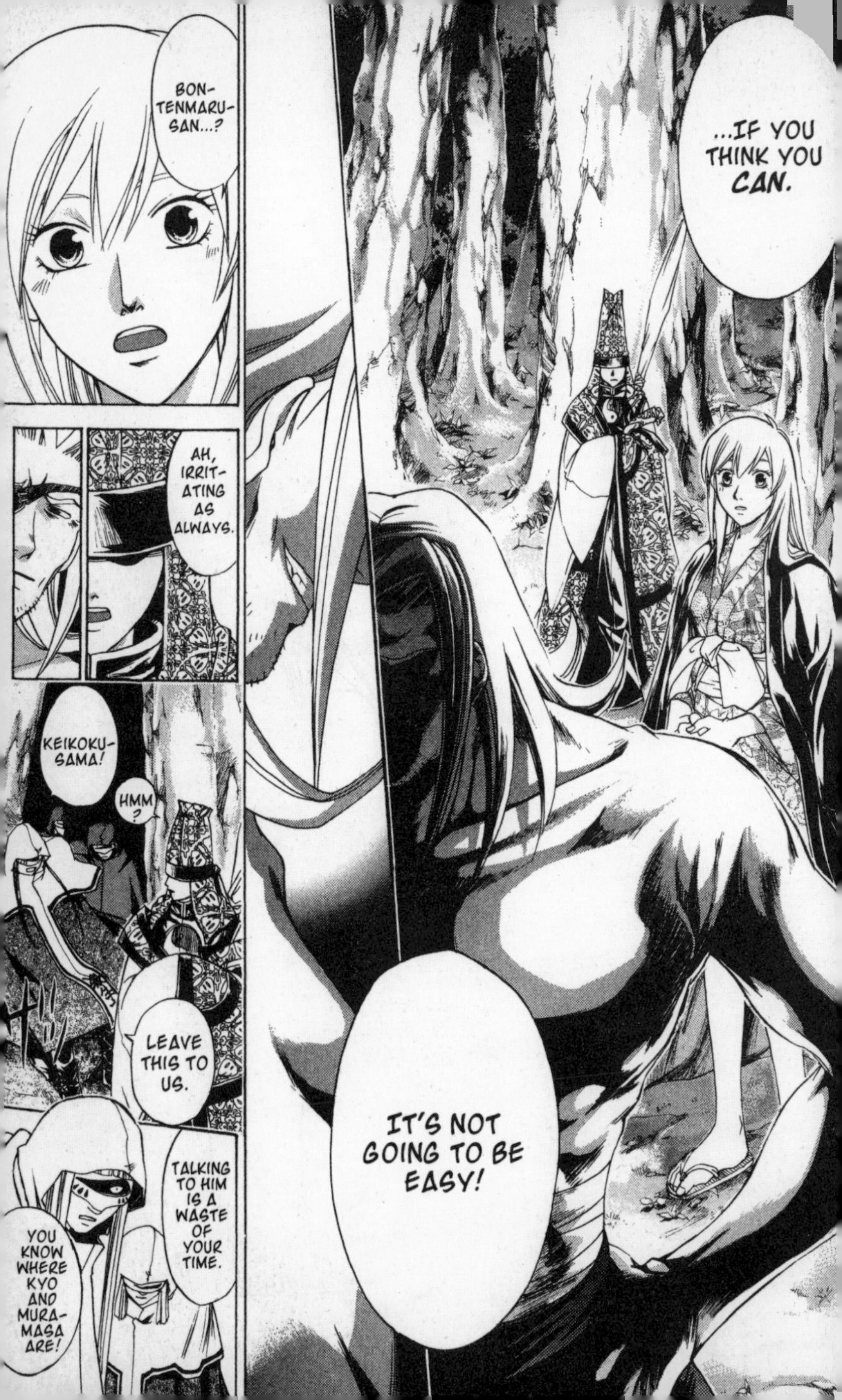
...IF YOU THINK YOU CAN.
IT'S NOT GOING TO BE EASY!
BON-TENMARU-SAN...?
AH, IRRIT-ATING AS ALWAYS.
KEIKOKU-SAMA!
HMM?
LEAVE THIS TO US.
TALKING TO HIM IS A WASTE OF YOUR TIME.
YOU KNOW WHERE KYO AND MURA-MASA ARE!

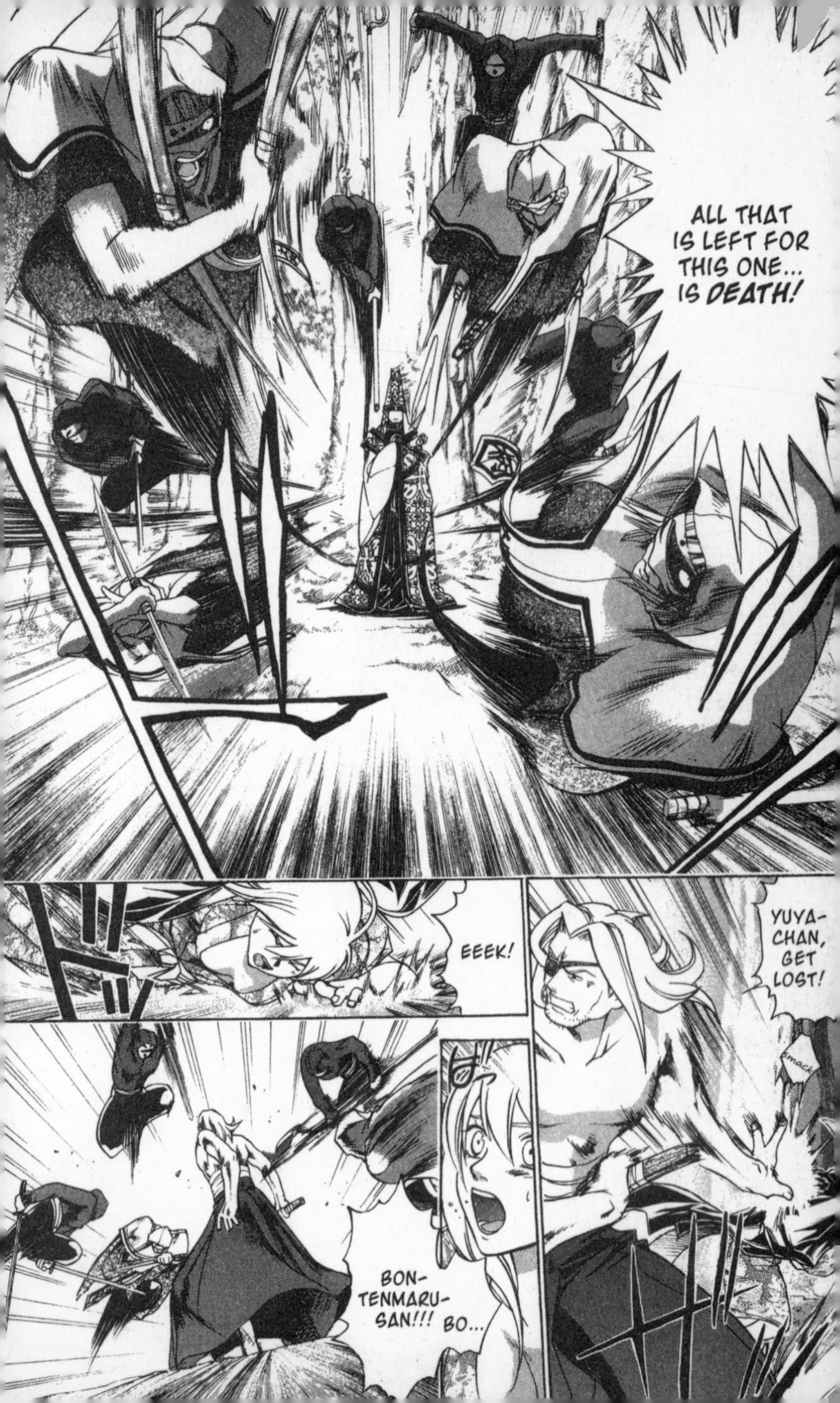
ALL THAT IS LEFT FOR THIS ONE... IS DEATH!
YUYA-CHAN, GET LOST!
smack
EEEK!
BO...
BON-TENMARU-SAN!!!

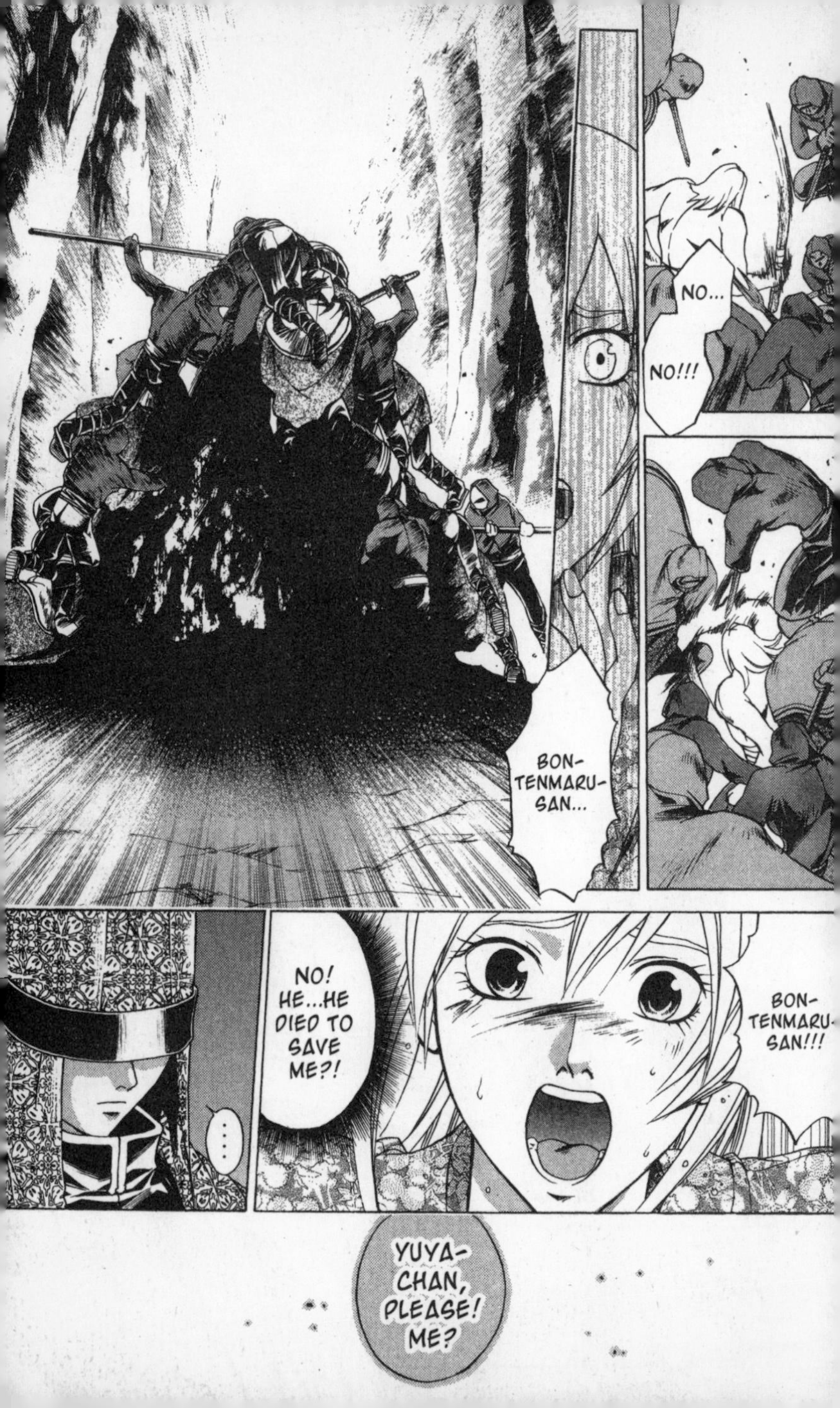
NO...
NO!!!
BON-TENMARU-SAN...
BON-TENMARU-SAN!!!
NO! HE...HE DIED TO SAVE ME?!
....
YUYA-CHAN, PLEASE! ME?

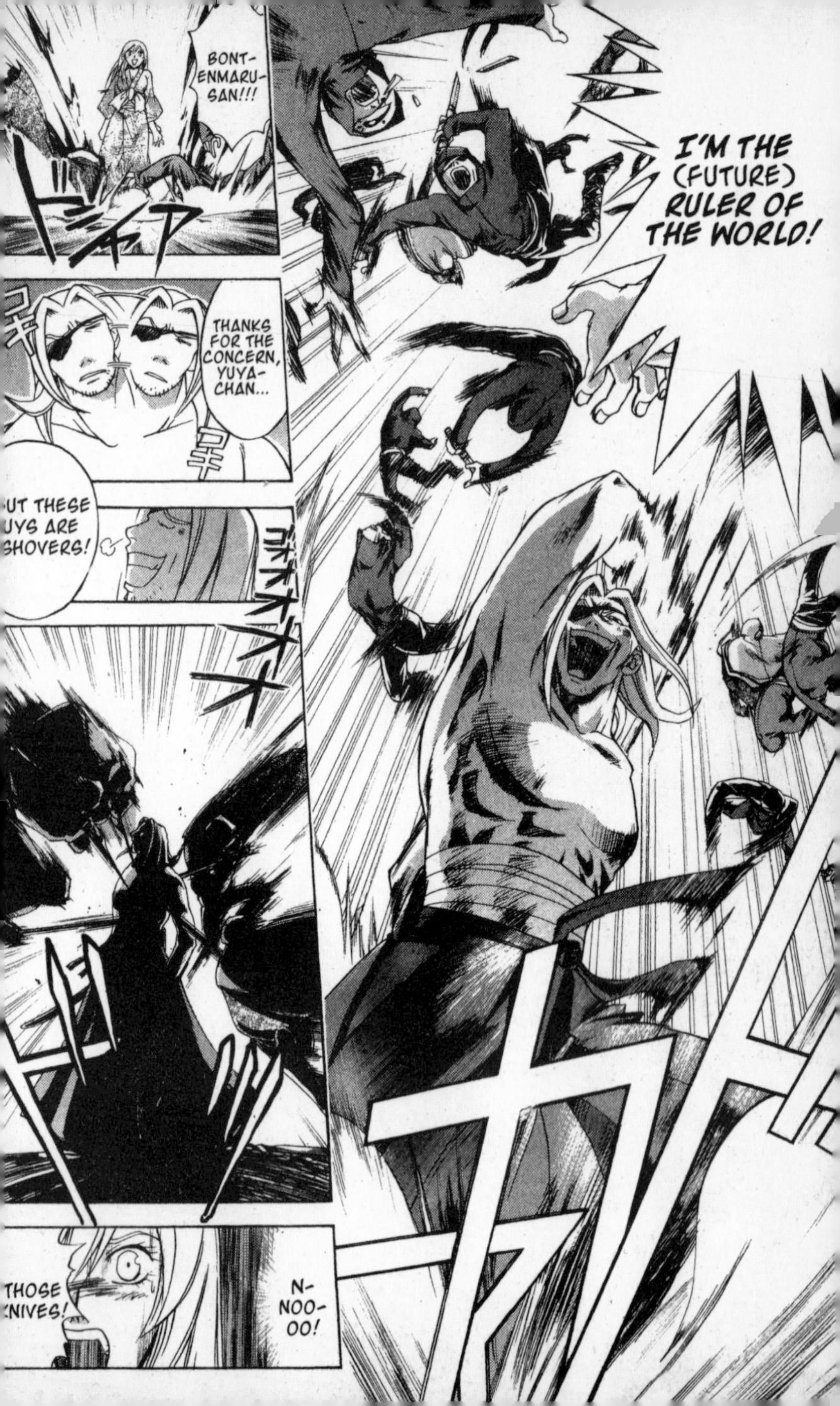
I'M THE (FUTURE) RULER OF THE WORLD!
BONT-ENMARU-SAN!!!
THANKS FOR THE CONCERN, YUYA-CHAN...
UT THESE
UYS ARE
SHOVERS!
N-NOOO-OO!
THOSE
NIVES!

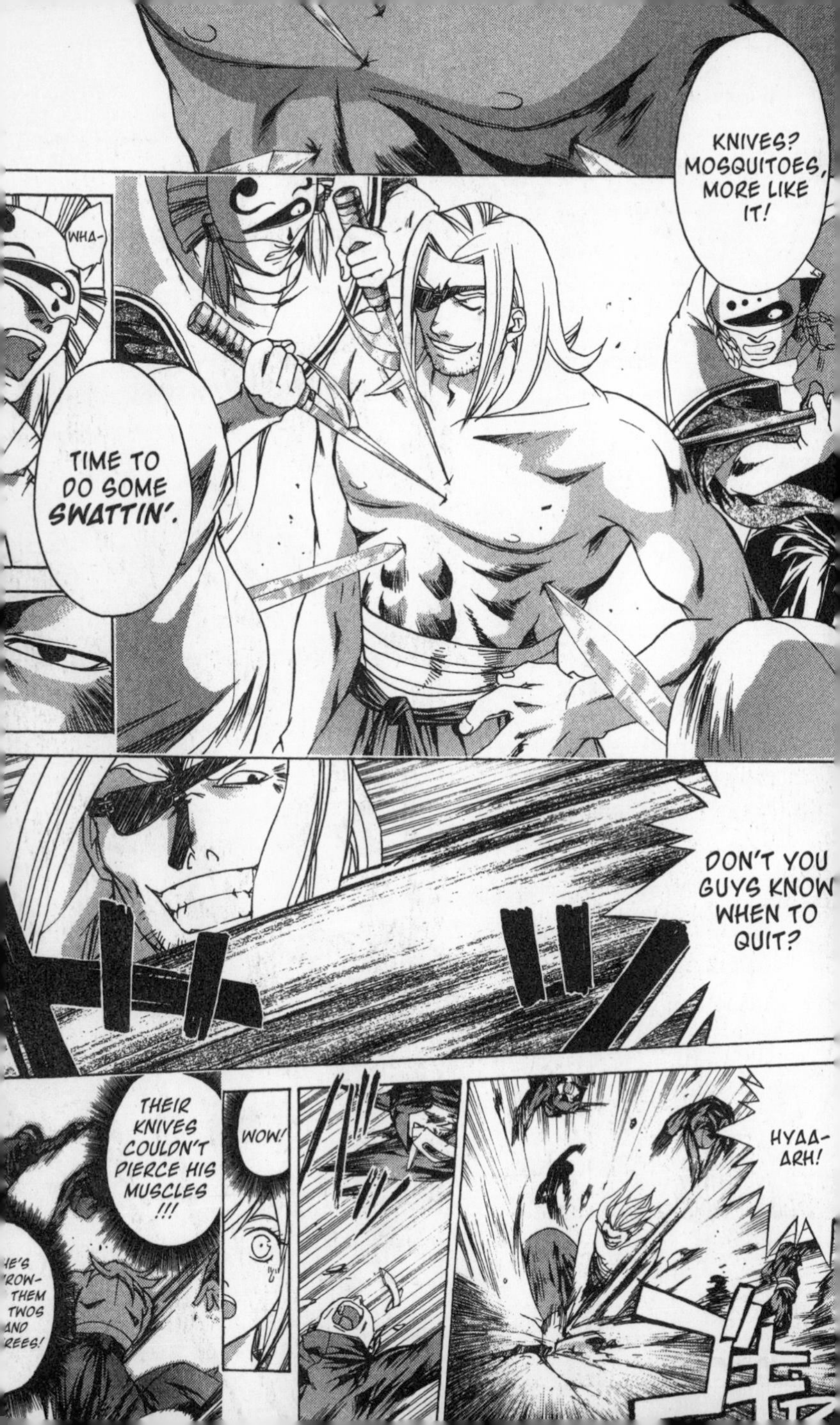
KNIVES? MOSQUITOES, MORE LIKE IT!
WHA-
TIME TO DO SOME SWATTIN'.
DON'T YOU GUYS KNOW WHEN TO QUIT?
HYAA-ARH!
WOW!
THEIR KNIVES COULDN'T PIERCE HIS MUSCLES!!!
HE'S ROW- THEM TWOS AND REES!

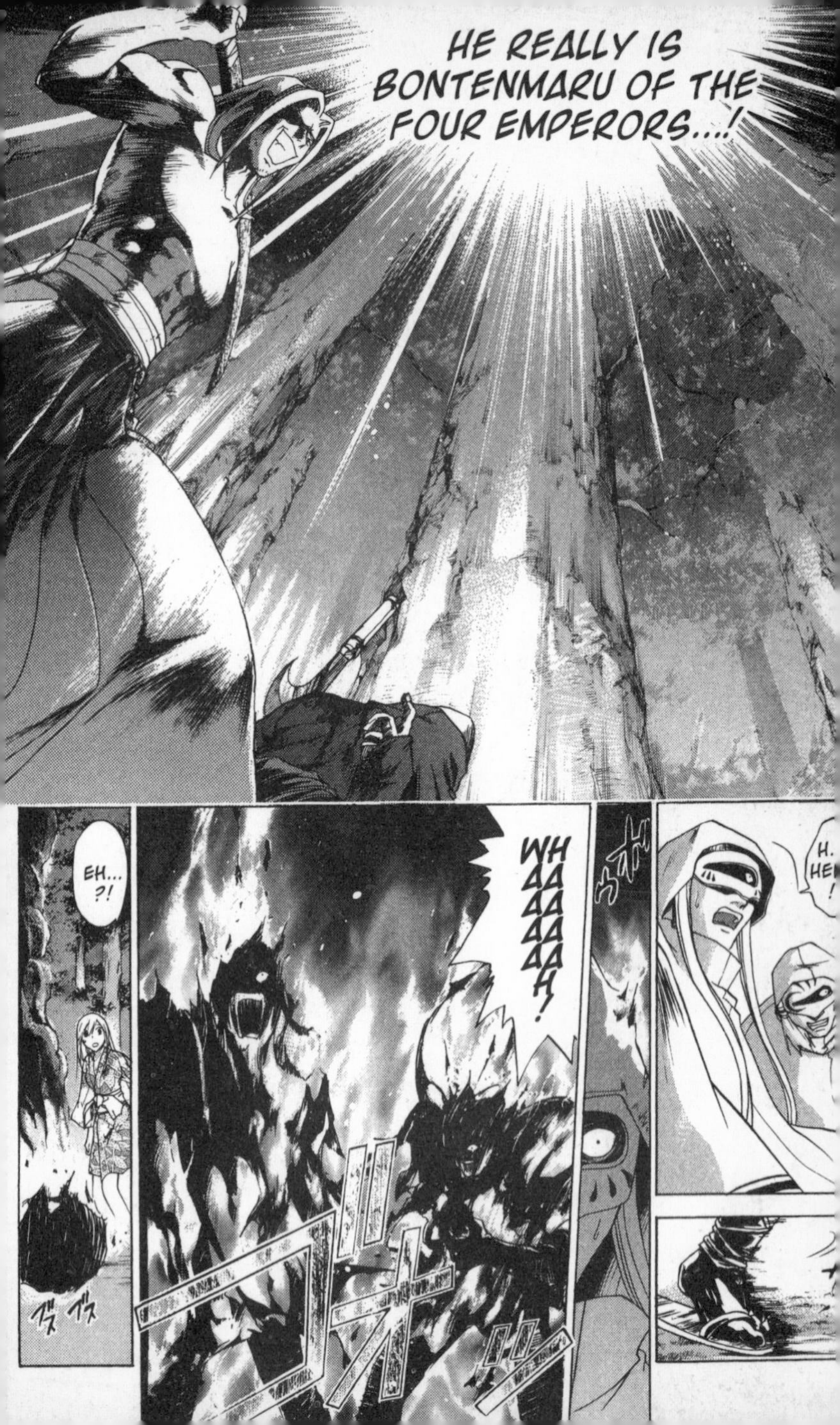
HE REALLY IS BONTENMARU OF THE FOUR EMPERORS...!
H. HE !
WHAAAAAAAH!
EH... ?!

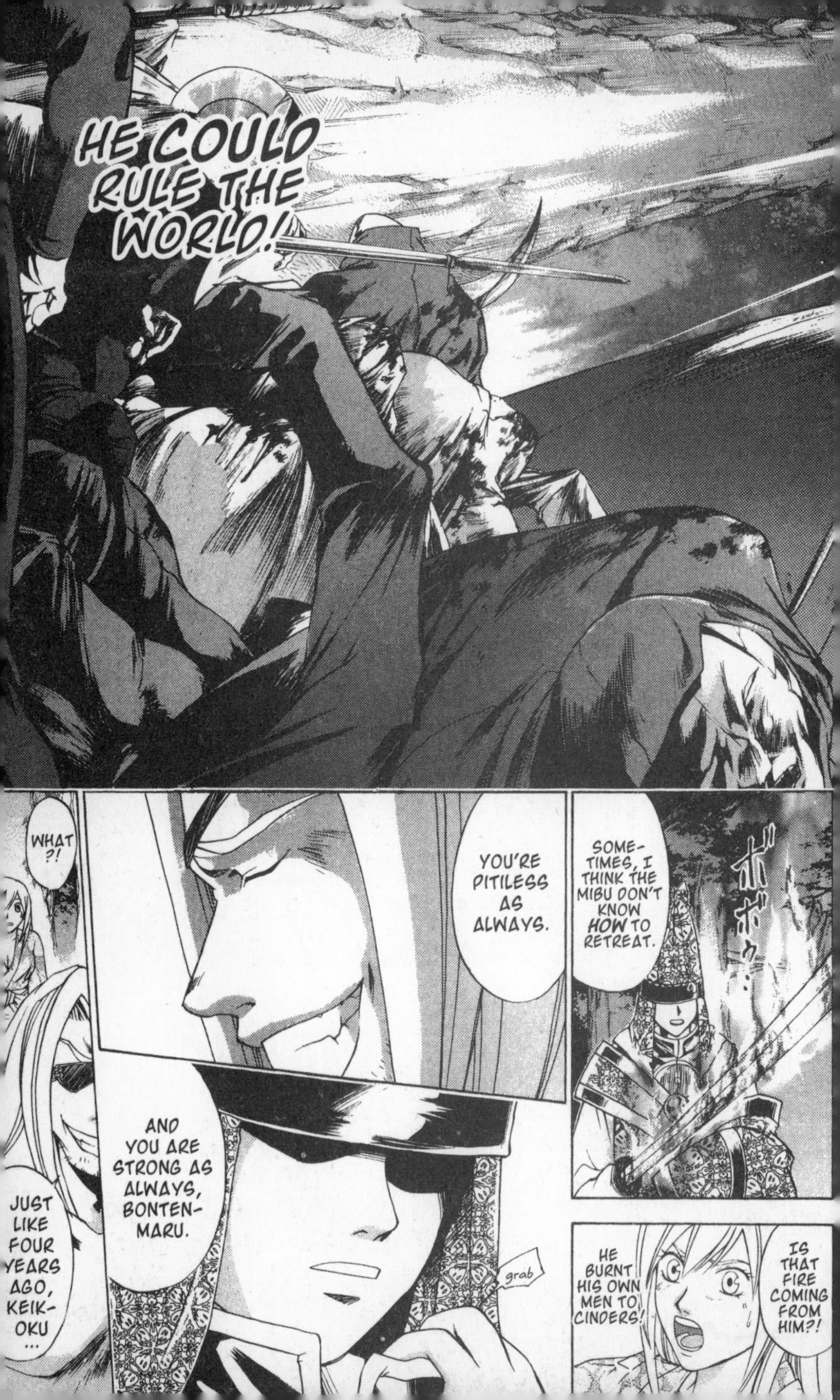
HE COULD RULE THE WORLD!
SOME-TIMES, I THINK THE MIBU DON'T KNOW HOW TO RETREAT.
YOU'RE PITILESS AS ALWAYS.
WHAT ?!
IS THAT FIRE COMING FROM HIM?!
HE BURNT HIS OWN MEN TO CINDERS!
AND YOU ARE STRONG AS ALWAYS, BONTEN-MARU.
grab
JUST LIKE FOUR YEARS AGO, KEIK-OKU ...

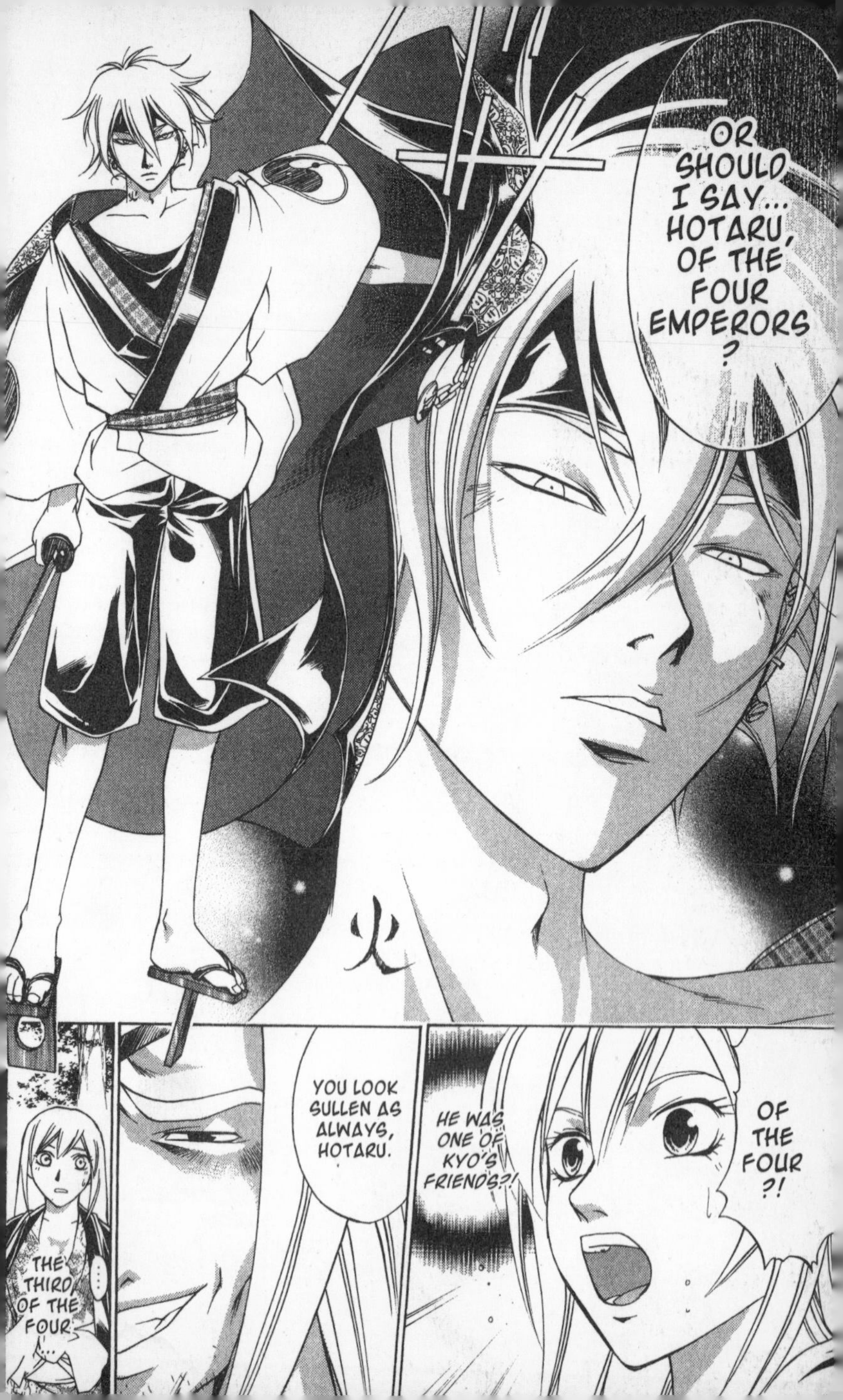
OR SHOULD I SAY... HOTARU, OF THE FOUR EMPERORS?
OF THE FOUR?!
HE WAS ONE OF KYO'S FRIENDS?!
YOU LOOK SULLEN AS ALWAYS, HOTARU.
...
THE THIRD OF THE FOUR...

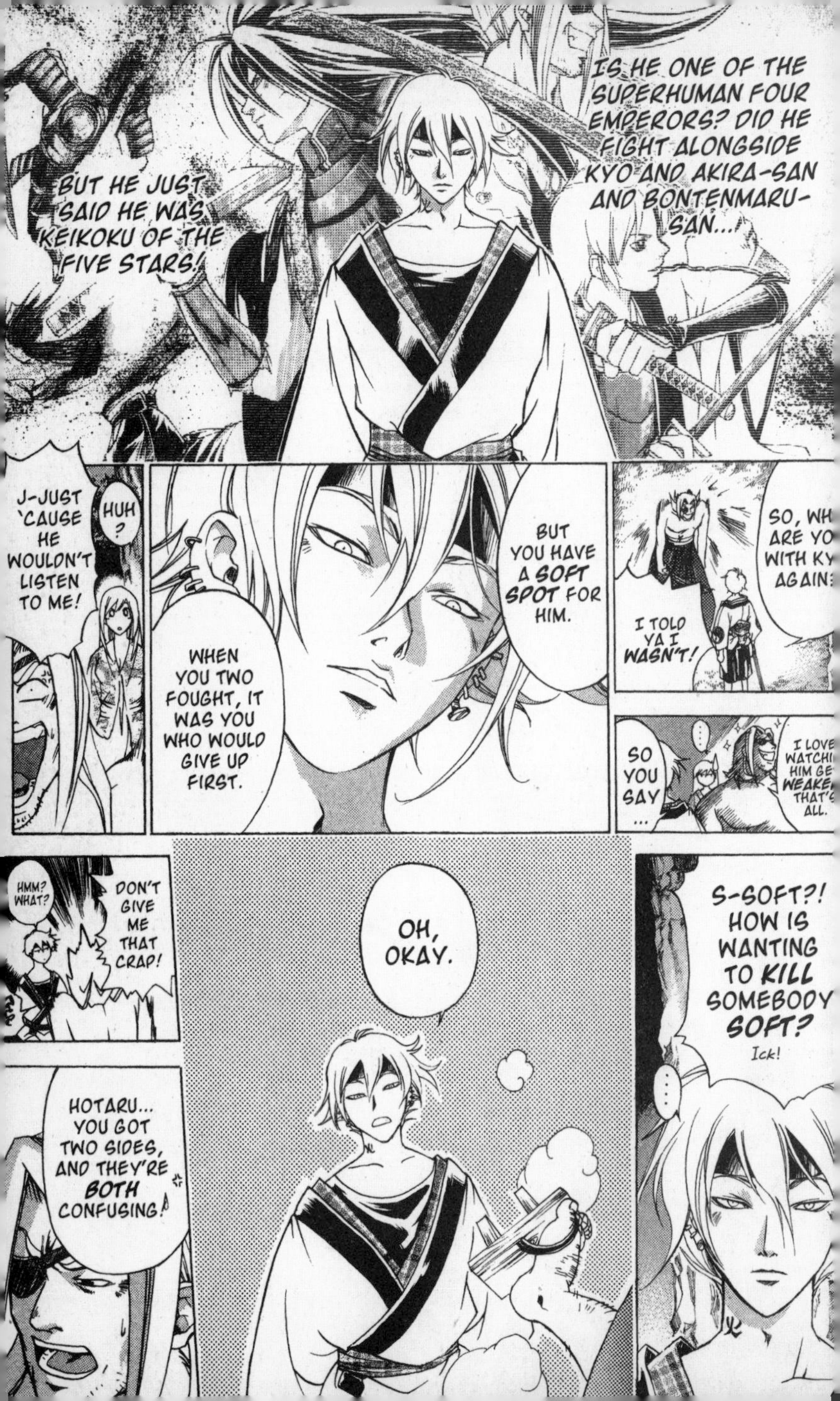

IS HE ONE OF THE SUPERHUMAN FOUR EMPERORS? DID HE FIGHT ALONGSIDE KYO AND AKIRA-SAN AND BONTENMARU-SAN...
BUT HE JUST SAID HE WAS KEIKOKU OF THE FIVE STARS!
SO, WH ARE YO WITH KY AGAIN
I TOLD YA I WASN'T!
I LOVE WATCHI HIM GE WEAKE THAT'S ALL.
...
SO YOU SAY ...
BUT YOU HAVE A SOFT SPOT FOR HIM.
WHEN YOU TWO FOUGHT, IT WAS YOU WHO WOULD GIVE UP FIRST.
HUH?
J-JUST 'CAUSE HE WOULDN'T LISTEN TO ME!
S-SOFT?! HOW IS WANTING TO KILL SOMEBODY SOFT?
Ick!
....
OH, OKAY.
DON'T GIVE ME THAT CRAP!
HMM? WHAT?
HOTARU... YOU GOT TWO SIDES, AND THEY'RE BOTH CONFUSING!

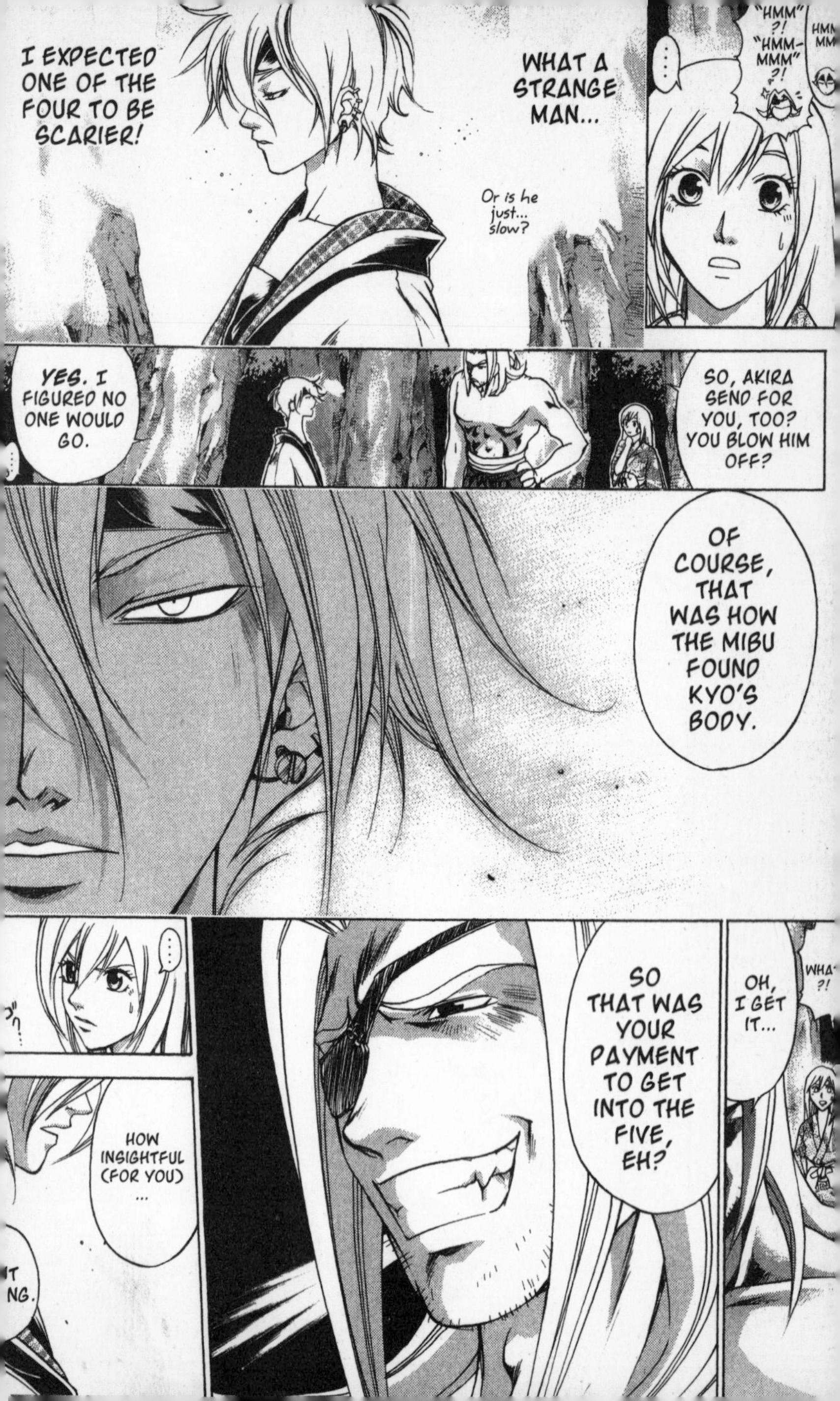
"HMM" ?! "HMM-MMM" ?!
...
WHAT A STRANGE MAN...
Or is he just... slow?
I EXPECTED ONE OF THE FOUR TO BE SCARIER!
SO, AKIRA SEND FOR YOU, TOO? YOU BLOW HIM OFF?
YES. I FIGURED NO ONE WOULD GO.
OF COURSE, THAT WAS HOW THE MIBU FOUND KYO'S BODY.
WHA- ?!
OH, I GET IT...
SO THAT WAS YOUR PAYMENT TO GET INTO THE FIVE, EH?
...
HOW INSIGHTFUL (FOR YOU) ...

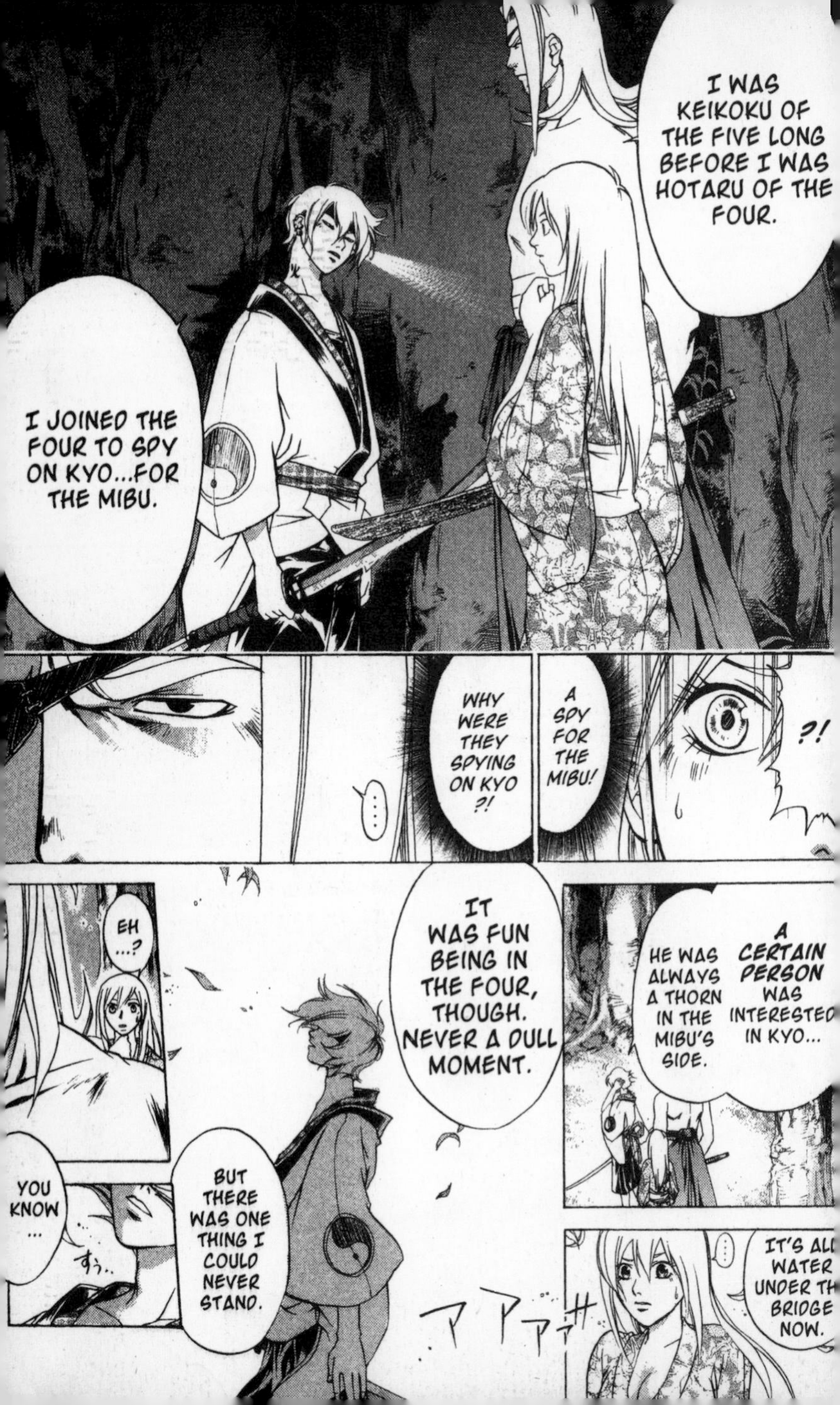
I WAS KEIKOKU OF THE FIVE LONG BEFORE I WAS HOTARU OF THE FOUR.
I JOINED THE FOUR TO SPY ON KYO...FOR THE MIBU.
?!
A SPY FOR THE MIBU!
WHY WERE THEY SPYING ON KYO ?!
......
A CERTAIN PERSON WAS INTERESTED IN KYO...
HE WAS ALWAYS A THORN IN THE MIBU'S SIDE.
IT'S AL WATER UNDER TH BRIDGE NOW.
...
IT WAS FUN BEING IN THE FOUR, THOUGH. NEVER A DULL MOMENT.
アアァ
BUT THERE WAS ONE THING I COULD NEVER STAND.
EH ...?
YOU KNOW ...
...
すぅ..

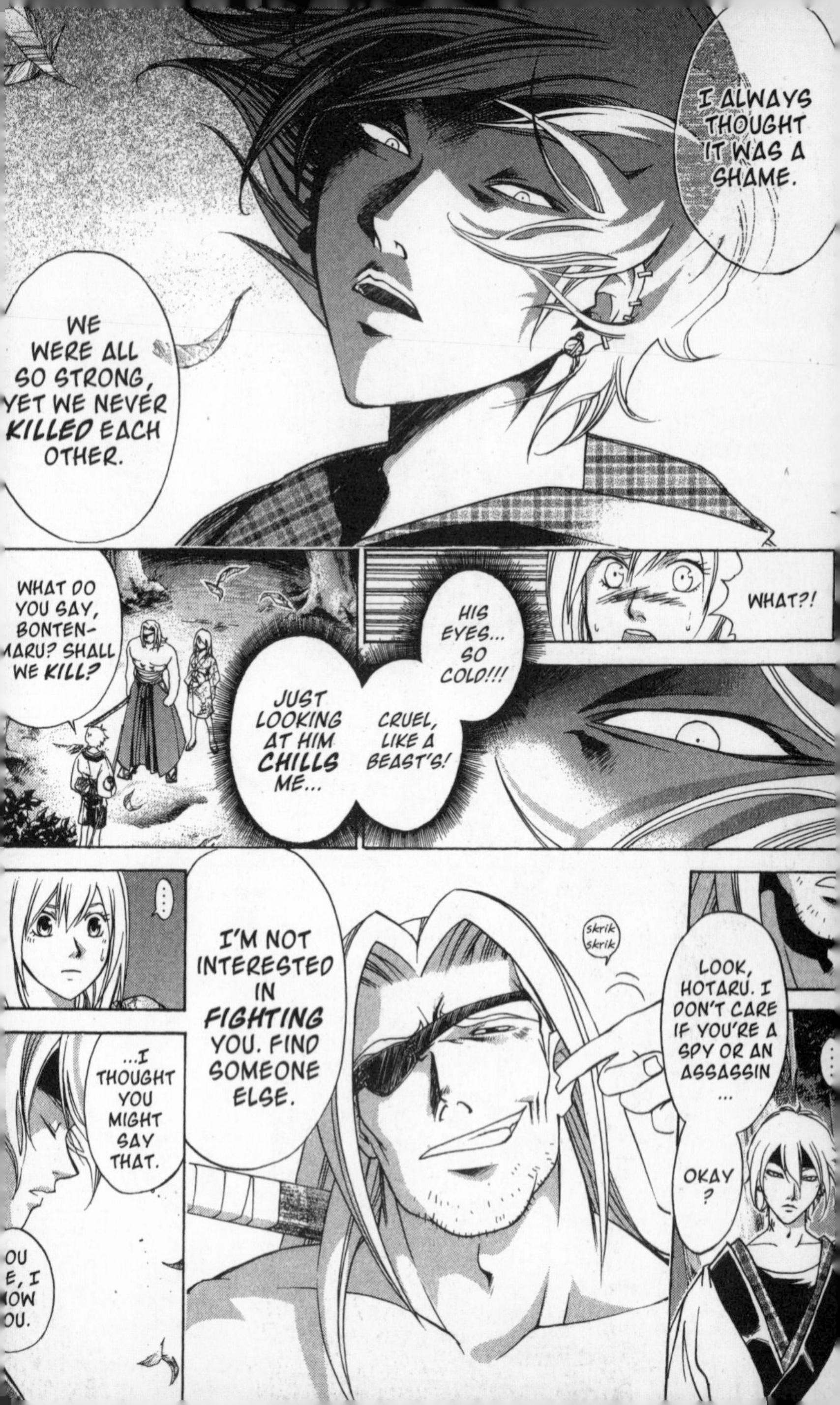
I ALWAYS THOUGHT IT WAS A SHAME.
WE WERE ALL SO STRONG, YET WE NEVER **KILLED** EACH OTHER.
WHAT?!
HIS EYES... SO COLD!!!
CRUEL, LIKE A BEAST'S!
JUST LOOKING AT HIM **CHILLS** ME...
WHAT DO YOU SAY, BONTEN-MARU? SHALL WE **KILL**?
LOOK, HOTARU. I DON'T CARE IF YOU'RE A SPY OR AN ASSASSIN ...
OKAY ?
skrik skrik
I'M NOT INTERESTED IN **FIGHTING** YOU. FIND SOMEONE ELSE.
...
...I THOUGHT YOU MIGHT SAY THAT.
OU E, I OW OU.

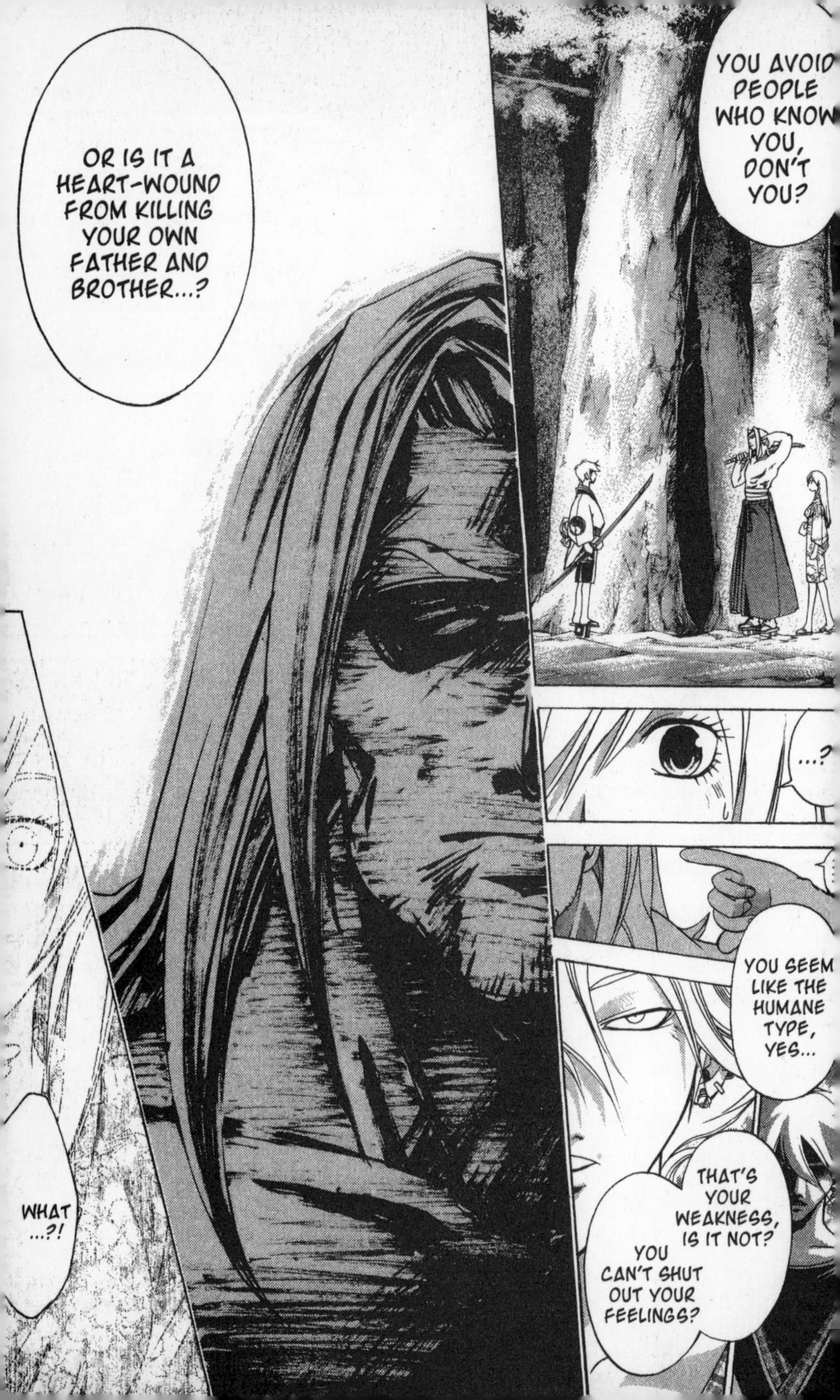
YOU AVOID PEOPLE WHO KNOW YOU, DON'T YOU?
...?
YOU SEEM LIKE THE HUMANE TYPE, YES...
THAT'S YOUR WEAKNESS, IS IT NOT?
YOU CAN'T SHUT OUT YOUR FEELINGS?
OR IS IT A HEART-WOUND FROM KILLING YOUR OWN FATHER AND BROTHER...?
WHAT ...?!

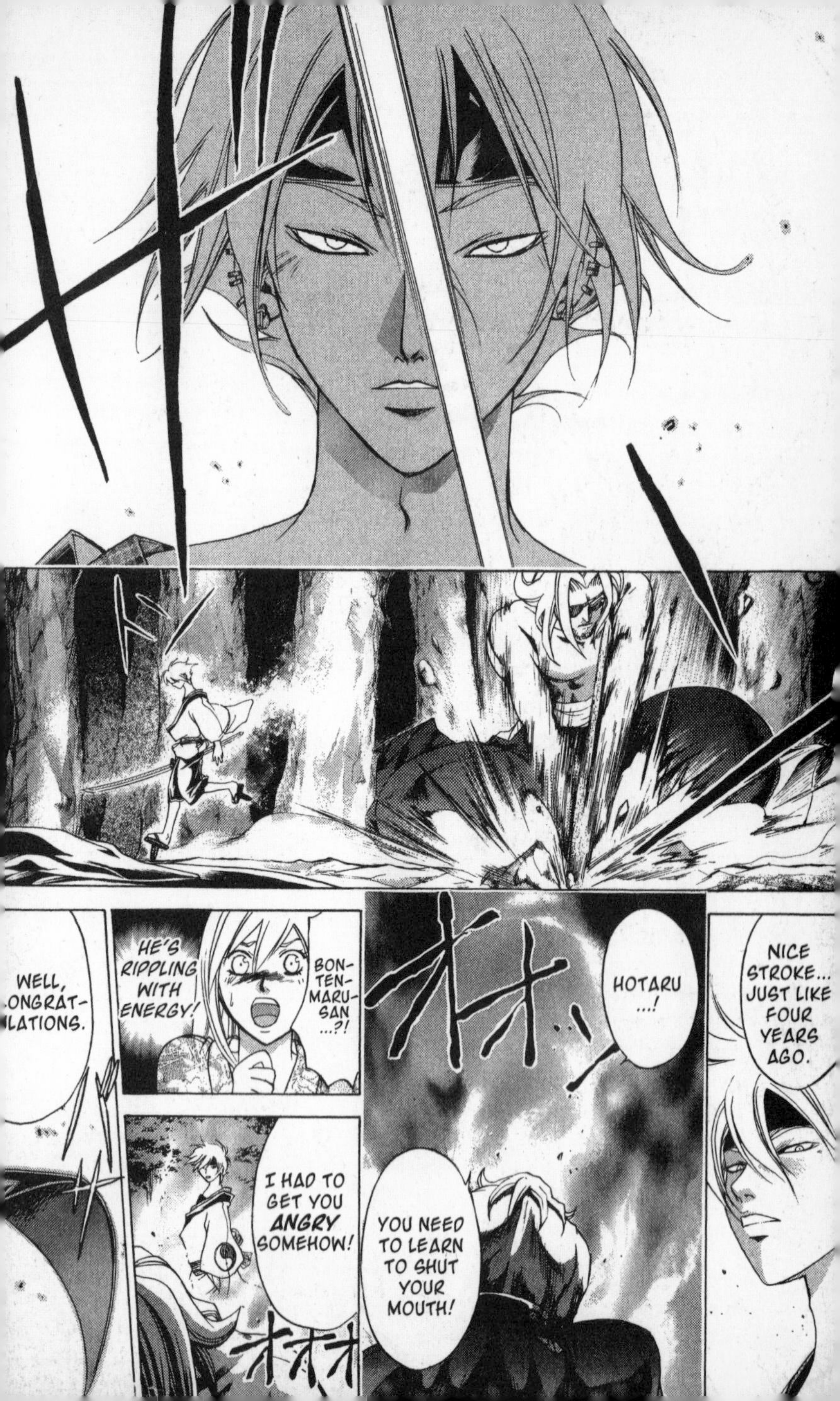
NICE STROKE... JUST LIKE FOUR YEARS AGO.
HOTARU ...!
YOU NEED TO LEARN TO SHUT YOUR MOUTH!
BON-TEN-MARU-SAN ...?!
HE'S RIPPLING WITH ENERGY!
I HAD TO GET YOU ANGRY SOMEHOW!
WELL, ONGRAT-LATIONS.

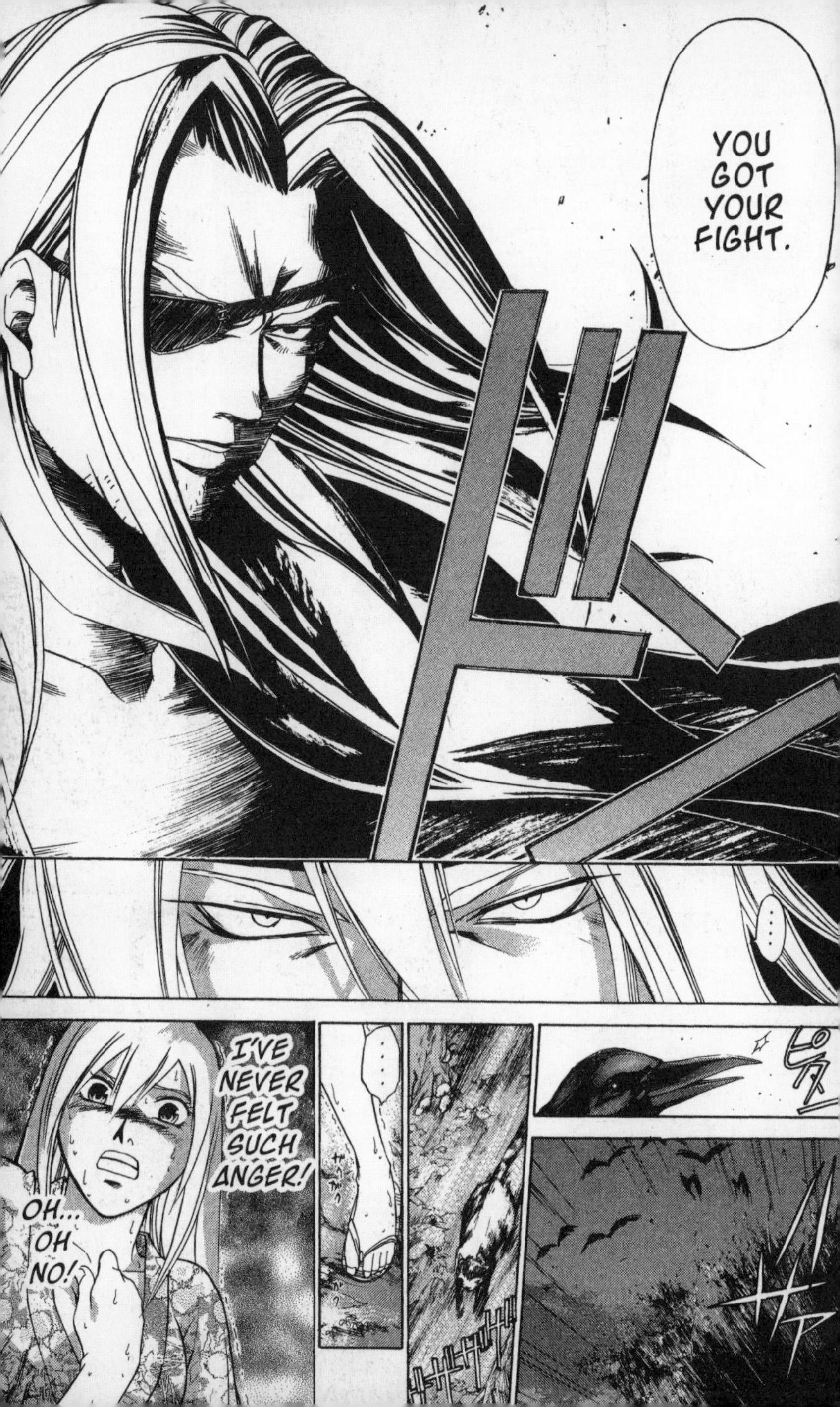

YOU GOT YOUR FIGHT.
...
...
I'VE NEVER FELT SUCH ANGER!
OH... OH NO!

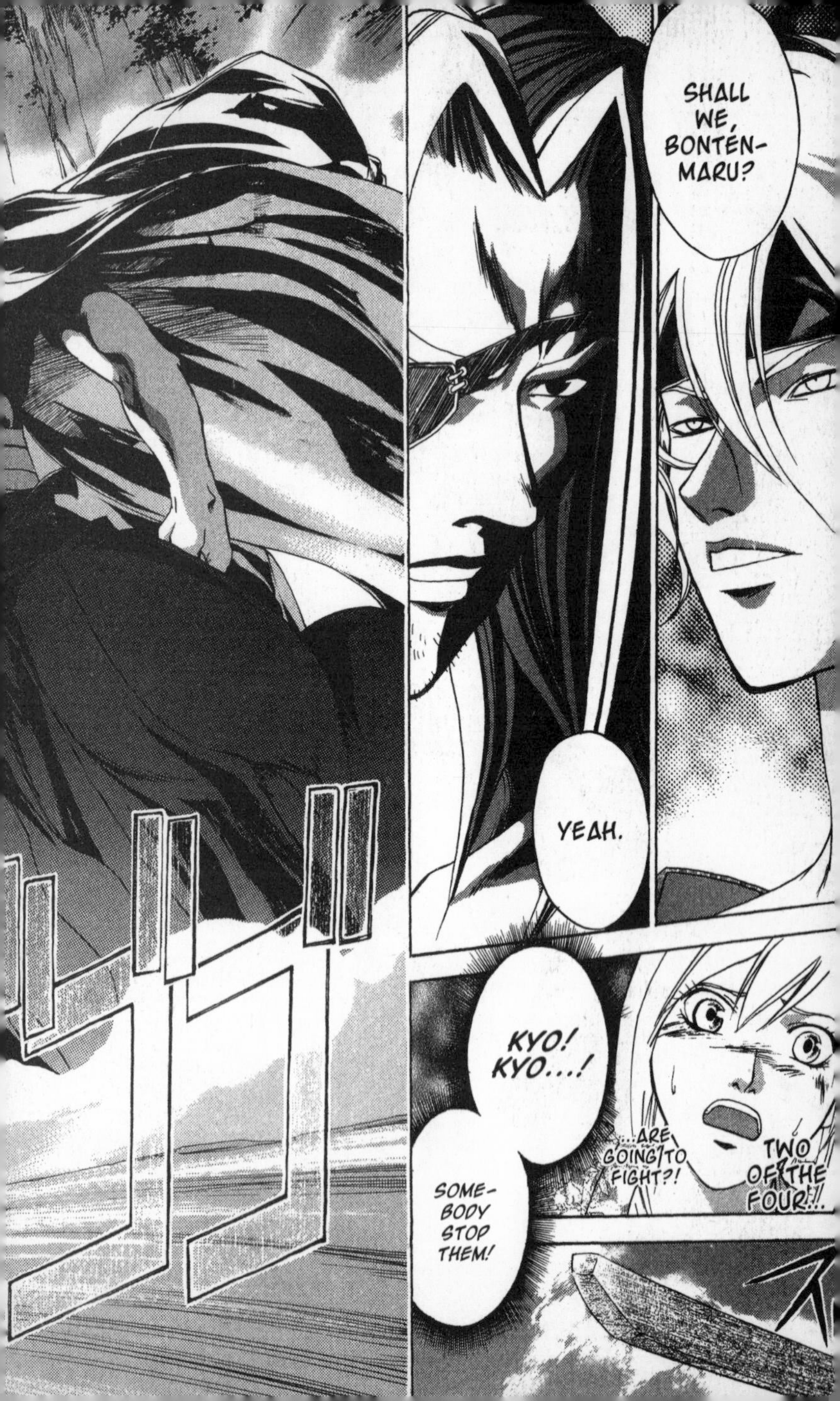
SHALL WE, BONTEN-MARU?
YEAH.
TWO OF THE FOUR...!!
...ARE GOING TO FIGHT?!
KYO! KYO...!
SOME-BODY STOP THEM!

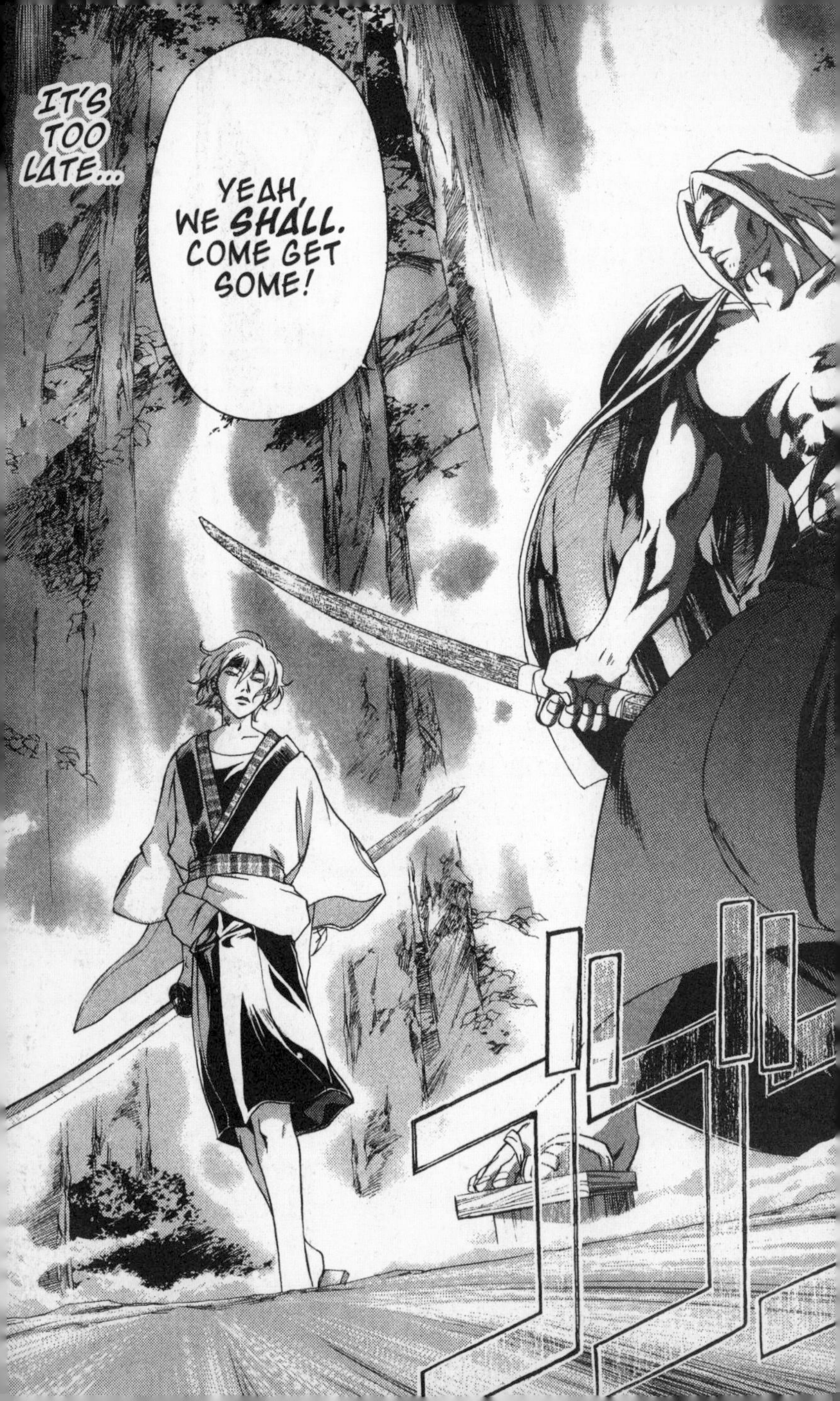
YEAH, WE SHALL. COME GET SOME!
IT'S TOO LATE...

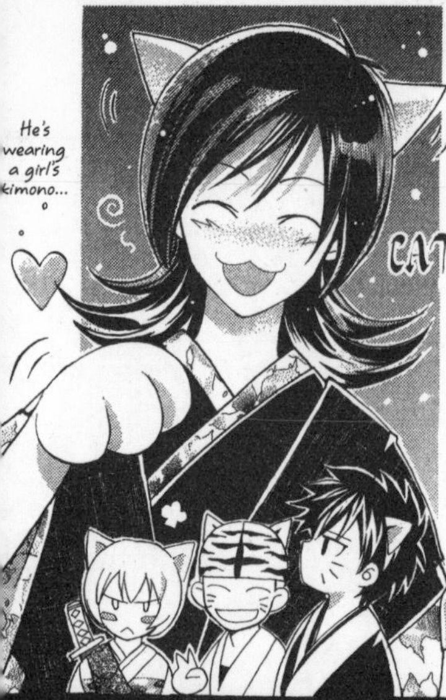
He's wearing a girl's kimono...
CAT

SIX MON (MON=OLD JAPANESE COIN!)

Recently. (Well, always)

THINGS I'VE FOUND ODD.

1. I'M SURROUNDED BY DOG-PEOPLE.
2. KAMIJYO-SENSEI NEVER SEEMS TO EAT.
3. WHEN DOES KAMIJYO-SENSEI EAT?
4. HE DOES EAT, RIGHT?
5. ACTUALLY, YOU LOOK A LITTLE PALE...(PURPLE?!)
6. TAKE BETTER CARE OF YOURSELF! (TO CHANGE THE SUBJECT.)
7. WHAT'S UNDER SHINDARA'S CLOAK? THIS HAS BEEN BOTHERING ME FOR OVER HALF A YEAR.
8. ME? SUB-CHIEF? I'M BARELY AN ASSISTANT! NOT TO GIVE ANYTHING AWAY, BUT THIS ILLUSTRATION WAS A COOPERATIVE EFFORT BY ME AND KAMIJYO-SENSEI!

Enjoy!

KAMIJYO: THANKS FOR ALL THE HARD WORK, GUYS! NOW, A QUIZ: WHAT PART OF THE ILLUSTRATION HE
[ANSWER: THE PRINTING TONE! ...COOPERATION?!]

HAZUKI ASAMI

STAFF

TAKAYA NAGAO (THE CHIEF)
HAZUKI ASAMI (THE SUB-CHIEF)
KEN'ICHI SUETAKE
SOMA AKATSUKI
MR. PUMPKIN
SHIBA TATEOKA
RISA (FROM CHAPTER 108...IN THE NEXT VOLUME!)

RECENTLY, MR. SUETAKE LEFT OUR TEAM. HE WAS WITH US THROUGH THICK AND THIN FROM THE VERY FIRST EPISODE. IT WAS SUETAKE WHO MADE KYO'S KATANA LOOK LIKE IT COULD CUT! AND THAT'S THE LIFE OF ANY SAMURAI MANGA. THANKS FOR EVERYTHING, AND FOLLOW YOUR DREAMS!

MR. PUMPKIN (BY ANOTHER NAME!) WILL BE PUBLISHING HIS OWN WORK IN THE JANUARY 2002 EDITION OF "MAGAZINE FRESH"! CHECK IT OUT!

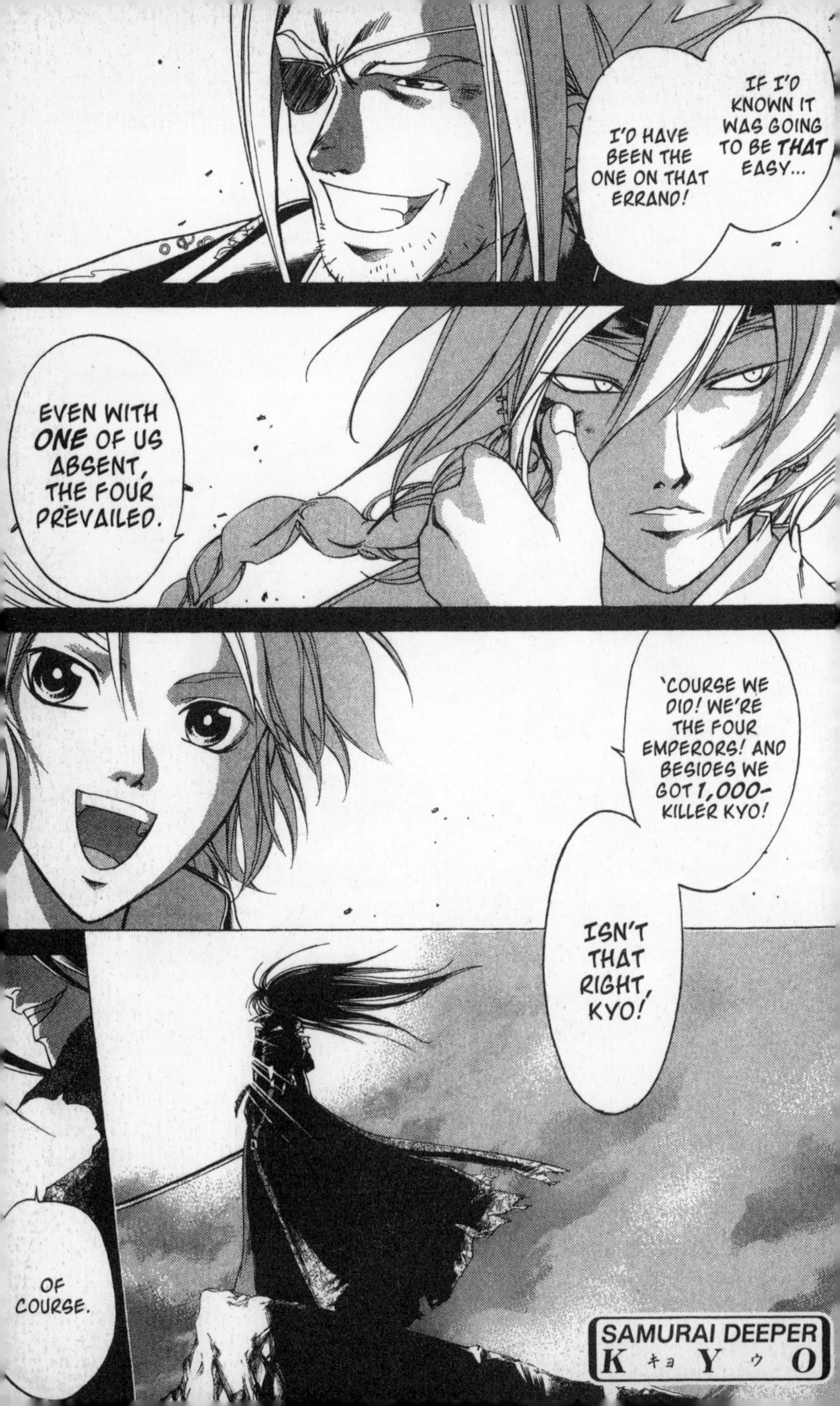
IF I'D KNOWN IT WAS GOING TO BE THAT EASY...
I'D HAVE BEEN THE ONE ON THAT ERRAND!
EVEN WITH ONE OF US ABSENT, THE FOUR PREVAILED.
'COURSE WE DID! WE'RE THE FOUR EMPERORS! AND BESIDES WE GOT 1,000-KILLER KYO!
ISN'T THAT RIGHT, KYO!
OF COURSE.
SAMURAI DEEPER KYO

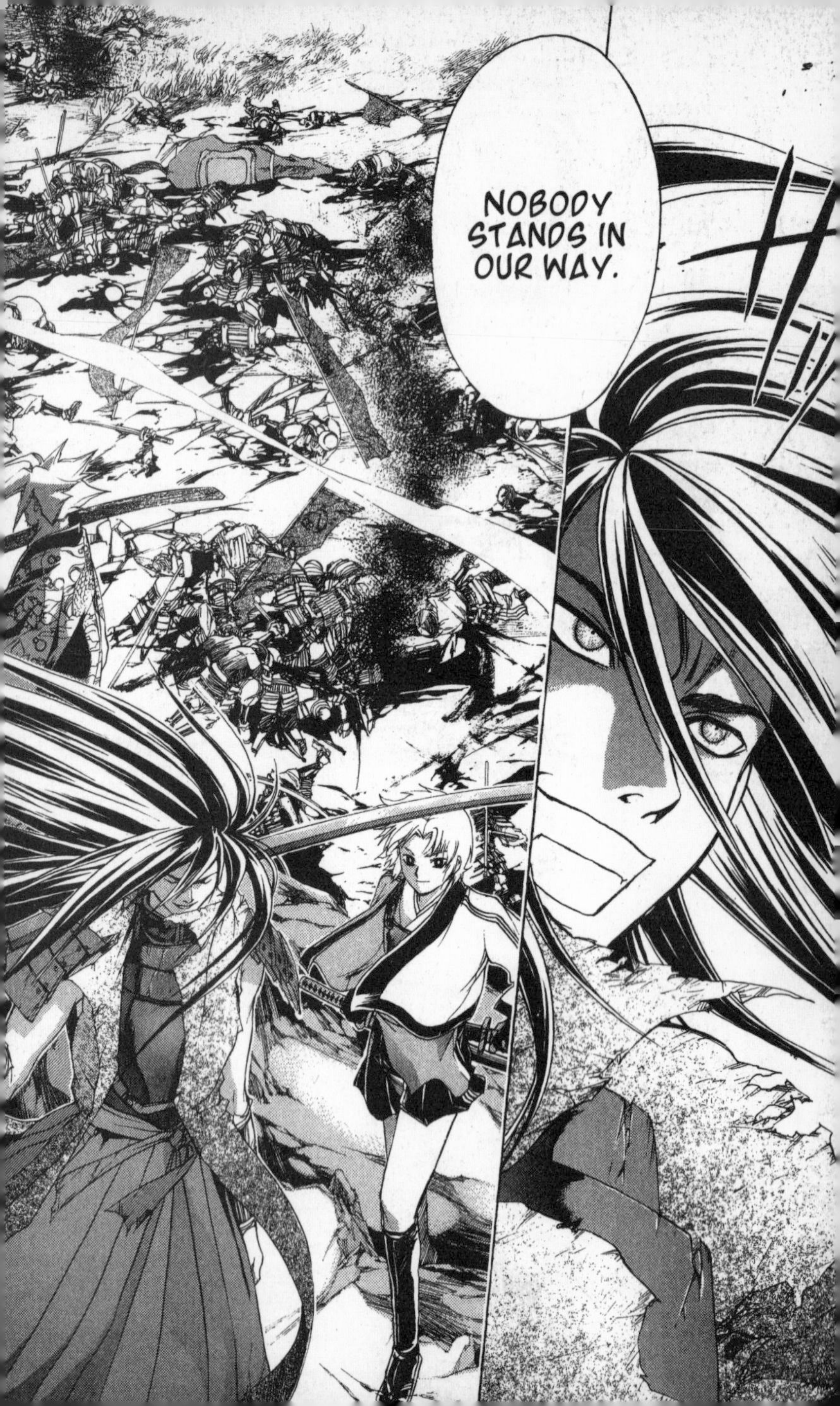
NOBODY STANDS IN OUR WAY.

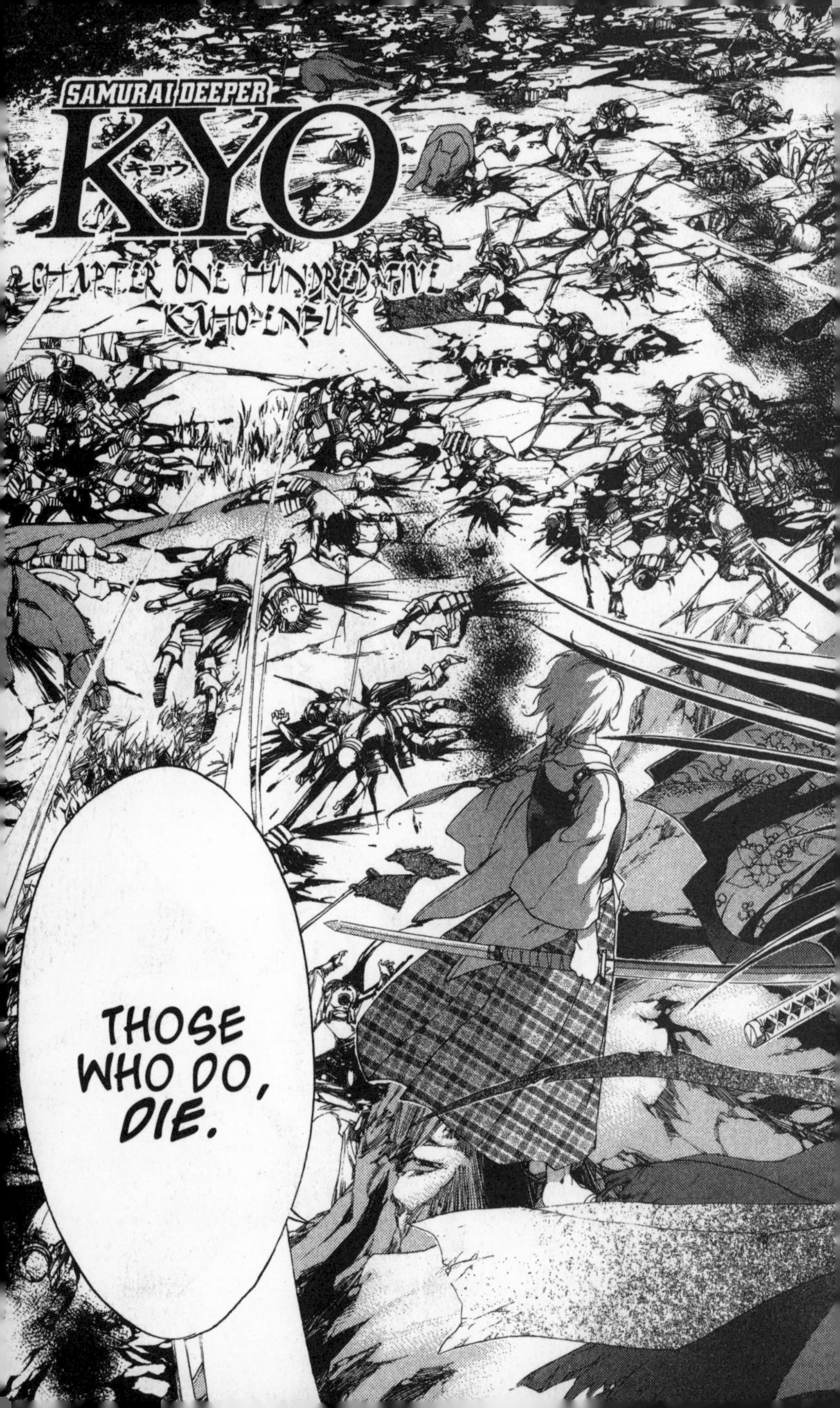
SAMURAI DEEPER
KYO
キョウ
CHAPTER ONE HUNDRED FIVE
KAHO-ENBU
THOSE WHO DO, DIE.

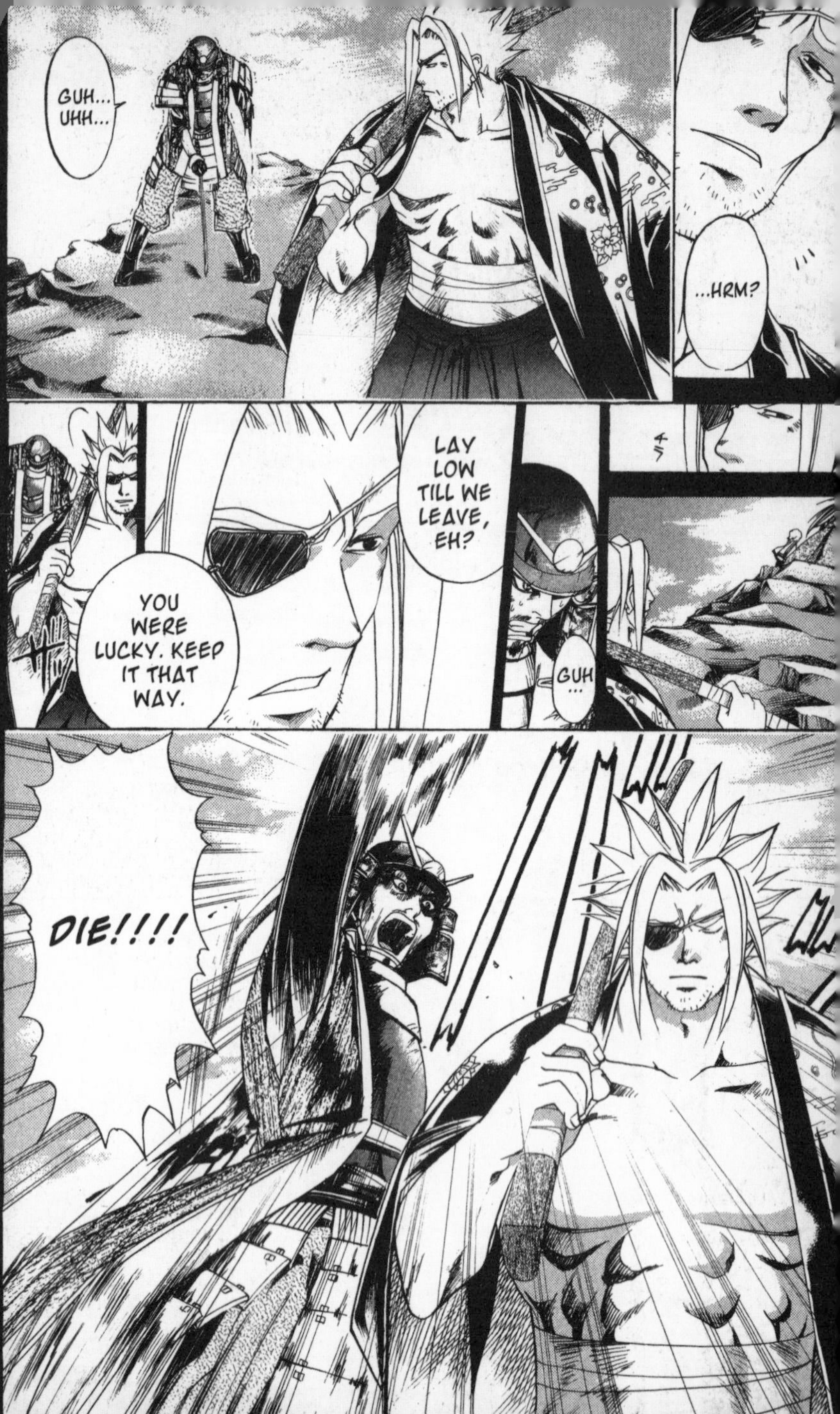
...HRM?
GUH... UHH...
GUH ...
LAY LOW TILL WE LEAVE, EH?
YOU WERE LUCKY. KEEP IT THAT WAY.
DIE!!!!

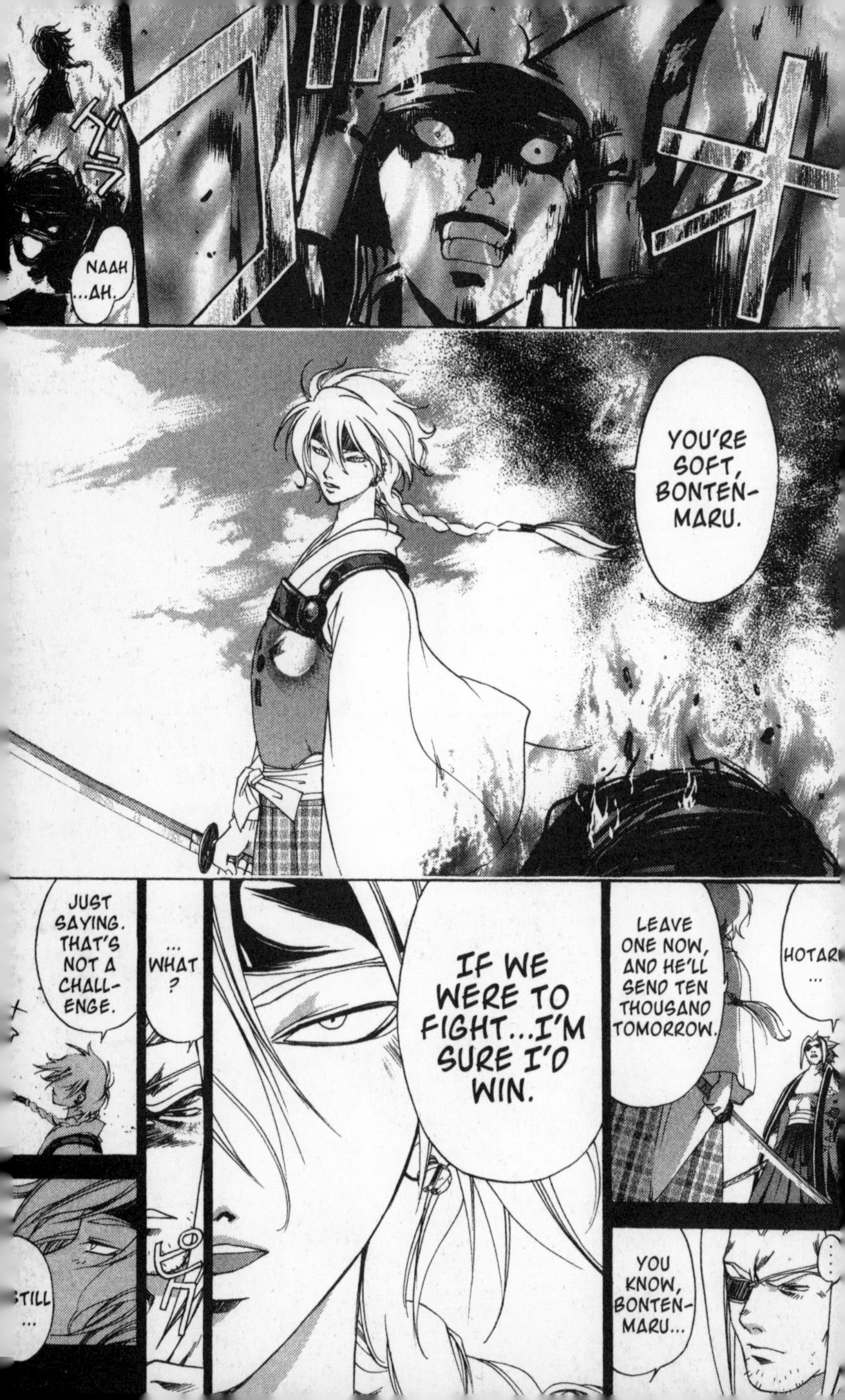
NAAH ...AH.
YOU'RE SOFT, BONTEN-MARU.
HOTAR ...
LEAVE ONE NOW, AND HE'LL SEND TEN THOUSAND TOMORROW.
...
YOU KNOW, BONTEN-MARU...
IF WE WERE TO FIGHT...I'M SURE I'D WIN.
... WHAT ?
JUST SAYING. THAT'S NOT A CHALLENGE.
STILL ...

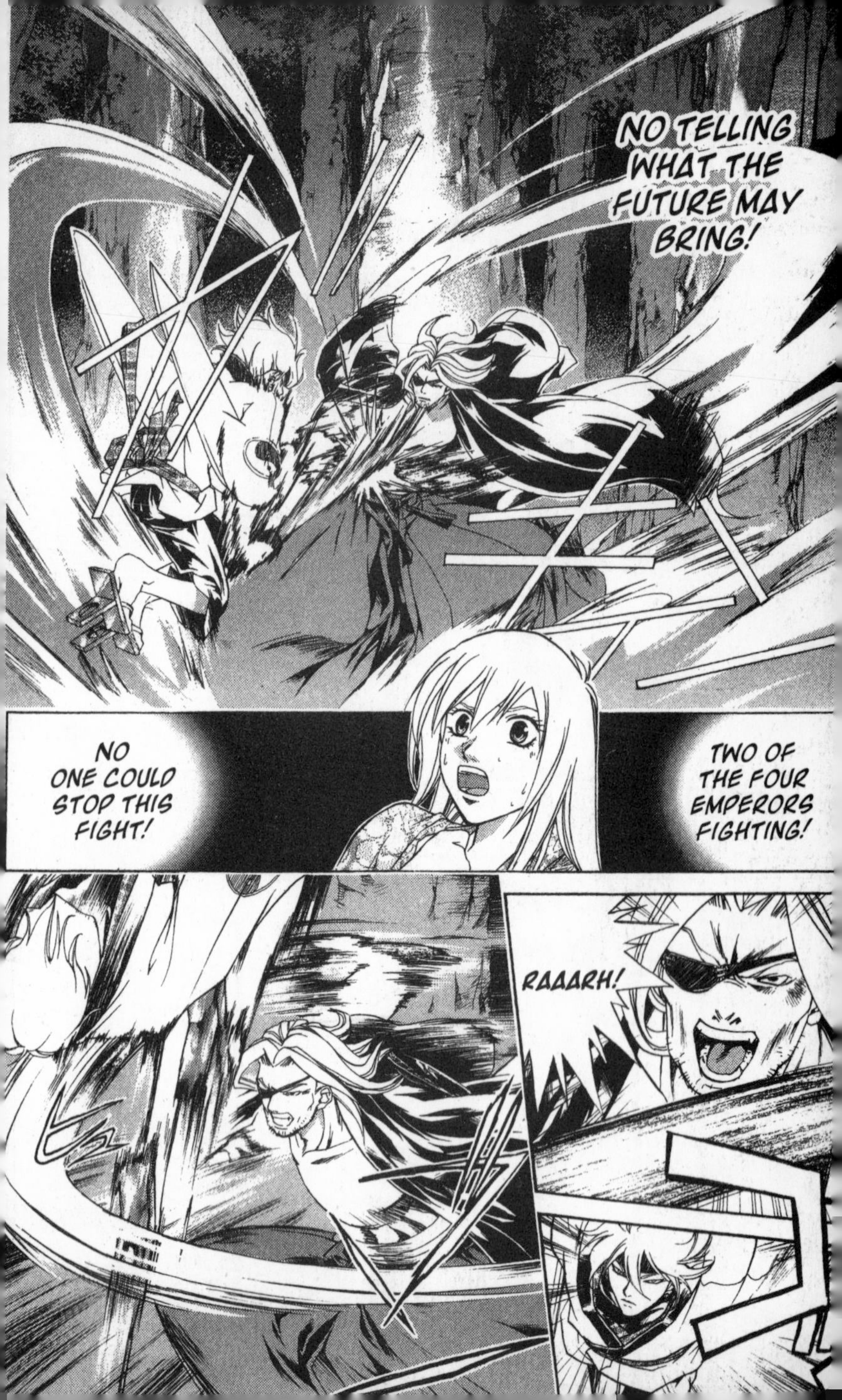
NO TELLING WHAT THE FUTURE MAY BRING!
TWO OF THE FOUR EMPERORS FIGHTING!
NO ONE COULD STOP THIS FIGHT!
RAAARH!

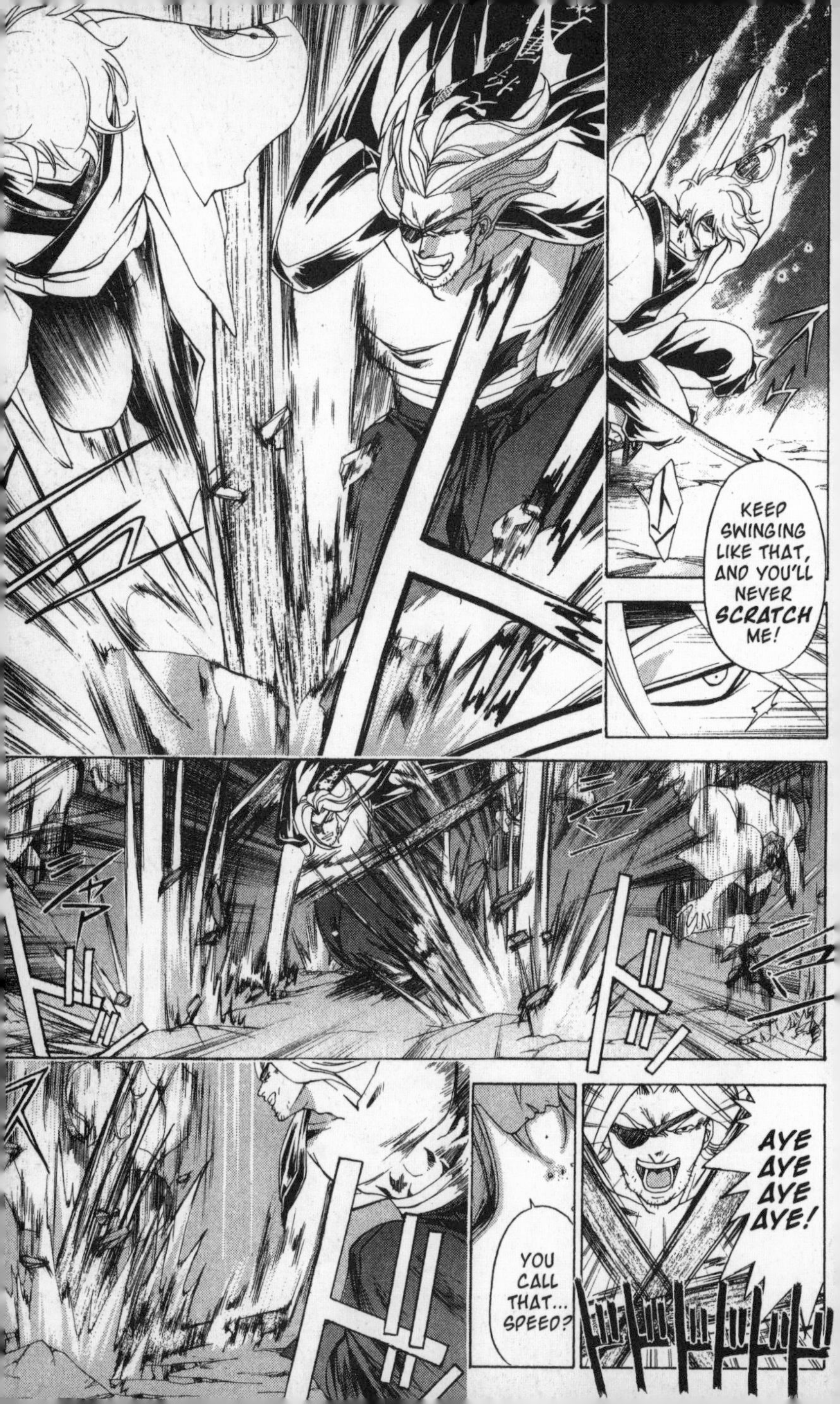

KEEP SWINGING LIKE THAT, AND YOU'LL NEVER SCRATCH ME!
AYE AYE AYE AYE!
YOU CALL THAT... SPEED?

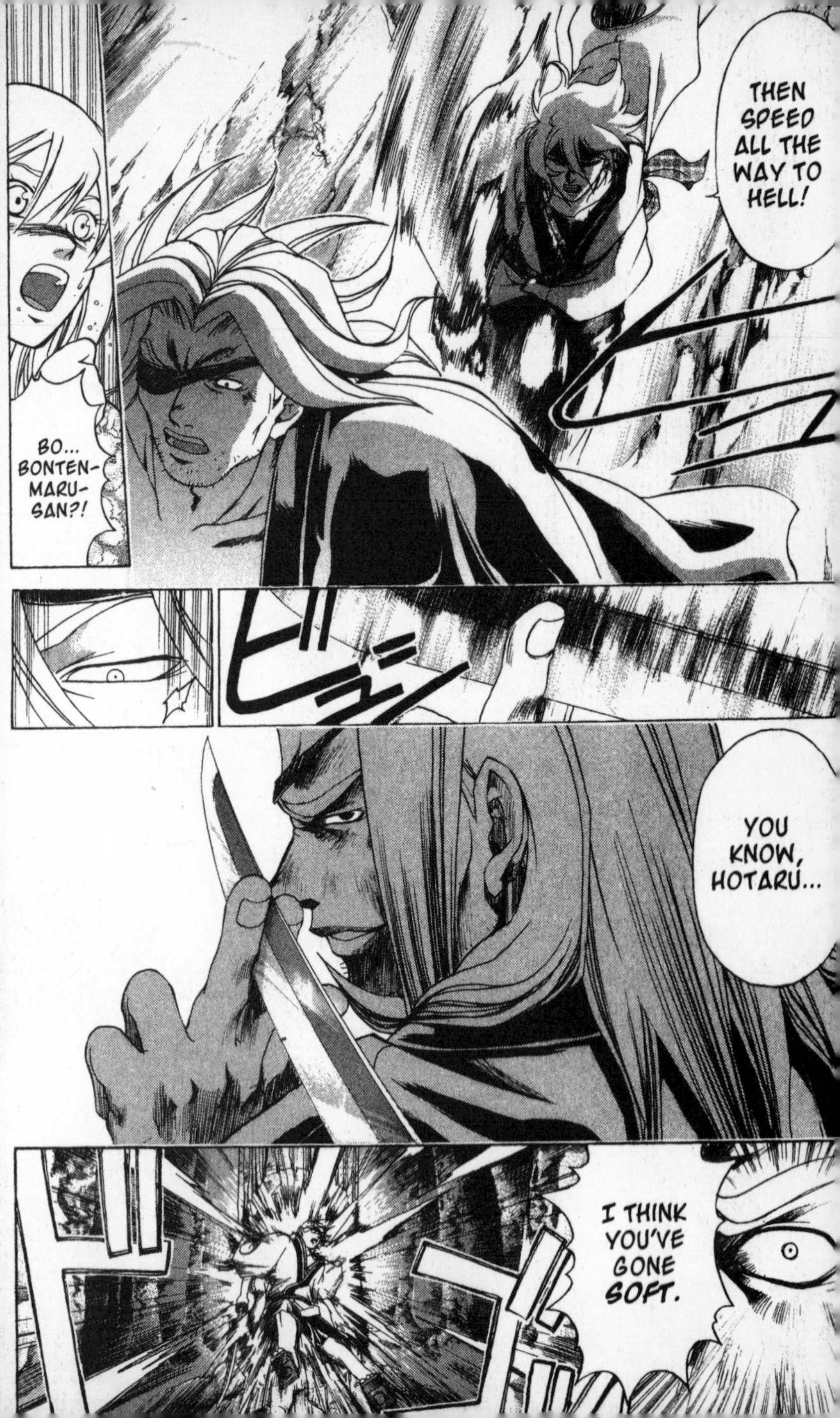
THEN SPEED ALL THE WAY TO HELL!
BO... BONTEN-MARU-SAN?!
YOU KNOW, HOTARU...
I THINK YOU'VE GONE **SOFT**.

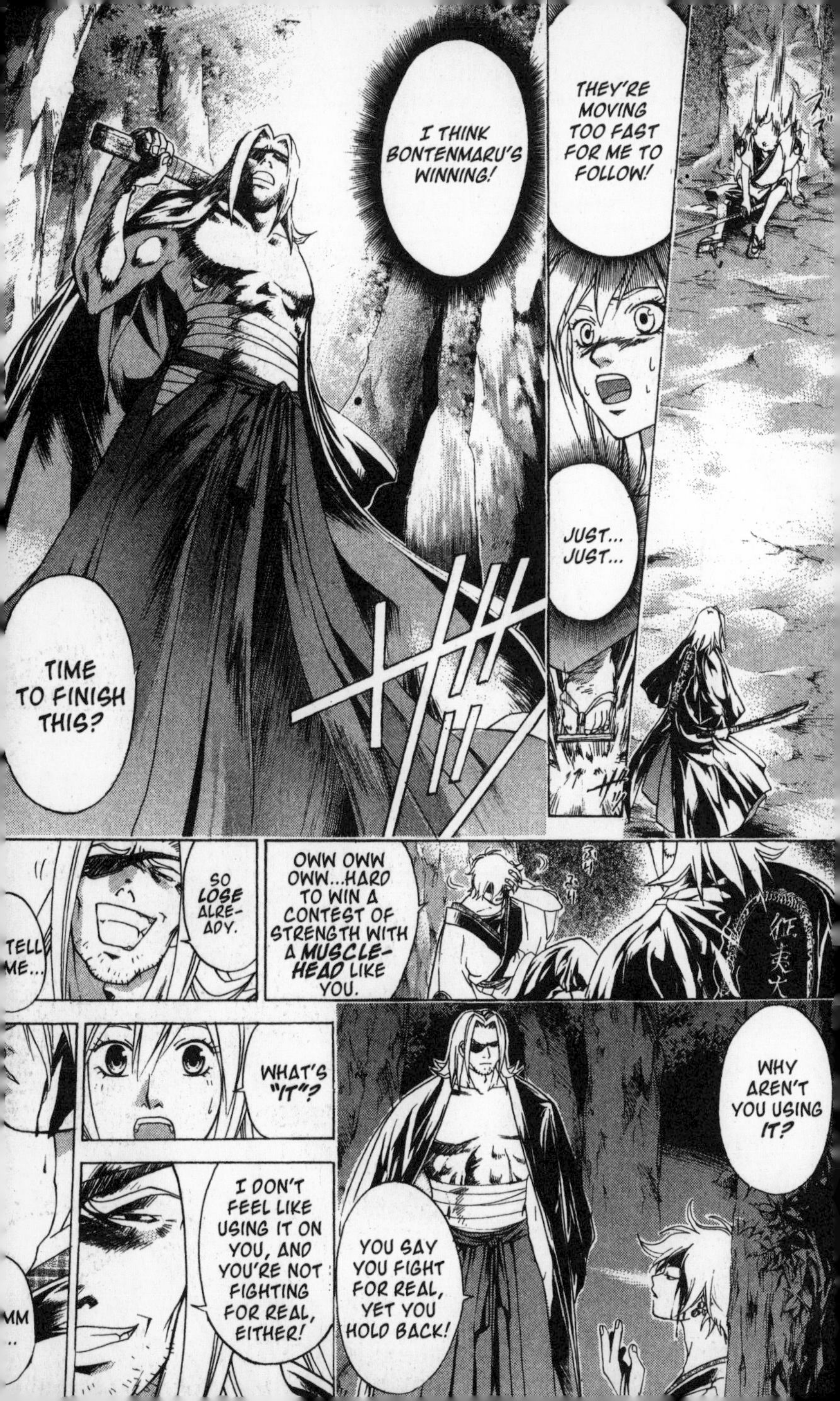

THEY'RE MOVING TOO FAST FOR ME TO FOLLOW!
JUST... JUST...
I THINK BONTENMARU'S WINNING!
TIME TO FINISH THIS?
OWW OWW OWW...HARD TO WIN A CONTEST OF STRENGTH WITH A MUSCLE-HEAD LIKE YOU.
SO LOSE ALREADY.
TELL ME...
WHY AREN'T YOU USING IT?
YOU SAY YOU FIGHT FOR REAL, YET YOU HOLD BACK!
WHAT'S "IT"?
I DON'T FEEL LIKE USING IT ON YOU, AND YOU'RE NOT FIGHTING FOR REAL, EITHER!
MM ..

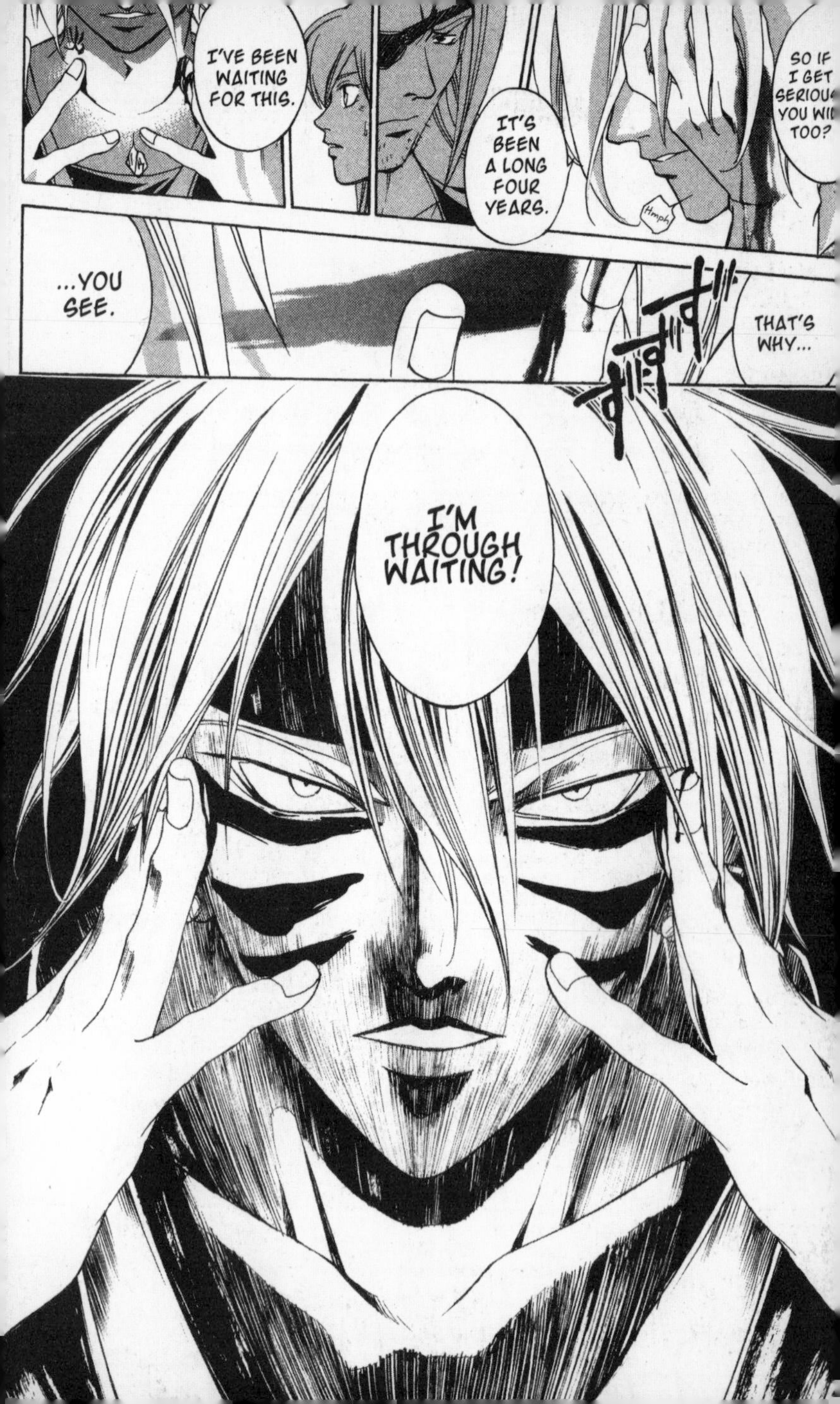
SO IF I GET SERIOU YOU WI TOO?
Hmph
IT'S BEEN A LONG FOUR YEARS.
I'VE BEEN WAITING FOR THIS.
THAT'S WHY...
ずずず
...YOU SEE.
I'M THROUGH WAITING!

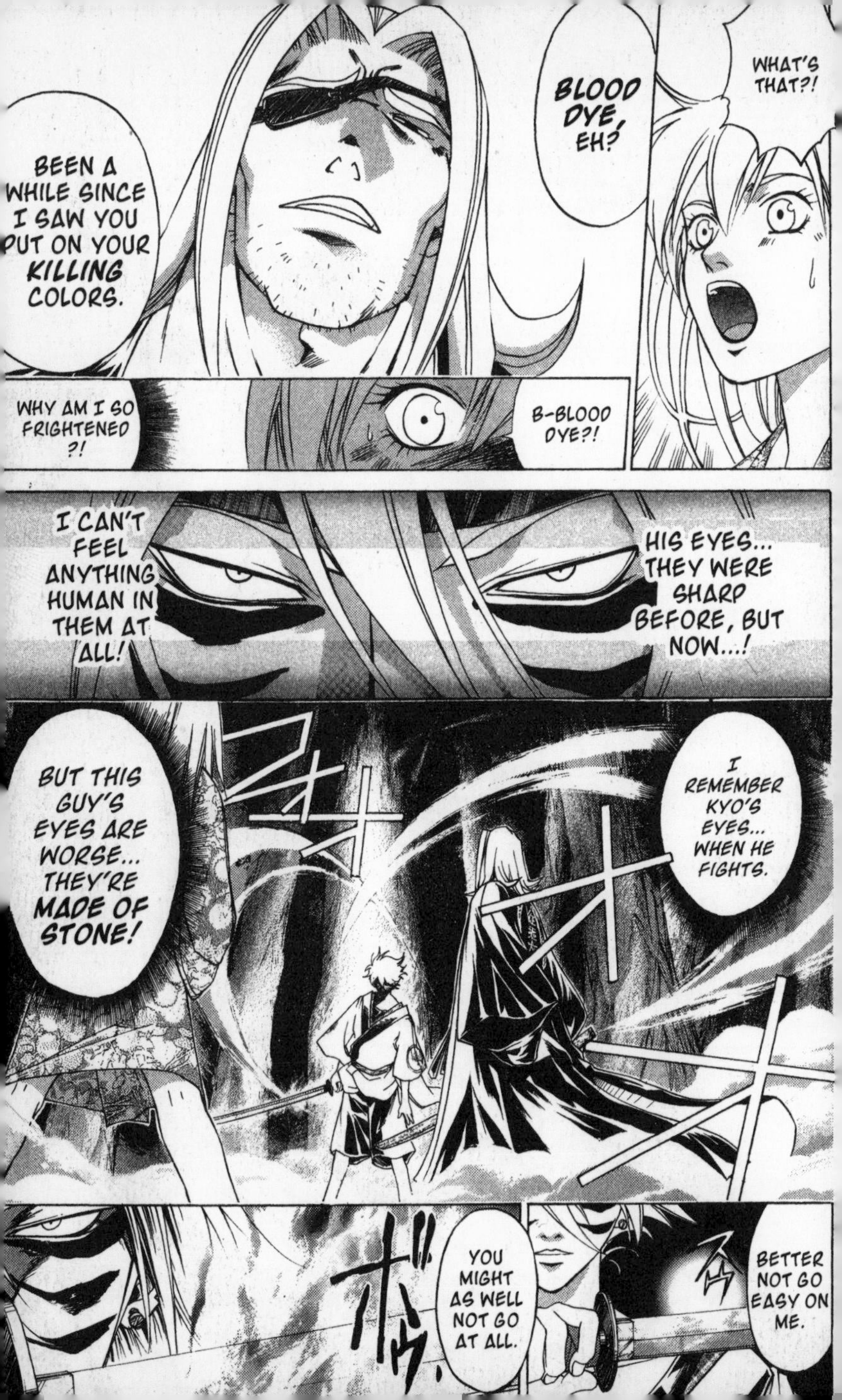
WHAT'S THAT?!
BLOOD DYE, EH?
BEEN A WHILE SINCE I SAW YOU PUT ON YOUR KILLING COLORS.
B-BLOOD DYE?!
WHY AM I SO FRIGHTENED?!
HIS EYES... THEY WERE SHARP BEFORE, BUT NOW...!
I CAN'T FEEL ANYTHING HUMAN IN THEM AT ALL!
I REMEMBER KYO'S EYES... WHEN HE FIGHTS.
BUT THIS GUY'S EYES ARE WORSE... THEY'RE MADE OF STONE!
BETTER NOT GO EASY ON ME.
YOU MIGHT AS WELL NOT GO AT ALL.

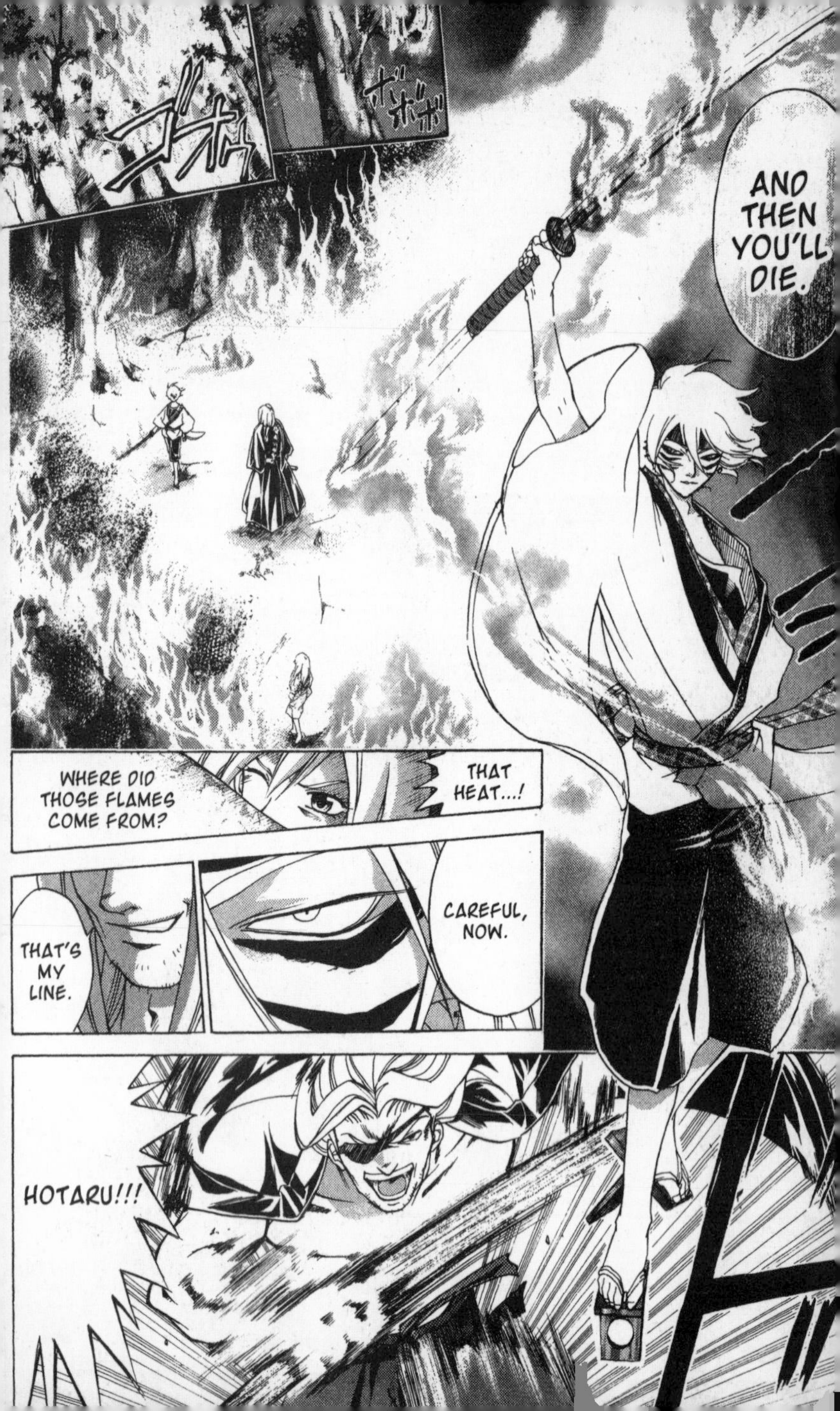
AND THEN YOU'LL DIE.
THAT HEAT...!
WHERE DID THOSE FLAMES COME FROM?
CAREFUL, NOW.
THAT'S MY LINE.
HOTARU!!!

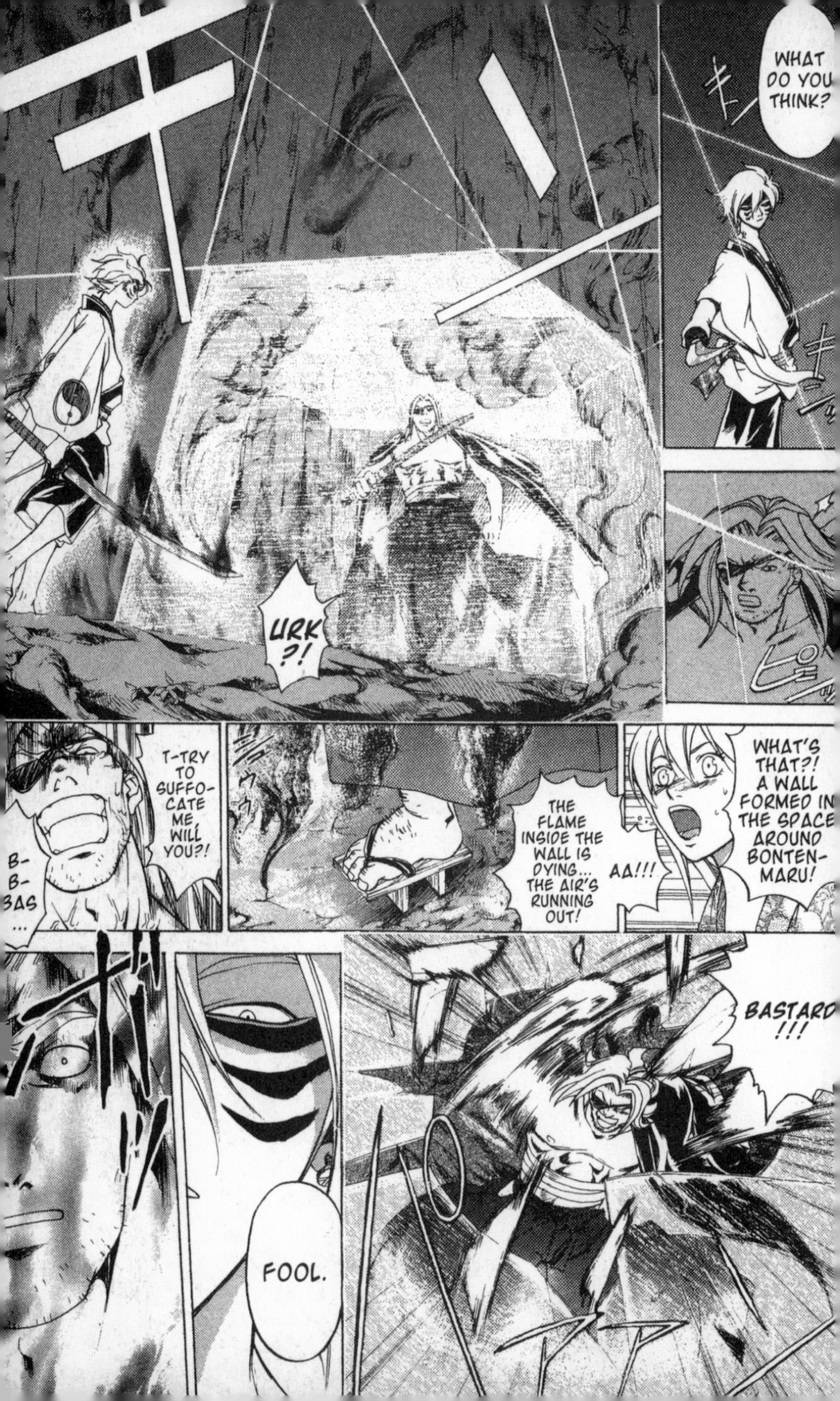
WHAT DO YOU THINK?
URK ?!
WHAT'S THAT?! A WALL FORMED IN THE SPACE AROUND BONTEN-MARU!
AA!!!
THE FLAME INSIDE THE WALL IS DYING... THE AIR'S RUNNING OUT!
T-TRY TO SUFFO-CATE ME WILL YOU?!
B-B-BAS...
BASTARD!!!
FOOL.

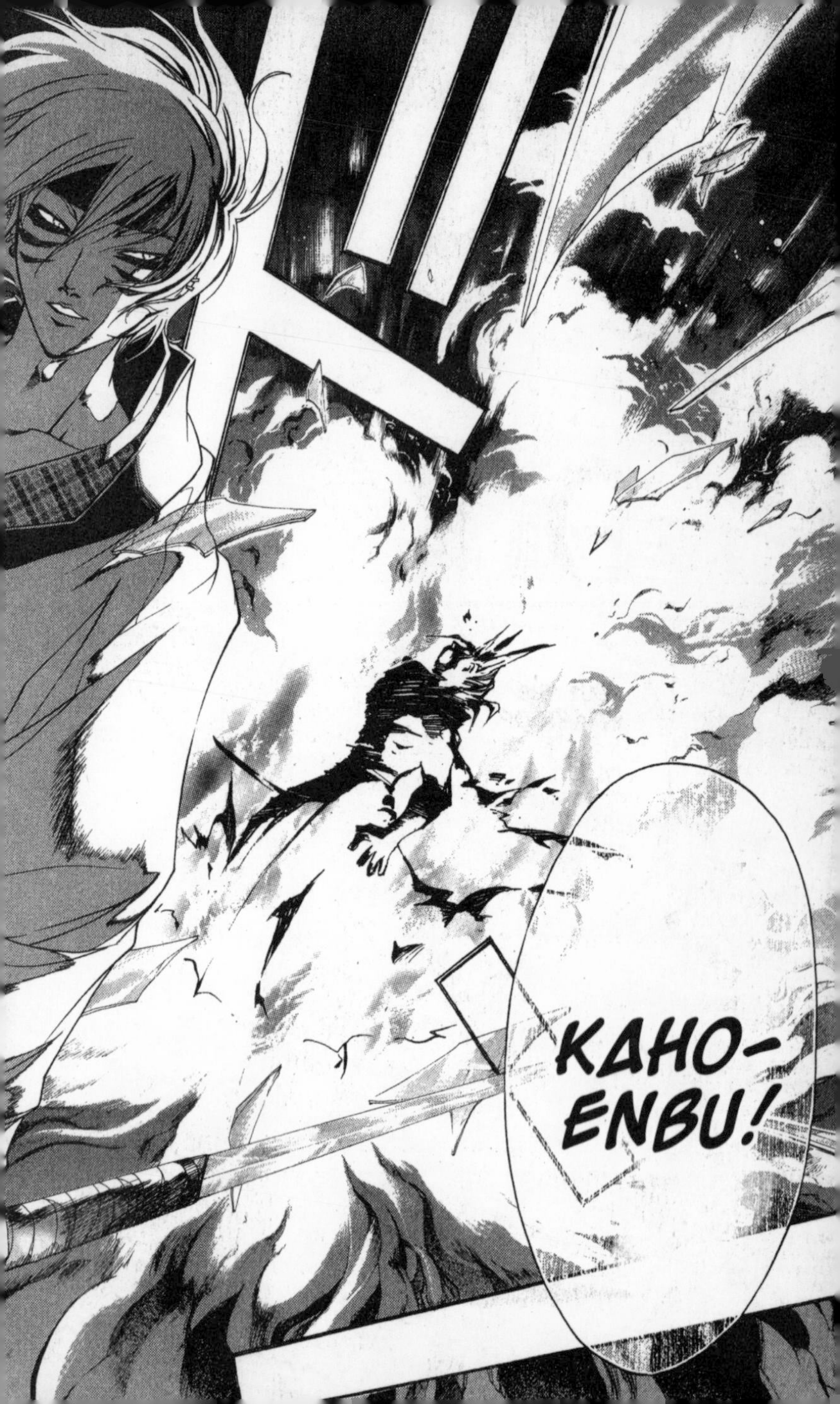
KAHO-
ENBU!

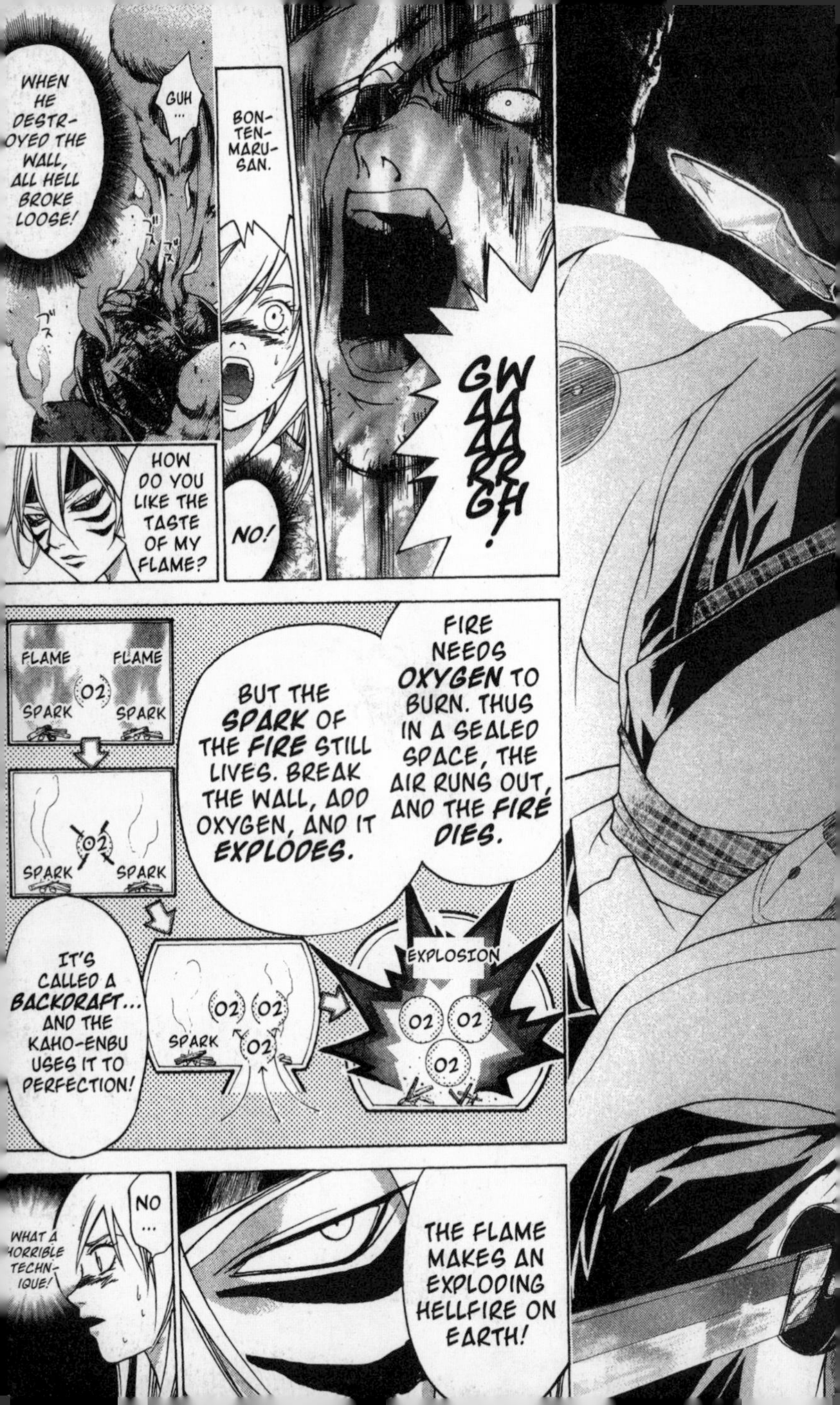

GWAAAARGH!
BON-TEN-MARU-SAN.
NO!
GUH...
WHEN HE DESTROYED THE WALL, ALL HELL BROKE LOOSE!
HOW DO YOU LIKE THE TASTE OF MY FLAME?
FIRE NEEDS **OXYGEN** TO BURN. THUS IN A SEALED SPACE, THE AIR RUNS OUT, AND THE **FIRE DIES**.
BUT THE **SPARK** OF THE **FIRE** STILL LIVES. BREAK THE WALL, ADD OXYGEN, AND IT **EXPLODES**.
FLAME
FLAME
O2
SPARK
SPARK
O2
SPARK
SPARK
O2
O2
O2
SPARK
EXPLOSION
O2
O2
O2
IT'S CALLED A **BACKDRAFT**... AND THE KAHO-ENBU USES IT TO PERFECTION!
THE FLAME MAKES AN EXPLODING HELLFIRE ON EARTH!
NO...
WHAT A HORRIBLE TECHNIQUE!

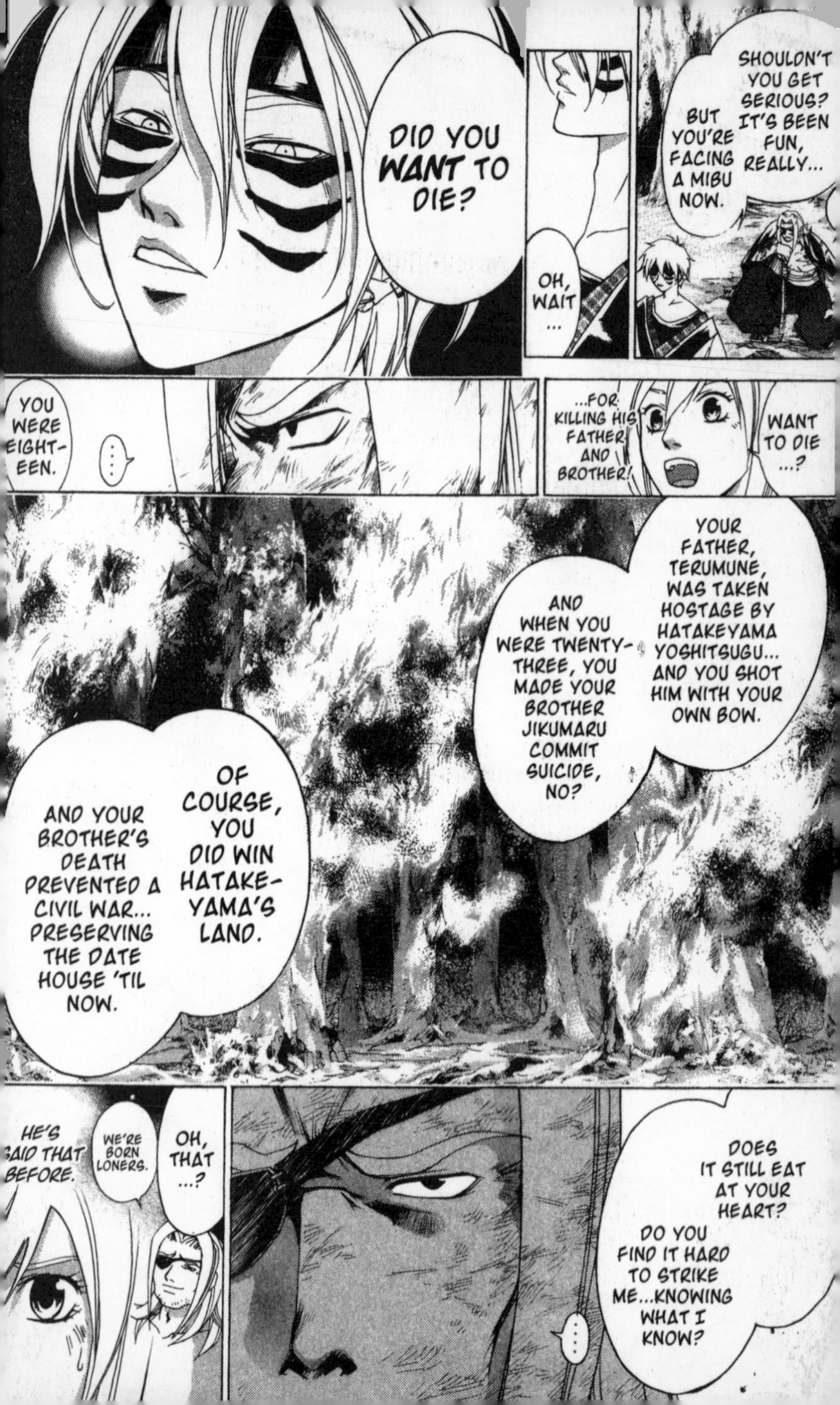
SHOULDN'T YOU GET SERIOUS? IT'S BEEN FUN, REALLY...
BUT YOU'RE FACING A MIBU NOW.
OH, WAIT...
DID YOU **WANT** TO DIE?
WANT TO DIE...?
...FOR KILLING HIS FATHER AND BROTHER!
...
YOU WERE EIGHTEEN.
YOUR FATHER, TERUMUNE, WAS TAKEN HOSTAGE BY HATAKEYAMA YOSHITSUGU... AND YOU SHOT HIM WITH YOUR OWN BOW.
AND WHEN YOU WERE TWENTY-THREE, YOU MADE YOUR BROTHER JIKUMARU COMMIT SUICIDE, NO?
OF COURSE, YOU DID WIN HATAKEYAMA'S LAND.
AND YOUR BROTHER'S DEATH PREVENTED A CIVIL WAR... PRESERVING THE DATE HOUSE 'TIL NOW.
DOES IT STILL EAT AT YOUR HEART?
DO YOU FIND IT HARD TO STRIKE ME...KNOWING WHAT I KNOW?
...
OH, THAT...?
WE'RE BORN LONERS.
HE'S SAID THAT BEFORE.

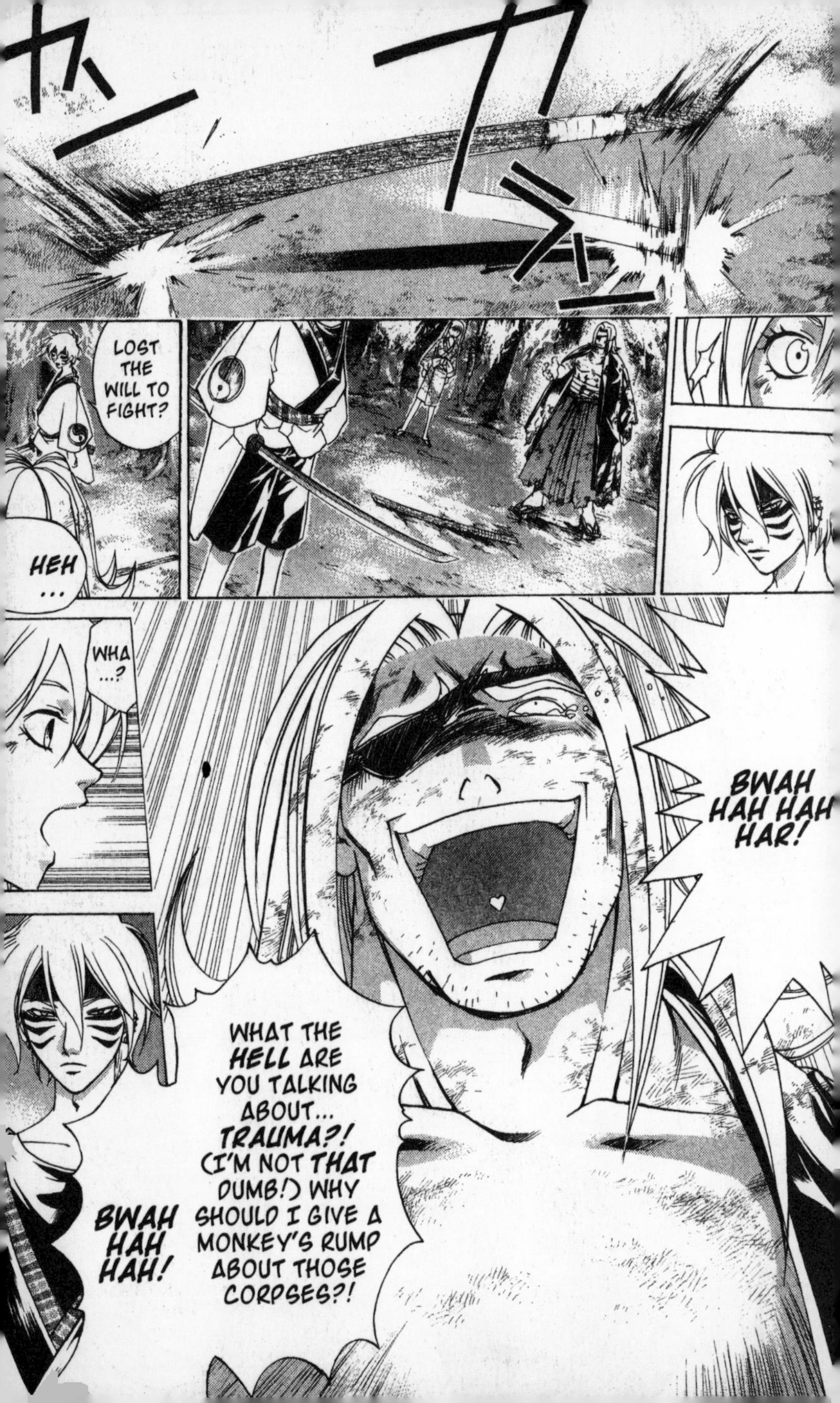
LOST THE WILL TO FIGHT?
HEH ...
BWAH HAH HAH HAR!
WHAT THE HELL ARE YOU TALKING ABOUT... TRAUMA?! (I'M NOT THAT DUMB!) WHY SHOULD I GIVE A MONKEY'S RUMP ABOUT THOSE CORPSES?!
WHA ...?
BWAH HAH HAH!

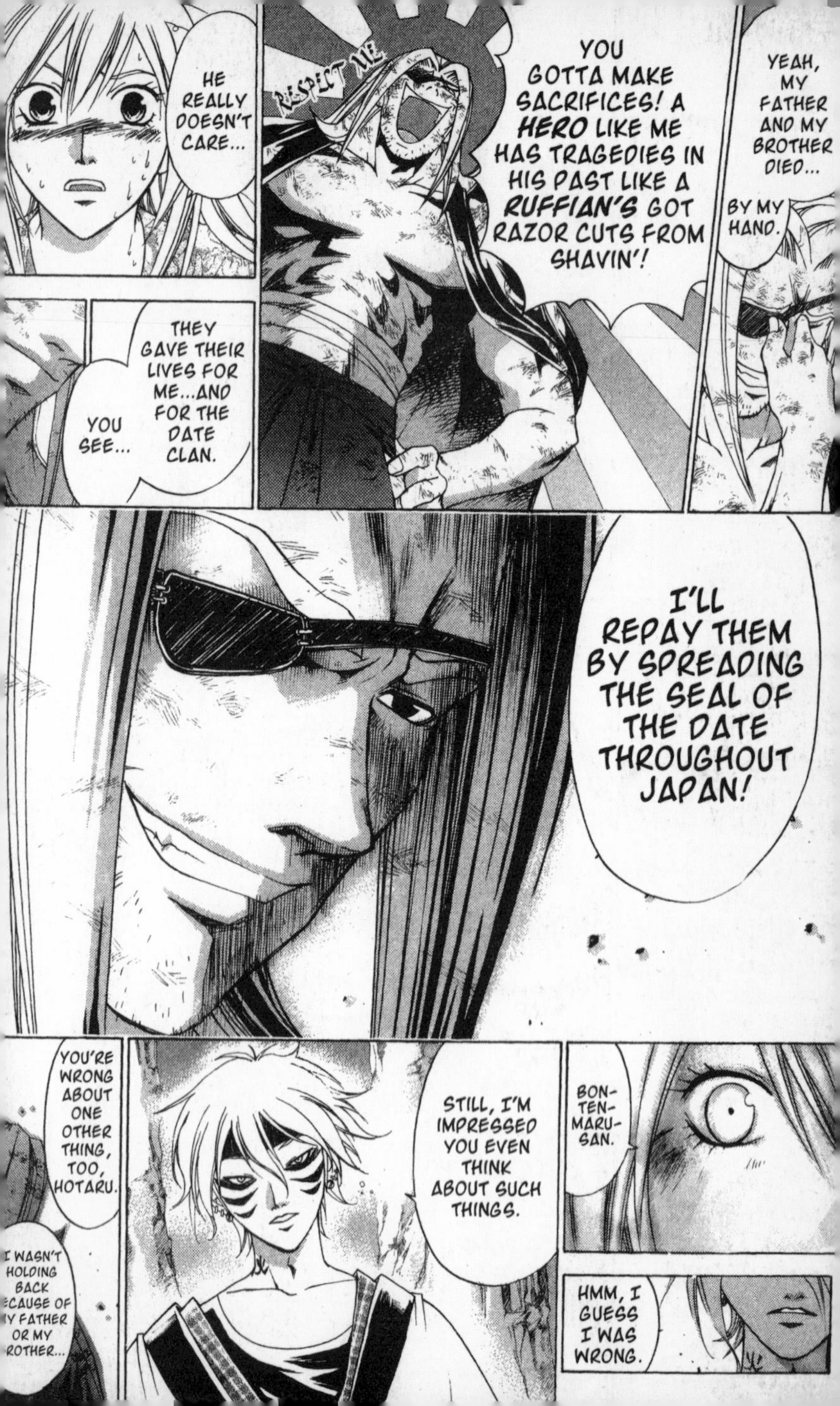
YEAH, MY FATHER AND MY BROTHER DIED...
BY MY HAND.
RESPECT ME
YOU GOTTA MAKE SACRIFICES! A HERO LIKE ME HAS TRAGEDIES IN HIS PAST LIKE A RUFFIAN'S GOT RAZOR CUTS FROM SHAVIN'!
HE REALLY DOESN'T CARE...
THEY GAVE THEIR LIVES FOR ME...AND FOR THE DATE CLAN.
YOU SEE...
I'LL REPAY THEM BY SPREADING THE SEAL OF THE DATE THROUGHOUT JAPAN!
BON-TEN-MARU-SAN.
HMM, I GUESS I WAS WRONG.
STILL, I'M IMPRESSED YOU EVEN THINK ABOUT SUCH THINGS.
YOU'RE WRONG ABOUT ONE OTHER THING, TOO, HOTARU.
I WASN'T HOLDING BACK ECAUSE OF Y FATHER OR MY ROTHER...

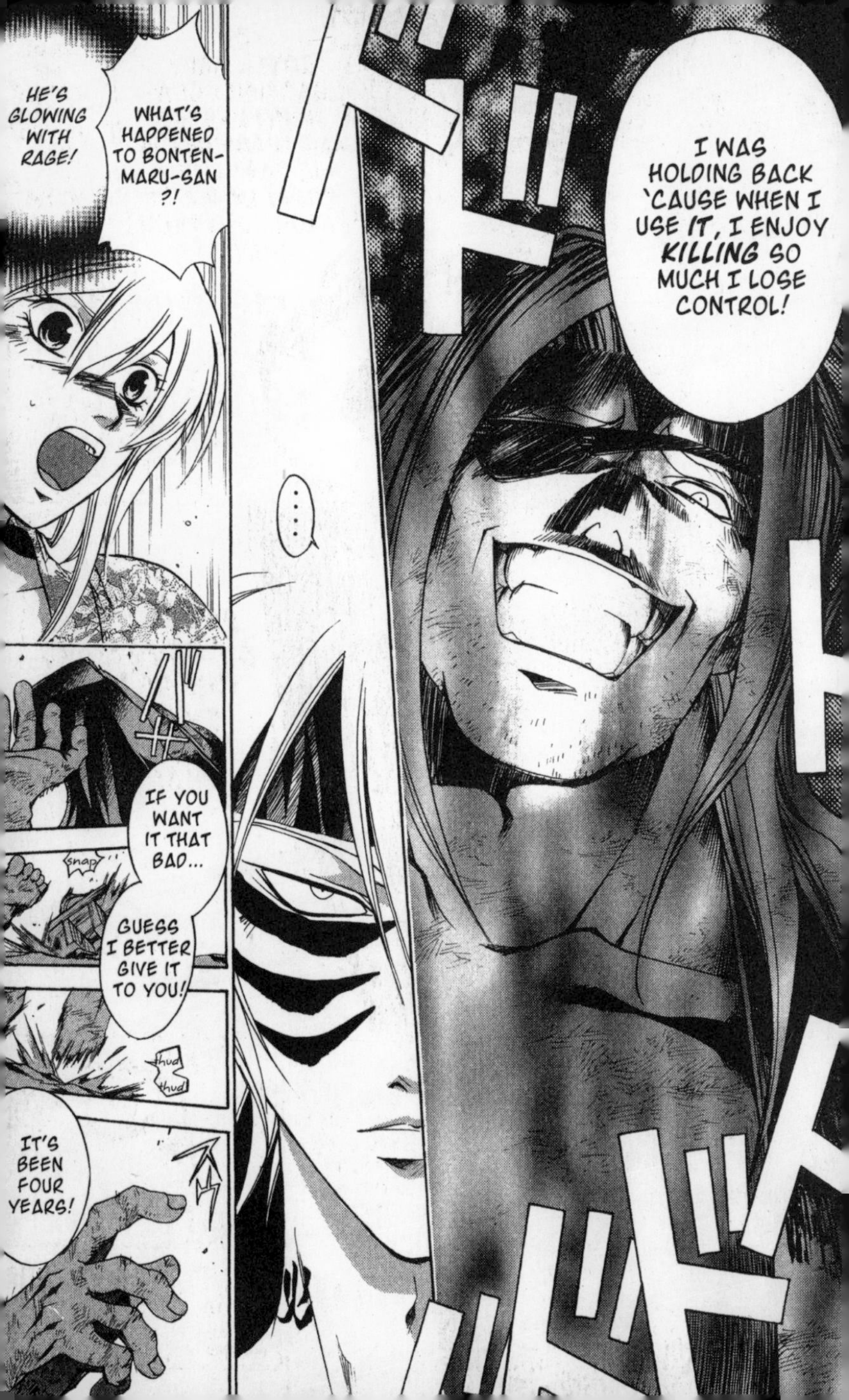
I WAS HOLDING BACK `CAUSE WHEN I USE IT, I ENJOY KILLING SO MUCH I LOSE CONTROL!
.....
WHAT'S HAPPENED TO BONTEN-MARU-SAN ?!
HE'S GLOWING WITH RAGE!
IF YOU WANT IT THAT BAD...
snap
GUESS I BETTER GIVE IT TO YOU!
thud thud
IT'S BEEN FOUR YEARS!

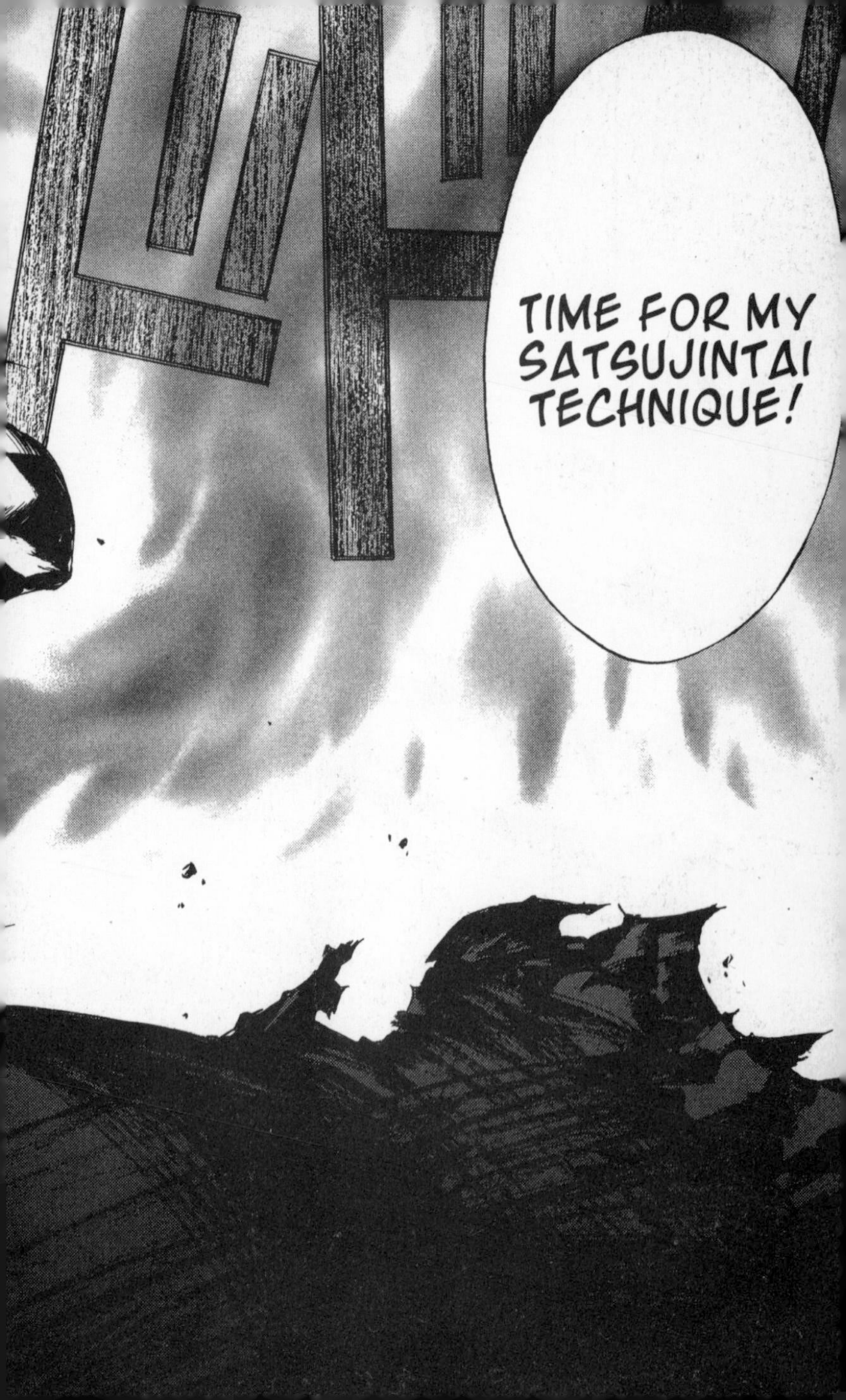
TIME FOR MY SATSUJINTAI TECHNIQUE!

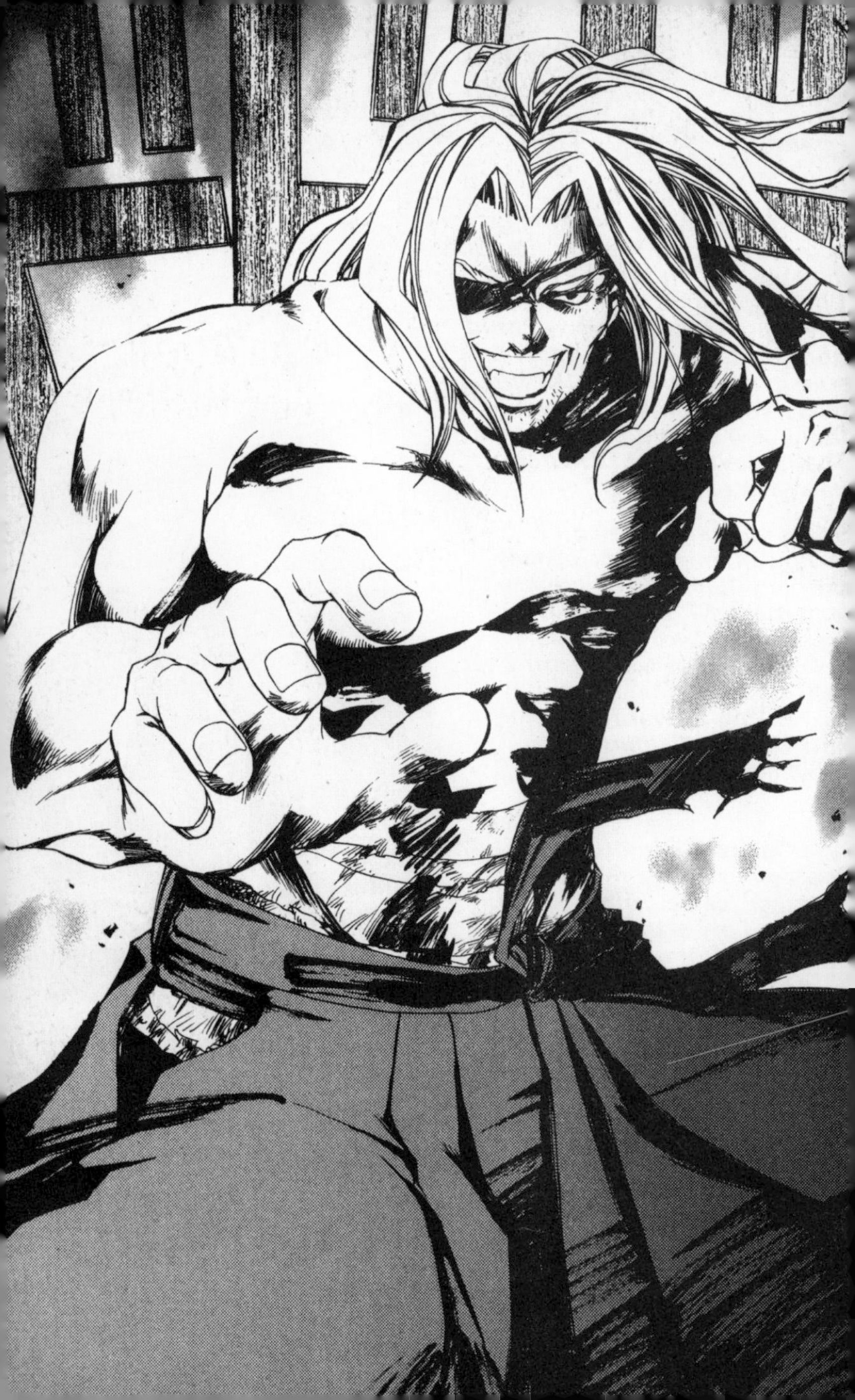

Yo! Kamijyo here, "looking beat," according to my friends. (lol) SDK is at vol. 13, thanks to all you! When I think of 13 volumes of anything, I start to worry about bookshelf space. (You too?) SDK's sure getting up there! (Ayup!) Every volume means I have to thank you all that much more! Thanks, everyone! (You gotta have perseverance!)

Some stuff about fan mail:
In Taiwan, instead of "sensei" they say "laoshi" -- it means "old master." So I'm "Old Master Kamijyo"...sounds powerful! (Drunken Brush? Eh heh)
I'm looking forward to seeing how they do "Hotaru" in Taiwanese... (thanks!)

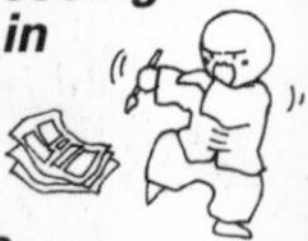

I was amazed someone figured out where the name "Sakuya" came from! Not even my staff knows that one... Our readers are STRONG, I tell you! (lol) I'll probably reveal it in the pages of SDK soon enough, so I won't let on here...but everyone try and guess!

Reading all your letters makes me happy! Thanks so much! I'll keep trying to make a manga with characters that are COOL. Keep reading!

SPECIAL SECRET STORY

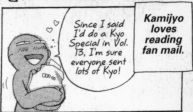

Kamijyo loves reading fan mail.
Since I said I'd do a Kyo Special in Vol. 13, I'm sure everyone sent lots of Kyo!
BUT
W- where's KYO?!
Yuya
Okuni
Yukimura
Sasuke
Yukimura & Sasuke
Muramasa
Shinrei
Kyoshiro
Akira
Tora
I mean, I got a ton of cards...but so little Kyo!
W- why?!
He's been losing lately, and all he says is "..." and what good is a manga without a hero?!
Is Kyo in danger of...being forgotten?!
Then again, vol. 12 just came out last week.
(We're usually working on the next volume already when one comes out.)
That said... send more Kyo art!

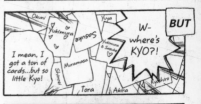

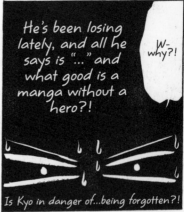

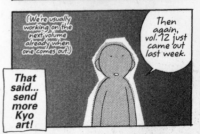

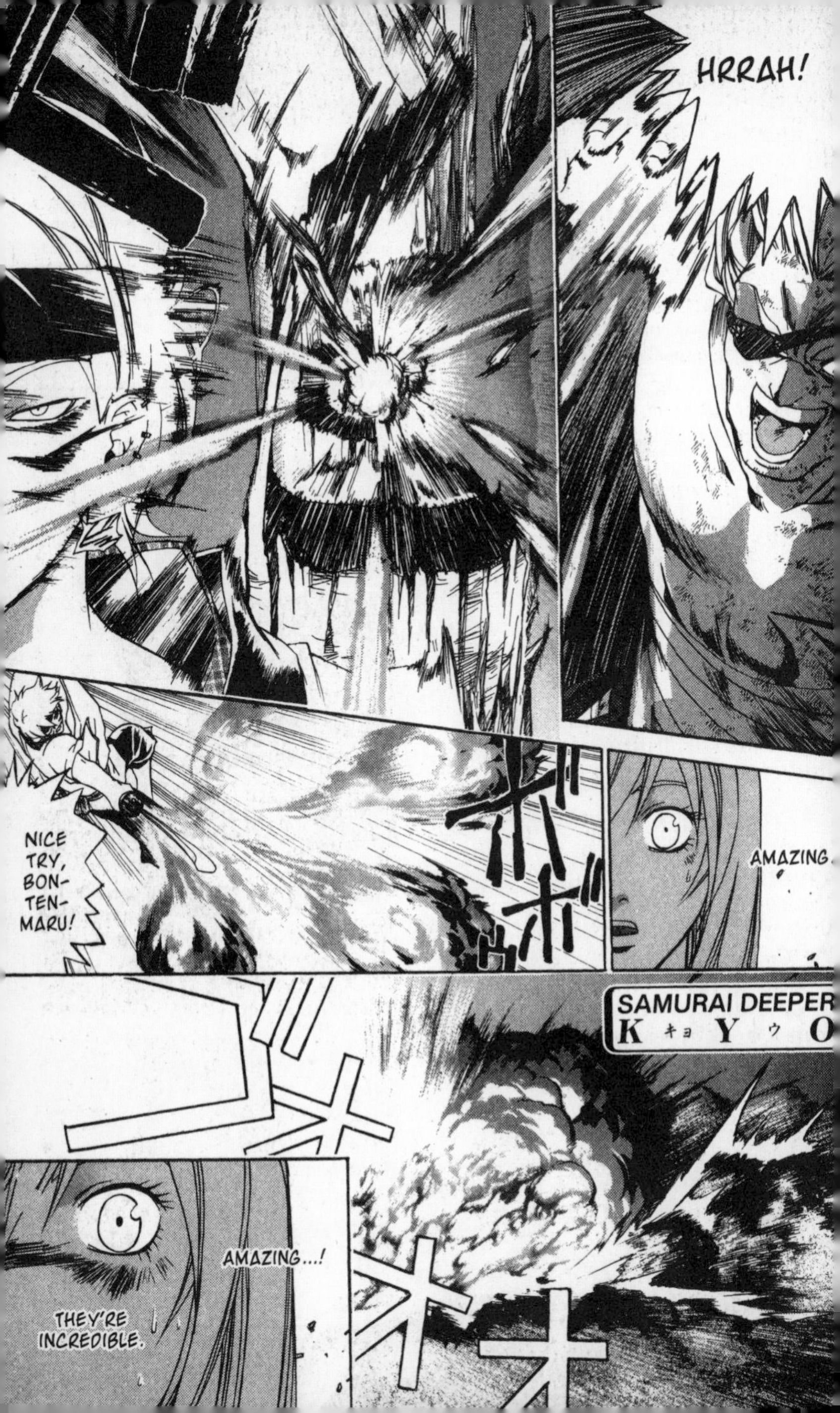
HRRAH!
AMAZING...
NICE TRY, BONTEN-MARU!
SAMURAI DEEPER
K キョ Y ウ O
AMAZING...!
THEY'RE INCREDIBLE.

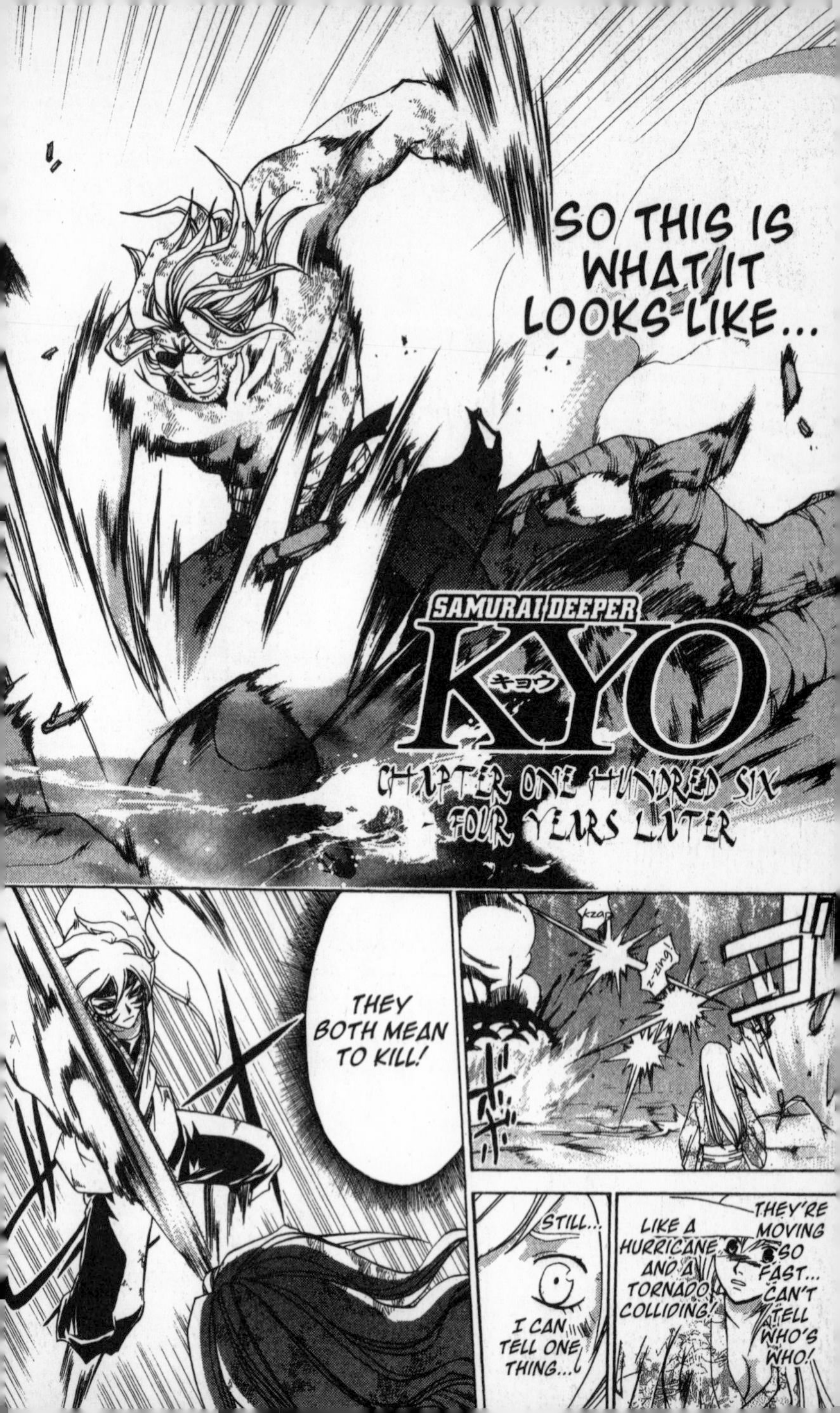
SO THIS IS WHAT IT LOOKS LIKE...
SAMURAI DEEPER
KYO
キョウ
CHAPTER ONE HUNDRED SIX - FOUR YEARS LATER
kzap
z-zing!
THEY'RE MOVING SO FAST... CAN'T TELL WHO'S WHO!
LIKE A HURRICANE AND A TORNADO COLLIDING!
STILL...
I CAN TELL ONE THING...
THEY BOTH MEAN TO KILL!

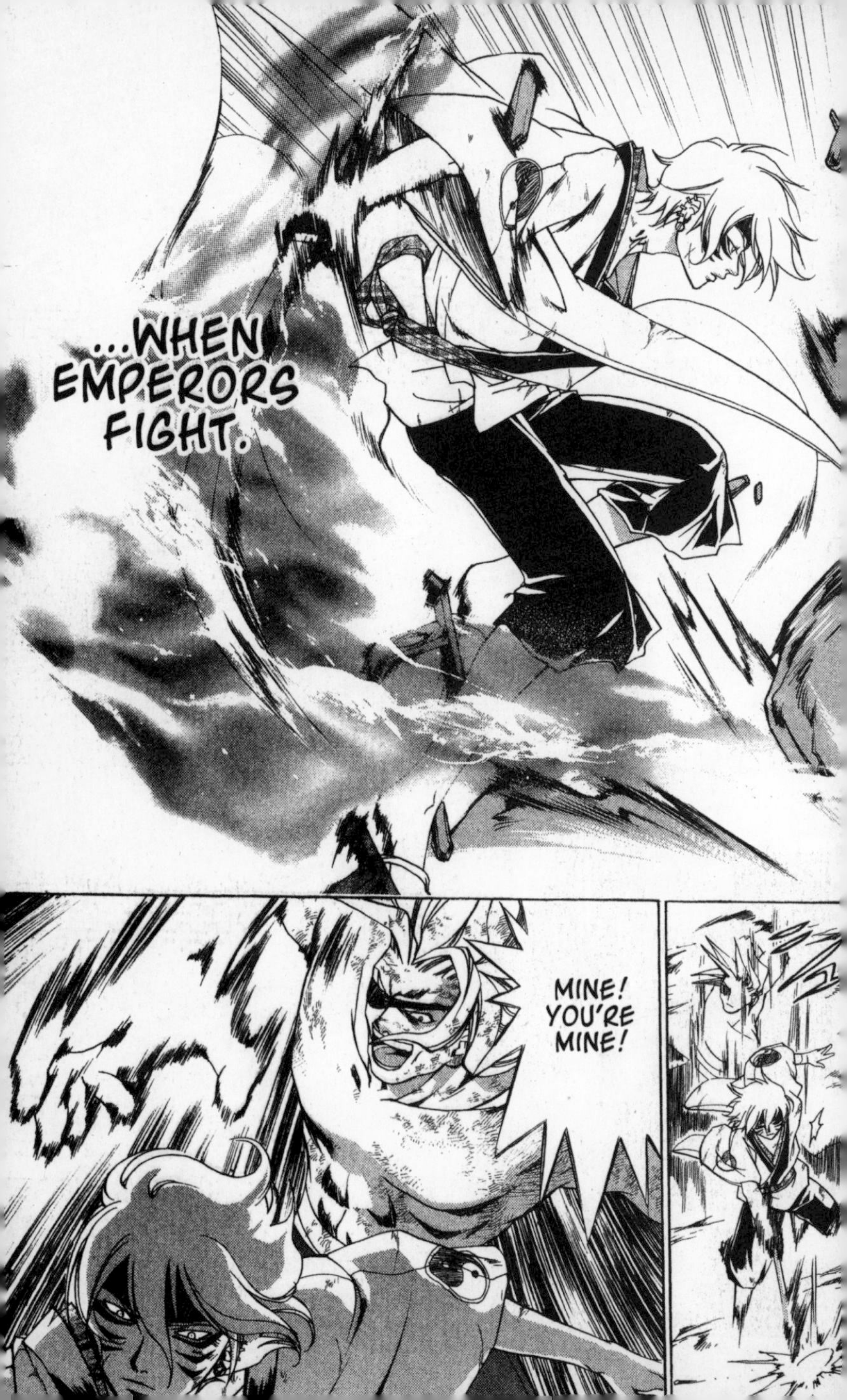
...WHEN EMPERORS FIGHT.
MINE! YOU'RE MINE!

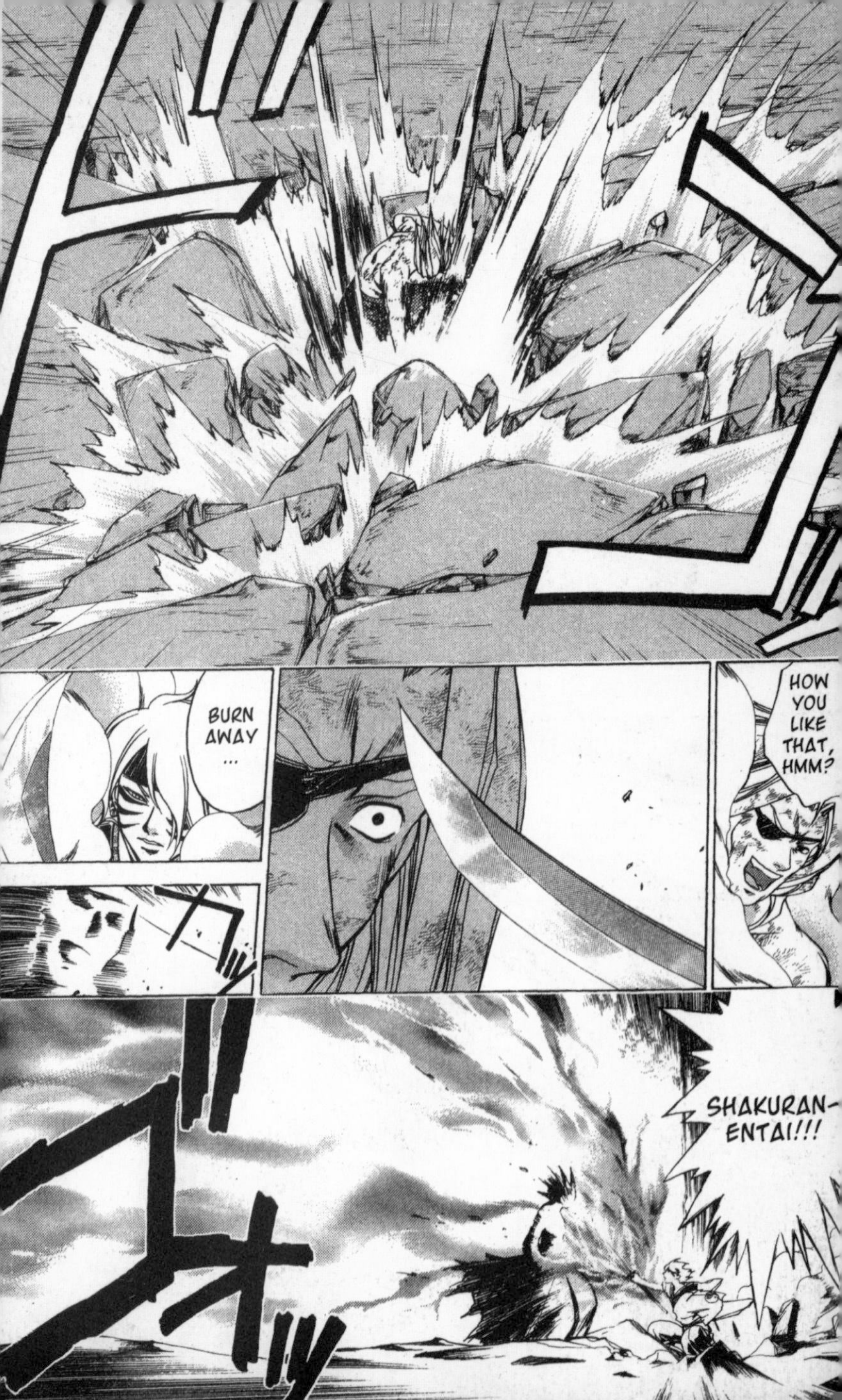
HOW YOU LIKE THAT, HMM?
BURN AWAY ...
SHAKURAN-ENTAI!!!

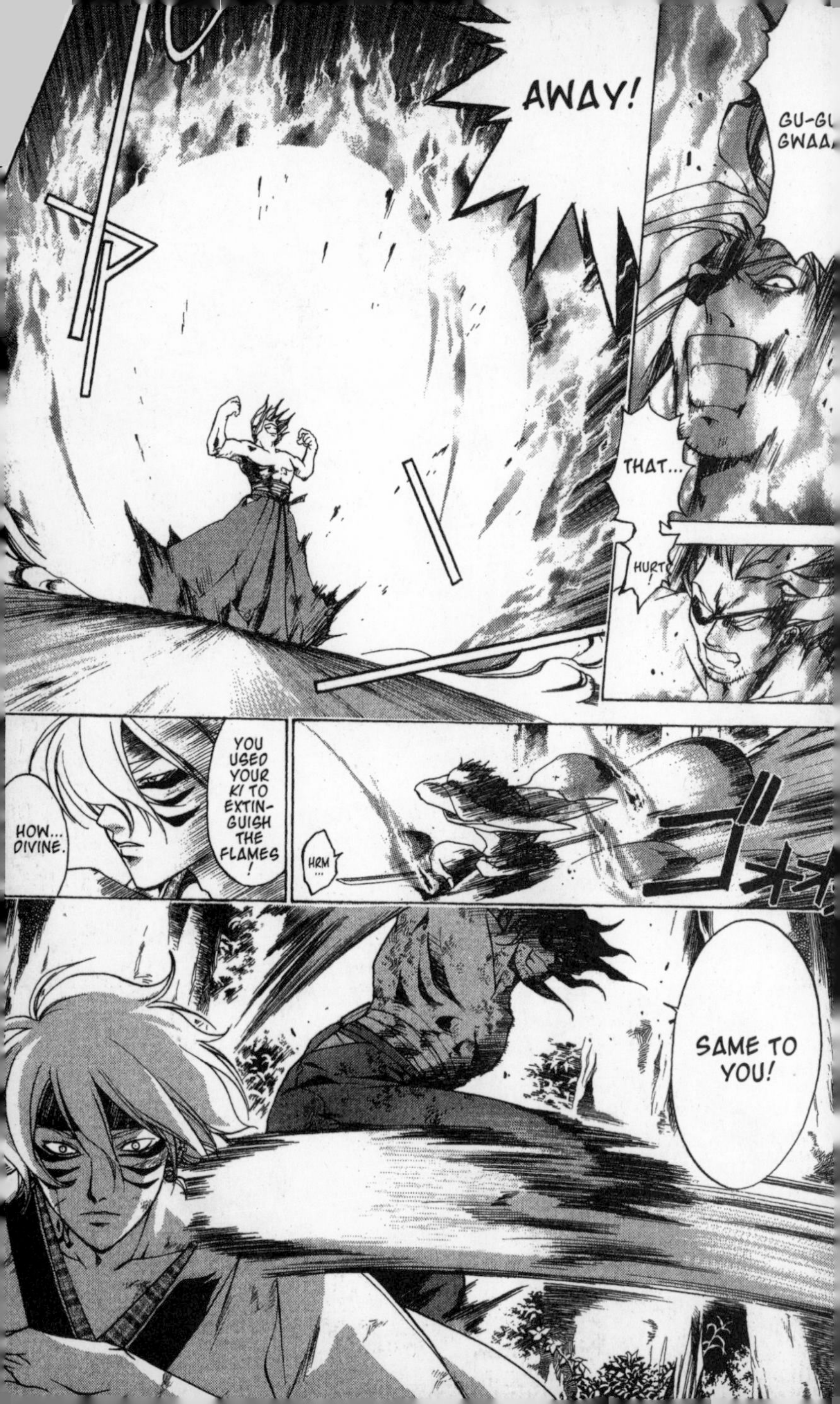
GU-GI GWAA
THAT...
HURT!
AWAY!
HRM...
YOU USED YOUR KI TO EXTIN-GUISH THE FLAMES!
HOW... DIVINE.
SAME TO YOU!

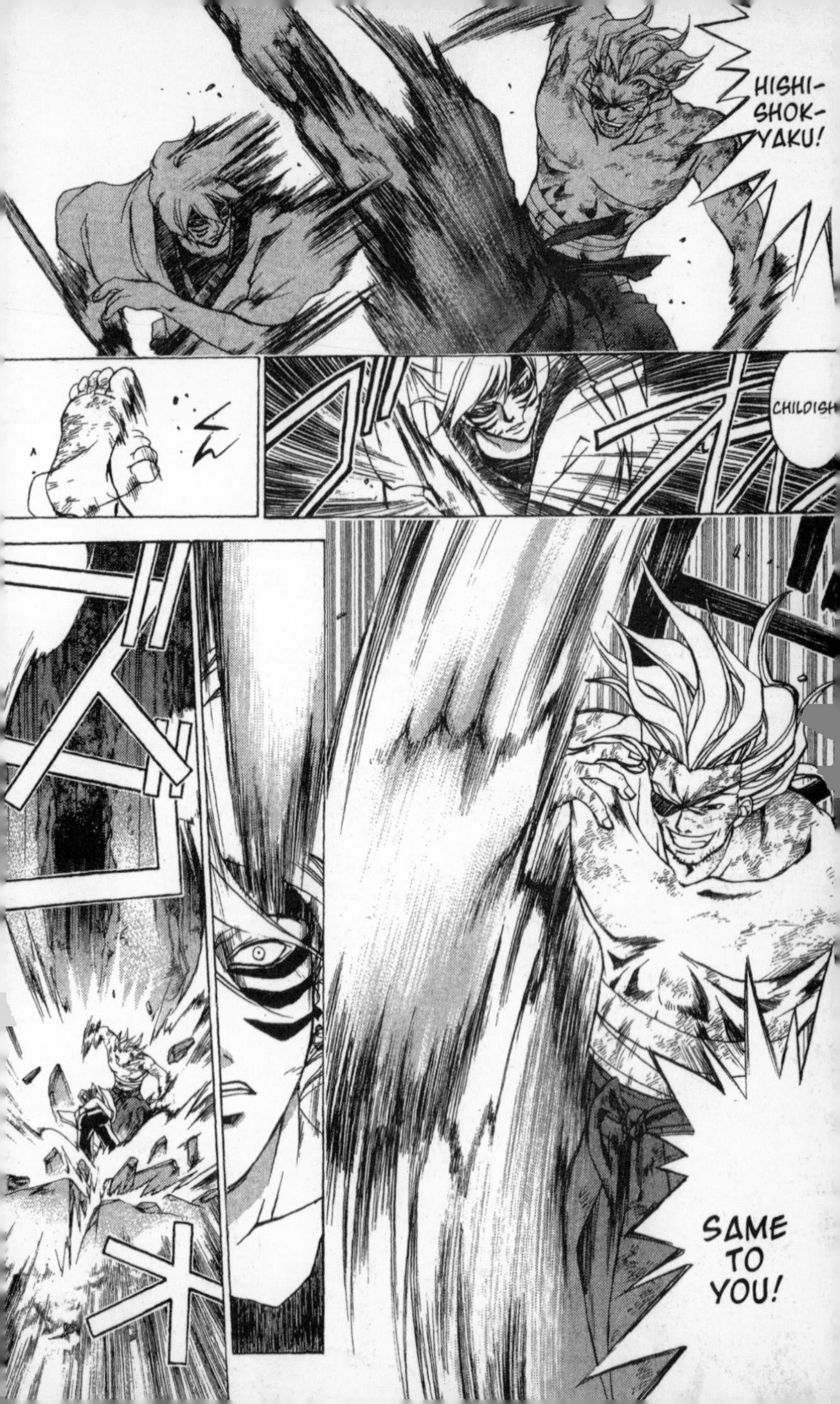

HISHI-SHOK-YAKU!
CHILDISH
SAME TO YOU!

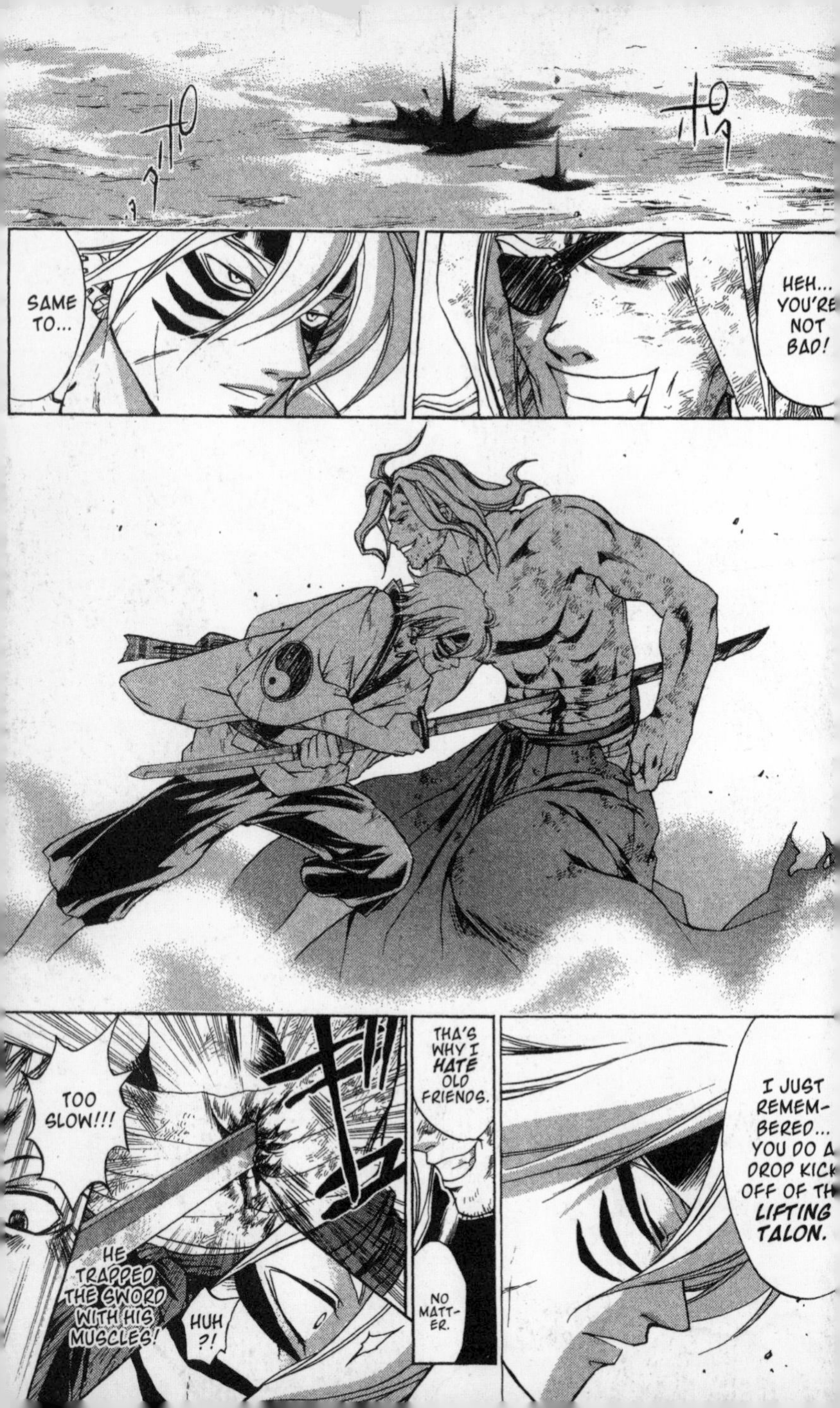
HEH... YOU'RE NOT BAO!
SAME TO...
I JUST REMEMBERED... YOU DO A DROP KIC OFF OF TH LIFTING TALON.
THA'S WHY I HATE OLD FRIENDS.
NO MATTER.
TOO SLOW!!!
HE TRAPPED THE SWORD WITH HIS MUSCLES!
HUH ?!

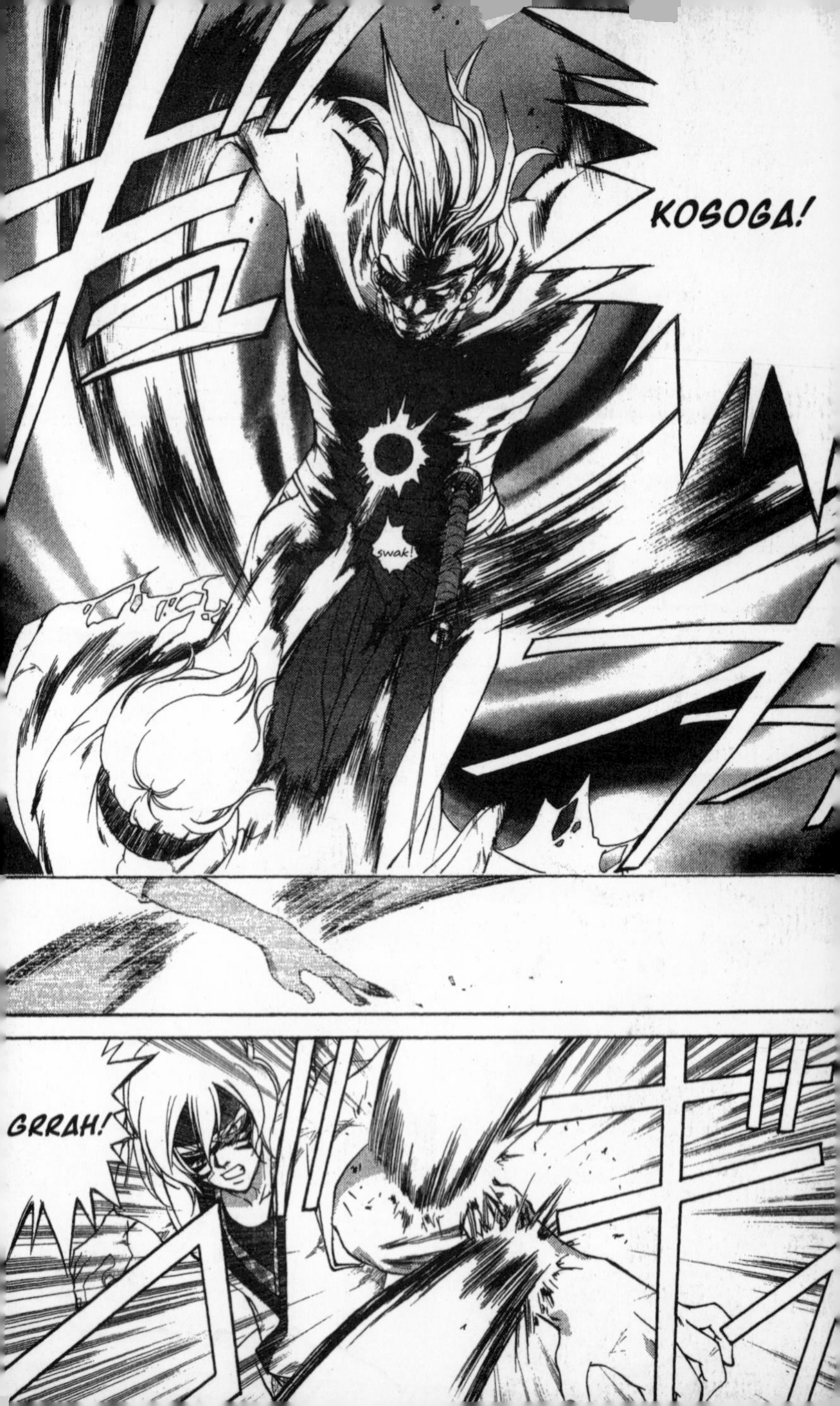
KOSOGA!
swak!
GRRAH!

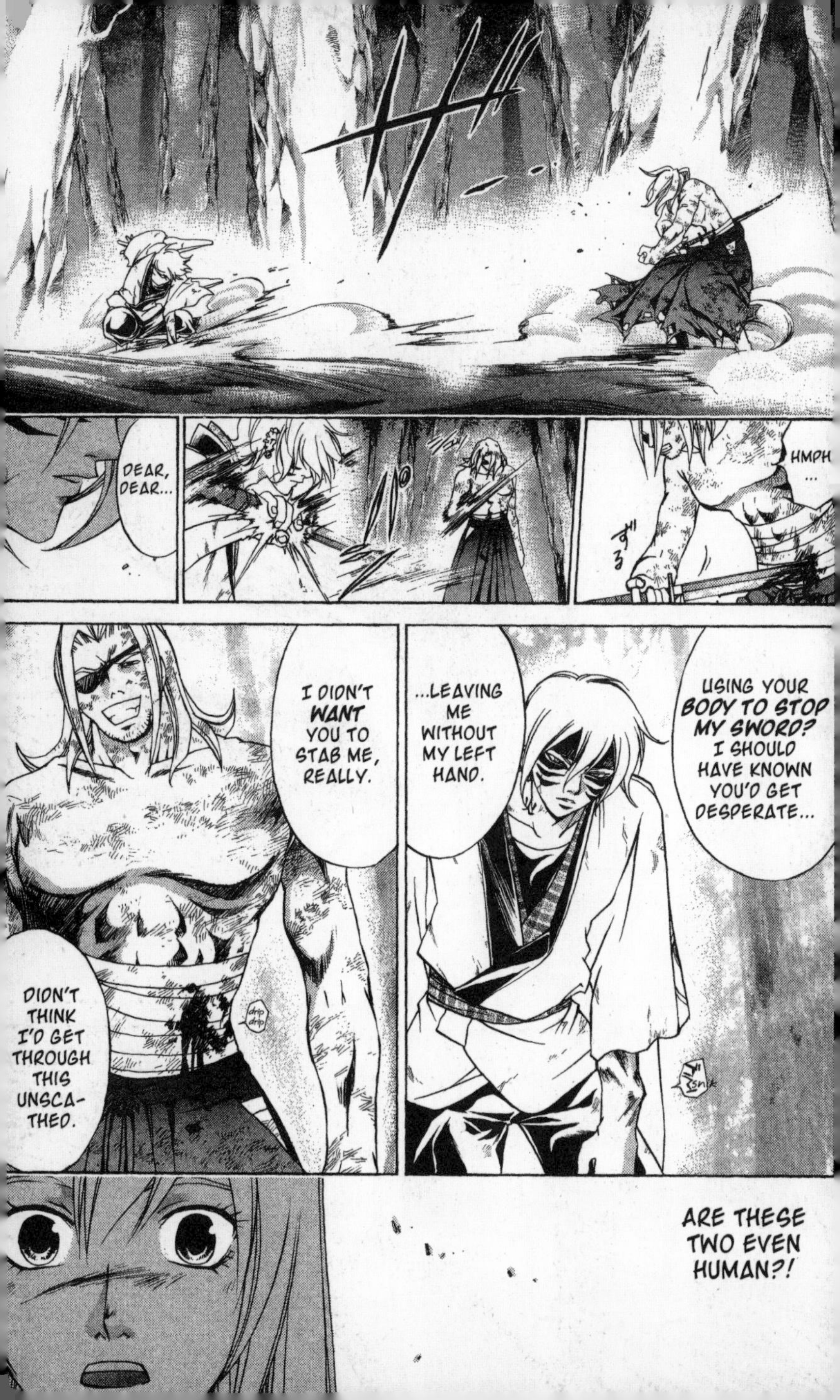
HMPH ...
ずる
DEAR, DEAR...
USING YOUR BODY TO STOP MY SWORD? I SHOULD HAVE KNOWN YOU'D GET DESPERATE...
...LEAVING ME WITHOUT MY LEFT HAND.
snik
I DIDN'T WANT YOU TO STAB ME, REALLY.
drip drip
DIDN'T THINK I'D GET THROUGH THIS UNSCA-THED.
ARE THESE TWO EVEN HUMAN?!

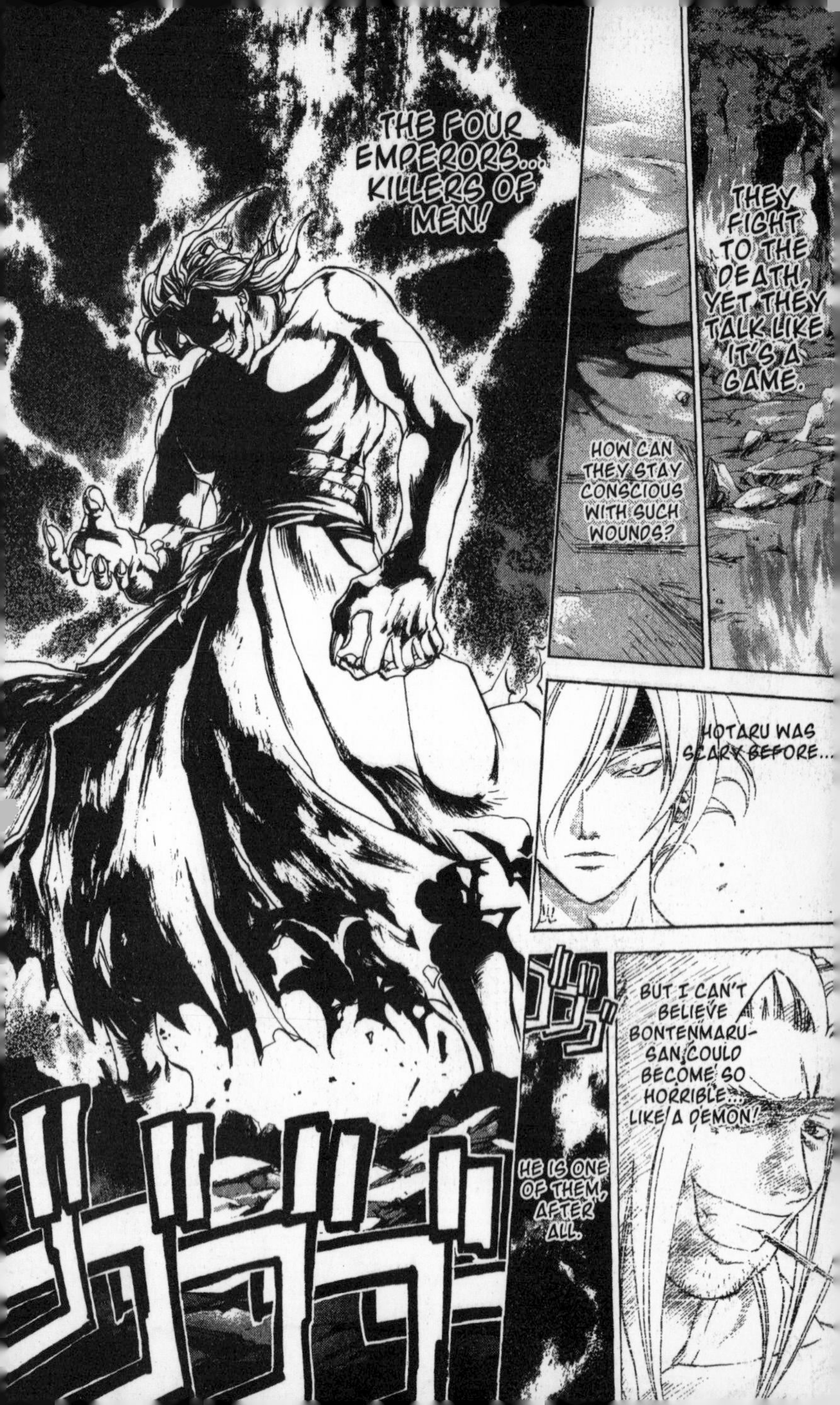
THEY FIGHT TO THE DEATH, YET THEY TALK LIKE IT'S A GAME.
HOW CAN THEY STAY CONSCIOUS WITH SUCH WOUNDS?
HOTARU WAS SCARY BEFORE...
BUT I CAN'T BELIEVE BONTENMARU-SAN COULD BECOME SO HORRIBLE... LIKE A DEMON!
HE IS ONE OF THEM, AFTER ALL.
THE FOUR EMPERORS... KILLERS OF MEN!

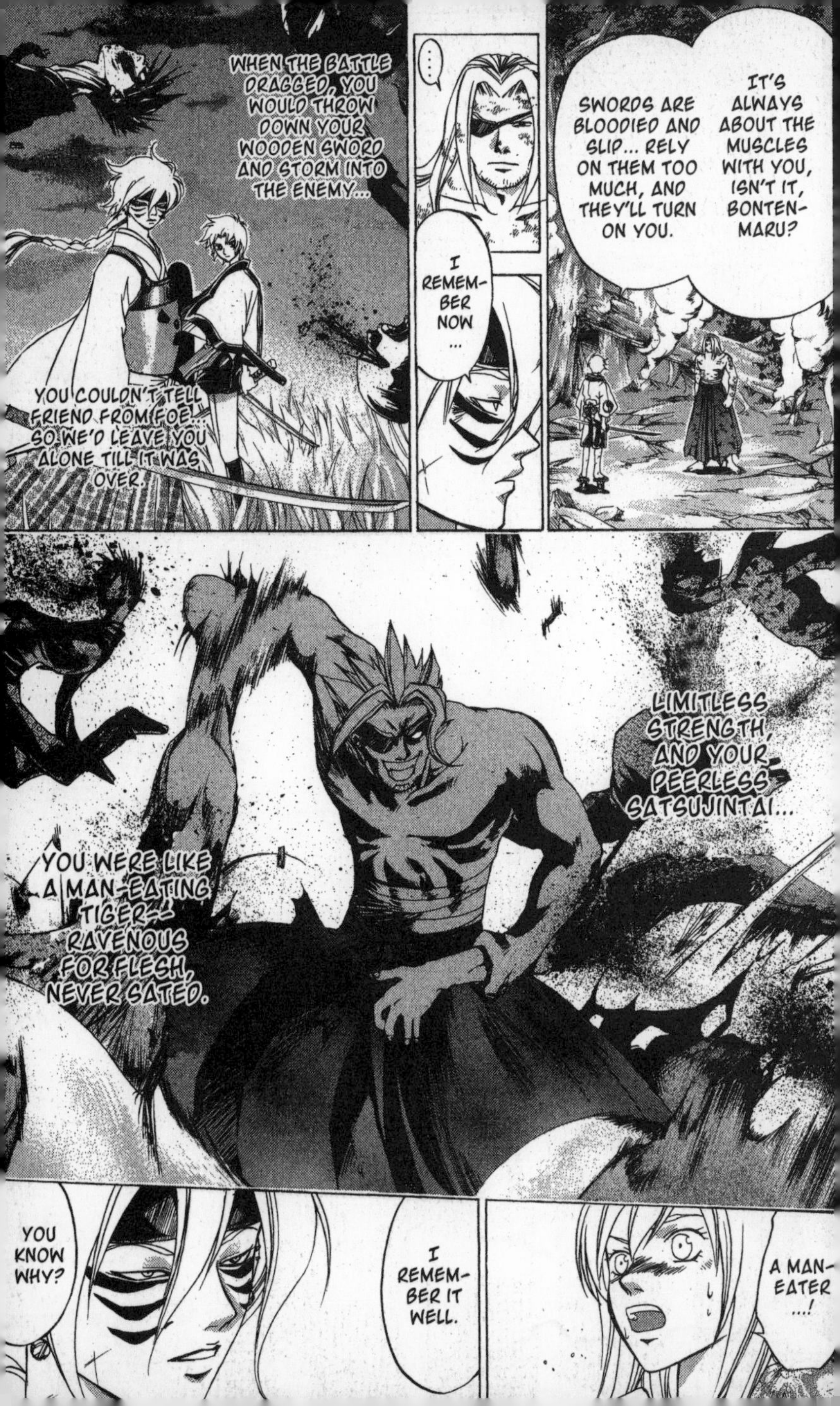
IT'S ALWAYS ABOUT THE MUSCLES WITH YOU, ISN'T IT, BONTEN-MARU?
SWORDS ARE BLOODIED AND SLIP... RELY ON THEM TOO MUCH, AND THEY'LL TURN ON YOU.
...
I REMEMBER NOW...
WHEN THE BATTLE DRAGGED, YOU WOULD THROW DOWN YOUR WOODEN SWORD AND STORM INTO THE ENEMY...
YOU COULDN'T TELL FRIEND FROM FOE... SO WE'D LEAVE YOU ALONE TILL IT WAS OVER.
LIMITLESS STRENGTH, AND YOUR PEERLESS SATSUJINTAI...
YOU WERE LIKE A MAN-EATING TIGER-- RAVENOUS FOR FLESH, NEVER SATED.
A MAN-EATER...!
I REMEMBER IT WELL.
YOU KNOW WHY?

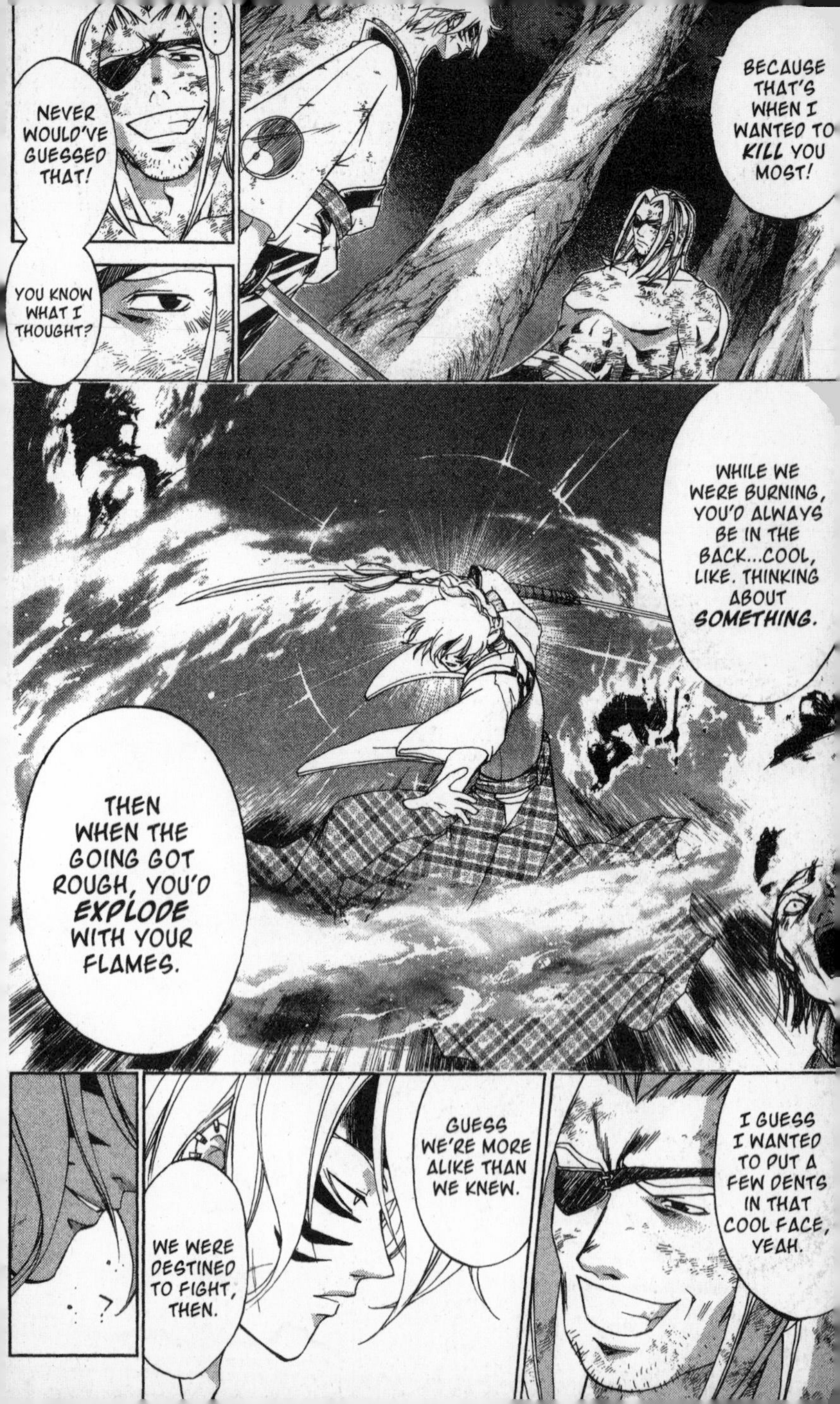
BECAUSE THAT'S WHEN I WANTED TO KILL YOU MOST!
NEVER WOULD'VE GUESSED THAT!
YOU KNOW WHAT I THOUGHT?
WHILE WE WERE BURNING, YOU'D ALWAYS BE IN THE BACK...COOL, LIKE. THINKING ABOUT SOMETHING.
THEN WHEN THE GOING GOT ROUGH, YOU'D EXPLODE WITH YOUR FLAMES.
I GUESS I WANTED TO PUT A FEW DENTS IN THAT COOL FACE, YEAH.
GUESS WE'RE MORE ALIKE THAN WE KNEW.
WE WERE DESTINED TO FIGHT, THEN.

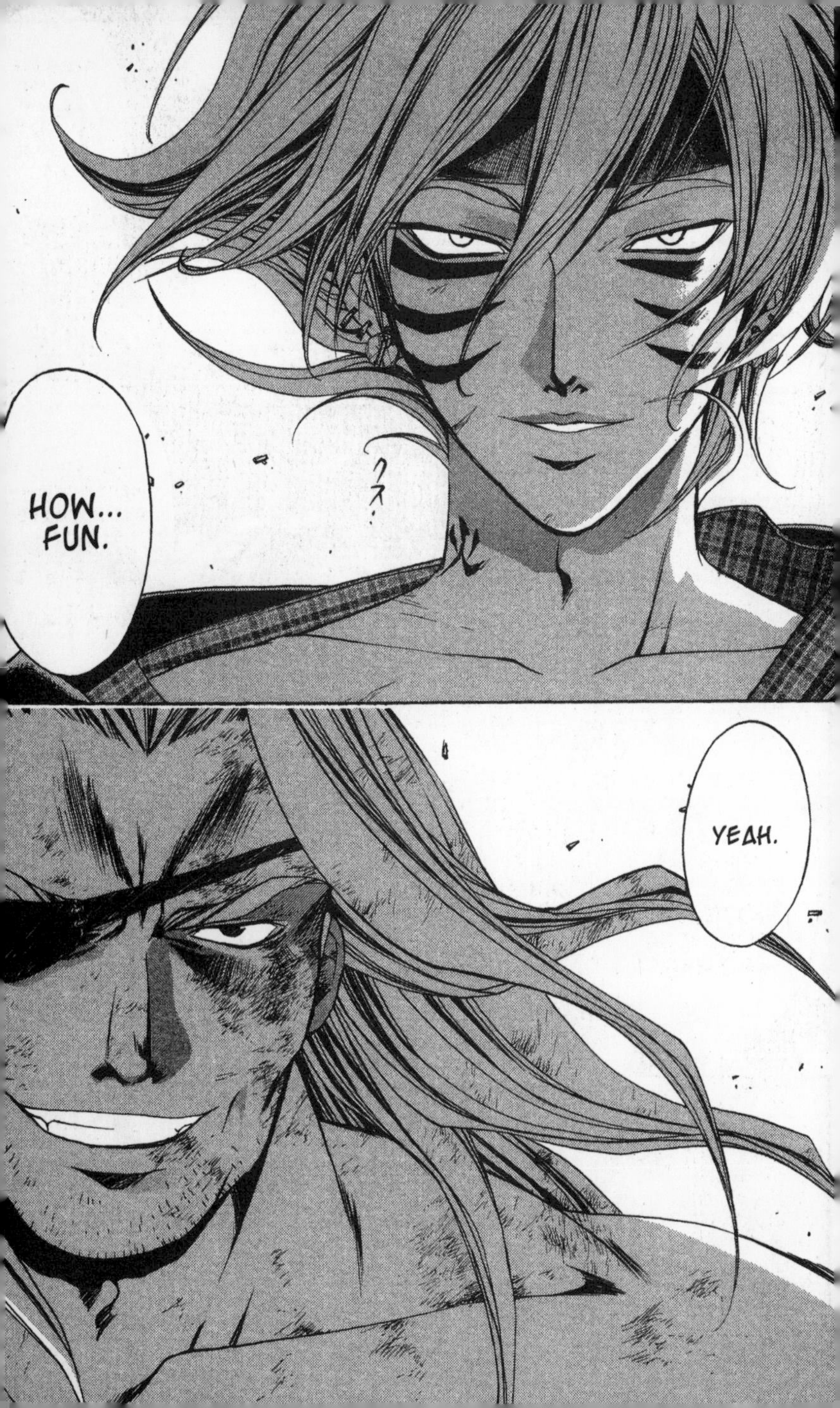
クス・・
HOW... FUN.
YEAH.

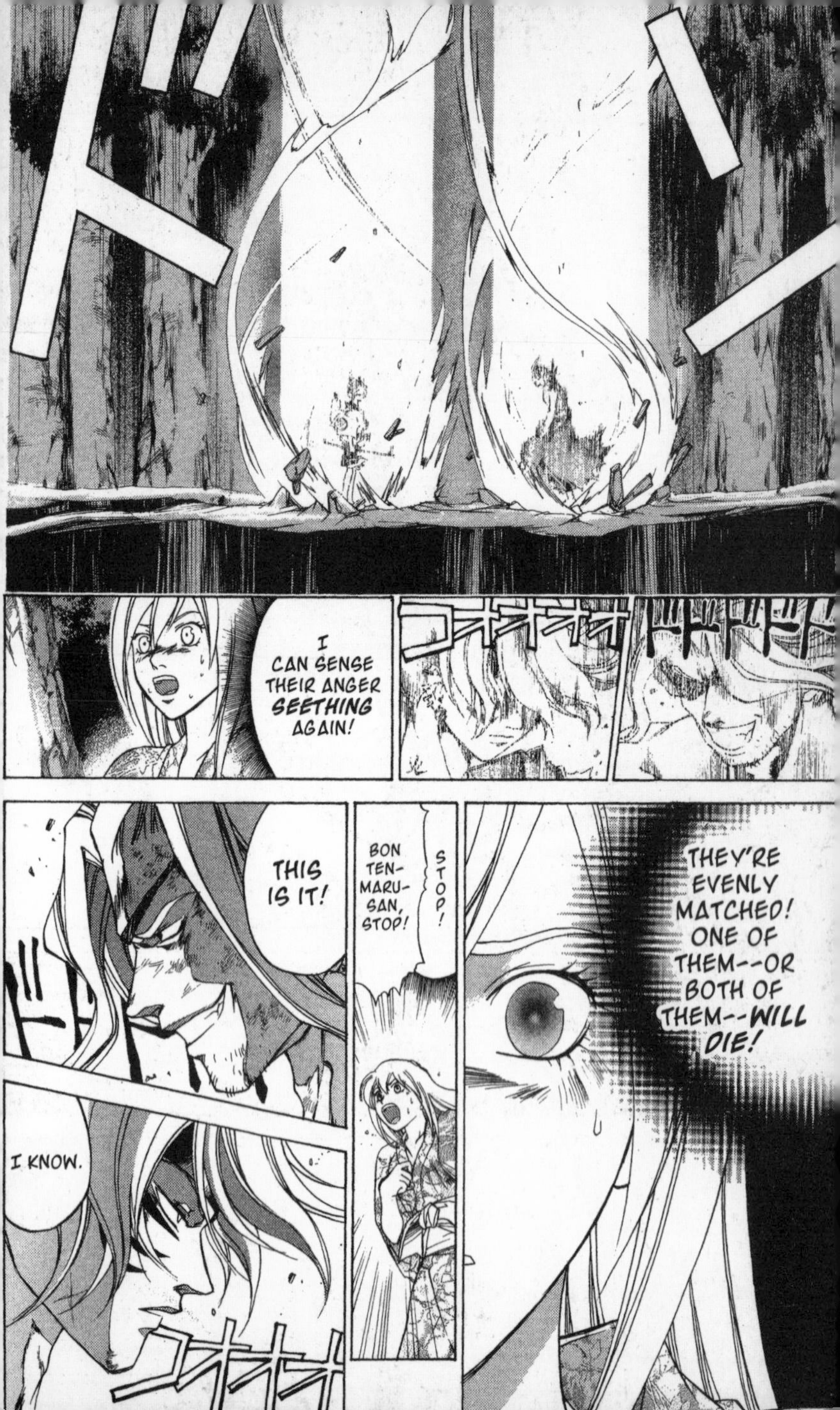
I CAN SENSE THEIR ANGER SEETHING AGAIN!
THEY'RE EVENLY MATCHED! ONE OF THEM--OR BOTH OF THEM--WILL DIE!
STOP!
BONTEN-MARU-SAN, STOP!
THIS IS IT!
I KNOW.

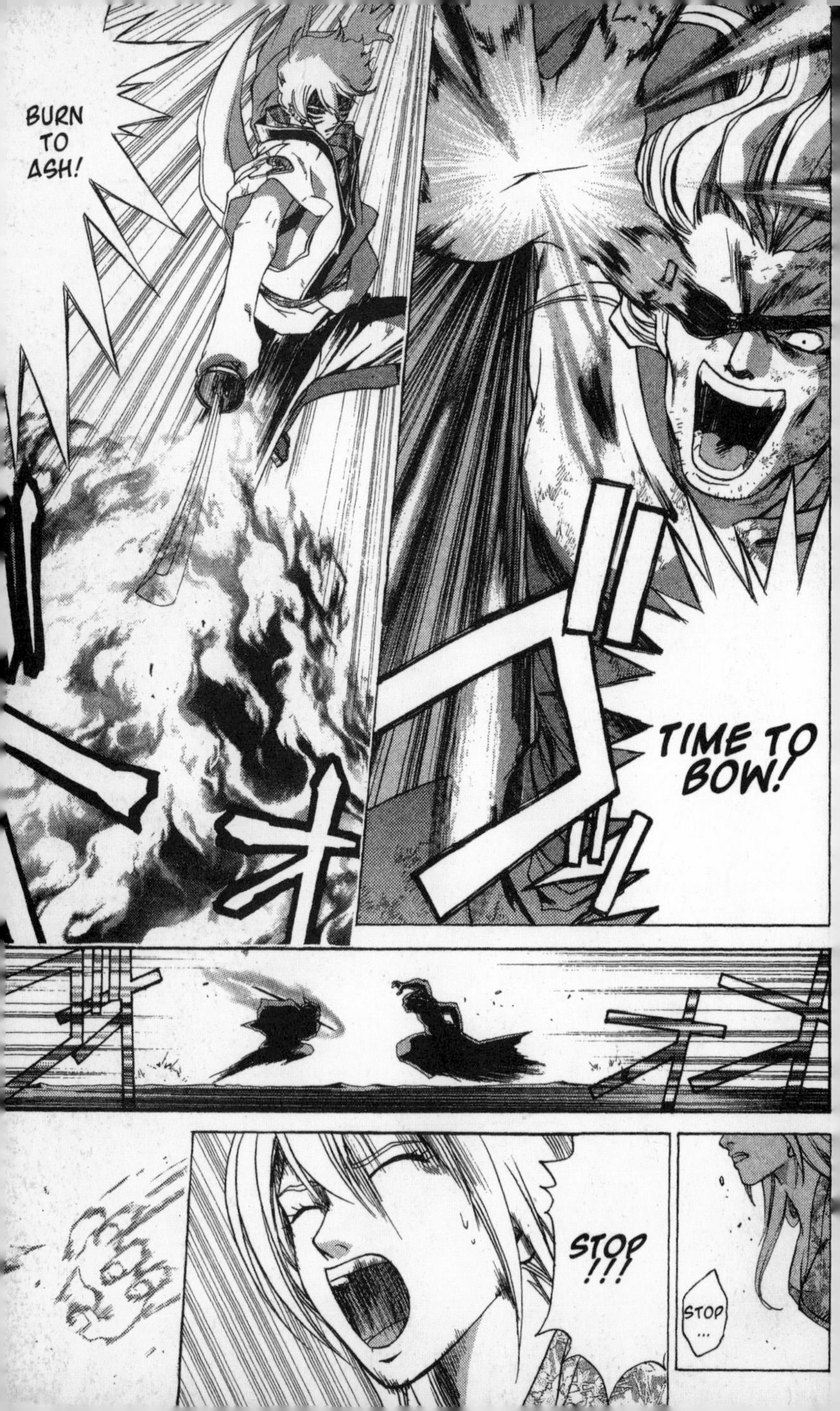
TIME TO BOW!
BURN TO ASH!
STOP ...
STOP !!!

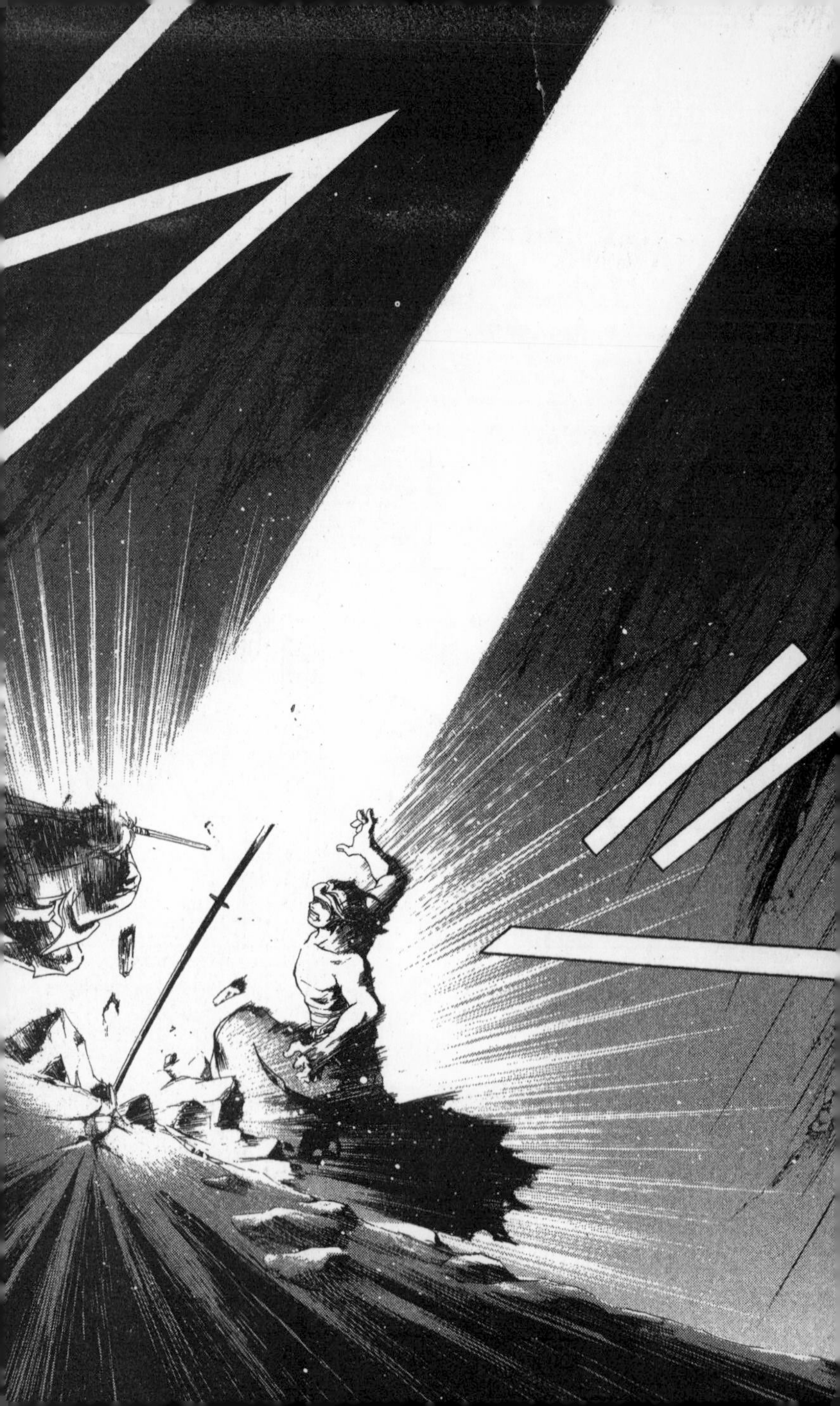

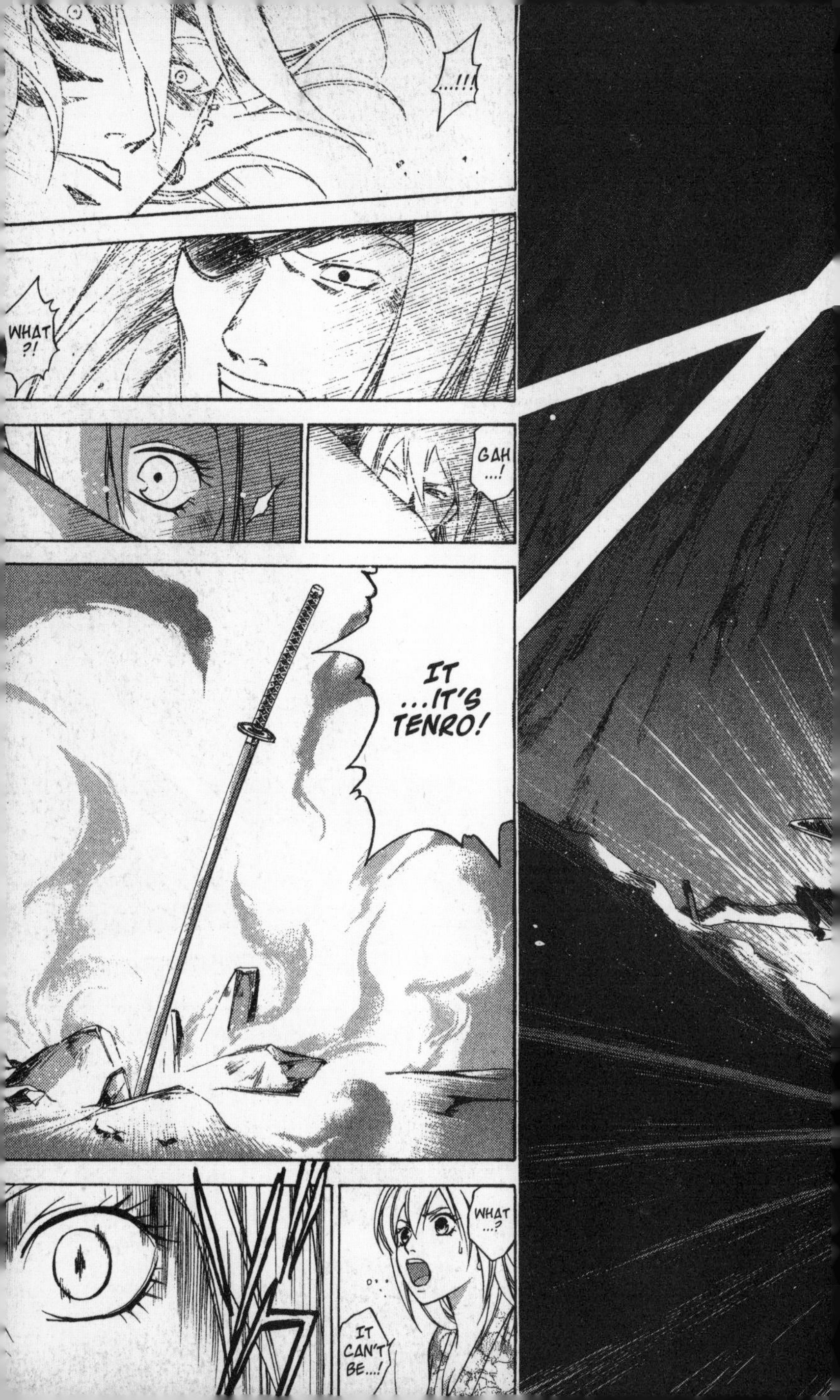

...!!!
WHAT ?!
GAH ...!
IT ...IT'S TENRO!
WHAT ...?
IT CAN'T BE...!

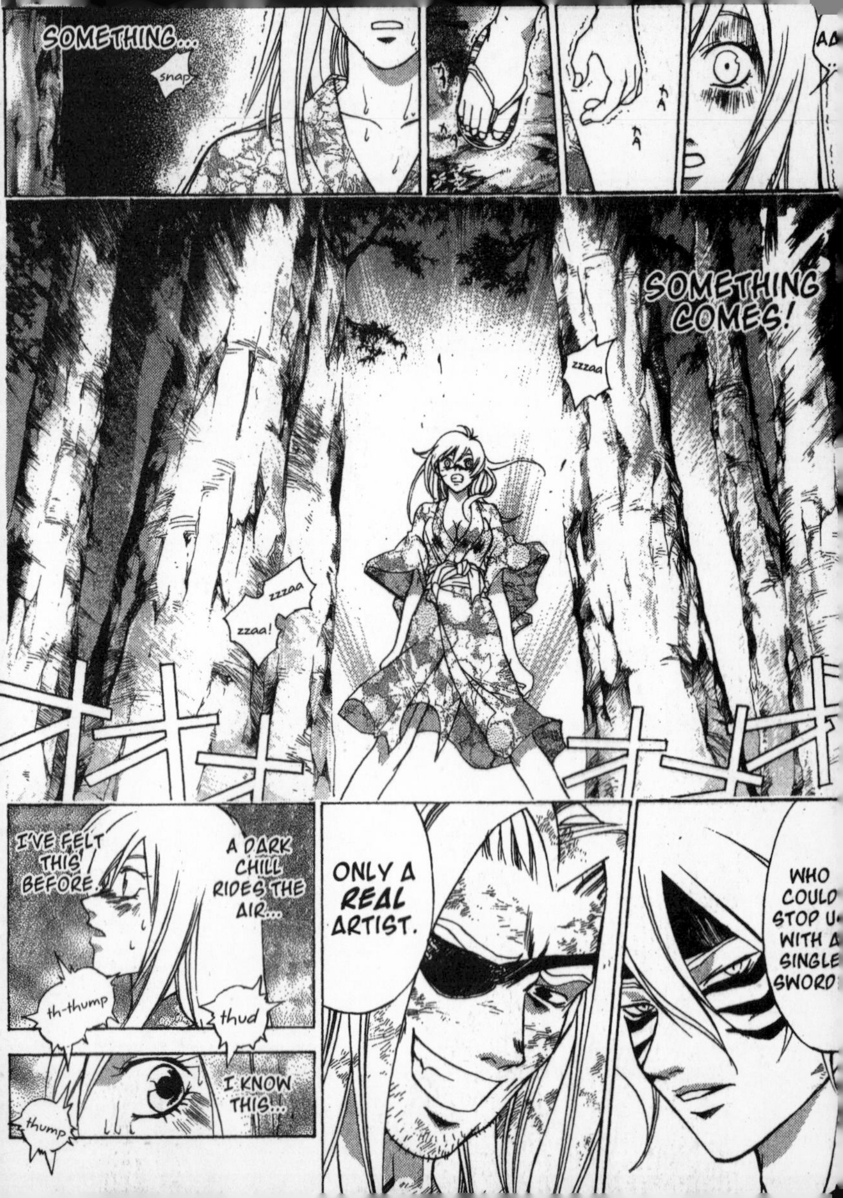
AA...
SOMETHING...
snap
SOMETHING COMES!
zzzaa
zzzaa
zzaa!
WHO COULD STOP U WITH A SINGLE SWORD
ONLY A REAL ARTIST.
A DARK CHILL RIDES THE AIR...
I'VE FELT THIS BEFORE.
thud
th-thump
I KNOW THIS...
thump

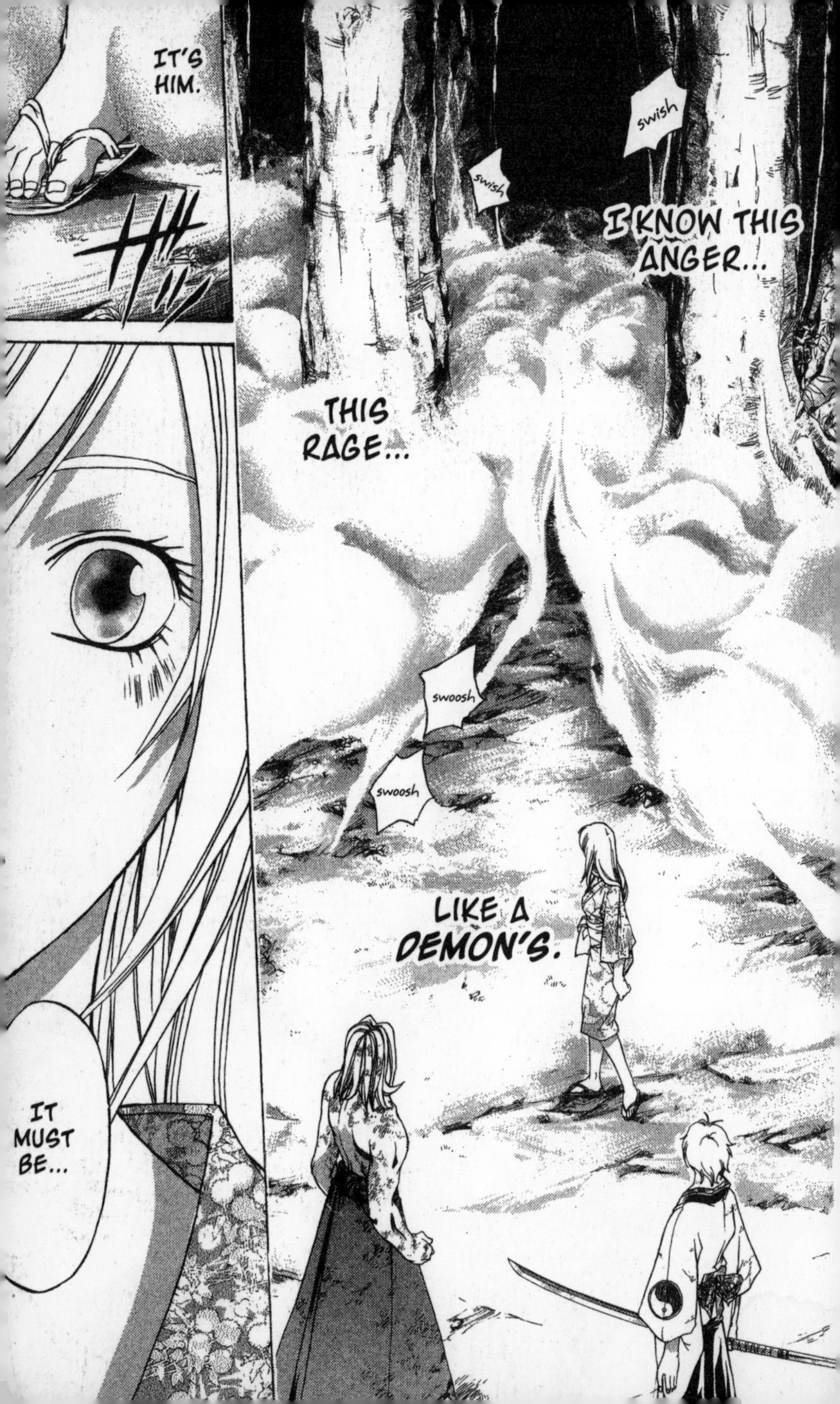
swish
swish
I KNOW THIS ANGER...
THIS RAGE...
swoosh
swoosh
LIKE A DEMON'S.
IT'S HIM.
IT MUST BE...

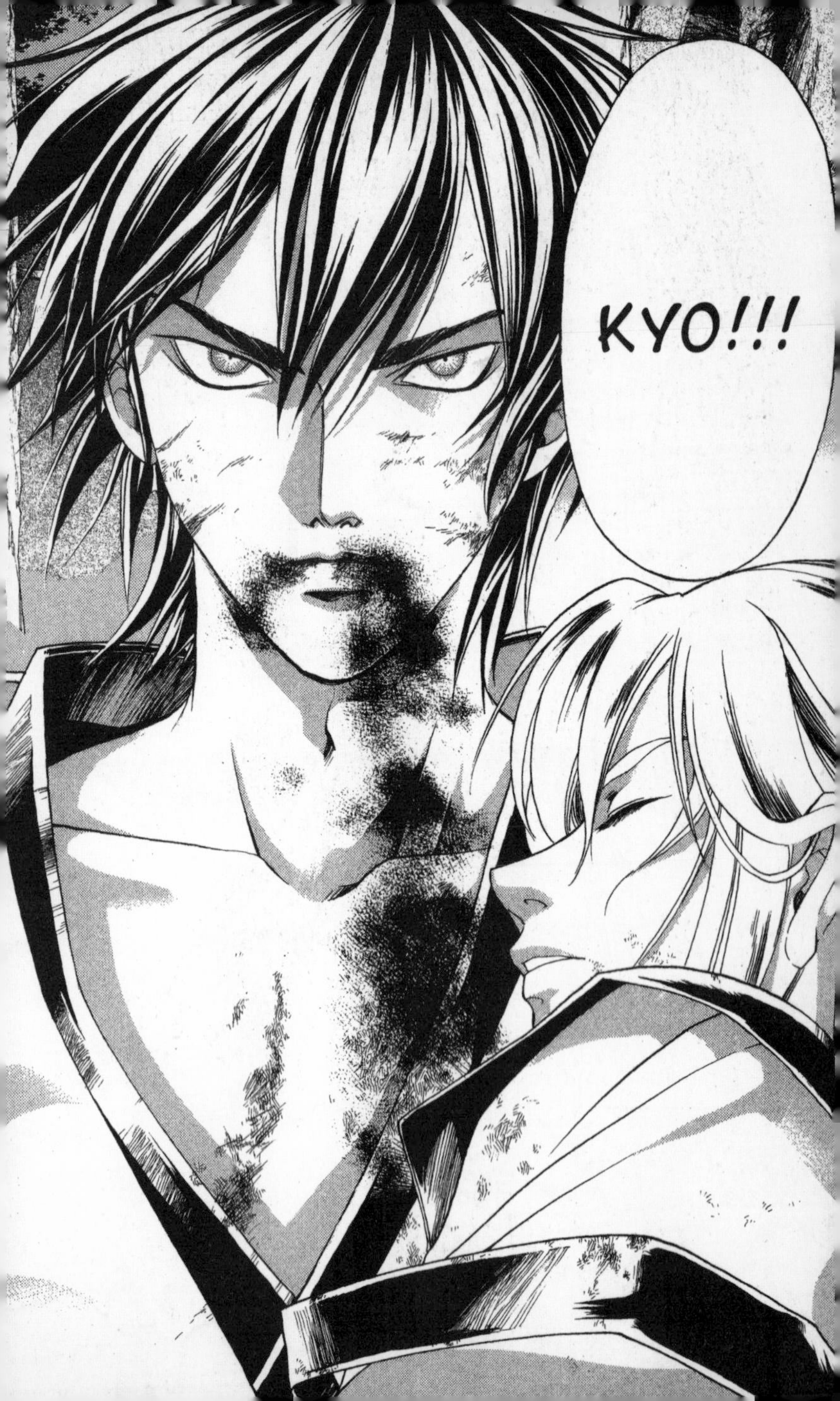
KYO!!!

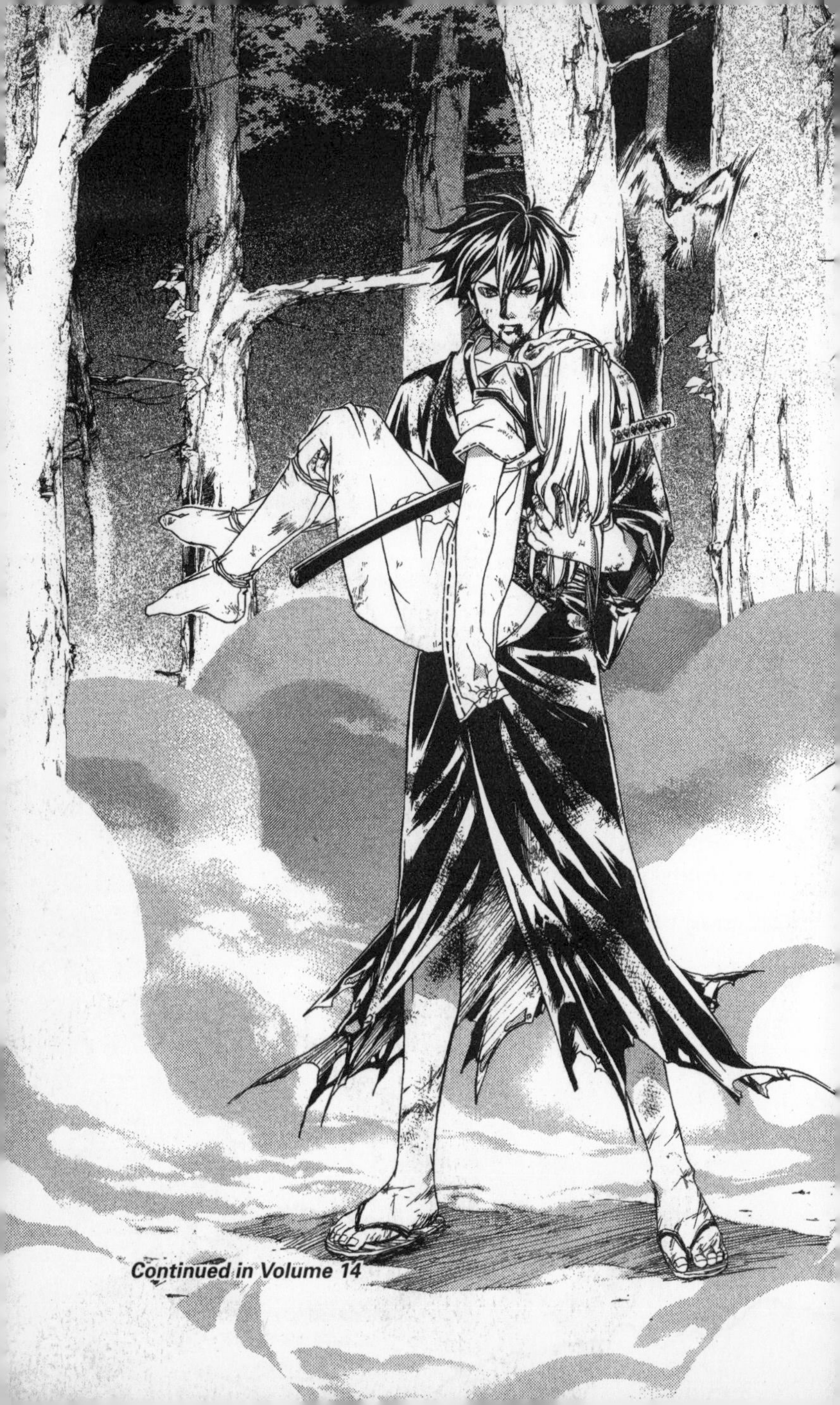
Continued in Volume 14

Character Profile

Kamijyo **K** Once again it's...a character profile! And what better fit than our reappearing Spider-Master...Mahiro? What has she been up to since Vol. 5?

Mahiro **M** Ninja never reveal their actions.

K I...er...I see! Must be tough! Let's hear your profile!

M Mahiro, Spider-Master. Age 19, Female, Height 165cm. Weight 48kg, Blood Type A, Bust 86cm (D-Cup) Waist 59cm, Hips87cm, Ninja for Ieyasu-sama. Of the Iga School. Ninja can't be picky, but I hate irresponsible men!

K T-thanks! I wasn't expecting so much detail from...a ninja! I mean, I thought you didn't talk about yourselves!?

M (Whoops! Damn!) I...I never said I was telling the truth!

K ...But it was true, wasn't it?

M (Gah!)

K Maybe you aren't cut out for the ninja life?

M N-never! I am the strongest ninja ever! And I will kill Kyo!

K I...I see... At least you know what you want. You're my kind of woman!

M (Blushes) Y-You want to die!? (sound of spiders rustling)

K Eek! J-just kidding! Any parting words?

M Kyo! You're next! (rustle rustle)

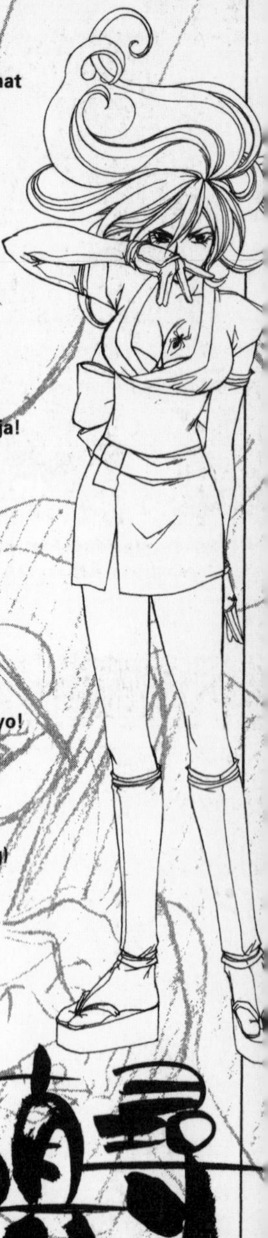

MAHIRO SPIDER-MASTER

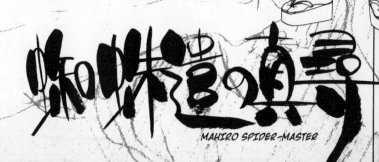

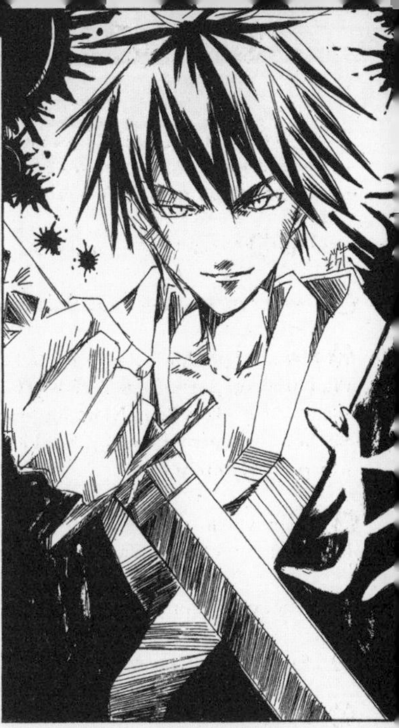

[Tsuzuki Eku / Hyogo Prefecture] He's teh sexy!

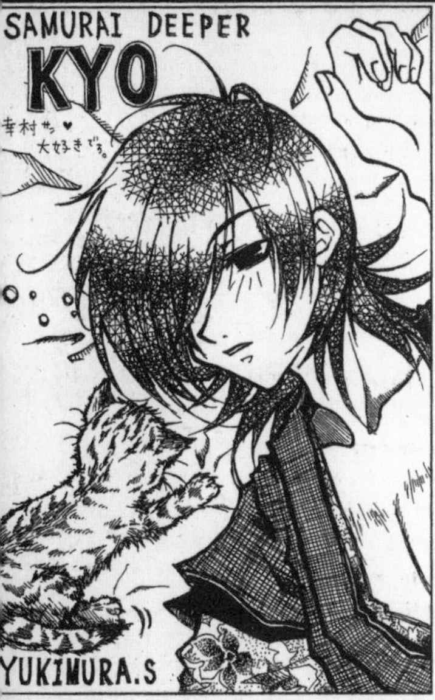
SAMURAI DEEPER KYO
幸村サン♥
大好きです。
YUKIMURA.S

[Yukio / Kagoshima Prefecture] Yukimura = Cat Person!

Draw Like Akimine Kamijyo

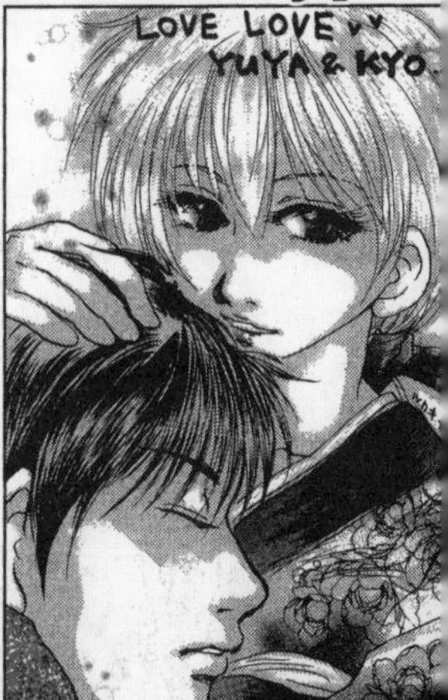
LOVE LOVE ♥♥
YUYA & KYO

[Tsukao Kazumi / Hiroshima Prefecture] The face of a grown woman?

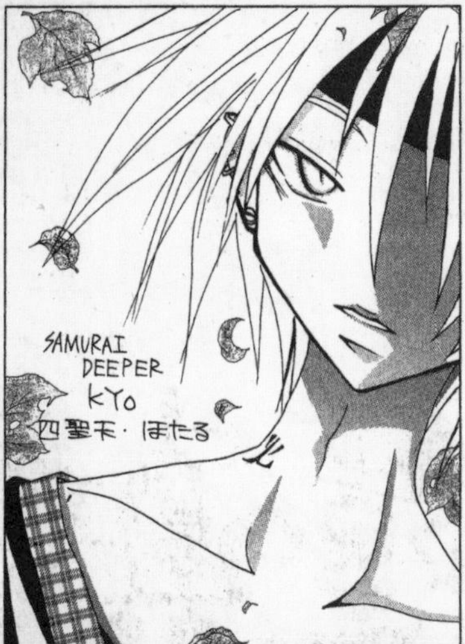
SAMURAI DEEPER KYO
四聖天・ほたる

[Fujisaki Fuji / Hokkaido] Yep, those are definitely Hotaru's eyes and lips!

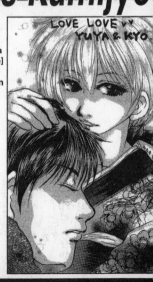

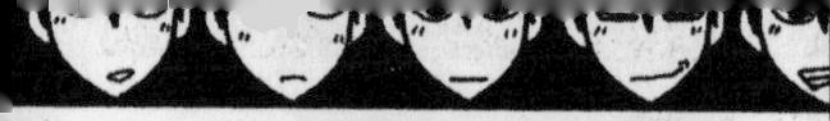

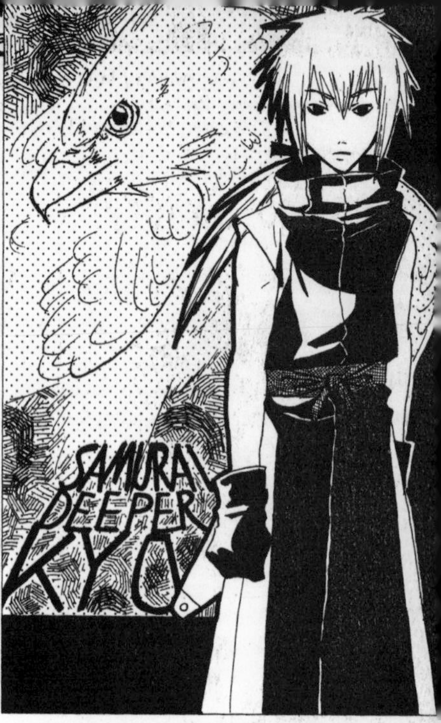
SAMURAI DEEPER KYO

[Okatani Ariki / Kochi Prefecture]
The challenge in an eagle's eyes!

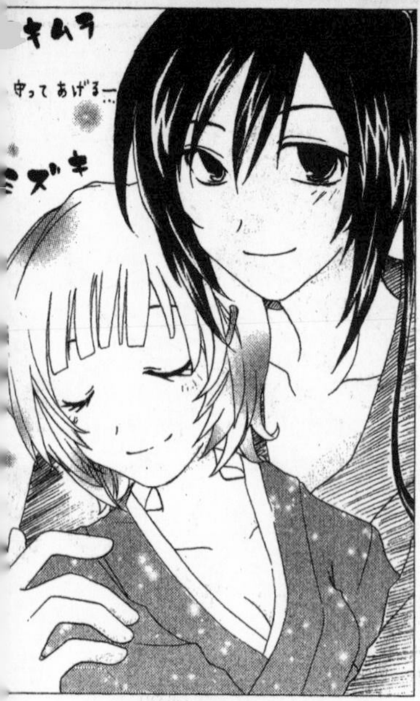
キムラ
守ってあげる…
ミズキ

[Kisaragi Aya]
They look happier than they looked in my story ♡

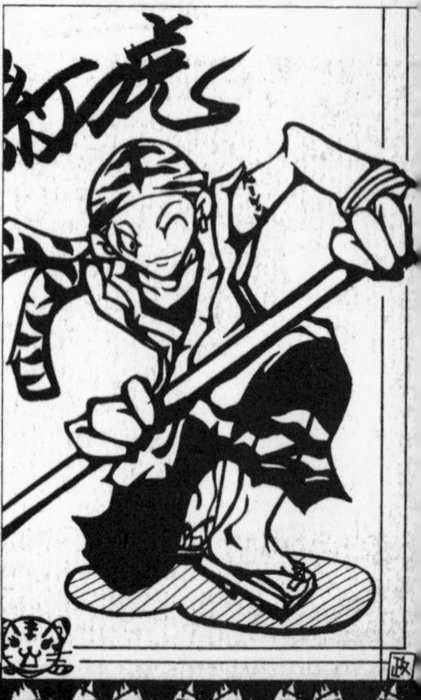

[Masani / Osaka]
In Taiwanese, Benitora is "Honfu"! Cool!

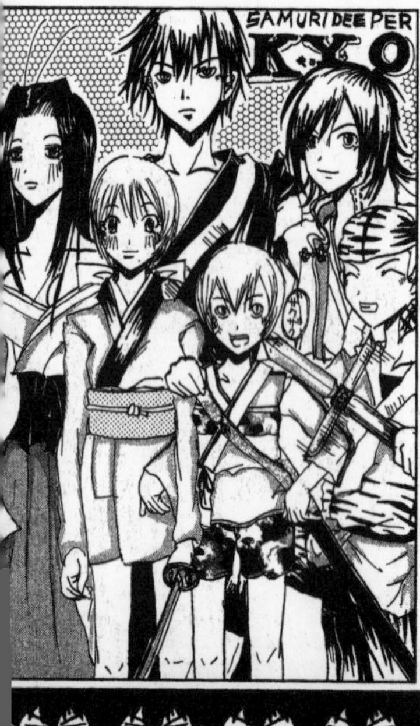
SAMURI DEEPER KYO

[Honda Kozue / Fukushima Prefecture]
H-hey! Is that thing sticking in Sasuke's neck!?

Kyoshiro Gallery!

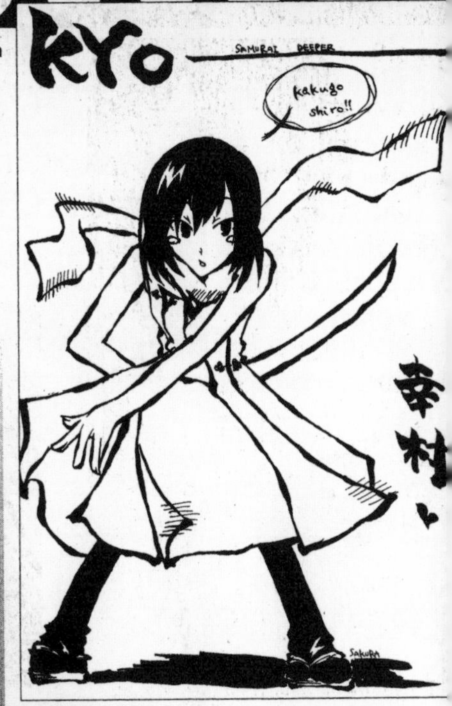
KYO
SAMURAI DEEPER
kakugo shiro!!
幸村♥
SAKURA

[Sakura Kotowa / Fukuoka Prefecture]
Fasion Yukimura! ♡

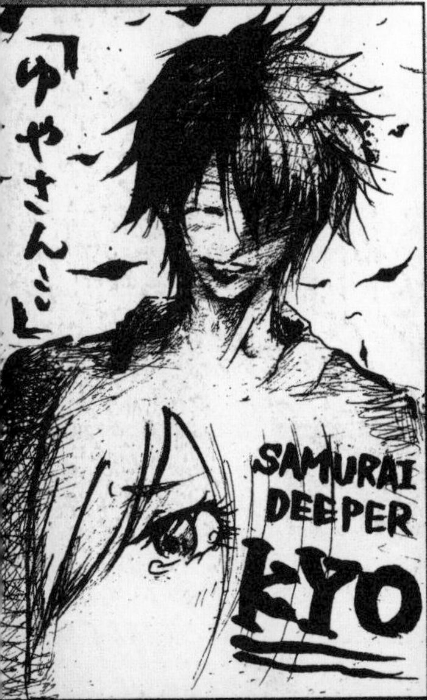
「ゆやさん…」
SAMURAI DEEPER KYO

[Arigo / Gifu Prefecture]
It's somehow...sad!

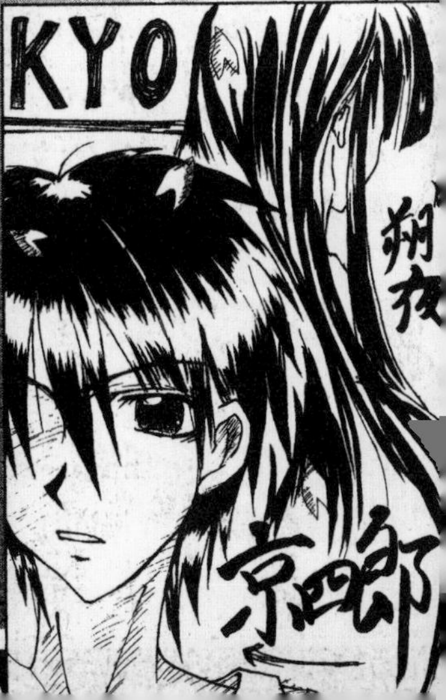
KYO
朔夜
京四郎

[AIRU / Niigata Prefecture]
He's serious when he's thinking about Sakuya.

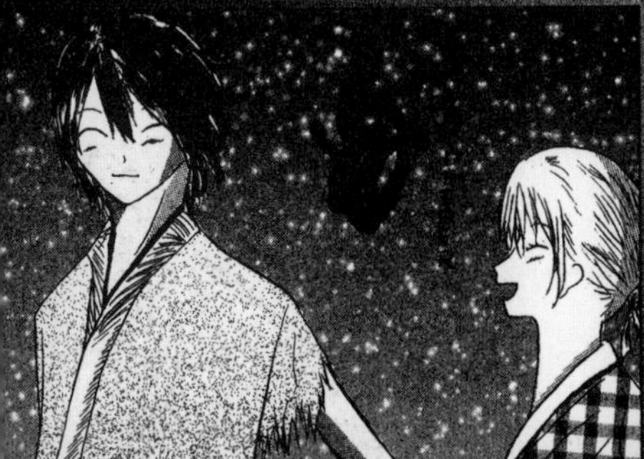

[Korihama Nana / Mie Prefecture]
We get a lot of Kyoshiro/Yuya shots.

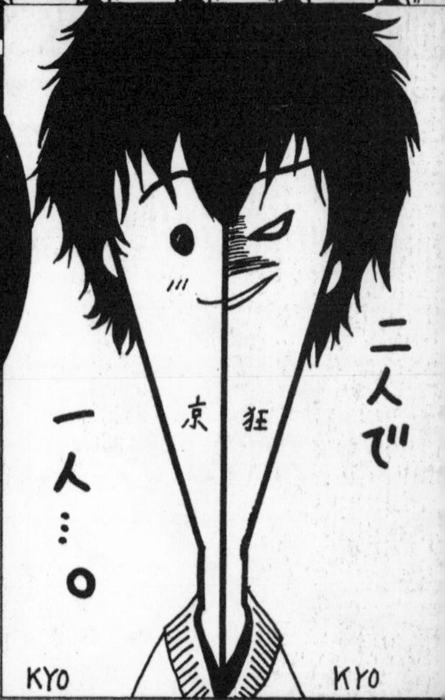
二人で
一人…。
京
狂
KYO
KYO

[Tsukamoto/Kumamoto Prefecture]
I want one of these! (what is it!?)

A message from Akimine Kamijyo:
♡

Next time: Shiina Yuya special! We want cute! We want sexy! (Look for the yo special next volume!)

[Isao Kazuma / Ehime Prefecture]
Gotta be sharp!

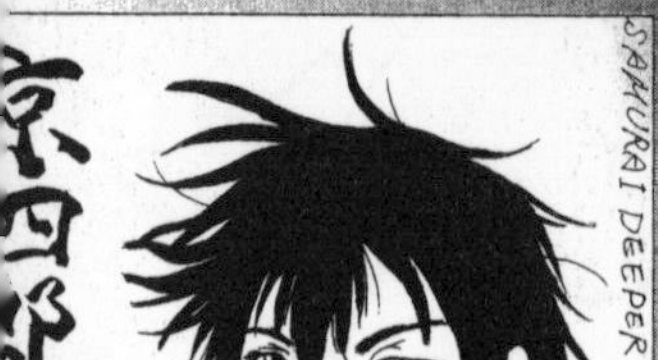
SAMURAI DEEPER KYO
SAMURAI
K.K.

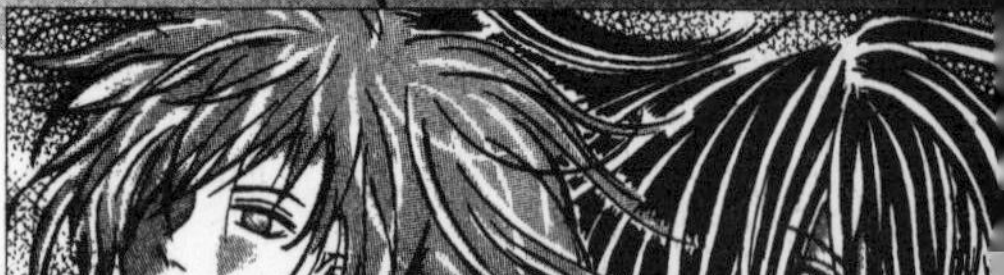
SAMURA
DEEPER
KYO

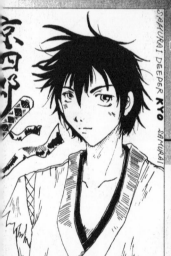

[Kusarebito / Kanagawa Prefecture]
A picture from the past... nice!

Fan Art Info

Submission Info

How to submit:

1) Send your work via regular mail (NOT e-mail) to:

SAMURAI DEEPER KYO FAN MAIL
C/O TOKYOPOP
5900 WILSHIRE BLVD., SUITE 2000
LOS ANGELES, CA 90036

2) All work should be in black-and-white and no larger than 8.5"x11". (And try not to fold it too many times!) 3) Anything you send will not be returned. If you want to keep your original, it's fine to send us a copy. 4) Please include your full name, age, city and state for us to print with your work. If you'd rather us use a pen name, please include that too. 5) IMPORTANT: If you're under the age of 18, you must have your parent's permission in order for us to print your work. Any submissions without a signed note of parental consent will not be used. 6) For full details, please check out http://www.tokyopop.com/aboutus/fanart.php

Disclaimer: Anything you send to us becomes the property of TOKYOPOP Inc. and will not be returned to you. We will have the right to print, reproduce, distribute or modify the artwork for use in future volumes of Samurai Deeper Kyo or on the Web without payment to you.

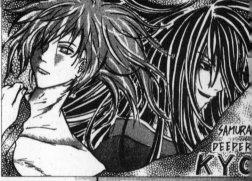

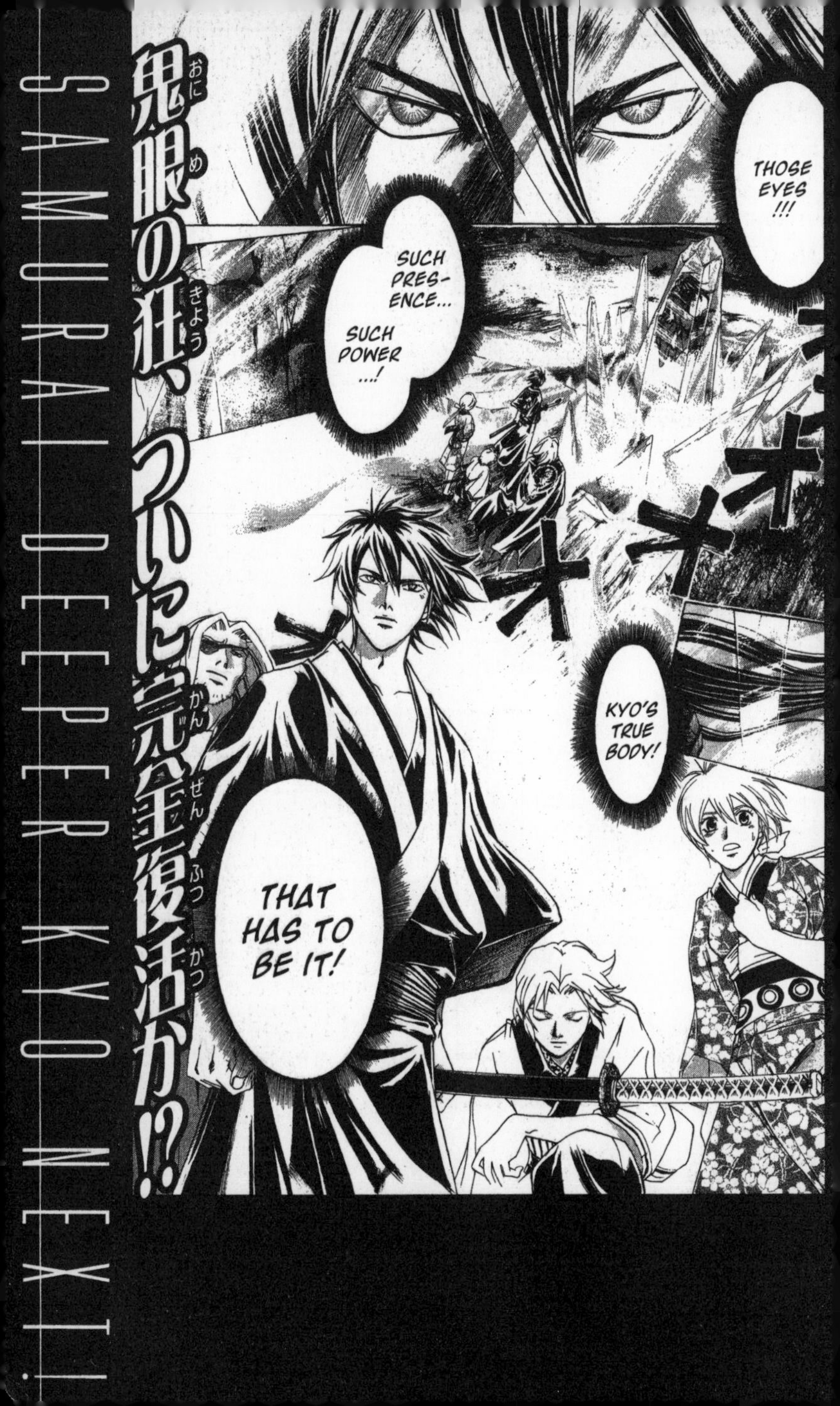
SAMURAI DEEPER KYO NEXT!
鬼眼の狂、ついに完全復活か!?
THOSE EYES!!!
SUCH PRESENCE... SUCH POWER...!
KYO'S TRUE BODY!
THAT HAS TO BE IT!

EDITORS' PICKS

TOKYOPOP MANGA SUPPLEMENT

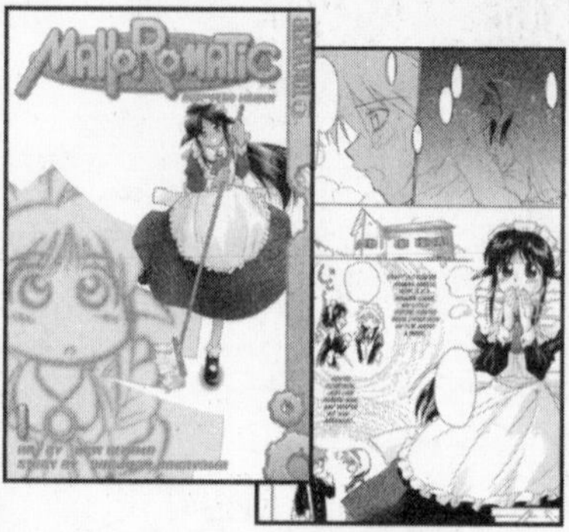
MaHoRoMaTic

BY BUNJURO NAKAYAMA
AND BOW DITAMA

MAHOROMATIC: AUTOMATIC MAIDEN

Mahoro is a sweet, cute, female battle android who decides to go from mopping up alien invaders to mopping up after Suguru Misato, a teenaged orphan boy... and hilarity most definitely ensues. This series has great art and a slick story that easily switches from truly funny to downright heartwarming...but always with a large shadow looming over it. You see, only Mahoro knows that her days are quite literally numbered, and the end of each chapter lets you know exactly how much—or how little—time she has left!

~Rob Tokar, Sr. Editor

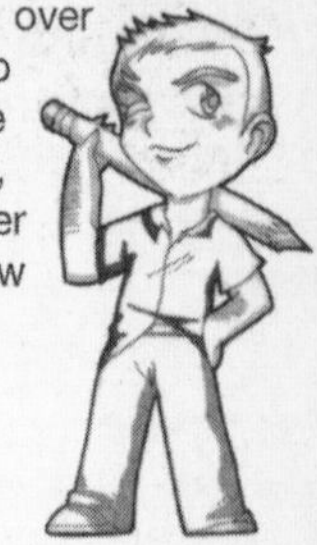

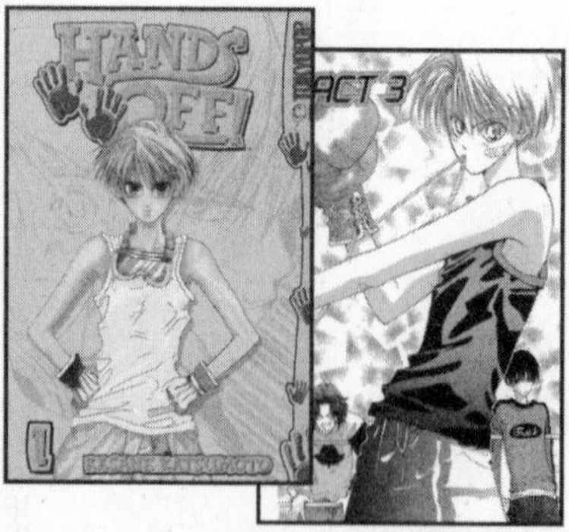
HANDS OFF!
ACT 3

BY KASANE KATSUMOTO

HANDS OFF!

Cute boys with ESP who share a special bond... If you think this is familiar (e.g. *Legal Drug*), well, you're wrong. *Hands Off!* totally stands alone as a unique and thoroughly enjoyable series. Kotarou and Tatsuki's (platonic!) relationship is complex, fascinating and heart-wrenching. Throw in Yuuto, the playboy who can read auras, and you've got a fantastic setup for drama and comedy, with incredible themes of friendship running throughout. Don't be put off by Kotarou's danger-magnet status, either. The episodic stuff gradually changes, and the full arc of the characters' development is well worth waiting for.

~Lillian Diaz-Przybyl, Jr. Editor

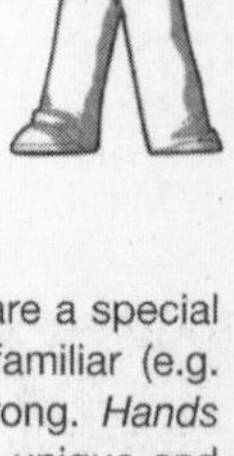

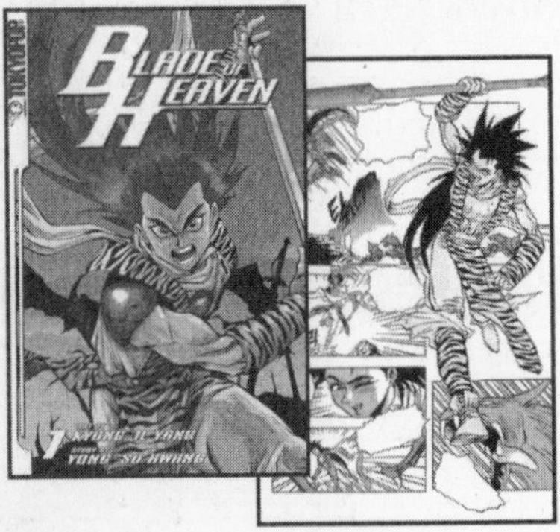
BLADE of HEAVEN
TOKYOPOP

BY YONG-SU HWANG
AND KYUNG-IL YANG

BLADE OF HEAVEN

Wildly popular in its homeland of Korea, *Blade of Heaven* enjoys the rare distinction of not only being a hit in its own country, but in Japan and several other countries, as well. On the surface, Yong-Su Hwang and Kyung-Il Yang's fantasy-adventure may look like yet another "Heaven vs. Demons" sword opera, but the story of the mischievous Soma, a pawn caught in a struggle of mythic proportions, is filled with so much humor, pathos, imagination—and yes, action, that it's easy to see why *Blade of Heaven* has been so popular worldwide.

~Bryce P. Coleman, Editor

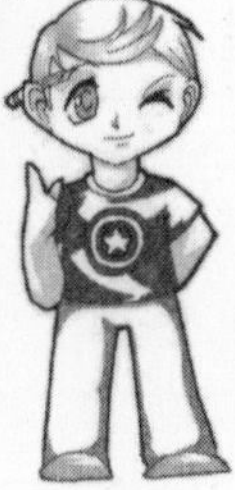

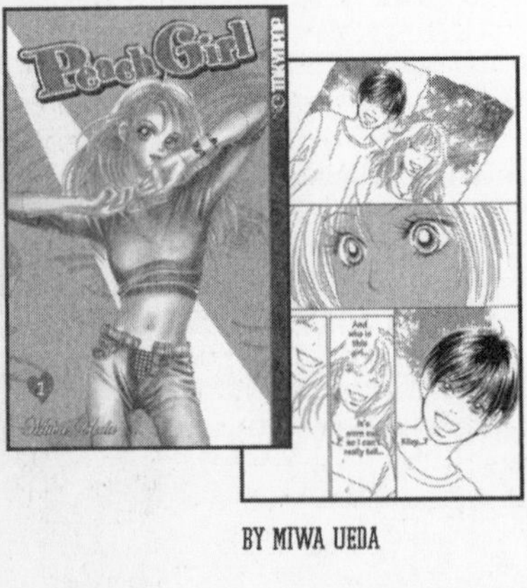
Peach Girl
TOKYOPOP

BY MIWA UEDA

PEACH GIRL

Am I the only person who thinks that *Peach Girl* is just like *The O.C.*? Just imagine Ryan as Toji, Seth as Kiley, Marissa as Momo and Summer as Sae. (The similarities are almost spooky!) Plus, Seth is way into comics and manga—and I'm sure he'd love *Peach Girl*. It has everything that my favorite TV show has and then some—drama, intrigue, romance and lots of will-they-or-won't-they suspense. I love it! *Peach Girl* rules, seriously. If you haven't read it, do so. Now.

~Julie Taylor, Sr. Editor

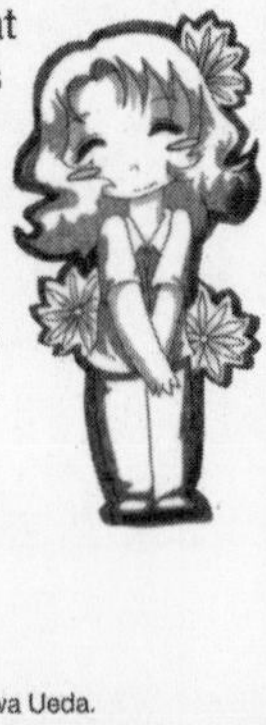

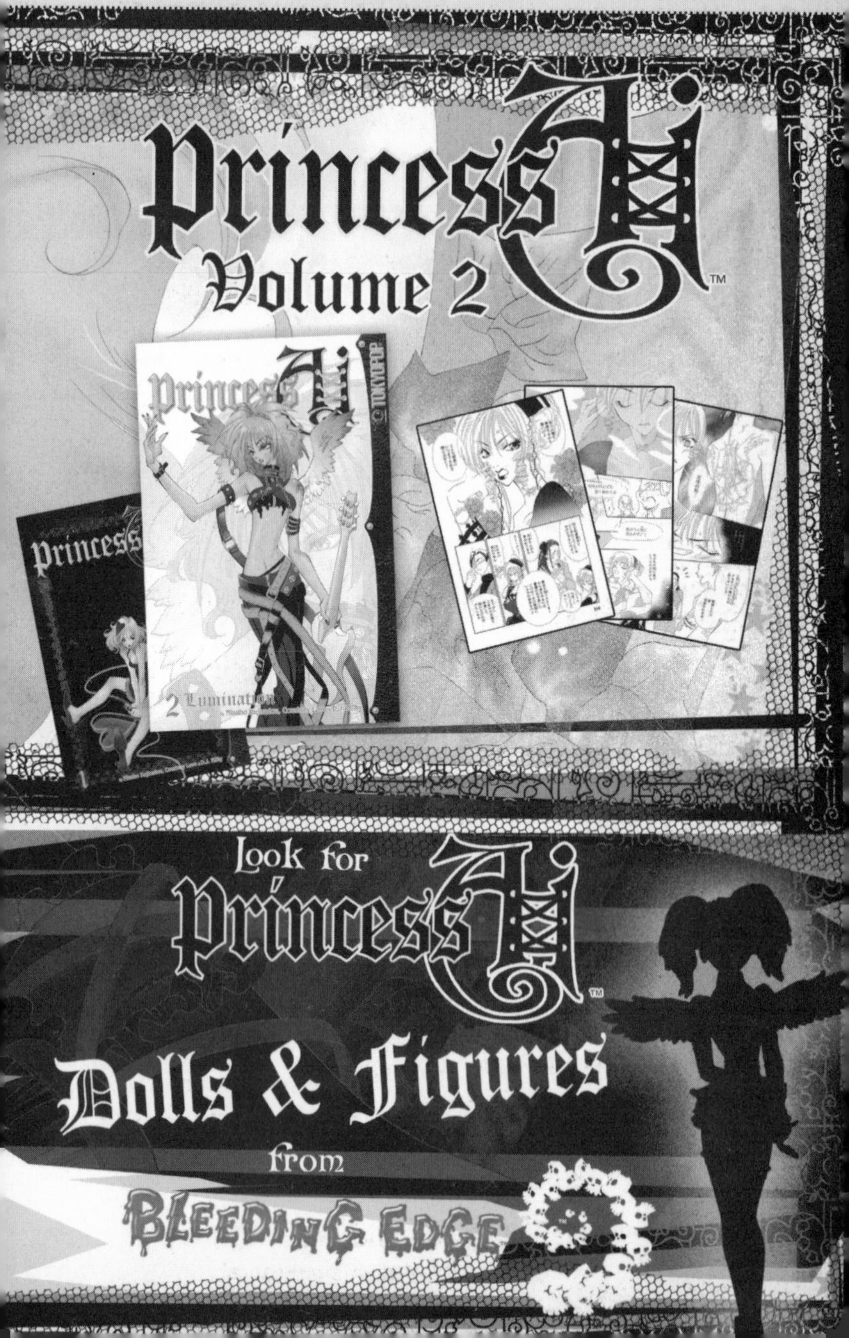
Princess Ai™
Volume 2
Look for
Princess Ai™
Dolls & Figures
from
BLEEDING EDGE

PRINCESS AI

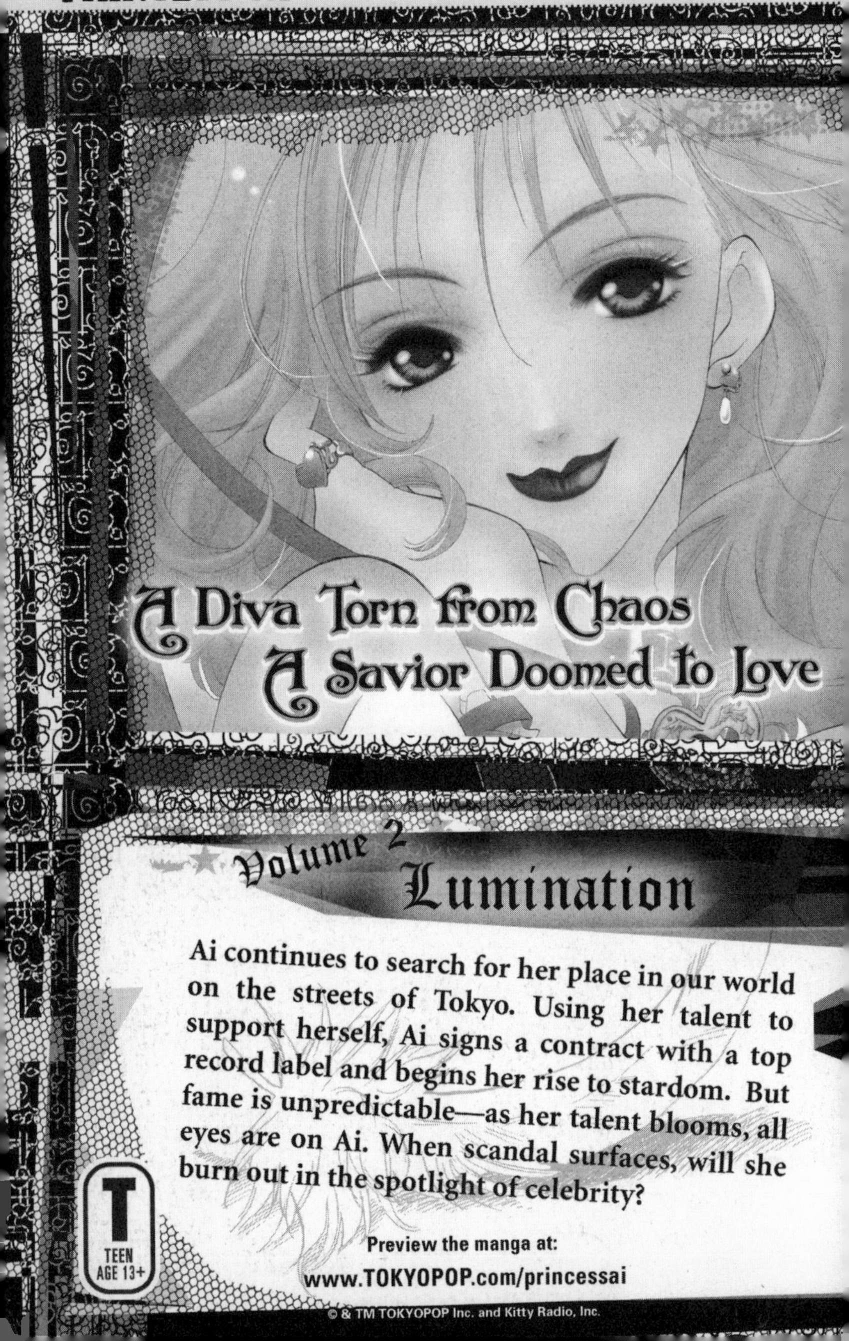
A Diva Torn from Chaos
A Savior Doomed to Love

Volume 2 Lumination

Ai continues to search for her place in our world on the streets of Tokyo. Using her talent to support herself, Ai signs a contract with a top record label and begins her rise to stardom. But fame is unpredictable—as her talent blooms, all eyes are on Ai. When scandal surfaces, will she burn out in the spotlight of celebrity?

T
TEEN
AGE 13+

Preview the manga at:

www.TOKYOPOP.com/princessai

BECK: MONGOLIAN CHOP SQUAD

OT
OLDER TEEN
AGE 16+

ROCK IN MANGA!

Yukio Tanaka is one boring guy with no hobbies, a weak taste in music and only a small vestige of a personality. But his life is forever changed when he meets Ryusuke Minami, an unpredictable rocker with a cool dog named Beck. Recently returned to Japan from America, Ryusuke inspires Yukio to get into music, and the two begin a journey through the world of rock 'n' roll dreams! With cameos of music's greatest stars—from John Lennon to David Bowie—and homages to supergroups such as Led Zeppelin and Nirvana, anyone who's anyone can make an appearance in *Beck*...even Beck himself! With action, music and gobs of comedy, *Beck* puts the rock in manga!

HAROLD SAKUISHI'S HIGHLY ADDICTIVE MANGA SERIES THAT SPAWNED A HIT ANIME HAS FINALLY REACHED THE STATES!

©Harold Sakuishi

FOR MORE INFORMATION VISIT: WWW.TOKYOPOP.COM

TOKYOPOP SHOP

THIS IS THE BACK OF THE BOOK.
You wouldn't want to spoil a great ending!

This book is printed "manga-style," in the authentic Japanese right-to-left format. Since none of the artwork has been flipped or altered, readers get to experience the story just as the creator intended. You've been asking for it, so TOKYOPOP® delivered: authentic, hot-off-the-press, and far more fun!

DIRECTIONS

If this is your first time reading manga-style, here's a quick guide to help you understand how it works.

It's easy… just start in the top right panel and follow the numbers. Have fun, and look for more 100% authentic manga from TOKYOPOP®!